CONCERT AND OPERA CONDUCTORS

Recent Titles in the Music Reference Collection
Series Advisers: Donald L. Hixon
Adrienne Fried Block

Music for Oboe, Oboe D'Amore, and English Horn: A Bibliography of Materials at the Library of Congress
Virginia Snodgrass Gifford, compiler

A Bibliography of Nineteenth-Century American Piano Music: With Location Sources and Composer Biography-Index
John Gillespie and Anna Gillespie

The Resource Book of Jewish Music: A Bibliographical and Topical Guide to the Book and Journal Literature and Program Materials
Irene Heskes, compiler

American Vocal Chamber Music, 1945-1980: An Annotated Bibliography
Patricia Lust, compiler

Concert and Opera Singers: A Bibliography of Biographical Materials
Robert H. Cowden, compiler

Music History from the Late Roman through the Gothic Periods, 313-1425: A Documented Chronology
Blanche Gangwere

Guide to the Hymns and Tunes of American Methodism
Samuel J. Rogal, compiler

Musical Settings of American Poetry: A Bibliography
Michael Hovland, compiler

Henrich Schütz: A Bibliography of the Collected Works and Performing Editions
D. Douglas Miller and Anne L. Highsmith, compilers

Hawaiian Music: An Annotated Bibliography
Bryan C. Stoneburner, compiler

Cross Index Title Guide to Classical Music
Steven G. Pallay, compiler

Source Book of Proposed Music Notation Reforms
Gardner Read

As the Black School Sings: Black Music Collections at Black Universities and Colleges with a Union List of Book Holdings
Jon Michael Spencer

CONCERT AND OPERA CONDUCTORS

A Bibliography of Biographical Materials

Compiled by Robert H. Cowden

Music Reference Collection, Number 14

Greenwood Press
New York • Westport, Connecticut • London

Library of Congress Cataloging-in-Publication Data

Cowden, Robert H.
Concert and opera conductors.

(Music reference collection, ISSN 0736-7740 ; no. 14)
Bibliography: p.
Includes index.
1. Conductors (Music)—Biography—Bibliography.
I. Title. II. Series.
ML128.B3C68 1987 016.785'092'2 [B] 87-11821
ISBN 0-313-25620-9 (lib. bdg. : alk. paper)

Library of Congress Catalog Card Number: 87-11821
ISBN: 0-313-25620-9
ISSN: 0736-7740

First published in 1987

Greenwood Press, Inc.
88 Post Road West, Westport, Connecticut 06881

Printed in the United States of America

The paper used in this book complies with the Permanent Paper Standard issued by the National Information Standards Organization (Z39.48-1984).

10 9 8 7 6 5 4 3 2 1

To afficionados, collectors,
dealers, and music reference
librarians worldwide
but especially to
LIM M. LAI
for his substantial contributions
to this compilation

Contents

Preface

Concert and Opera Singers: a Bibliography of Biographical Materials by Robert H. Cowden (Greenwood Press, 1985) was received with a great deal of enthusiasm by dealers and collectors worldwide. The response encouraged me to compile a companion volume devoted to conductors, a work which has profited from access to the materials and expertise of my colleague, Lim M. Lai. The number of collective works related to conductors and conducting is limited in comparison to those that I documented in the vocal field, perhaps due to the fact that the modern conductor is a relatively recent phenomenon. Since von Weber and Berlioz there have been only a handful of conductors who could compete for the attention of the public with the numerous singers who have dominated the classical music world since the Italian Camerata launched their experiments in expressive text settings. The occasional Beecham, Toscanini, or Furtwaengler had to have mastered fearsome elements indeed in order to claim their rightful place in the esteem of a fickle musical public. Opportunities were few; the demands of virtuosi, impresarios, and orchestras were great; and the public was and always has been forever ready to change allegiance at the beginning of a downbeat. This situation offered a challenge to chart the variety of materials by and about these singular individualists who have achieved such power and notoriety in such a short time. The pages that follow will contain, I hope, some pleasant surprises for every reader; some fascinating avenues to pursue in the quest for insights, knowledge, and entertainment.

CHOICE OF CONDUCTORS

In order to be included in "PART C: Individual Conductors, A-Z," each artist had to be cited in at least one of the standard music biographical dictionaries or encyclopedias, had to have written an autobiography or substantive contribution to the pedagogy of conducting, and/or had to have been the subject of a biographical study. Articles in major musical periodicals and/or mention in some other publication, e.g. the extensive material on Hans von Buelow in Ernest Newman's biography of Richard Wagner (C1175.4), was not considered sufficient recognition by itself. Occasionally, as in the case of Vilem Tausky, an edited autobiography (Vilem Tausky Tells His Story: a Two-Part Setting. London, 1979) does exist, but no other sources were discovered that fit my guidelines. On the other hand, many conductors are included in two of the standard reference works who are not mentioned in any other published materials, and such individuals are a part of this compilation. Some difficult judgments had to be made regarding conductors in the popular, entertainment, and commercial fields. Well-known names such as Paul Whiteman, Fred Waring, Skitch Henderson, Giuseppe Creatore, Tommy

Dorsey, and Percy Faith are not to be found here. A much more difficult task arose in conjunction with composers and performers who also managed to conduct, some with relative frequency and success. Anton Rubinstein was the czar's pianist and conductor in Russia; Vincent d'Indy "although he never held an official position as a conductor...frequently, and with marked success, appeared in that capacity..." (BAKER 7); and Yehudi Menuhin increasingly turned to conducting after the 1950s. Copland, Hindemith, and Stravinsky often conducted, but here, at last, is a crucial point. Practically every composer conducts at one time or another; Beethoven did and Brahms did. In fact, the latter had fully expected to succeed Friedrich Grund in Hamburg. Alexander Buchner's study of Franz Liszt in Bohemia goes into some detail about Liszt as a composer and conductor in Prague. And to make matters that much more interesting for the compiler, Konrad Huschke authored Beethoven als Pianist und Dirigent (Berlin: Schuster & Loeffler, 1919) as well as Johannes Brahms als Pianist, Dirigent und Lehrer (Karlsruhe: F.G. Verlag, 1935). But neither conductor had a permanent orchestral post or a group of instrumentalists he could call his own -- and that is the critical difference between Beethoven and Brahms on the one hand and Wagner, Richard Strauss, and Gustav Mahler, three of the more prominent composer/conductors who are listed. Felix Mendelssohn, due to his work with the famous Gewandhaus Orchestra in Leipzig, merits an entry; Igor Stravinsky despite his many guest appearances and recordings, does not! On the other hand, John Philip Sousa, the noted American bandmaster can be found here as can Frederick Fennell, both for outstanding contributions to the concept of the symphonic band in the United States. Unquestionably, there will be some honest disagreement, not so much with inclusions as with exclusions, but the guidelines are, overall, quite inclusive and fair: (a) a minimum of two entries from the first four categories of information which will be explained later in the Preface, and (b) appointment as the conductor of a permanent ensemble that presented major instrumental compositions.

As to some of the smaller details, I feel obliged to quote from William S. Newman's Preface to the initial volume of his definitive study of the elusive sonata: The Sonata in the Baroque Era, rev. ed. (Chapel Hill: The University of North Carolina Press, 1966).

> One matter concerns a minor fact of editorial policy. The reader needs to be cautioned that the spelling and punctuation, though not necessarily the capitalization, of titles and other direct quotations are retained here as they were found in the 'best' (usually the earliest) sources available to me. Once a start is made toward 'correcting' or modernizing such spelling and punctuation there is no place to draw the line. Instead, one grand SIC must be offered here, to be applied ad libitum throughout the book. To be sure, that sic could be a carte blanche for carelessness on the author's part. And allowance must always be made, in any case, for the inevitable human errors, especially in a study so filled with fussy details.

To which one emphatically says, "AMEN," and encourages each reader to check back, consider the alternatives, and realize that "arbitrary decisions are often necessary."

There is one final point that should be addressed with regard to the inclusion of book titles. Over ninety-eight percent of the books listed have been personally inspected. A lack of specifics or a comment on the unavailability of the titles make the unseen items obvious. In the case of major conductor/composers such as Mahler, Mendelssohn, Richard Strauss, and Wagner, however, the sheer number of books made any attempt at comprehensiveness both impractical and inappropriate. Most studies deal almost exclusively with each individual as a composer rather than as a conductor. Therefore, a concentrated attempt was made to include only those titles that dealt specifically with conducting involvement and/or shed light on personal life and artistic orientation. I am well aware of a number of titles that would have been included had I been able to secure a copy; and the numerous references to a bibliography after the dictionary and encyclopedia entries suggest further avenues to the serious researcher. The cross that any bibliographer must bear is engraved with the countless titles that have not or cannot be located. They are probably somewhere, but where? This bibliography includes most of what has been published in this area, and omissions certainly suggest where additional work must be done.

REFERENCE WORKS AND PERIODICALS

Initially, thirteen reference works in four languages and fourteen periodicals in five languages were selected for inclusion; the final list includes seven and ten respectively. The number of such sources should and will be increased eventually, but length considerations had to be taken into account in this initial effort. Each of the seventeen titles has been assigned a bibliographical abbreviation, and a coded list of the reference works with their abbreviations immediately follows this Preface.

FACTUAL DATA AND LANGUAGES

BAKER 7, which was edited by the justly renowned lexicographer Nicolas Slonimsky, has been the primary source for the spelling of names, as well as date and place of birth and death. Only fifteen of the twelve hundred forty-nine artists listed here are not found in BAKER 7 (see Appendix II for details) in which case the source of data is indicated specifically. Perhaps due to fact that the professional conductor is a relatively recent phenomenon, almost all of the conductors listed in this bibliography are to be found in at least two basic encyclopedias or dictionaries.

A conscious effort was made to include all known biographical material in the Germanic and Italic branches of the Indo-European language family. Citations from the Balto-Slavic branch are occasionally listed only because they were immediately available, but some knowledgeable colleague will have to be responsible for a comprehensive listing of such titles sometime in the future. Thus the important writings of J. Burghauser, Rimas Geniusas, Leo Ginzburg, and Vladimir Sefl (to mention only a few) will not be found in this bibliography.

ORDER OF MATERIALS

This work is divided into three major sections. The first, "COLLECTIVE WORKS: Books on Conductors," includes fifty-four titles devoted entirely or primarily to concert and opera conductors. The entries are code numbered A0001 through A0054; authors, co-authors, and editors in this section also appear in the Index. Those titles with roughly forty or fewer artists include the name of each conductor in the annotation, and these names are cross-indexed under the entries for individual conductors. Annotations are specifically designed to be informational. The second section, "COLLECTIVE WORKS: Related Books," contains one hundred sixty-nine titles, with additional material on many of the conductors mentioned in section one. As in the previous section, the entries are code numbered (B0001 through B0169) and authors, co-authors, and editors are listed in the Index. Any conductors mentioned in the annotations are cross-referenced in section three.

The final section, "INDIVIDUAL CONDUCTORS: A-Z," includes twelve hundred forty-nine artists from Claudio Abbado to Fritz Zweig listed alphabetically and numbered from C0001 through C1249. Along with essential birth and death information, each entry may include information from five different types of sources: (1) entries in any of the seven reference works listed in the bibliographical abbreviations section, including the edition and volume number if appropriate. Bibliographic references not duplicated in this compilation are indicated, e.g. BAKER 7 (Bibliography); (2) articles of a biographical or autobiographical nature from any of the ten periodicals listed in the abbreviations section; (3) autobiographies or books by the conductor related directly to pedagogy or interpre-tation; (4) biographies about the conductor and compilations of memora-bilia, scores, reviews, etc.; (5) other books containing important material; for example, because Sir Thomas Beecham is mentioned prominently in Ivor Newton's autobiography, this reference appears under the code number C0079.5. This section can act as its own index and, used in conjunction with the collective works, should provide an abundance of sources to pursue for information. Appendix I suggests a few additional reference sources which may be unknown to even the serious amateur, and Appendix II provides a comprehensive index to the sixteen hundred fifteen conductors included in Nicolas Slonimsky's seventh edition of Baker's Biographical Dictionary of Musicians. Any commonality with the twelve hundred forty-nine artists listed in this bibliography is indicated by the appropriate code number which precedes the name. The fact that fewer than two percent of the artists are not to be found in BAKER 7 attests to Slonimsky's outstanding work.

This compilation has been a labor of love and extends back over several decades. I will continue to add artists, expand the number of encyclopedias, dictionaries, and periodicals that are cross-referenced, and therefore, each reader is encouraged to inform me of any additions, deletions, or corrections through the publisher. The number of titles that have come to light during the compilation of this book has been a constant source of pleasure. Bibliographies are by definition process rather than product, and I trust that this particular process will continue ad infinitum with or without William Newman's "one grand SIC"!

ACKNOWLEDGMENTS

The undertaking of such a work usually entails the cooperation of a number of libraries, funding sources, and individuals. I should first of all like to thank Lim M. Lai for his unique and valuable contributions to this project. His expertise and constant support make him a valued colleague indeed. And I must express special gratitude to the following: the Library of Congress in Washington and the Music Library at the University of California/Berkeley; the National Endowment for the Humanities and the San José State University Foundation; and Professor Gus C. Lease, Chairman of the Department of Music at San José State University. Far too many individuals have, over the years, been of assistance. Their names would read like a Who's Who among dealers, collectors, researchers, and talented dilettantes. Such unheralded heroes provide the network of support upon which compilers like myself have come to depend. As a collector for over half my lifetime, I have countless reasons to deeply appreciate their anonymous contributions. And finally, my dear wife and better half, Jacqueline Mailloux Cowden, has proven to be indispensible for her computer expertise, her patient proofreading and editorial suggestions, and her tireless support of an incurable "book nut."

Robert H. Cowden
Monte Sereno, California
December, 1986

Bibliographical Abbreviations

The abbreviations listed below are used in the text of this bibliography, especially in the third section on individual conductors. The abbreviations chosen are widely used, and readers should find them easy to remember and use.

Encyclopedias and Dictionaries

BAKER 7

Baker's Biographical Dictionary of Musicians. 7th edition. Revised by Nicolas Slonimsky. New York: Schirmer Books, 1984.

EdS

Enciclopedia dello spettacolo. 9 vols. Roma: Casa Editrice le Maschere, 1954-62. Aggiornamento 1955-1965. Roma: Unione Editoriale, 1966.

GROVE 6

Sadie, Stanley, ed., The New Grove Dictionary of Music and Musicians. 20 vols. London: Macmillan Publishers Limited, 1980.

GROVE-AM

Hitchcock, H. Wiley and Stanley Sadie, eds. The New Grove Dictionary of American Music. 4 vols. London: Macmillan Publishers Limited, 1986.

MGG

Blume, Friedrich, ed. Die Musik in Geschichte und Gegenwart: allgemeine Enzyklopaedie der Musik.... 14 vols. Kassel: Baerenreiter Verlag, 1949-67. Supplement. Kassel, 1973/1979. Register. Kassel, 1986.

PAB-MI/2

McNeil, Barbara and Miranda C. Herbert, eds. Performing Arts Bibliography Master Index: a Consolidated Guide to over 270,000 Bibliographical Sketches of Persons Living and Dead, as They Appear in over 100 of the Principal Biographical Dictionaries Devoted to the Performing Arts. 2nd edition. Detroit: Gale Research Company, 1982.

RIEMANN 12

Gurlitt, Wilibald, ed. Riemann Musik-Lexikon: Personenteil. 2 Vols.

12. voellig neubearbeitete Auflage. Mainz: B. Schott's Soehne, 1959-1967. Ergaenzungsband. Mainz, 1972/1975.

Periodicals

GR

The Gramophone. Vol. 44 (1966-67) to Vol. 63 (1985-86).
Note: Prior to volume 45 there was no table of contents.

HiFi/MusAm

High Fidelity and Musical America. Vol. 20 (1970) to Vol. 35 (1985).
Note: Musical America was merged into High Fidelity beginning with Vol. 23 (1973).

JCG

Journal of the Conductor's Guild. Vol. 1, #1 (1980) to Vol. 4, #4 (1983).

LS

La Scala Rivista. #1 (1949) to #133 (1960).

LGB

Le Grand Baton. Vol. 1, #1 (1964) to Vol. 20, #56 (1983).
Note: Published by The Sir Thomas Beecham Society, Inc.

MQ

Musical Quarterly. Vol. 1 (1915) to Vol. 45 (1959).

ON

Opera News. Vol. 1 (1936) to Vol. 47 (1982-83).

OPERA

Opera. Vol. 1 (1950) to Vol. 36 (1985).

OW

Opernwelt. Vol. 1 (1960) to Vol. 26 (1985).

RS

British Institute of Recorded Sound. As of 1961 the publication was called Recorded Sound. No. 1 (Summer 1956) to No. 86 (1984).

CONCERT AND OPERA CONDUCTORS

PART A.

COLLECTIVE WORKS:
Books on Conductors

A0001. Blaszczyk, Leon Tadeusz. Dyrygenci polscy i obey w Polsce dzialajacy w XIX i XX wieku. Kraków: Polskie Wydawnictwo Muzyczne, 1964. 358, [3] p., illus., 38-item bibliography, chronology, list of appointments by country and city, supplement.

An important reference source listing about 1,500 conductors, some with pictures and/or bibliographic references.

A0002. Blaukopf, Kurt. Great Conductors. Translated by Miriam Blaukopf. London: Arco Publishers Limited, 1955. xii, 13-194 p., 16 illus., selected LP discography, 42-item bibliography.

Twenty-two of the outstanding 20th century conductors including Ansermet, Barbirolli, Beecham, van Beinum, Boehm, Boult, Fricsay, Furtwaengler, Jochum, von Karajan, Kleiber, Klemperer, Kletzki, Knappertsbusch, Krauss, Krips, Sacher, Sargent, Scherchen, Stokowski, Toscanini, and Walter.

A0003. Brook, Donald. Conductor's Gallery: Biographical Sketches of Well-known Orchestral Conductors including Notes on the Leading Symphony Orchestras, and a Short Biography of the Late Sir Henry Wood. London: Rockliff, 1945. xii, 188 p., 45 illus.

Biographies of thirty-two conductors including Richard Austin, Barbirolli, Beecham, Boult, Braithwaite, Cameron, Carner, Coates, Cohen, Cundell, Fagan, Fistoulari, Harrison, Irving, Jacques, Lambert, Mathieson, Menges, Miles, Neel, Newman, Raybould, Kathleen Riddick, Robinson, Sargent, Sherman, Statham, Warrak, Weldon, Whyte, Woodgate, and Wood.

A0004. Brook, Donald. International Gallery of Conductors. London: Rockliff Publishing Corporation Ltd., 1951. ix, 232, [1] p., 36 illus., index.

Thirty-six conductors with a number of changes from the author's A0003. Ansermet, Richard Austin, Barbirolli, Beecham, van Beinum, Boult, Basil Cameron, Del Mar, Furtwaengler, Goossens, John Hollingsworth, von Karajan, Klemperer, Richard Korn, Koussevitzky, Nikolai Malko, Herbert Menges, Maurice Miles, Mitropoulos, Boyd Neel, Ormandy, Paray, Karl Rankl, Clarence Raybould, Hugo Rignold, Stanford Robinson, Rodzinski, de Sabata, Sargent, Rudolf Schwarz, Fabien Sevitzky, Stokowski, Susskind, Toscanini, Walter, and Weldon.

A0005. Burghauser, Jarmil. Slavní čeští dirigenti. Praha: Statni hudebni vydavatelstvi, 1963. 158, [1] p., 20 illus.

291 conductors many of whom are totally unknown. A colleague provided an annotation of the same title with twenty-two illustrations and a list of 193 referenced conductors.

A0006. Camner, James, ed. Great Conductors in Historic Photographs: 193 Portraits from 1860 to 1960. New York: Dover Publications, Inc., 1982. 89 p., 193 black-and-white photographs.

Legendary conductors from Claudio Abbado to Felix Weingartner in single and multiple poses. Similar to the editor's books on composers, instrumentalists, and opera stars.

A0007. Chesterman, Robert, ed. Conversations with Conductors. Totowa (NJ): Rowman and Littlefield, 1976. 128 p., 11 illus.

Walter, Boult, Bernstein, Ansermet, Klemperer, and Stokowski are interviewed by Chesterman, Albert Goldberg, Peter Heyworth, and Glenn Gould.

A0008. Couturier, Louis. Dirigenten van dezen tijd. Uitgave: J. Philip Kruseman 'S-Gravenhage, n.d. [1938]. 112 p., 8 illus.

Mengelberg, van Beinum, van Anrooy, Schuurman, Flipse, Cornelis, van Otterloo, Kuiler, Spaanderman, Hermans, Muck, Monteux, Walter, Schuricht, Rhené-Baton, Schneevoigt, Nikisch, Toscanini, Jirak, Furtwaengler, and Stokowski.

A0009. Craven, Robert R., ed. Symphony Orchestras of the United States: Selected Profiles. Westport (CT): Greenwood Press, 1986. xxiii, 521 p., chronology of 126 profiled orchestras, 72-item bibliography, index, list of 114 contributors.

Each profile includes a chronology of music directors which makes this work valuable for tracing both major and minor artists. A companion volume covering orchestras of the world is forthcoming.

A0010. Ewen, David. Dictators of the Baton. Chicago: Alliance Book Corporation, 1943. 305, [5] p., 30 illus., 44-item bibliography, list of major American orchestras, index.

Toscanini, Stokowski, Koussevitzky, Mitropoulos, Iturbi, Walter Damrosch, Stock, Walter, Fritz Busch, Beecham, Monteux, Barbirolli, Ormandy, Leinsdorf, Reiner, Rodzinski, Golschmann, Sevitzky, Smallens, Kindler, Kolar, Goossens, Krueger, Barlow, Black, Wallenstein, Rapee, Solomon, Dixon, and Levin.

A0011. Ewen, David. Musicians Since 1900: Performers in Concert and Opera. New York: H.W. Wilson Company, 1978. ix, 974 p., numerous portraits.

Among the 432 performers listed are 111 conductors from Claudio Abbado to Eugene Ysayë. Not intended for the serious scholar.

A0012. Ewen, David. The Man with the Baton: the Story of Conductors and Their Orchestras. New York: Thomas Y. Crowell Company, 1937. 374 p., 26 illus., biographical guide to 192 conductors, 88-item bibliography, index.

Biographical material on most of the 192 conductors is limited, but there are major chapters on Nikisch, Muck, Weingartner, Toscanini, Stokowski, and Koussevitzky who authored the introductory chapter, "Concerning Interpretation."

A0013. Ferro, Enzo Valenti. Los directores: Teatro Colón 1908-1984. Buenos Aires: Ediciones de Arte Gaglianone, 1985. 406 p., 175 portraits, 42-item bibliography, index of conductors.

This limited edition of 1,500 copies includes material on 451 conductors, many of whom are not mentioned elsewhere.

A0014. Galkin, Elliott Washington. The Theory and Practice of Orchestral Conducting Since 1752. Ph.D. diss., Cornell University, 1960. ix, 650 p., 42 illus., 341-item bibliography.

A major contribution by a conductor-scholar which should be required reading for the serious student. The excellent bibliography includes a number of references not duplicated here. A respected conductor (see his individual entry C0376), Galkin was also a music critic for the Baltimore Sun and served as the director of the Peabody Conservatory of Music.

A0015. Gandrup, Victor. Fem taktstokkens mestre. København: Rosenkilde og Bagger, 1957. 43, [1] p., 5 illus.

Nikisch, Johan Svendsen, Muck, Franz Schalk, and Toscanini.

A0016. Geitel, Klaus, ed. Grosse deutsche Dirigenten: 100 Jahre Berliner Philharmoniker. Berlin: Severin und Siedler, 1981. 221 p., illus., 6-item bibliography.

Includes a very interesting chronology 1882-1981. Important material on von Buelow, Nikisch, Strauss, Klemperer, Walter, Furtwaengler, and von Karajan.

A0017. Hart, Philip. Conductors: a New Generation. New York: Charles Scribner's Sons, 1979. xviii, 302 p., 8 illus., recordings, index.

Important material on Barenboim, Andrew Davis, Abbado, Riccardo Muti, Mehta, Ozawa, De Waart, and Levine.

A0018. Hart, Philip. Orpheus in the New World: the Symphony Orchestra as an American Cultural Institution. New York: W.W. Norton & Company, Inc., 1973. xix, 562 p., 43 tables and graphs, 14 statistical and informational graphs, notes, 184-item bibliography, index.

Both notes and bibliography are excellent. A magnificent contribution to the literature which has aged marvelously well.

A0019. Herzfeld, Friedrich. Magie des Takstocks: die Welt der grossen Dirigenten, Konzerte, und Orchester. Berlin: Verlag Ullstein, A.G., 1953. 207 p., 70 illus., index.

A general history which is an excellent introduction to the subject.

A0020. Holmes, John L. Conductors on Record. London: Victor Gollancz Ltd., 1982. xv, 734 p., 21-item bibliography.

An interesting solo effort in which the entries include birth and death year, short biography, discography up to 1977, some repertoire, and comments.

A0021. Holsinger, Clyde William. A History of Choral Conducting with Emphasis on the Time-Beating Techniques used in the Successive Historical Periods. Ph.D. diss., University of Illinois, 1954. v, 351, [1] p., 177-item bibliography.

"The attempt is made here to examine numerous significant existing works, or their translations, which deal with our study, and evolve basic principles which probably guided music conductors in the different eras in music history."

A0022. Humphrey, Martha Burnham. An Eye for Music. Boston: H.M. Teich and Company, 1949. 108 p., numerous drawings.

Koussevitzky, Richard Burgin, Munch, Bernstein, de Carvalho, Walter, Milhaud, Fabian Sevitzky, Reiner, Nicolai Malko, Taumo Hannikainen, Stanley Chapple, Szell, Goossens, Barbirolli, Desire Defauw, Boult, Paray, Stokowski, Mitropoulos, and Stravinsky.

A0023. Jacobson, Bernard. Conductors on Conducting. Frenchtown (NJ): Columbia Publishing Company, Inc. 1979. 237 p., 20 illus., index.

Informative interviews with James Levine, Nikolaus Harnoncourt, Charles Mackerras, Colin Davis, Bernard Haitink, Jose Serebrier, Adrian Boult, and Carlo Maria Giulini.

A0024. Jaeger, Stefan, ed. Das Atlantisbuch der Dirigenten: eine Enzyklopaedie. Zuerich: Atlantis Musikbuch Verlag AG, 1985. 415 p., 205 illus., index of names, 49-item bibliography.

Clearly the outstanding book of its kind presently available, this reference work includes sixty-nine major conductors among the 783 who merited inclusion.

A0025. Jordá, Enrique. El director de orquesta ante la partitura (bosquejo de interpretación de la música orquestal). Madrid: Espasa-Calpe, S.A., 1969. 159, [1] p.

The author is a well known conductor who has led a number of orchestras including the San Francisco Symphony.

A0026. Juramie, Ghislaine. Les grands chefs d'orchestre. Nancy: Editions Love Me Tender, 1983. 135 p., illus.

This coffee table book with magnificent color illustrations includes 126 conductors.

A0027. Koury, Daniel J. Orchestral Performance Practices in the Nineteenth Century: Size, Proportions, and Seating. Ann Arbor (MI): UMI Research Press, 1986. xiv, [iii], 409 p., notes, 290-item bibliography, index of names.

This is a revision of the author's 1981 Ph.D. dissertation at Boston University.

A0028. Krebs, Carl. Meister des Taktstocks. Berlin: Verlegt bei Schuster & Loeffler, 1919. 229 p., 69-item bibliography, index of names.

One of the better early histories which is worthwhile due to its period orientation as well as its bibliographical references. Great conductors in the persons of Mahler and Nikisch had introduced the public to a new category of musical stars.

A0029. Krueger, Karl. The Way of the Conductor: His Origins, Purpose and Procedures. New York: Charles Scribner's Sons, 1958. 250 p., 44 illus., index.

"This little book is for the musical amateur to whom we musicians owe so much."

A0030. Loebmann, Hugo. Zur Geschichte des Taktierens und Dirigierens. Duesseldorf: Druck und Verlag von L. Schwann, 1913. [2], 104 p.

A very minor contribution at best.

A0031. Matheopoulos, Helena. Maestro: incontri con i grandi direttori d'orchestra. Milano: Garzanti Editore s.p.a., 1983. 551, [3] p., 75 illus., notes, 35-item bibliography, index of names.

Twenty-three of the top contemporary conductors are discussed in some depth: Bernstein, Boulez, Previn, Abbado, Boehm, Boult, Davis, Giulini, Haitink, von Karajan, Levine, Maazel, Mackerras, Mehta, Muti, Ozawa, Solti, Tennstedt, Carlos Kleiber, Ašhkenazy, Rostropovich, Riccardo Chailly, and Simon Rattle.

A0032. May, Robin. Behind the Baton: a Who's Who of Conductors. London: Frederick Muller Limited, 1981. 152 p., select discography, 33-item bibliography.

Short biographies of 575 conductors from Claudio Abbado to Hermann Zumpe who in 1873 aided Wagner in preparing the "Ring Cycle."

A0033. Melichar, Alois. Der volkommene Dirigent: Entwicklung und Verfall einer Kunst. Muenchen: Georg Mueller Verlag, 1981. 399, [2] p., 7 illus.

A0034. Metz, Louis. Over dirigeren, dirigenten en orkesten. Amsterdam: 'De Tijdstroom', Lochem, 1956. 333 p., 100 illus., list of conductors with birth and death dates/locations, selective discography.

Short summaries of forty-five 20th century conductors including some relative unknowns. The second enlarged edition published in 1968 expands the list to ninety conductors, and there is a 101-item bibliography.

A0035. Nebdal, Karel and Vilém Pospišil. Slavni světovi dirigenti. Praha: Státní hudební vydavatelství, 1963. 183, [2] p., 28 illus., select discography.

A general chronological overview with special attention given to sixty-three important figures from von Buelow to von Karajan.

A0036. Neumeister, Werner and Guenter Hausswald. Dirigenten - Bild und Schrift. Berlin: Rembrandt Verlag, 1965. 103 p., 40 portraits, 40 autographed statements.

Little material which is not available elsewhere.

A0037. Norlind, Tobias. Dirigerings konstens historia. Stockholm: Nordiska Musikfoerlaget, 1944. 79 p., 25-item bibliography.

Norlind is best known for his Allmaent Musiklexikon (rev. ed., 1927-28) which is the standard Swedish reference work for the period.

A0038. Poessiger, Guenter. Die grossen Saenger und Dirigenten. Muenchen: Wilhelm Heyne Verlag, 1968. 220 p., 55 illus., 21-item bibliography.

Fifty-five conductors share the spotlight with 151 vocalists. The coverage is quite brief and lacks depth.

A0039. Pricope, Eugen. Dirijori si orchestre. Bucuresti: Editura Muzicală, 1971. 461, [1] p., 50 illus., 75-item bibliography.

Another unusual item which includes some artists difficult to trace elsewhere. The bibliography provides scholars familiar with the language a number of suggestions.

A0040. Ringbom, Nils-Eric. Orkesterhoevdingar: dokument om dirigenter. Ekenaes: Soederstroem & C:O Foerlags AB, 1981. 144 p., 25 illus.

Sibelius, Kajanus, Schnéevoigt, Jaernefelt, Hannikainen, Funtek, Ansermet, Barbirolli, Beecham, Dixon, Ferencsik, Jorda, van Beinum, Kletzki, Ormandy, Munch, von Karajan, Szell, Mravinskij, Kubelik, Sargent, Stokowski, Monteux, and Wolff.

A0041. Schonberg, Harold C. The Great Conductors. New York: Simon and Schuster, 1967. 384 p., 48 illus., index.

"Basically this book is a study in style, an attempt to present, in continuous evolution, the musical attitudes and techniques of the great conductors." Schonberg is a journalist of unusual breadth whose musical knowledge is far above that of most of his colleagues. A working bibliography would have substantially increased the value of this important contribution.

A0042. Schreiber, Ottmar. Orchester und Orchesterpraxis in Deutschland zwischen 1780 und 1850. Berlin: Triltsch & Luther, 1938. Reprint 1978. 322 p., extensive bibliographical footnotes, index of cities.

A valuable contribution for the period.

A0043. Schuenemann, Georg. Geschichte des Dirigierens. Hildesheim: Georg Olms, 1965 [original: Leipzig, 1913]. ix, 359 p., index.

This is the first authoritative history of conducting. Interesting features include orchestra seating plans and conducting patterns.

A0044. Seidl, Arthur. Moderne Dirigenten. Berlin: Schuster & Loeffler, 1902. 48 p.

A student of Spitta, Seidl was primarily a teacher and writer on aesthetics.

A0045. Shore, Bernard. The Orchestra Speaks. London: Longmans, Green and Co., 1938. Reprint 1972. 217, [1] p.

Beecham, Boult, Casals, Coates, Goossens, Barbirolli, Heward, Julius Harrison, Harty, Koussevitzky, Mengelberg, Sargent, Toscanini, and Wood.

A0046. Sordet, Dominique. Douze chefs d'orchestre. Paris: Librairie Fischbacher, 1924. 107, [2] p.

A rare and very important publication which includes information about a number of obscure conductors. Camille Chevillard, André Caplet, Philippe Gaubert, Rhené-Baton, Albert Wolff, Henri Busser, François Ruehlmann, Maurice Frigara, Paul Paray, Vladimir Golschmann, D.-E. Inghelbrecht, and Gabriel Pierné.

A0047. Šrom, Karel. Orchestr a dirigent. Praha: Panton, 1960. 130, [3] p., 4 illus., 10-item bibliography.

The author was a music critic in Prague for almost two decades and served as head of the Music Section of Czech Radio (1945-50).

A0048. Stoddard, Hope. Symphony Conductors of the U.S.A.. New York: Thomas Y. Crowell Company, 1957. [iii], 405 p., index.

Thirty-two major conductors are covered in some detail with thumbnail sketches of 443 lesser figures. Abravanel, Alessandro, Bernstein, Saul Caston, Dorati, Massimo Freccia, Golschmann, Harrison, Hendl, Alexander Hilsberg, Thor Johnson, Jorda, Krips, Leinsdorf, Howard Mitchell, Mitropoulos, Monteux, Munch, Ormandy, Paray, Reiner, Hans Schwieger, Izler Solomon, Sopkin, Steinberg, Stokowski, Benjamin Swalin, Szell, van Beinum, Wallenstein, Walter, and Robert Whitney.

A0049. Voss, Egon. Die Dirigenten der Bayreuther Festspiele. Regensburg: Gustav Bosse Verlag, 1976. 156 p., 56 illus., discography, index of names.

Includes a brief lexicon of forty-six conductors from Abendroth to Zender. The discography covers thirty-one of these artists.

A0050. Waldorff, Jerzy. Diably i anioly. Kraków: Polskie Wydawnietwo Muzyczne, 1971. 316, [3] p., illus.

von Buelow, Nikisch, Toscanini, Monteux, Emil Mlynarski, Furtwaengler, Stokowski, Grzegorz Fitelberg, Georgescu, Pawelklecki, Václav Talich, Bohdan Wodiczko, von Karajan, Witold Rowicki, Markévitch, Jan Krenz, and Bernstein.

A0051. Weissmann, Adolf. Der Dirigent im 20. Jahrhundert. Berlin: Propylaeen-Verlag, 1925. 195, [3] p., 20 illus., 11-item bibliography.

This is a brief history from Gluck through Beecham.

A0052. Witeschnik, Alexander, Elfriede Hanak and Winnie Jakob. Dirigenten charakterisiert, photographiert, karikiert. Wien: Verlagsanstalt Forum Verlag GmbH, 1965. 144 p., illus.

Coverage of thirty-one conductors: Volkmar Andreae, Ansermet, Boehm, Cluytens, Fricsay, Furtwaengler, Hindemith, Jochum, von Karajan, Keilberth, Kempe, Kertész, Klemperer, Knappertsbusch, Krauss, Krips, Kubelik, Maazel, Mehta, Mitropoulos, Monteux, Mrawinski, Ormandy, Paumgartner, Prêtre, Rossi, Sawallisch, Schuricht, Solti, Szell, and Walter.

A0053. Wooldridge, David. Conductor's World. New York: Praeger Publishers, 1970. xiv, 379 p., orchestral layouts under various conductors, table of six major American orchestras with the terms of office of the respective permanent conductors, select discography, index.

A general history of conducting from Weber to Bernstein. In addition to the table of six major American orchestras, there is a table of ten leading German and Austrian opera houses and symphony orchestras from 1800 until World War II listing conductors.

A0054. Young, Percy. The Concert Tradition: From the Middle Ages to the Twentieth Century. New York: Roy Publishers, Inc., 1965. x, 278 p., 23 illus., 109-item bibliography, index.

A good general study which concentrates on the connections between the musical and social events of each period.

A0055. Young, Percy M. World Conductors. London: Abelard-Schuman Limited, 1965. 160 p., 20 illus., 6 musical examples and drawings, 19-item bibliography, list of suggested recordings, index.

PART B.

COLLECTIVE WORKS:
Related Books

B0001. Abdul, Raoul. Blacks in Classical Music: a Personal History. New York: Dodd, Mead & Company, 1977. 253 p., 16 illus., notes, chronology, index.

Seven conductors are included among the twenty-six artists: Dean Dixon, Everett Lee, Henry Lewis, James De Priest, Hall Johnson, Eva Jessye, and Leonard de Paur.

B0002. Alcari, C. Parma nella musica. Parma: M. Fresching, 1931. 259 p.

Biographical dictionary of famous musicians from Parma including conductors.

B0003. Aldrich, Richard. Concert Life in New York 1902-1923. New York: G.P. Putnam's Sons, 1941. Reprint 1971. 795 p., index, list of Sunday New York Times articles.

Reviews of major orchestras and conductors by one of America's most respected critics. Numerous conductors are mentioned, e.g. Bodansky, Damrosch, and von Dohnanyi, but there is considerable material on Gabrilowitsch.

B0004. Alonso, Luis. 40 años orquesta nacional. Madrid: Dirección General de Música y Teatro, 1982. 677 p., illus., list of conductors, chronology.

Includes short biographies with a portrait for 199 conductors.

B0005. Arditi, Luigi. My Reminiscences. Edited by Baroness von Zedlitz. 2nd edition. London: Skeffington and Son, 1896. Reprint 1977. xxv, 352 p., 38 illus., appendices include compositions and arrangements, operas produced, and singers who appeared under his direction. This composer-conductor also appears in section three.

B0006. Armsby, Leonora Wood. Musicians Talk. New York: Dial Press, Inc., 1935. xiii, 242 p., 7 illus.

The managing director of the Philharmonic Society of San Mateo County (CA) records her impressions of Hadley, Hamilton Harty, Alfred Hertz, Walter, Gabrilowitsch, Bernardino Molinari, Arbos, Toscanini, Smallens, Coates, Damrosch, Monteux, Goossens, Stock, Richard Lert, Rodzinski, Hanson.

B0007. Arteaga y Pereira, Fernando. Celebridades musicales. Barcelona: Editorial Artistico de I.T.M. Gegui, 1886. 676 p., illus.

This is really a very interesting source considering the period. Along with fifty-seven singers, there are nineteen conductors: Zerrahn, Balatka, Damrosch, Mackenzie, Stanford, Cowen, Smart, Randegger, Manns, Rosa, Barnett, Barnby, Thomas, Lucas, Bottesini, Nicolau, Casamitjana, Delmau, and Goula.

B0008. Baker-Carr, Janet. Evening at Symphony: a Portrait of the Boston Symphony Orchestra. Boston: Houghton Mifflin Company, 1977. 172 p., 61 illus., 24-item bibliography, index.

Primary focus on Koussevitzky, Leinsdorf, Munch, Monteux, Muck, and Ozawa. Unfortunately, any comprehensive documentation of major orchestras is almost as rare as that of leading opera houses. The opportunity is there for any serious scholar!

B0009. Batten, Joe. The Story of Sound Recording. London: Rockliff, 1956. xiv, 201 p., 30 illus., 3 appendices including "Recording Artistes' First Engagements, 1904-1914," index.

A pioneer English recording manager shares his recollections of Beecham, Coates, Goossens, Mackenzie, and Sargent.

B0010. Bennett, Joseph. Forty Years of Music 1865-1905. London: Methuen & Co., 1908. xvi, 415 p., 24 illus., index.

Numerous conductors but especially Costa, Hallé, Mendelssohn, Rosa, Sullivan, and Wood.

B0011. Bennwitz, Hanspeter. Interpretenlexikon der Instrumentalmusik. Bern: Francke Verlag, 1964. 326 p.

This surprisingly rare volume includes conductors.

B0012. Berutto, Guglielmo. Il Piemonte e la musica 1800-1984. Torino: privately printed for the author, 1984. 419, [2] p., illus.

Section one of this basic study includes 100 conductors.

B0013. Bescoby-Chambers, John. The Archives of Sound Including a Selective Catalogue of Historical Violin, Piano, Spoken, Documentary, Orchestral, and Composer's Own Recordings. Bolton (Lancashire): The Oakwood Press, n.d. [1964]. 153 p., 7 illus., 28-item bibliography.

A fascinating compilation which is full of factual information and short biographical sketches. The entire area of recordings, as opposed to live concerts, needs to be documented so that this critical phase of each artist's career can be properly considered.

B0014. Blackman, Charles. Beyond the Baton. New York: Charos Enterprises, Inc., 1964. 223 p., index of [61] contributors.

Many but not all of the contributors are active conductors.

B0015. Boult, Adrian C. Thoughts on Conducting. London: Phoenix House Ltd., 1963. xv, 79 p., 11 illus., 24-item bibliography.

Included in this thin volume are discussions of the methods of Nikisch, Toscanini, Weingartner, Furtwaengler, Beecham, Wood, Strauss, and Walter. As the organizer of the BBC Symphony and principal conductor of the London Philharmonic Orchestra, Boult was eminently qualified to comment on his peers.

B0016. Bragaglia, Leonardo. Verdi e i suoi interpreti (1839-1978): vita senica delle opere del cigno di Busseto attraverso una antologia critica e uno studio delle ventotto opere di Giuseppe Verdi. Roma: Bulzoni Editore, 1979. 375, [3] p., illus., index of names.

Along with over 500 interpreters of Verdian roles are six famous conductors of the master's works: DeFabritiis, De Sabata, Gui, von Karajan, Serafin, and Toscanini.

B0017. Brower, Harriet. The World's Great Men of Music. New York: Frederick A. Stokes Company, 1922. v, [v], 400 p., 5 illus.

Also published as Story-Lives of Master Musicians, Ms. Brower's book includes Mendelssohn, Wagner, Toscanini, Stokowski, and Koussevitzky.

B0018. Brown, Maynard, ed. Operatic and Dramatic Album. London: E. Matthews & Sons, n.d. [c.1877]. unpaginated, 61 illus.

Especially notable for Campanini and Carl Rosa.

B0019. Buffen, Frederick F. Musical Celebrities. London: Chapman & Hall, Limited, 1889. 116 p., 18 illus.

Interviews from The Lady typical of the journalism of the period. Excellent portraits. von Buelow, and Hallé.

B0020. Buffen, Frederick F. Musical Celebrities. second series. London: Chapman & Hall, Limited, 1893. viii, 125 p., 25 illus.

A companion volume to B0019, Manns and William George Cusins are the principal conductors.

B0021. Cairns, David. Responses: Musical Essays and Reviews. New York: Alfred A. Knopf, Inc., 1973. xiv, 266 p., musical examples.

In an expanded and edited version of previously printed articles, Cairns offers sensitive insights about Klemperer, Beecham, Furtwaengler, and von Karajan. His edited translation of Berlioz's memoirs is an absolutely first-class piece of literary scholarship.

B0022. Cardus, Neville. Full Score. London: Cassell & Company Ltd., 1970. 217 p.

The chief musical critic of the Manchester Guardian includes personal observations of Klemperer, and Furtwaengler. His portrait of Beecham (1961) and of Mahler (1965) are typical of his energetic style.

B0023. Carse, Adam. Orchestral Conducting: a Textbook for Students and Amateurs. London: Augener Ltd., 1929.

A teacher of composition and harmony who indulged a lifelong passion for the orchestra, particularly wind instruments. No copy located.

B0024. Carse, Adam. The Orchestra from Beethoven to Berlioz: a History of the Orchestra in the First Half of the 19th Century, and of the development of Orchestral Baton-conducting. Cambridge: W. Heffer & Sons Ltd., 1948. xiii, 514 p., 23 plates + numerous other illus., appendix of selected orchestral personnel, 236-item bibliography, index.

An outstanding example of research. Note especially the chapter on conducting and the following one on conductors. Carse also wrote a catalogue (1951) for the superb collection of over three hundred wind instruments he donated to the Horniman Museum in London.

B0025. Carse, Adam. The Orchestra in the XVIIIth Century. Cambridge: W. Heffer & Sons Limited., 1940. Reprint 1950. vii, 176 p., 1 plate, 105-item bibliography, index.

Still the authoritative study of the early formally organized orchestra. Carse attempts "to piece together the story of how the orchestra grew, from its infancy at the end of the 17th century to its adolescence at the end of the 18th century..."

"One of the things that must be completely cut out of the picture of the 18th century orchestra is our conception of the orchestral conductor. The time-beating, interpretative orchestral conductor did not exist...it should be understood that the word 'conductor' was applied to the musician who was in charge of a performance, but that orchestras were not controlled by a time-beating conductor."

B0026. Chorley, Henry F. Music and Manners in France and Germany: a Series of Traveling Sketches of Art and Society. 3 vols. London: Longman, Brown, Green, and Longmans, 1844. Reprint 1983. viii, 299 p.; viii, 302 p.; xii, 299 p.

A very important first-hand account as it were of Mendelssohn and Berlioz. As the influential critic of the Athenaeum, the author supported musical conservatives such as Mendelssohn while attacking Chopin, Schumann, and Wagner. He was also the author of a rather bizarre novel A Prodigy: a Tale of Music (1866).

B0027. Coar, Birchard. The Masters of the Classical Period as Conductors. DeKalb (IL): privately printed for the author, 1949. [ii], vii, 126 p., index, 50-item bibliography.

Includes material on Bach, Handel, Haydn, Mozart, and Beethoven as conductors. Note Carse's caveat in B0025! One of the fascinating aspects of any involvement in the origins of conducting is precisely when, where, and how musical leadership was established.

B0028. Cox, John Edmund. Musical Recollections of the Last Half-Century. 2 vols. London: Tinsley Brothers, 1872. xv, 345 p.; vi, 370 p.

An important period source (1818-1867), most of the material is taken from the Quarterly Musical Magazine and Review (1818-1828), The Harmonicon (1823-1833), and The Athenaeum, the Times, and the Spectator for the remaining years.

B0029. Croger, T.R. Notes on Conductors and Conducting. 3rd edition revised and enlarged. London: William Reeves, n.d. 76 p., portrait.

A very cursory account beginning with Ludwig Spohr (1810) and ending with Felix Mottl.

"...I wish it to be distinctly understood that I have nothing to suggest to conductors of established reputation, but address myself to those who are seeking information on a technical subject."

B0030. Culshaw, John. Putting the Record Straight; the Autobiography of John Culshaw. Edited posthumously by Erik Smith. New York: The Viking Press, 1968. 362 p., index.

As Decca's chief producer he played a crucial role in Solti's complete recording of the Ring Cycle. Important material on Ansermet, Beecham, von Karajan, Kleiber, Knappertsbusch, Krips, Solti, and Szell.

B0031. Culshaw, John. Ring Resounding: the Recording in Stereo of 'Der Ring des Nibelungen'. London: Secker & Warburg, 1967. 284 p., 20 illus., cast listings, index.

An all too rare look into the inner world of financial and political manipulation as well as artistic egos. A special edition with new illustrations was issued in 1972. Furtwaengler, Knappertsbusch, and Solti.

B0032. Davison, Henry, comp. From Mendelssohn to Wagner Being the Memoirs of J.W. Davison Forty Years Music Critic of "The Times". London: Wm. Reeves, 1912. xviii, 539 p., 61 illus., [incomplete] list of articles, index.

Basic source for the period 1835-1885 in England compiled by the author's son from memoranda and documents. Useful for Berlioz, Jullien, and Wagner. As editor of the Musical World (1844-85) as well as music critic of the Times (1846-79), Davison was one of the most influential critics of his generation.

B0033. de Curzon, Henri. L'Oeuvre de Richard Wagner a Paris et ses interprètes (1850-1914). Paris: Maurice Senart et Cie, Editeurs, n.d. 92, [2] p., 24 illus., index of names.

Alban, Bréville, Chevillard, Colonne, Cortot, Danbé, Delsart, Harcourt, Lamoureux, Luigini, Messager, Mottl, Nikisch, Pasdeloup, Rabaud, Richter, Ruehlmann, Sechiari, Seghers, Taffanel, and Weingartner.

B0034. de Grial, Hugo. Musicos Mexicanos. México, D.F.: Editorial Diana, S.A., 1965. 275, [8] p.

Conductors are included among the 129 artists covered.

B0035. della Corte, Andrea. L'Interpretazione musicale e gli interpreti. Torino: Unione Tipografico-Editrice Torinese, 1951. xvi, 574 p., 12 portraits, 263 illus.

Spohr, Mendelssohn, Habeneck, Deldevez, Seidl, Costa, Nicolai, Richter, Mottl, Levi, von Buelow, Nikisch, Weingartner, Toscanini, Furtwaengler, and Walter.

B0036. Desarbres, Nérée. Deux siècles a l'Opéra (1669-1868). Paris: E. Dentu, Editeur, 1868. 297 p.

Quite valuable period publication which includes a number of rather obscure conductors. Cambert, Lalouette, Colasse, Marais, J. Rebel, Lacoste, Mouret, F. Francoeur, Niel, Chéron, Lagarde, Danvergne, Aubert, Berton, L.-J. Francoeur, Rey, Persuis, Kreutzer, Habeneck, Girard, Dietsch, and George [Francois?] Hainl.

B0037. Diósy, Bela. Ungarischer Kuenstler Almanach: das Kuenstler Ungarns in Wort und Bild. Budapest: Koeniglich Ungarische Universitaetsdruckerei, 1929. 383 p., illus., index of names.

Nine conductors are included with a picture, biography and/or repertoire and/or press notices. Anton Fleischer, Eugen Kereszty, Wilhelm Komor, Desider Márkus, Emmerich Petoe, Ferdinand Rékai, Stephan Strasser, Ernst Unger, and Viktor Vaszy.

B0038. Downes, Irene, ed. Olin Downes on Music: a Selection of His Writings During the Half-century 1906-1955. New York: Simon and Schuster, 1957. xxxi, 473 p., index.

Many conductors are mentioned in passing but especially valuable for Muck, Monteux, Koussevitzky, Gabrilowitsch, Mengelberg, Beecham, Toscanini, and Morel.

B0039. Ebel, Arnold, ed. Berliner Musikjahrbuch 1926. Leipzig: Verlagsanstaldt Deutscher Tonkuenstler A.-G., 1926. 246 p., 10 illus.

Heinz Tiessen, Walter, and Furtwaengler.

B0040. Ertel, Paul. Kuenstler-Biographieen. 10 vols. Berlin: Concert-Direction Hermann Wolff, 1898-1907.

Gabrilowitsch (v. 1), Schnéevoigt (v. 2), and Koussevitzky (v. 10).

B0041. Espinoza, Adolfo Parra. Antologia de artistas, compositores y profesionales Ecuatorianos. Cuenca: Publicaciones y Papeles, 1983. 296 p., illus.

Very helpful for conductors from Ecuador.

B0042. Estavan, Lawrence, ed. W.P.A. Project 10677: the History of Opera in San Francisco. 2 vols. San Francisco: The W.P.A., 1938. 136 p., 41-item bibliography; 164 p., 41-item bibliography.

Volume one is important for conductors of the Tivoli Opera House 1880-1900. Volume two includes Gaetano Merola, Alfred Hertz, and Pelletier at the Civic Auditorium (1923-1932) as well as those who conducted at the War Memorial Opera House (1933-1938) especially Bodanzky, Leinsdorf, and Reiner.

B0043. Ewen, David. Encyclopedia of Concert Music. New York: Hill and Wang, 1959. ix, 566 p., selected readings on music and musicians.

Brief entries on over 150 conductors. "In addition, brief histories are provided for over a hundred symphony orchestras, chamber music ensembles, two-piano teams, music festivals, and summer concert series (European as well as American), and the foremost auditoriums in which these performances take place."

B0044. Ewen, David. Men and Women Who Make Music. New York: Thomas Y. Crowell Company, 1939. xiv, 274 p., 16 illus., index.

Toscanini, Koussevitzky, Ormandy, Rodzinski, and Stokowski. Entries in the 1945 and 1949 editions may differ and should be checked.

B0045. Fernandez Cid, Antonio. Musicos que fueron nuestros amigos. Madrid: Editora Nacional, 1967. 243 p., 26 illus.

Eduardo Toldra, Bartolome Perez Casas, Jesus Arambarri, Ataulfo Argenta, Carl Schuricht, and Victorino Echevarria.

B0046. Finck, Henry T. My Adventures in the Golden Age of Music. New York: Funk & Wagnalls Company, 1926. Reprint 1971. xvi, 462 p., 31 illus., index.

Finck was the music editor at the New York Evening Post for over four decades (1881-1924). These personal recollections probe beneath the surface commonplaces and include Thomas, Campanini, Seidl, Toscanini, and Mahler. Famous for his vendetta against the Dramrosch family.

B0047. Firner, Walter, ed. Wir von der Oper: ein kritisches Theater-bildbuch. Muenchen: Verlag F. Bruckmann AG, 1932. 126 p., 40 portraits.

Insights into the personal life and professional work of Busch, Furtwaengler, Kleiber, Klemperer, and Walter.

B0048. Gaisberg, F.W. Music on Record. London: Robert Hale Limited, 1946. Reprint 1977. 269 p., 33 illus., index.

Of the many conductors who are mentioned, Beecham, Koussevitzky, Nikisch, Ronald, Toscanini, and Walter merit in-depth coverage.

B0049. Ganz, Wilhelm. Memories of a Musician: Reminiscences of Seventy Years of Musical Life. London: John Murray, 1913. xv, 357 p., 19 illus., list of compositions, index.

Trained as a pianist, Ganz organized the Ganz Orchestra Concerts in London and premiered many Berlioz and Liszt works. Campanini, Hallé, Mengelberg, Nikisch, Richter, and Sullivan.

B0050. Garcia, Francisco Moncada. Pequeñas biografias de grandes musios Mexicanos. Primera Serie. México, D.F.: Ediciones Framong, 1966. 291 p., 62 illus., 21-item bibliography.

Fourteen conductors are included among the sixty artists. Alberto M. Alvarado Lopez, Daniel Ayala Pérez, Salvador Contreras Sánchez, Carlos Chávez Ramírez, José Mariano Elízaga Prado, José Antonio Gomez, Eduardo Hernández Moncada, Carlos J. Meneses Ladrón de Guevara, José Pablo Moncayo García, Salvador Ochoa Fernández, Cenobio Paniagua Vázquez, Silvestre Revueltas Sánchez, Luis Sandi Meneses, and José Francisco Váquez Cano.

B0051. Gatti-Casazza, Giulo. Memories of the Opera. New York: Charles Scribner's Sons, 1941. Reprint 1977. xii, 326 p., 18 illus., index.

Memoirs by directors of leading musical organizations are typically bland, and this is not an exception. Considering that he guided the Metropolitan Opera during its "Golden Age", surely there was more to tell! Bodanzky, Campanini, Hertz, and Toscanini.

B0052. Gelatt, Roland. Music Makers: Some Outstanding Musical Performers of Our Day. New York: Alfred A. Knopf, 1953. xvi, 286, xiv p., 21 illus., index.

"Each chapter attempts to analyze its subject's special gifts, the reasons why he performs as he does, and his influence on other musicians." Penetrating insights into the work of Ansermet, Beecham, Mitropoulos, Munch, Ormandy, Toscanini, and Walter.

B0053. Glennon, James. Australian Music & Musicians. Adelaide: Rigby Limited, 1968. [vii], 291 p., 11 illus.

Short biographies including Bellhouse, Cade, Chinner, Deane, Douglas, Foote, Hall, Heinze, Hopkins, Jones, Henry Krips, Linger, Mayer, Slapoffski, Thomas, Alberto Zelman, and Albert Zelman. SEE: B0108.

B0054. Gollancz, Victor. Journey Towards Music: a Memoir. New York: E.P. Dutton & Company, Inc., 1965. 238 p., 36 illus., appendix (nine months' opera season), index of names and places.

Beecham, Klemperer, Richter, Toscanini, Walter, Weingartner, and Wood.

B0055. Graf, Max. Die Wiener Oper. Wien: Humboldt-Verlag, 1955. 384 p., 28 illus.

Longtime (1900-1938) critic of the Wiener Allgemeine Zeitung celebrates the reopening of the Staatsoper in 1955 with recollections which include Richter, Mottl, Mahler, Walter, Weingartner, Furtwaengler, Toscanini, and Boehm.

B0056. Graves, Charles L. Post-Victorian Music With Other Studies and Sketches. Port Washington: Kennikat Press, 1971 [1st edition 1911]. xi, 369 p., index.

This book serves as an enlightening historical record of the period. Alfred Ridewald and August Manns.

B0057. Gregor, Hans. Die Welt der Oper - dic Oper der Welt: Bekenntnisse. Berlin: Ed. Bote & G. Bock, 1931. x, 3-423 p., 25 illus., index.

Recollections from one of the golden eras of European music. Mahler, Mottl, Nikisch, Richter, Strauss, and Weingartner.

B0058. Grew, Sydney. Favourite Musical Performers. London: T.N. Foulis, Limited, 1923. 266 p., 10 illus.

Wood, Beecham, Julius Harrison, and Landon Ronald.

B0059. Hadden, J. Cuthbert. Modern Musicians. Edinburgh: T.N. Foulis, 1918 [1st edition London 1913]. 267 p., 21 illus.

Nikisch, Weingartner, Wood, Ronald, Safonov, Michael Balling, Mengelberg, and Emil Mlynarski.

B0060. Haggin, B.H. 35 Years of Music. New York: Horizon Press, 1974 [first published as Music Observed, 1964]. 297, [4] p., index.

The author was music critic of the Nation for over twenty years and cultivated a confrontational style. Many of his articles are published in book form. Beecham, Bernstein, Cantelli, Furtwaengler, Koussevitzky, Monteux, Sargent, Stokowski, Toscanini, and Walter.

B0061. Hart, Philip. Orpheus in the New World: the Symphony Orchestra as an American Cultural Institution. New York: W.W. Norton & Company, Inc., 1973. xix, 562 p., 15 appendices, notes, 184-item bibliography, index.

The bibliography provides extensive leads for further investigation.

B0062. Hartford, Robert, comp./ed. Bayreuth, the Early Years: an Account of the Early Decades of the Wagner Festival as seen by the Celebrated Visitors and Participants. London: Victor Gollancz Ltd., 1980. 284, [3] p., 4 appendices (Personalia, Statistics 1876-1914, Chronology, Early Influences), notes, 117-item bibliography, index.

Among those conductors prominently mentioned are Weingartner, Wood, Sullivan, Beecham, Boult, Levi, Mottl, and Richter.

B0063. Hartmann, Rudolf. Das Geliebte Haus: mein Leben mit der Oper. Muenchen: Deutscher Taschenbuch Verlag, 1979 [1st edition 1975]. 456 p., 56 illus., repertoire list 1952-67, index.

Noted both as a producer and as an administrator, Hartmann was Intendant of the Bavarian State Opera between 1952 and 1967, a period of high artistic achievement. He worked with many of the leading conductors of opera including Boehm, Christoph Dohnanyi, Fricsay, Furtwaengler, Hollreiser, von Karajan, Keilberth, Kempe, Carlos Kleiber, Knappertsbusch, Krauss, Tietjen, and Walter.

B0064. Heylbut, Rose and Aime Gerber. Backstage at the Opera. New York: Thomas Y. Crowell Company, 1937. Reprint 1977 as Backstage at the Metropolitan Opera. ix, 325 p., 19 illus., index.

"Personal recollections and observations" which highlight Bodanzky, Hertz, and Toscanini among many others. Another piece of readable journalism from the Metropolitan Opera.

B0065. Howe, M.A. DeWolfe. The Boston Symphony Orchestra: an Historical Sketch. Boston: Houghton Mifflin Company, 1914. ix, [i], 279, [1] p., 16 illus., 3 appendices including repertoire, index.

Informative for the early conductors such as Georg Henschel, Wilhelm Gericke, Arthur Nikisch, Emil Paur, Karl Muck, and Max Fiedler.

B0066. Hurd, Michael. The Orchestra. New York: Facts on File, Inc., 1980. 224 p., numerous illus., index.

Handsome, lavishly illustrated "coffee table" book. There is a section (pp. 194-216) which includes short biographies of 101 conductors from Claudio Abbado to Sir Henry Wood.

B0067. Jacobson, Robert M. with photographs by Christian Steiner. Opera People. Introduction by Michael Scott. New York: The Vendome Press, 1982. 112 p., illus.

Artistic illumination through image and anecdote: Herbert von Karajan, Erich Leinsdorf, Karl Boehm, James Levine, Lorin Maazel, Claudio Abbado, Georg Solti, and Leonard Bernstein. The authors attempted to capture the "very particular quality", the "superior intelligence", and the "indefinable charisma" of the great stars.

B0068. Jacobson, Robert. Reverberations: Interviews with the World's Leading Musicians. New York: William Morrow & Company, Inc., 1974. 308 p.

The lack of an index is a real handicap in using this otherwise informative volume. Boulez, Barenboim, Copland, Giulini, Menuhin, Stokowski, and Michael Tilson Thomas.

B0069. Kaindl-Hoenig, Max, ed. Resonanz: 50 Jahre Kritik der Salzburger Festspiele. Forward by Bernhard Paumgartner. Salzburg: SN Verlag, 1971. 594 p., index of names, chronological register and index.

Prominently mentioned are Bernstein, Boehm, Furtwaengler, von Karajan, Klemperer, Knappertsbusch, Krauss, Krips, Mitropoulos, Paumgartner, Schalk, Szell, Toscanini, and Walter.

B0070. Kennedy, Michael. The Hallé Tradition: a Century of Music. Manchester: Manchester University Press, 1960. xiv, 424 p., 43 illus., 6 appendices, 24-item bibliography, index.

Charles Hallé, Richter, Michael Balling, Beecham, Hamilton Harty, and Barbirolli.

B0071. Kenyon, Nicholas. The BBC Symphony Orchestra: the First Fifty Years 1930-1980. Forward by Sir Adrian Boult. London: British Broadcasting Corporation, 1981. xv, 543, [20] p., 81 illus., 65-item bibliography, 6 appendices including first performances 1930-1980 and a discography, index.

Numerous conductors but especially Boult, Sargent, Rudolf Schwarz, Dorati, Boulez, Pritchard, Mackerras, and Rozhdestvensky.

B0072. Key, Pierre. Pierre Key's Music Year Book 1925-26: the Standard Music Annual. New York: Pierre Key, Inc., 1925. 379 p., illus.

Key served as the music critic for three Chicago newspapers as well as holding a similar responsibility with the New York World between 1907 and 1919. His compilations provide valuable source materials for active performers between the two world wars. This is a fascinating series loaded with obscure as well as famous artists. The initial volume includes Bodanzky, Coates, Gabrilowitsch, Louis Hasselmans, Gennaro Papi, Reiner, Serafin, Smallens, Willem van Hoogstraten, and Frank Waller. The title of the third edition is changed to Pierre Key's International Music Year Book 1928: the Standard Music Annual and includes Bodanzky, Reiner, Sokoloff, Coates, Sandor Harmati, Georg Schnéevoigt, Mengelberg, Smallens, Albert Stoessel, and Georges Zaslawsky. Anyone doing research on the period should consult each volume in the series.

B0073. Key, Pierre. Pierre Key's Musical Who's Who: a Biographical Survey of Contemporary Musicians. New York: Pierre Key, Inc., 1931. 498 p., illus.

"Material compiled and arranged by Irene E. Haynes." This is another valuable source for obscure but important artists.

B0074. Klein, Hermann. Thirty Years of Musical Life in London 1870-1900. New York: The Century Company, 1903. Reprint 1978. xvii, 483 p., 106 illus., index.

Music critic for both the Sunday Times in London (1881-1901) and the New York Herald (1902-1909), Klein heard all of the foremost artists of his era. Having studied voice with Manuel Garcia, his most penetrating comments concern singers, but his personal observations afford us a different perspective.

B0075. Klein, Hermann. The Golden Age of Opera. London: George Routledge & Sons, Ltd., 1933. Reprint 1979. xxvi, 275 p., 12 illus., index.

Beecham, Campanini, Costa, Richter, Rosa, Seidl, Sullivan, and Wood.

B0076. Klein, Hermann. Musicians and Mummers. London: Cassell and Company, Ltd., 1925. xi, 340 p., 12 illus., index.

A valuable period memoir with mention of Beecham, von Buelow, Costa, Goossens, Hallé, Manns, Mottl, Richter, and Sullivan.

B0077. Kloss, Erich, ed. Richard Wagner an seine Kuenstler. Zweiter Band der "Bayreuther Briefe" (1872-1883). Leipzig: Schuster & Loeffler, 1908. 414 p., index of names.

Most of the expected names but especially Richter and Seidl.

B0078. Koerke, Fritz A. Almanach der Kuenstler von Schauspiel, Operette, Oper und Konzert. Ausgabe 1947. Nuernberg: Verlag Die Egge-Rudolf Tauer, 1947. 800 p., illus.

An important period source which indicates then current affiliation and address. Conductors are included (pp. 643-659).

B0079. Kohut, Adolph. Beruehmte israelitische Maenner und Frauen in der Kulturgeschichte der Menschheit: Lebens- und Charakterbilder aus Vergangenheit und Gegenwart. 2 vols. Leipzig-Reudnitz: Druck und Verlag von A.H. Payne, n.d. 433 p., illus.; 432 p., illus.

Costa, Damrosch, Felix Dessoff, Alexis Hollaender, Levi, Mahler, and Julius Stern.

B0080. Kolodin, Irving, ed. The Composer as Listener: a Guide to Music. New York: Horizon Press, 1958. 300 p.

Translated excerpts on conducting by Berlioz, Wagner, and Richard Strauss. Also included are translated articles on Berlioz by Moscheles, on von Buelow by Liszt, and on Mahler by Schoenberg.

B0081. Krehbiel, Henry Edward. Chapters of Opera Being Historical and Critical Observations and Records Concerning the Lyric Drama in New York from Its Earliest Days down to the Present Time. New York: Henry Holt and Company, 1908. xvii, 435 p., 72 illus., index.

A critic of great influence, he authored program notes for the New York Philharmonic Society, published and edited the English version of Thayer's Beethoven, and served as the American editor of GROVE 2.

B0082. Krehbiel, Henry Edward. More Chapters of Opera Being Historical and Critical Observations and Records Concerning the Lyric Drama in New York from 1908 to 1918. New York: Henry Holt and Company, 1919. xvi, 474 p., 43 illus., appendix of performance records at the Met and the Manhattan Opera, index.

Intended as a sequel to B0081, this is essentially a rewrite of material printed in the New York Tribune between 1908 and 1918.

B0083. Krehbiel, Henry Edward. Review of the New York Musical Season 1885-1886 Containing Programmes of Noteworthy Occurrences, with Numerous Criticisms. New York: Novello, Ewer & Co., 1886. xxi, 233 p., index.

Primarily reprints of articles contributed to the New York Tribune. The initial volume of the five volume series includes Seidl and Theodore Thomas. Volume two (1886-87) contains material on Seidl. Volume three (1887-88) includes Leopold Damrosch, Seidl, Spontini, Thomas, and Wagner. Volume four (1888-89) covers Seidl, Thomas, and von Buelow. The final volume (1889-90) again mentions Thomas and von Buelow AND also includes an appendix of American choral societies and conductors. An important period source.

B0084. Kuehle, Gustav. Kuenstler-Album: eine Sammlung von Bildern und Biographien beruehmter Kuenstler und Kuenstlerinnen der Gegenwart auf der Gebiete der Musik. Band I. Leipzig: Kommissions-Verlag Nestmann & Wittig, n.d. 82 p., 16 illus.

The title implies a continuing series, but no additional volumes have come to light. Franz Mikorey, Franz Fischer, and Arthur Koennemann.

B0085. Kuhe, Wilhelm. My Musical Recollections. London: Richard Bentley and Son, 1896. xxviii, 394 p., 17 illus., index.

A musician's recollections of numerous contemporaries. Conductors include Costa, Jullien, Benedict, Mackenzie, Wagner, Sullivan, Manns, Henschel, Spohr, Richter, and Carl Rosa among the more famous. Excellent period source for numerous major and minor figures who conducted during the 19th century.

B0086. Kupferberg, Herbert. Tanglewood. New York: McGraw-Hill Book Company. 1976. 280 p., illus., chronology, 15-item bibliography, index.

Koussevitzky, Bernstein, Munch, and Leinsdorf.

B0087. Kurucz, Ladislao. Vademecum musical Argentino. Buenos Aires: Edicion Vamuca, n.d. [1982]. 142 p., illus.

"Directores de orquestas" (pp. 27-36) includes fifty-seven conductors most of whom are given a short biography.

B0088. Lawrence, Robert. The World of Opera. New York: Thomas Nelson & Sons, 1956. 208 p., index.

Beecham, Bodanzky, Reiner, Serafin, Toscanini, and Walter.

B0089. Lengyel, Cornel. ed. W.P.A. Project 10377: the History of Music in San Francisco. vol. 4. Celebrities in El Dorado 1850-1906. New York: AMS Press, 1972 [1st edition 1938 with illus.]. 270 p., selected bibliography, index.

Casals, Damrosch, Gabrilowitsch, Mascagni, Fritz Scheel, Seidl, Sousa, and Thomas.

B0090. LePage, Jane Weiner. Women Composers, Conductors and Musicians of the Twentieth Century: Selected Biographies. 2 vols. Metuchen (NJ): Scarecrow Press, 1980/83. vii, 293 p., 17 illus., index; x, 373 p., 17 illus., index.

Volume one includes Victoria Bond, Antonia Brico, Margaret Hillis, Thea Musgrave, Eve Queler, and Rosalyn Tureck. Volume two covers Dalia Atlas, Sarah Caldwell, and Frederique Petrides. Material on women is particularly difficult to locate so this work is most welcome.

B0091. Liebermann, Rolf. OpernJahre: Erlebnisse und Erfahrungen vor, auf und hinter der Buehne grosser Musiktheater. Translated by Eva Schoenfeld from Actes et entractes (Paris, 1976). Muenchen: Scherz Verlag, 1977. 320 p., index.

As the highly successful director of the Hamburg State Opera and the Paris Opera, Liebermann worked closely with many of the finest artists of his time. Boehm, Furtwaengler, von Karajan, and Solti.

B0092. Lipman, Samuel. The House of Music: Art in an Era of Institutions. Boston: David R. Godine Publisher, 1984. xi, 331 p., index.

Prominently covered among others are Bernstein, Boulez, Furtwaengler, von Karajan, Levine, Mehta, Solti, Szell, and Toscanini.

B0093. Lombardo, Giuseppe A. Annuario della arte lirica e coreografica Italiana 1897-98 - prima edizione. Milano: Arturo Demarchi, 1898. iv, 310 p., illus.

There is a listing of concert masters and conductors, but Emanuel Natale, Marino Giacomo, Pintorno Vincenzo, and Rossi Cesare are given special treatment. There are other volumes in this series.

B0094. Lualdi, Adriano. L'Arte di dirigere l'orchestra: antologia e guida. Milano: Editore Ulrico Hoepli, 1940. xv, [i], 413 p., 120 musical examples.

Professional involvement as an opera conductor, music critic, administrator, composer, and director of the conservatories in both Naples and Florence, Lualdi was a prolific writer on musical subjects. His travel memoirs including South America and Russia make entertaining reading. Section two of this book is an anthology of the writings of Berlioz, Gui, Saminski, Gounod, Serafin, Weingartner, and Wagner.

Seconda edizione aggiornata e molto accresciuta con nuovi capitoli. Milano, 1949. xvi, 592 p., 200 musical examples, index. Adds Liszt, Schumann, and Wood.

B0095. Macdonald, Nesta. Diaghilev Observed by Critics in England and the United States 1911-1929. London: Dance Books Ltd., 1975. xvi, 400 p., illus., list of forty-seven books referenced, index.

Conductors of the premieres: Beecham, Goossens, and Monteux.

B0096. Mackenzie, Compton, ed. The Gramophone Jubilee Book 1923-1973. Harrow, Middlesex: The Gramophone, 1973. x, 310 p.

Articles reprinted from The Gramophone include those by Ansermet, Barbirolli, Boult, Casals, Goossens, Ronald, and Sargent. One of the first publishing ventures of its kind, The Gramophone represents an important and singular source of reviews, articles, and information about recorded musical events during the last six decades.

B0097. Mann, Ernst, and Bruno Vogler, Heinz Voss, Hans Gerloff. Deutschlands Oesterreich-Ungarns und der Schweiz, Musiker in Wort und Bild: eine illustrierte Biographie der gesamten alldeutschen Musikwelt. 1. Ausgabe 1909/10. Leipzig-Gohlis: Bruno Vogler Verlagsbuchhandlung, 1909. vi, 525 p.

A number of obscure conductors are included.

B0098. Mapleson, James Henry. The Mapleson Memoirs 1848-1888. New York: Belford, Clarke & Co., 1888. 2 vols. xi, 372 p., portrait; viii, 319 p., appendix of singers and operas, index.

A valuable period source which must be used with caution. Harold Rosenthal edited and annotated a new edition in 1966.

B0099. Marsh, Robert C. The Cleveland Orchestra. Cleveland: The World Publishing Company, 1967. [vi], 205 p., 130 illus., 5 appendices including a discography.

Marsh was music critic of the Chicago Sun Times, and he wrote tastefully on a wide variety of subjects including Bertrand Russell and Arturo Toscanini's conducting style (C1140.4). Included here are Nikolai Sokoloff, Artur Rodzinski, Leinsdorf, and Szell.

B0100. Martin, Jules. Nos artistes: portraits et biographies suvis d'un notice sur les droits d'auteurs, l'Opéra, la Comédie-Française, les associations artistiques, etc.... Paris: Librairie de l'Annuaire Universel, 1895. 448 p., 369 portraits.

Includes a number of conductors.

B0101. Matz, Mary Jane. Opera Stars in the Sun: Intimate Glimpses of Metropolitan Opera Personalities. New York: Farrar, Strauss & Cudahy (sponsored by the Metropolitan Opera Guild), 1955. Reprint 1973. xiv, 349 p., 72 illus., culinary index.

An unabashed piece of popular journalism which includes Cleva, Monteux, Kempe, Mitropoulos, and Max Rudolf.

B0102. May, Robin. A Companion to the Opera. New York: Hippocrene Books, Inc., 1977. 364 p., 32 illus., index of names, index of operas.

114 conductors (pp. 215-66) are covered briefly.

B0103. von Mensi-Klarbach, Alfred. Alt-Muenchner Theater-erinnerungen: Bildnisse aus der glanzzeit der Muenchner Hofbuehnen. 2nd enlarged edition. Muenchen: Verlag von Knorr & Hirth, G.M.B.H., 1924. 255 p., 32 illus.

A leading theater critic in Munich includes Levi, Mottl, Walter, and Knappertsbusch among others.

B0104. Meyer, Torben, and Josef Mueller-Marein, Hannes Reinhardt. Musikalske selvportraetter. København: Jul. Gjellerups Forlag, 1966. 325 p., 40 illus.

Bernstein, Ehrling, Øivin Fjeldstad, Fricsay, Pierino Gamba, Kubelik, Paumgartner, and Walter.

B0105. Mildberg, Bodo. Das Dresdner Hoftheater in der Gegenwart: Biographien und Charakteristiken. Dresden: F. Piersons Verlag, 1902. 270 p., 112 portraits.

Ninety-seven conductors and coaches are included.

B0106. Milke, S.J. Auais. Algo de la opera: guia practica del aficianado al teatro lirico. Mexico, D.F.: Ediciones Selectas, 1982. 2 vols. 672, [4] p., illus.; 673-1352, [4] p., illus., index of composers, 49-item bibliography.

Little if any original material; a cut-and-paste job which could provide some challenging detective work for an interested authority.

B0107. Moore, Jerrold Northrop. A Voice in Time: the Gramophone of Fred Gaisberg 1873-1951. London: Hamish Hamilton Ltd., 1976. viii, 248 p., 24 illus., index.

Landon Ronald, Toscanini, and Bruno Walter.

B0108. Moresby, Isabelle. Australia Makes Music. Melbourne: Longmans, Green and Co., 1948. x, 197 p., 20 illus., appendix of choral societies, selected list of recordings, 19-item bibliography.

Chapter six, "The Man with the Baton," highlights twelve conductors: G.W.L. Marshall-Hall, Henri Verbrugghen, Slapoffski, Fritz Hart, Arundel Orchard, Edgar Bainton, Alberto Zelman, Bernard Heinze, Percy Code, William Cade, Joseph Post, and John Farnsworth Hall.

B0109. Mueller, Martin and Wolfgang Mertz, eds. Diener der Musik: unvergessene Soloisten und Dirigenten unserer Zeit im Spiegel der Freunde. Tuebingen: Rainer Wunderlich Verlag Hermann Leins, 1965. 275 p., 20 illus., 13-item bibliography, discography.

A marvelous collection of essays each written by a personal friend of the conductor: Pierre Monteux by Paul Cronheim, Bruno Walter by Thomas Mann, Erich Kleiber by Hans Gal, Hans Rosbaud by Marius Meng, Ferenc Fricsay by Maria Stader, Fritz Busch by Otto Erhardt, Willem Mengelberg by E.B. Heemskerk, Thomas Beecham by Otto Erhardt, and Wilhelm Furtwaengler by Paul Hindemith. Observations by friends and professional colleagues offer rare insights into the creative lives of some memorable artists.

B0110. Mueller-Marein, Josef and Hannes Reinhardt. Das musikalische Selbstportrait von Komponisten, Dirigenten, Instrumentalisten, Saengerinnen und Saengern unserer Zeit. Hamburg: Nannen-Verlag GmbH, 1963. 508 p., 55 illus., select discography, index of names.

Fifty well-known artists including eight conductors were asked to provide autobiographical insights and commentary. Bruno Walter, Boehm, Szell, Rosbaud, Schmidt-Isserstedt, Fricsay, Mitropoulos, and Jochum.

B0111. Nanquette, Claude. Anthologie des interprètes. Paris: Editions Stock, 1979. 745, [4] p., index.

Pages 251-472 are devoted to fifty conductors whose careers flourished after World War II.

B0112. Nanquette, Claude. Les grands interprètes romantiques. Paris: Librairie Arthème Fayard, 1982. 367 p., 60 illus., 406-item bibliography.

Principal conductors, instrumentalists, and singers from the early nineteenth century to the present day. Habeneck, Berlioz, Mendelssohn, Wagner, Pasdeloup, von Buelow, Lamoureux, Colonne, Richter, Nikisch, Mottl, Mahler, Weingartner, and Strauss.

B0113. Newton, Ivor. At the Piano: the World of an Accompanist. London: Hamish Hamilton Ltd, 1966. viii, [i], 309 p., 21 illus., index.

Primarily a source for Sir Thomas Beecham, but there are comments on a number of conductors.

B0114. Niggli, Paul. Musiker Medaillen. Hofheim am Taunus: Verlag Friedrich Hofmeister, 1965. 268 p., illus.

A limited edition of 1,500 which lists eight conductors: Abendroth, von Buelow, von Dohnanyi, Furtwaengler, von Karajan, Knappertsbusch, Krauss, and Levi.

B0115. Noble, Helen. Life with the Met. New York: G.P. Putnam's Sons, 1954. 250 p., index.

A secretary at the old Metropolitan Opera comments on a host of conductors but especially Bodanzky.

B0116. O'Connell, Charles. The Other Side of the Record. New York: Alfred A. Knopf, 1947. Reprint 1970. xi, 332 xi p., index.

A well-known recording industry executive serves up required reading for the period 1924-44. Iturbi, Ormandy, Toscanini, Fiedler, Monteux, Koussevitzky, and Stokowski.

B0117. Oehlmann, Werner. Das Berliner Philharmonische Orchester. Kassel: Baerenreiter-Verlag, 1974. 199 p., 131 illus., personnel, chronology, 21-item bibliography.

von Buelow, Nikisch, Furtwaengler, and von Karajan. The most definitive work to date on the Berlin Philharmonic is Peter Muck's Einhundert Jahre Berliner Philharmonisches Orkester: Darstellung in Dokumenten. 3 vols. Tutzing: Verlegt bei Hans Schneider, 1982. xi, 512 p., illus., 46-item bibliography; vii, 484 p., 46-item bibliography; viii, 509 p.

B0118. Parker, H.T. Eighth Notes: Voices and Figures of Music and the Dance. New York: Dodd, Mead and Company, 1922. 238 p.

Reprints of reviews originally published in the Boston Evening Transcript. Not trained as a musician Parker nevertheless exhibited remarkable sensitivity. Toscanini, Muck, Mengelberg, Monteux, Stock, Stokowski, and Stravinsky.

B0119. Parkhurst, Winthrop and L.J. de Bekker. The Encyclopedia of Music and Musicians. New York: Crown Publishers, 1937. viii, 662 p., portrait.

Helpful for obscure performers.

B0120. Peltz, Mary Ellis. Spotlights on the Stars: Intimate Sketches of Metropolitan Opera Personalities. New York: The Metropolitan Opera Guild, Inc., 1943. 114 p., 63 illus., index.

Primarily devoted to singers on the 1942-43 roster, there is also information on Beecham, Walter, Szell, Paul Breisach, Pelletier, Cesare Sodero, and Frank St. Leger.

B0121. Perry, Bliss. Life and Letters of Henry Lee Higginson. Boston: The Atlantic Monthly Press, 1921. viii, [iii], 557 p., 7 illus., index.

Helpful for early conductors of the Boston Symphony: Muck, Henschel, Gericke, Rabaud, and Nikisch.

B0122. Pettitt, Stephen J. Philharmonia Orchestra: a Record of Achievement 1945-1985. London: Robert Hale Limited, 1985. 285 p., 47 illus., recordings, index.

The record of a unique achievement in which many conductors took part. Giulini, von Karajan, Klemperer, Maazel, and Muti.

B0123. Pincherle, Marc. The World of the Virtuosa. Translated by Lucile H. Brockway. London: Victor Gollancz Ltd., 1964 [1st English edition New York, 1963]. 192 p.

A leading authority on the history of violin play, Pincherle served for almost thirty years as artistic director of the Societe Pleyel. This work [original as Le Monde des virtuoses. Paris, 1961] includes Walter, Furtwaengler, and Koussevitzky.

B0124. Porter, Andrew. Music of Three Seasons: 1974-1977. New York: Farrar Strauss Giroux, 1978. xix, 667, [1] p., index.

Editor of the Musical Times (1960-67) and music critic of the New Yorker since 1972, Porter has established himself as one of the finest contemporary music critics. Comments on Beecham, Bernstein, Boulez, Caldwell, Ehrling, von Karajan, Rudel, and Solti.

B0125. Porter, Andrew. Music of Three More Seasons. New York: Alfred A. Knopf, 1981. 613 p., index.

One-liners on just about everybody but especially Abbado, Boehm, Boulez, Caldwell, Bernard Haitink, von Karajan, Levine, Maazel, Mehta, and Solti.

B0126. Rees, C.B. One Hundred Years of the Hallé. Forward by John Barbirolli. London: Macgibbon and Kee, 1957. 175 p., 8 illus.

Charles Hallé, Richter, Hamilton Harty, and Barbirolli.

B0127. Reichelt, Johannes. Erlebte Kostbarkeiten: Begegnungen mit Kuenstlern in Bekenntnisstunden. 2nd expanded edition. Dresden: Verlag Wodni & Lindecke, 1941. 421 p., 44 illus., index of names.

Twenty German and Austrian artists including Weingartner, von Schuch, and Nikisch.

B0128. Reis, Claire R. Composers Conductors and Critics. New York: Oxford University Press, 1955. xiii, 264 p., 9 illus., appendix of ten commissions offered to the League of Composers for its twenty-fifth anniversary, index.

A number of conductors are mentioned but particularly Copland, Koussevitzky, Stokowski, and Stravinsky.

B0129. Reissig, Elisabeth. Erlebte Opernkunst: Bilder und Gestalten der Berliner Staatsoper. 2 vols. 98 p., 12 illus.; 132 p., 16 illus.

Volume one includes Max von Schillings, Blech, and Kleiber.

B0130. Rich, Maria F. ed. Who's Who in Opera: an International Biographical Directory of Singers, Conductors, Directors, Designers, and Administrators; Also Including Profiles of 101 Opera Companies. New York: Arno Press, 1976. xxi, 684 p.

A sorely needed addition to the literature when it appeared in 1976, Rich's reference work deserves a revised edition. This first edition includes 287 conductors, and the "biographical information is current as of the 1974-75 season." As longtime editor of the Central Opera Service Bulletin, Ms. Rich has fostered an impressive record of assembling performance data. As the legitimate heir to B0135, any continuation would be most welcome.

B0131. Riess, Curt. Knauers Weltgeschichte der Schallplatte. Zuerich: Droemersche Verlagsanstalt AG, 1966. 447 p., 150 illus., 52-item bibliography, index of names.

Furtwaengler, Nikisch, Toscanini, and Walter.

B0132. Rohm, Wilhelm, ed. Mozartgemeinde Wien 1913-1963: Forschung und Interpretation. Wien: Mozartgemeinde, 1964. 395 p., 95 illus., list of participants, index of authors.

Articles by Fricsay, Paumgartner, Boehm, Furtwaengler, and Strauss. Articles about Strauss, Krips, and Boehm. A total of fifty-five conductors are mentioned.

B0133. Rohozinski, L. ed. Cinquante ans de musique française de 1874 à 1925. 2 vols. Paris: Les Editions Musicales de la Librairie de France, 1925. 394 p., illus.; 424 p., illus.

Handsome collectors edition with numerous illustrations including color plates. Chapter ten (pp. 271-316), "Les Chefs d'Orchestre," includes Oliver Métra, Edouard Colonne, Taffanel, Jules Danbé, Chevillard, Rhené-Bâton, Paray, Golschmann, Gaubert, d'Indy, Hahn, Busser, Luigini, Ruhlmann, and Lauweryns.

B0134. Rosenberg, Deena and Bernard. The Music Makers. New York: Columbia University Press, 1979. xiii, 466 p., 32 illus., index.

This is an oral history distilled from interviews with thirty-two individuals in the arts. Ormandy, Margaret Hillis, Neville Marriner, Michael Tilson Thomas, and Henry Mazer.

B0135. Ross, Anne, ed. The Opera Directory. London: John Calder (Publishers) Ltd, 1961. xii, 160, xxxii, 161-288, xxxiii-lxiv, 289-416, lxv-xcvi, 417-544, xcvii-civ, 545-566 p., glossary of abbreviations and foreign terms, glossary of cities with opera houses.

"Conductors and Musical Staff including Repetiteurs and Chorus Masters," pp. 135-167. This was planned as an annual publication which unfortunately did not materialize. With the present state of computers and communication, perhaps the effort can be revived.

B0136. Roussel, Hubert. The Houston Symphony Orchestra, 1913-1971. Austin: University of Texas Press, 1972. 247 p., 34 illus., appendix, index of names.

Valuable material on Fricsay, Beecham, Stokowski, and Barbirolli.

B0137. Sáenz, Gerardo, ed. Ecos teatrales [by Luis G. Urbina]. México, D.F.: Instituto Nacional de Bellas Artes, 1963. 256, [5] p., comprehensive thirty-three section bibliography including thirty-two periodicals.

Brief mention of some obscure conductors. The bibliography is especially helpful for research into uncharted territory.

B0138. Saleski, Gdal. Famous Musicians of a Wandering Race: Biographical Sketches of Outstanding Figures of Jewish Origin in the Musical World. New York: Block Publishing Company, 1927. xiv, 463 p., photo of each musician.

Fifty-two conductors including Blech, Bodanzky, Damrosch (3), Ronald, Klemperer, Koussevitzky, Levi, Monteux, Reiner, Smallens, and Walter.

2nd edition: Famous Musicians of Jewish Origin. New York, 1949. Sixty-four conductors with notable additions to the first edition including Abravanel, Bernstein, Dorati, Fiedler, Goldovsky, Katims, Kostelanetz, Leinsdorf, Nikisch, Ormandy, Rodzinski, Steinberg, Stiedry, and Szell. Both editions MUST be consulted.

B0139. Salter, Norbert, ed. The World Musical and Theatrical Guide. 2 vols. New York: p.p., 1929. 327 p.; 332 p., illus., index to both vols.

Volume two includes conductors (pp. 185-228).

B0140. Samazeuilh, Gustave, ed. Les écrits de Paul Dukas sur la musique. Paris: Société d'Editions Françaises et Internationales, 1948. 691, [10] p., portrait, index.

Chevillard, Colonne, Lamoureux, Mottl, Nikisch, and Weingartner.

B0141. Samazeuilh, Gustave. Musiciens de mon temps. Paris: Editions Marcel Daubin, 1947. 429 p.

Valuable material on Paul Paray, Strauss, Mottl, and Lili Boulanger.

B0142. Sandu, Augustin. Arpegii pentru patru anotimpuri. 2 vols. Iasi (Romania): Editura Junimea, 1976/1981. 253 p., illus.

Volume one includes Mehta, von Karajan, Markevitch, Kondrashin, and Barbirolli. Leitner, Dorati, and Ferencsik are in volume two.

B0143. Schoen-René, Anna Eugénia. America's Musical Inheritance: Memories and Reminiscences. New York: G.P. Putnam's Sons, 1941. xi, 244 p., 18 illus., index.

An important period source.

B0144. Schonberg, Harold C. Facing the Music. New York: Summit Books, 1981. 464 p., index.

Highly influential music critic with the New York Times for thirty years (1950-80), Schonberg mentions many artists but especially Bernstein, von Karajan, Solti, Boulez, Barbirolli, and Szell. As the author of The Great Conductors (A0041), a book which followed The Great Pianists, he was the first music critic awarded a Pulitzer Prize for criticism in 1971.

B0145. Schwaiger, Egloff, ed. Warum der Applaus: beruehmte Interpreten ueber ihre Musik. Muenchen: Ehrenwirth Verlag, 1968. 349 p., 48 illus., section of short biographies.

Ansermet, Boehm, Cluytens, Jochum, Keilberth, Kempe, Kubelik, Munch, Paumgartner, and Sawallisch.

B0146. Seeger, Horst. Opern Lexikon. Mitarbeit fuer die Gebiete Opernfiguren und -zitate: Eberhard Schmidt. Wilhelmshaven: Heinrichshofen's Druck, 1979. 6, 11-598 p.

Included because of the extensive coverage of eastern block artists.

B0147. Shanet, Howard. Philharmonic: a History of New York's Orchestra. Garden City: Doubleday & Company, Inc., 1975. xxi, 788 p. + 24 leaves of plates, 74 illus., repertoire of the New York Philharmonic 1842-1970, 17 p. comprehensive bibliography, 8 appendices, index.

Conductors associated with the New York Philharmonic. The extensive bibliography includes (a) books and articles, (b) periodicals, (c) dictionaries, encyclopedias, and directories, and (d) manuscripts and other materials in special collections.

B0148. Shaw, George Bernard. London Music in 1888-89 as Heard by Corno di Bassetto (Later Known as Bernard Shaw) With Some Further Autobiographical Particulars. London: Constable and Company Limited, 1950 [original 1937]. 420 p., index.

Reprints from the Star which include Costa, Hallé, Mottl, and Richter. These reviews, as were those in B0149, were written before Shaw became famous as a playwright but they are excellent examples of his penetrating wit and ability to manipulate the English language.

B0149. Shaw, George Bernard. Music in London 1890-94. 3 vols. London: Constable and Company Limited, 1956 [original 1932]. 302; 325; 320 p., index in the third volume.

Reprints from The World which include comments on a number of Shaw's baton wielding contemporaries.

B0150. Sheean, Vincent. First and Last Love. New York: Random House, 1956. 305 p., index.

The autobiography of a professional foreign correspondent contains personal insights into a number of conductors, especially Toscanini and Walter.

B0151. Sheean, Vincent. Oscar Hammerstein I: the Life and Exploits of an Impresario. New York: Simon and Schuster, 1936. xx, 363 p., 17 illus., index.

Based on material originally assembled by Arthur and Oscar II. The Manhattan Opera Company quickly emerged as a feared competitor of the Met, and Cleofonte Campanini was the principal conductor.

B0152. Sherman, John K. Music and Maestros: the Story of the Minneapolis Symphony Orchestra. Minneapolis: University of Minnesota Press, 1952. xiii, 357 p., 72 illus., personnel, repertoire, index.

One tends to overlook the presence of major artists in other than the five or so "talked about" centers. Emil Oberhoffer, Verbrugghen, Ormandy, Mitropoulos, and Dorati.

B0153. Siegmier, F.G., trans. Ueber den Ritter Gluck und seine Werke: Briefe von ihm und andern beruehmten Maennern seiner Zeit. Eine historisch-kritische Beurtheilung seiner Opern-Musik. 2nd edition. Berlin: In der Boss'schen Buchhandlung, 1837. viii, 384 p.

Another marvelous and important period reference.

B0154. Slonimsky, Nicolas. Music of Latin America. New York: Thomas Y. Crowell Company, 1945. [iv], 374 p., 49 illus., dictionary of Latin American musicians, song and dances, and musical instruments, index.

The great lexicographer compiled an early and important source for Latin American conductors. A composer and conductor of no mean accomplishments "beset by a chronic itch for novelty", Slonimsky has made singular contributions to the "information business."

B0155. Spark, William. Musical Memories. London: Swan Sonnenschein & Co., 1888. viii, 439 p., portrait.

Period source for Costa, Spohr, and Macfarren. William Reeves published a new revised edition [n.d.] with an index and sixteen illustrations which included Mendelssohn.

B0156. Stargardt-Wolff, Edith. Wegbereiter grosser Musiker: unter Verwendung von Tagebuchblaettern, Briefen und vielen persoenlichen Erinnerungen von Hermann und Louise Wolff, den Gruendern der ersten Konzertdirektion 1880-1935. Berlin: Ed. Bote & G. Bock, 1954. 312 p., 26 illus., index of names.

The daughter combines diaries, letters, and personal recollections to trace the life and professional accomplishments of the first great German agent. Anton Rubinstein, von Buelow, Nikisch, Weingartner, Muck, Strauss, Furtwaengler, and Walter are among a "Who's Who" of the artists of the period. SEE: B0040.

B0157. Stresemann, Wolfgang. ...und Abends in die Philharmonie: Erinnerungen an grosse Dirigenten. Muenchen: Georg Mueller Verlag GmbH, 1981. 280 p., 29 illus.

A conducted tour of the masters including Nikisch, Furtwaengler, Walter, Strauss, Klemperer, Toscanini, von Karajan, and Barbirolli.

B0158. Swoboda, Henry, ed. The American Symphony Orchestra. New York: Basic Books, Inc., Publishers, 1967. xiii, [iii], 208 p., index.

This compilation includes interviews with Maurice Abravanel, Howard Hanson, Josef Krips, Leinsdorf, Max Rudolf, Stokowski, and G. Wallace Woodworth.

B0159. Taubman, Howard. Music on My Beat: an Intimate Volume of Shop Talk. New York: Simon and Schuster, 1943. viii, 267 p.

Taubman followed Olin Downes as the chief music critic of The New York Times in 1955. These recollections date from the period during which he was a staff writer. Information on Beecham, Damrosch, Furtwaengler, Koussevitzky, Mitropoulos, Stokowski, and Toscanini.

B0160. Taullard, A. Historia de nuestros viejos teatros. Bueos Aires: Imprenta López, 1932. 500 p., illus.

Should be consulted for obscure conductors.

B0161. Thompson, Virgil. The Musical Scene. New York: Alfred A. Knopf, 1945. xiv, 301, xv p., index.

As editor of Musical America (1936-43) and music critic for the New York Evening Post (1928-34) and the New York Sun (1937-45), Thompson was very influential. Stokowski, Koussevitzky, Beecham, Mitropoulos, Toscanini, and Reginald Stewart. A multifaceted human being, Thompson composed Four Saints in Three Acts on a libretto by Gertrude Stein. What other music critic won a Pulitzer Prize for composition?

B0162. Upton, George P. Musical Memories: My Recollections of Celebrities of the Half Century 1850-1900. Chicago: A.C. McClurg & Co., 1908. xiv, 345 p., 47 illus., index.

As music critic for the Chicago Tribune, Upton's autobiography is an important period source. His book Women in Music (1880) was a highly unusual contribution for its time.

B0163. Vásárhelyi, Julius. Ungarn ein Land der Musik: Ungarischer Kuenstleralmanach. Budapest: Koeniglich Ungarische Universitaets-druckerei, 1930. 340 p., illus.

A very rare source with information on Eugen Adám, Emil von Abrányi, Otto Berg, Wilhelm Komor, Desider Márkus, Emmerich Petoe, Reiner, Michael Szenkár, and Viktor Vaszy.

This may be the second edition of Bela Diosy's book (SEE: B0037), but both titles were not available concurrently to confirm this.

B0164. Weinschenk, H.F. Kuenstler plaudern. Berlin: Wilhelm Limpert Verlag, 1938. 338 p., 177 illus.

Fifty artists including eight conductors discuss themselves. Abendroth, Beecham, Boehm, Elmendorff, Mengelberg, de Sabata, Carl Schuricht, and Tietjen.

B0165. Whelbourn, Hubert. Standard Book of Celebrated Musicians, Past and Present. revised and enlarged edition. New York: Garden City Publishing Co., Inc., 1937 [originally published as Celebrated Musicians, Past and Present. London, 1930]. xiii, 305 p., 7 illus.

344 musicians include some major and minor conductors.

B0166. Who is Who in Music: 1941 Edition. Chicago: Lee Stern Press, 1941. 782, cxxviii p., illus.

Included are short articles by Rodzinski, Barbirolli, Damrosch, Stock, Koussevitzky, Ormandy, Rudolf Ganz, Ernest Macmillan, Vladimir Golschmann. No complete set of this reference work was available.

B0167. Wiener, Hilda and D. Millar Craig. Pencil Portraits of Concert Celebrities. London: Sir Isaac Pitman & Sons, Ltd., 1937. xii, 198, [1] p., 100 portraits by Wiener.

Of the twenty-five conductors, there are some little-known names. Hugh Allen, Ansermet, Beecham, Boult, Fritz Busch, Désiré Defauw, Elmendorff, Furtwaengler, Inghelbrecht, Kleiber, Nikolai Malko, Pietro Mascagni, Mengelberg, Molinari, Monteux, Sargent, Scherchen, Johann Strauss, Richard Strauss, Vaclav Talich, Toscanini, Walter, Weingartner, Albert Wolff, and Wood.

B0168. Wyndham, Henry Saxe. Stories of the Operas and the Singers Containing the Plots of the Operas and Biographical Sketches with Portraits of the Artists. London: John Long, Ltd., 1910. 96 p., 61 illus.

Five Covent Garden conductors are included: Campanini, Frigara, Panizza, Richter, and Pitt.

B0169. Young, Kenneth. Music's Great Days in the Spas and Watering-Places. London: Macmillan and Co Ltd, 1968. 228 p., 48 illus., 17-item bibliography, index.

The author has provided a fascinating retrospective of a little known phenomenon. During the period 1880-1950 many resorts supported large orchestras, and this book reminds us of numerous unknowns who conducted these obscure ensembles.

PART C.

Individual Conductors, A-Z

This brief headnote is intended for those readers who bypassed the Preface which contains a detailed explanation of the type of information one will encounter in PART C: INDIVIDUAL CONDUCTORS, A-Z. The entries are alphabetical, are code numbered C0001 through C1249, and include at least two entries from the five sources of material which relate to that individual. These distinct catagories will always be listed in the following order: (1) A coded entry which indicates one of seven major performing arts' reference works. Titles and codes are in the Bibliographical Abbreviations section which follows the Preface. Titles were selected for their reliability and availability, and each entry will give the edition and volume number where appropriate. To alert the reader to additional bibliographic references NOT DUPLICATED in this work, the entry "(Bibliography)" will appear after the code, e.g. BAKER 7 (Bibliography); (2) A coded entry which refers to one of ten periodicals which have been checked for articles of a biographical or autobiographical nature. There are occasional additional references, e.g. Time or Newsweek where a special issue is concerned; (3) Autobiographies and books written by the conductor which relate directly to interpretation or pedagogy; (4) Biographies about a conductor including historical novels if there was good reason to believe that the content was based upon or influenced by actual events; (5) Additional sources as well as cross-references from Parts A, B, and C. Please note that cross-references particularly with regard to Parts A and B are not complete and mention only those artists itemized in the individual annotations.

C0001.
ABBADO, CLAUDIO. b. June 26, 1933, Milan, Italy.

1. BAKER 7; EdS/Supp.; GROVE 6/1; MGG/Supp.; PAB-MI/2 (Bibliography); RIEMANN 12/Supp.

2. ON 33/5; OW 13/5, 14/5, 20/12.

5. A0017, A0031, B0067, B0125.

C0002.
ABBADO, MARCELLO. b. October 7, 1926, Milan, Italy.

1. BAKER 7, PAB-MI/2 (Bibliography); RIEMANN/Supp.

C0003.
ABENDROTH, HERMANN. b. January 19, 1883, Frankfurt/M.; d. May 29, 1956, Jena, Germany.

1. BAKER 7; GROVE 6/1; MGG 1/1; PAB-MI/2 (Bibliography); RIEMANN 12.

5. B0114, B0164.

C0004.
ABRAVANEL, MAURICE. b. January 6, 1903, Saloniki, Greece.

1. BAKER 7; EdS 1/1; GROVE 6/1; GROVE-AM 1/1 (Bibliography); PAB-MI/2 (Bibliography).

2. HiFi/MusAm 24/8.

4. GROVE 6/1 mentions a biography by L.M. Durham in preparation, but no further information is available at this time.

5. A0048, B0138, B0158.

C0005.
ACKERMANN, OTTO. b. October 18, 1909, Bucharest, Romania; d. March 9, 1960, Wabern, near Bern, Switzerland.

1. BAKER 7; GROVE 6/1 (Bibliography); PAB-MI/2 (Bibliography); Riemann 12 + Supp.

C0006.
ADAM, JENŐ. b. December 12, 1896, Szigetszentmiklos; d. May 15, 1982, Budapest, Hungary.

1. BAKER 7; EdS 1/1; GROVE 6/1 (Bibliography); MGG/Supp. (Bibliography); PAB-MI/2 (Bibliography); RIEMANN 12/Supp.

C0007.
ADLER, KURT. b. March 1, 1907, Neuhaus, Bohemia; d. September 21, 1977, Butler, New Jersey.

1. BAKER 7; RIEMANN 12 + Supp.

3. Adler, Kurt. The Art of Accompanying and Coaching. revised ddition. New York: Da Capo Press, Inc., 1979 [original 1965]. [iii], 260 p., 258-item bibliography, index.

C0008.
ADLER, KURT HERBERT. b. April 2, 1905, Vienna, Austria.

1. BAKER 7; GROVE 6/1; GROVE-AM 1/1; PAB-MI/2 (Bibliography); RIEMANN 12 + Supp.

2. HiFi/MusAm 25/4; ON 32/2, 37/4, 38/4; OPERA 23/9, OW 15/7, 21/2.

4. The Adler Years 1954-1981. San Francisco: San Francisco Opera, 1981. 94, [2] p., 234 illus.

   San Francisco Opera: 25 Adler Years. San Francisco: San Francisco Opera, 1978. 188, [7] p., illus.

C0009.
ADLER, PETER HERMAN. b. December 2, 1899, Jablonec, Czechoslovakia.

1. BAKER 7; GROVE 6/1; GROVE-AM 1/1; PAB-MI/2 (Bibliography); RIEMANN 12 + Supp.

2. ON 37/12.

C0010.
AESCHBACHER, NIKLAUS. b. April 30, 1917, Trogen, Switzerland.

1. BAKER 7; GROVE 6/1; PAB-MI/2 (Bibliography); RIEMANN 12 + Supp.

C0011.
AHRONOVICH, YURI. b. May 13, 1932, Leningrad, Russia.

1. BAKER 7; GROVE 6/1 (Bibliography).

C0012.
AIBLINGER, JOHANN KASPAR. b. February 23, 1779, Wasserburg, Bavaria; d. May 6, 1867, Munich, Germany.

1. BAKER 7; EdS 1/1; GROVE 6/1 (Bibliography); MGG 1/1; RIEMANN 12 (Bibliography).

C0013.
ALBERT, HERBERT. b. December 26, 1903, Lausick; d. September 15, 1973, Bad Reichenhall, Germany.

1. BAKER 7; EdS 1/1; RIEMANN 12 + Supp.

C0014.
ALBRECHT, GEORGE ALEXANDER. b. February 15, 1935, Bremen, Germany.

1. BAKER 7; PAB-MI/2 (Bibliography); RIEMANN 12/Supp.

C0015.
ALBRECHT, GERD. b. July 19, 1935, Essen, Germany.

1. BAKER 7; GROVE 6/1; PAB-MI/2 (Bibliography); RIEMANN 12/Supp.

2. OW 23/2.

C0016.
ALBRECHT, KARL. b. August 27, 1807, Posen; d. March 8, 1863, Gatchina, near St. Petersburg, Russia.

1. BAKER 7; EdS 1/1; GROVE 6/1; MGG/Supp. (Bibliography); RIEMANN 12.

C0017.
ALBRECHT, MAX. b. March 14, 1890, Chemnitz; d. February 13, 1945, Dresden, Germany.

1. BAKER 7; EdS 1/1; RIEMANN 12.

C0018.
ALFVEN, HUGO. b. May 1, 1872, Stockholm; d. May 8, 1960 Falun, Sweden.

1. GROVE 6/1 (Bibliography); PAB-MI/2 (Bibliography); RIEMANN 12 (Bibliography) + Supp. (Bibliography).

3. GROVE 6/1 lists five autobiographical publications.

4. Hugo Alfvén: en svensktonsaettares liv och werk. Stockholm: P.A. Norstedt & Soeners Foerlag, 1973. 428 p., portrait, list of works, discography, index of names.

C0019.
ALLDIS, JOHN. b. August 10, 1929, London, England.

1. BAKER 7; GROVE 6/1; PAB-MI/2 (Bibliography).

C0020.
ALLEN, HUGH (PERCY). b. December 23, 1869, Reading; d. February 20, 1946, Oxford, England.

1. GROVE 6/1 (Bibliography); PAB-MI/2 (Bibliography); RIEMANN 12 (Bibliography).

4. Baily, C. Hugh Percy Allen. Oxford, 1948.

   No copy located.

5. B0167.

C0021.
ALLERS, FRANZ. b. August 6, 1905, Karlovy Vary, Czechoslovakia.

1. BAKER 7; PAB-MI/2 (Bibliography); RIEMANN 12/Supp.

C0022.
de **ALMEIDA, ANTONIO.** b. January 1, 1928, Paris, France.

1. BAKER 7; GROVE 6/1; RIEMANN 12/Supp.

2. ON 41/5.

C0023.
ALTSCHULER, MODEST. b. February 15, 1873, Mogilev, Russia; d. September 12, 1963, Los Angeles, California.

1. BAKER 7; RIEMANN 12.

3. BAKER 7 mentions an unpublished autobiography.

C0024.
ALWIN, KARL OSKAR. b. April 15, 1891, Koenigsberg, Germany; d. October 15, 1945, Mexico City, Mexico.

1. BAKER 7; EdS 1/1; RIEMANN 12.

C0025.
AMMANN, BENNO. b. June 14, 1904, Gersau, Switzerland.

1. BAKER 7; PAB-MI/2 (Bibliography); RIEMANN 12 + Supp. (Bibliography).

C0026.
AMY, GILBERT. b. August 29, 1936, Paris, France.

1. BAKER 7; GROVE 6/1 (Bibliography); PAB-MI/2 (Bibliography); RIEMANN 12/Supp. (Bibliography).

C0027.
ANCERL, KAREL. b. April 11, 1908, Tucapy; d. July 3, 1973, Toronto.

1. BAKER 7; EdS 1/1; GROVE 6/1; MGG/Supp.; PAB-MI/2 (Bibliography); RIEMANN 12.

C0028.
ANDRE, FRANZ. b. June 10, 1893; d. January 20, 1975, Brussels, Belgium.

1. BAKER 7; GROVE 6/1 (Bibliography); RIEMANN 12.

C0029.
ANDREAE, VOLKMAR. b. July 5, 1879, Bern; d. June 18, 1962, Zurich.

1. BAKER 7; EdS 1/1 (Bibliography); GROVE 6/1 (Bibliography); MGG + Supp.; PAB-MI/2 (Bibliography); RIEMANN 12 + Supp.

5. A0052.

C0030.
ANGERER, PAUL. b. May 16, 1927, Vienna, Austria.

1. BAKER 7; GROVE 6/1 (Bibliography); PAB-MI/2 (Bibliography); RIEMANN 12 + Supp.

C0031.
van **ANROOY, PETER.** b. October 13, 1879, Zalt-Boomel; d. December 31, 1954, The Hague, Holland.

1. BAKER 7; GROVE 6/1 (Bibliography); MGG/Supp.; RIEMANN 12.

5. A0008.

C0032.
ANSCHUETZ, KARL. b. January 10, 1818 (MGG), Koblenz; d. December 30, 1870, New York City.

1. BAKER 7; EdS 1/1; MGG 1/1; PAB-MI/2 (Bibliography).

C0033.
ANSERMET, ERNEST. b. November 11, 1883, Vevey; d. February 20, 1969, Geneva, Switzerland.

1. BAKER 7; EdS 1/1; GROVE 6/1 (Bibliography); MGG 1/1 (Bibliography) +

Supp. (Bibliography); PAB-MI/2 (Bibliography); RIEMANN 12 + Supp. (Bibliography).

2. GR 45/532; ON 27/1, 27/8, 33/23; RS 13, 14, 72.

3. Ansermet, Ernest with J.-Claude Piguet. Ecrits sur la musique. Neuchâtel: Editions de la Baconnière, 1971. 251, [2] p., notes.

4. Ansermet, Anne. Ernest Ansermet, mon père. Lausanne: Editions Payot, 1983. 190, [1] p., 77 illus.

Augsbourg, Gea. Ernest Ansermet et L'Orchestre de la Suisse Romande: une vie en images dessinée. Lausanne: L'Abbaye Du Livre, 1943. unpaginated [98 p.], illus. including portraits of all 84 members of the orchestra.

1000 copies plus 25 collector's deluxe copies.

Gavoty, Bernard. Ernest Ansermet. Translated by F.E. Richardson. Geneva: René Kister, 1961. 33, [1] p., 21 illus., discography.

Hudry, Francois. Ernest Ansermet: pionnier de la musique. Lausanne: Editions de l'Aire, 1983. 222, [8] p., 40 illus., discography, 19-item bibliography, list of 6 writings by Ansermet, list of 26 titles consulted, notes, index of names.

Piguet, Jean-Claude, ed. Ernest Ansermet Frank Martin Correspondence 1934-1968. Neuchâtel: Editions de la Baconnière, 1976. 169, [2] p., illus., 25-item bibliography, index of names.

Piguet, J.-Claude. La pensée d'Ernest Ansermet. Lausanne: Editions Payot, 1983. 110, [7] p.

Roulet, Alfred. Découverte d'Ansermet. Genève: Tribune Editions, 1978. 119, [4] p., 12 illus.

Tétaz, Numa F. Ernest Ansermet, interprète. Lausanne: Editions Payot, 1983. 149, [2] p., appendix of musical notation.

5. A0002, A0004, A0007, A0040, A0052, B0030, B0052, B0096, B0145, B0167.

C0034.
ANTON, MAX. b. August 2, 1887, Bornstedt; d. August 18, 1939, Bonn.

1. BAKER 7; RIEMANN 12 (Bibliography).

C0035.
ARAMBARRI y GARATE, JESUS. b. April 13, 1902, Bilbao, Spain; d. July 11, 1960, Madrid, Spain.

1. BAKER 7; GROVE 6/1 (Bibliography); MGG/Supp.; RIEMANN 12.

5. B0045.

C0036.
ARBOS, ENRIQUE FERNANDEZ. b. December 24, 1863, Madrid; d. June 2, 1939, San Sebastian, Spain.

1. BAKER 7; EdS 1/1; GROVE 6/1; RIEMANN 12.

3. Arbós wrote a book (Madrid, 1914) on the place of the violin in the evolution of music.

4. Espinós Moltó, V. El maestro Arbós: memorias (1863-1939). Madrid: Ediciones Cid, 1963. xxiii, 538 p., 62 illus., list of premiere performances, index of names.

5. B0006.

C0037.
ARCHANGELSKY, ALEXANDER. b. October 23, 1846, Penza, Russia; d. November 16, 1924, Prague, Czechoslovakia.

1. BAKER 7; MGG/Supp. (Bibliography); PAB-MI/2 (Bibliography); RIEMANN 12.

C0038.
ARCHER, FREDERICK. b. June 16, 1838, Oxford; d. October 22, 1901, Pittsburgh, Pennsylvania.

1. BAKER 7; GROVE 6/1; PAB-MI/2 (Bibliography).

C0039.
ARDITI, LUIGI. b. July 16, 1822, Crescentino, Piedmont; d. May 1, 1903, Hove, near Brighton, England.

1. BAKER 7; EdS 1/1 (Bibliography); GROVE 6/1; GROVE-AM 1/1 (Bibliography); MGG/Supp. (Bibliography); PAB-MI/2 (Bibliography); RIEMANN 12.

3. Arditi, Luigi. My Reminiscences. 2nd edition. London: Skeffington and Son, 1896. Reprint 1977. xxv, 352 p., 38 illus., appendices include a complete list of operas produced. Also listed as B0005.

C0040.
ARGENTA, ATAULFO. b. November 19, 1913, Castro Urdiales, Santander, Spain; d. January 21, 1958, Los Molinos, near Madrid, Spain.

1. BAKER 7; GROVE 6/1; RIEMANN 12 + Supp. (Bibliography).

4. Alonso, José Montero. Vida apasionada de Ataulfo Argenta. Santander: Antología de escritores y artistas Montañeses, 1959. ccclx, 99 p.

   Fernandez-Cid, Antonio. Ataulfo Argenta. Madrid: Biblioteca Nueva, 1958. 349 p., 59 illus.

   Fernandez-Cid, Antonio. Ataulfo Argenta. Valencia: Artes Gráficas Soler, S.A., 1971. 63 p., 12 illus., discography, chronology.

Gavoty, Bernard. Ataulfo Argenta. Genève: Editions René Kister, 1956. 29, [3] p., 30 illus., discography.

5. B0045.

C0041.
ARGENTA, PIETRO. b. March 7, 1909, Gioia del Colle, Italy.

1. BAKER 7; RIEMANN 12/Supp.

C0042.
ARMBRUSTER, KARL. b. July 13, 1846, Andernach-am-Rhein, Germany; d. June 10, 1917, London, England.

1. BAKER 7; EdS 1/1; RIEMANN 12.

C0043.
ARNDT, GUENTHER. b. April 1, 1907; d. December 25, 1976 Berlin, Germany.

1. BAKER 7; GROVE 6/1; RIEMANN 12 + Supp.

C0044.
ARNOLD, GUSTAV. b. September 1, 1831, Altdorf; d. September 28, 1900, Lucerne, Switzerland.

1. BAKER 7; GROVE 6/1 (Bibliography).

C0045.
ASHKENAZY, VLADIMIR. b. July 6, 1937, Gorkey, Russia.

1. BAKER 7; GROVE 6/1; PAB-MI/2 (Bibliography); RIEMANN 12/Supp.

2. GR 63/748; HiFi/MusAm 28/5.

4. Parrott, Jasper and Vladimir Ashkenazy. Beyond Frontiers. London: William Collins Sons & Co. Ltd., 1984. 239 p., 17 illus., discography compiled by John Kehoe, recordings in progress, index.

5. A0031.

C0046.
ATHERTON, DAVID. b. January 3, 1944, Blackpool, England.

1. BAKER 7; GROVE 6/1; PAB-MI/2 (Bibliography).

C0047.
ATTENHOFER, KARL. b. May 5, 1837, Wettingen; d. May 22, 1914, Zurich.

1. BAKER 7; GROVE 6/1 (Bibliography); RIEMANN 12.

C0048.
ATZMON, MOSHE. b. July 30, 1931, Budapest, Hungary.

1. BAKER 7; GROVE 6/1; PAB-MI/2 (Bibliography); RIEMANN 12/Supp.

C0049.
AUBERSON, JEAN-MARIE. b. May 2, 1920, Chavornay, Switzerland.

1. BAKER 7; RIEMANN 12/Supp.

C0050.
AURIACOMBE, LOUIS. b. February 22, 1917, Paris, France.

1. BAKER 7; GROVE 6/1.

C0051.
AVERKAMP, ANTON. b. February 18, 1861, Willige Langerak; d. June 1, 1934, Bussum, Holland

1. BAKER 7; MGG/Supp. (Bibliography); RIEMANN 12 (Bibliography).

C0052.
BAINTON, EDGAR. b. February 14, 1880, London; d. December 8, 1956, Sydney, Australia.

1. GROVE 6/2 (Bibliography); PAB-MI/2 (Bibliography); RIEMANN 12.

5. B0108.

C0053.
BAKALA, BRETISLAV. b. February 12, 1897, Frystak; d. April 1, 1958, Brno, Czechoslovakia.

1. BAKER 7; GROVE 6/2 (Bibliography); RIEMANN 12 + Supp. (Bibliography).

C0054.
BALATKA, HANS. b. February 26, 1825, Hoffnungsthal, Moravia; d. April 17, 1899, Chicago, Illinois.

1. BAKER 7; GROVE 6/2 (Bibliography); GROVE-AM 1/1 (Bibliography); RIEMANN 12.

5. B0007.

C0055.
BALFE, MICHAEL WILLIAM. b. May 15, 1808, Dublin; d. October 20, 1870, Rowney Abbey, Hertfordshire, England.

1. BAKER 7; EdS 1/1; GROVE 6/2 (Bibliography); MGG 1/1; PAB-MI/2 (Bibliography); RIEMANN 12.

2. GR 3/4.

4. Barrett, William Alexander. Balfe: His Life and Work. London: Remington and Co., 1882. v, 313 p., 6 illus., index.

   Kenney, Charles Lamb. A Memoir of Michael William Balfe. London: Tinsley Brothers, 1875. x, 309 p., 3 illus.

C0056.
BALKWILL, BRYAN. b. July 2, 1922, London, England.

1. BAKER 7; GROVE 6/2; PAB-MI/2 (Bibliography).

C0057.
BALLING, MICHAEL. b. August 27, 1866, Heidingsfeld, near Wuertzburg; d. September 1, 1925, Darmstadt, Germany.

1. BAKER 7; PAB-MI/2 (Bibliography); RIEMANN 12 (Bibliography).

5. B0059, B0070.

C0058.
BALMER, LUC. b. July 13, 1898, Munich, Germany.

1. BAKER 7; EdS 1/1; GROVE 6/2 (Bibliography); MGG/Supp. (Bibliography); RIEMANN 12 + Supp.

C0059.
BAMBERGER, CARL. b. February 21, 1902, Vienna, Austria.

1. BAKER 7; PAB-MI/2 (Bibliography); RIEMANN 12 + Supp.

3. He wrote _The Conductor's Art_ which was published in 1965, but no copy has been located.

C0060.
BAMBOSCHEK, GIUSEPPE. b. June 12, 1890, Trieste; d. June 24, 1969, New York City.

1. BAKER 7; EdS 1/1; PAB-MI/2 (Bibliography).

5. SEE: Null, Gary & Carl Stone. _The Italian Americans_. Harrisburg: Stackpole Books, 1976. 220 p., 132-item bibliography, index of names.

C0061.
BAND, ERICH. b. May 10, 1876, Berlin; d. May 13, 1945, Waidhofen.

1. BAKER 7; RIEMANN 12.

C0062.
BARATI, GEORGE. b. April 13, 1913, Gyoer, Hungary.

1. BAKER 7; GROVE-AM 1/1; PAB-MI/2 (Bibliography); RIEMANN 12/Supp.

C0063.
BARBIERI, CARLO EMMANUELE. b. October 22, 1822, Genoa, Italy; d. September 28, 1867, Budapest, Hungary.

1. BAKER 7; EdS 1/1; GROVE 6/2; MGG/Supp.; RIEMANN 12.

C0064.
BARBIROLLI, JOHN. b. December 2, 1899, London; d. July 29, 1970, London.

1. BAKER 7; EdS 1/1; GROVE 6/2; GROVE-AM 1/1 (Bibliography); MGG 1/1 (Bibliography); PAB-MI/2 (Bibliography); RIEMANN 12.

2. GR 45/532, 47/559, 48/568, 569; LGB 7/4; ON 34/6; OPERA 2/11, 21/3, RS 50/51.

4. Atkins, Harold & Peter Cotes. The Barbirollis: a Musical Marriage. London: Robson Books Ltd., 1983. 238 p., 28 illus., 44-item select bibliography, index.

   Kennedy, Michael. Barbirolli: Conductor Laureate. New York: Da Capo Press, 1982 [original London, 1971]. xii, 416 p., 34 illus., discography by Malcolm Walker, index.

   Reid, Charles. John Barbirolli: a Biography. New York: Taplinger Publishing Company, 1971. xviii, 446 p., 17 illus., 4 appendices (appendix four is a discography 1949-1970), index.

   Rigby, Charles. John Barbirolli. Altrincham: John Sherratt and Son, 1948. 191 p., 15 illus.

5. A0002, A0003, A0004, A0010, A0022, A0040, A0045, B0070, B0096, B0126, B0136, B0142, B0144, B0157, B0166.

   SEE: Cardus, Neville. Talking of Music. London, 1957.

   SEE: Kennedy, Michael. Hallé Orchestra. Manchester, 1968, rev. 1976.

C0065.
BARCEWICZ, STANISLAW. b. April 16, 1858, Warsaw; d. September 1, 1929, Warsaw, Poland.

1. BAKER 7; GROVE 6/2 (Bibliography); MGG/Supp. (Bibliography); RIEMANN 12/Supp.

C0066.
BARDOS, LAJOS. b. October 1, 1899, Budapest, Hungary.

1. BAKER 7; GROVE 6/2; MGG/Supp. (Bibliography); RIEMANN 12 + Supp. (Bibliography)

C0067.
BARENBOIM, DANIEL. b. November 15, 1942, Buenos Aires, Argentina.

1. BAKER 7: GROVE 6/2; PAB-MI/2 (Bibliography); RIEMANN 12/Supp.

2. GR 50/592; HiFi/MusAm 22/1.

5. A0017, B0068

   SEE: Wordsworth, William, ed. Jacqueline du Pré: Impressions. New York: The Vanguard Press, 1983. 141, [3] p., 45 illus., list of honors, discography.

   Contributors include Menuhin, Mehta, and Zukerman.

C0068.
BARLOW, HOWARD. b. May 1, 1892, Plain City, Ohio; d. January 31, 1972, Bethel, Conneticut.

1. BAKER 7; GROVE-AM 1/1 (Bibliography); PAB-MI/2 (Bibliography); RIEMANN 12.

5. A0010.

C0069.
BARNBY, JOSEPH. b. August 12, 1838, York; d. January 28, 1896, London, England.

1. BAKER 7; GROVE 6/2 (Bibliography); MGG/Supp. (Bibliography); PAB-MI/2 (Bibliography); RIEMANN 12.

5. B0007.

C0070.
BARNETT, JOHN FRANCIS. b. October 16, 1837, London; d. November 24, 1916, London, England.

1. GROVE 6/2 (Bibliography); RIEMANN 12.

3. GROVE 6/2 mentions <u>Musical Reminiscences and Impressions</u> (1906).

5. B0007.

C0071.
BARSHAI, RUDOLF. b. September 28, 1924, Labinskaya, Russia.

1. BAKER 7; GROVE 6/2 (Bibliography); PAB-MI/2 (Bibliography).

C0072.
BARTOLETTI, BRUNO. b. June 10, 1926, Sesto Fiorentino, Italy.

1. BAKER 7; EdS/Supp.; GROVE 6/2; PAB-MI/2 (Bibliography); RIEMANN 12/Supp.

C0073.
BARZIN, LEON EUGENE. b. November 27, 1900, Brussels, Belgium.

1. BAKER 7; GROVE 6/2; GROVE-AM 1/1; PAB-MI/2 (Bibliography).

C0074.
BAUDO, SERGE. b. July 16, 1927, Marseilles, France.

1. BAKER 7; GROVE 6/2; PAB-MI/2 (Bibliography); RIEMANN 12/Supp.

2. ON 35/24.

C0075.
BAUER-THEUSSL, FRANZ. b. September 25, 1928, Zillingdorf, Germany.

1. BAKER 7; PAB-MI/2 (Bibliography); RIEMANN 12/Supp.

C0076.
BAYER, JOSEF. b. March 6, 1852, Vienna; d. March 12, 1913, Vienna.

1. BAKER 7; EdS 1/2; GROVE 6/2; MGG/Supp.; RIEMANN 12.

C0077.
BECK, JOHANN HEINRICH. b. September 12, 1856, Cleveland; d. May 26, 1924, Cleveland, Ohio.

1. BAKER 7; GROVE 6/2; GROVE-AM 1/1 (Bibliography); PAB-MI/2 (Bibliography).

C0078.
BEDFORD, STUART. b. July 31, 1939, London, England.

1. BAKER 7; GROVE 6/2 (Bibliography); PAB-MI/2 (Bibliography).

C0079.
BEECHAM, THOMAS. b. April 29, 1879, St. Helens, near Liverpool; d. March 8, 1961, London, England.

1. BAKER 7; EdS 1/2; GROVE 6/2 (Bibliography); MGG 1/1; PAB-MI/2 (Bibliography); RIEMANN 12 + Supp. (Bibliography).

2. GR 56/671; HiFi/MusAm 30/8; LGB (vol. 1/1964 - vol. 20/1983); ON 25/23; OPERA 9/10, 10/5, 30/4-7; OW 23/11.

3. Beecham, Thomas. A Mingled Chime; an Autobiography. New York: G.P. Putnam's Sons, 1943. 330 p., index.

   The only title from a planned series, this volume covers the period up to 1924. Interesting comments on a number of performers.

4. Atkins, Harold & Archie Newman, eds. Beecham Stories: Anecdotes, Sayings and Impressions of Sir Thomas Beecham. New York: St. Martin's Press, 1979. 96 p., 12 illus.

   Highly dependent upon books by Neville Cardus, Berta Geissmar, Humphrey Procter-Gregg, Charles Reid, Thomas Russell, and Bernard Shore.

   Cardus, Neville. Sir Thomas Beecham: a Memoir. London: Collins, 1961. 125, [1] p., 7 illus.

   Geissmar, Berta. The Baton and the Jackboot: Recollections of Musical Life. London: Hamish Hamilton, 1944. 403, [1] p., index.

   She was the private secretary to Furtwaengler and Beecham during a turning point in world history.

   Gilmour, J.D., ed. Sir Thomas Beecham, the North American Tour, 1950: a Documentary Presentation of News Media Articles. Ocean Shores (WA): North Beach Printing Co., Inc., 1979. xv, 136, [1] p., 24 illus.

Gray, Michael H. Beecham: a Centenary Discography. London: Duckworth, 1978. xiv, 129 p., index of composers and works, index of performers.

Jefferson, Alan. Sir Thomas Beecham: a Centenary Tribute. London: World Records Limited by arrangement with Macdonald and Jane's Publishers Ltd., 1979. 256 p., 43 illus., 67-item bibliography, index.

Procter-Gregg, Humphrey. Beecham Remembered. London: Gerald Duckworth & Company Limited, 1976. viii, [i], 212 p., 10 illus., list of musicians and other colleagues associated with Beecham, list of recordings without specifics, 38-item select bibliography, index.

A preliminary edition was privately issued in 1973: Sir Thomas Beecham, Conductor and Impresario, as Remembered by His Friends and Colleagues. 206 p., illus., bibliography.

Reid, Charles. Thomas Beecham: an Independent Biography. New York: E.P. Dutton & Co., Inc., 1962. 256 p., 8 illus., index.

Sir Thomas Beecham Discography. Westport (CT): Greenwood Press, 1978. ix, 81 p.

Compiled by the Sir Thomas Beecham Society based on materials from Le grand baton.

Smyth, Ethel Mary. Beecham and Pharoah: Thomas Beecham (Fantasia in B# Major). Egypt Before England's Exodus (a Fragment of an Autobiography). London: Chapman & Hall Ltd, 1935. 181 p., 3 illus.

5. A0002, A0003, A0004, A0010, A0040, A0045, B0009, B0015, B0021, B0030, B0038, B0048, B0052, B0054, B0058, B0060, B0062, B0070, B0075, B0076, B0088, B0095, B0109, B0113, B0120, B0124, B0136, B0159, B0161, B0164, B0167.

SEE: Blunt, Wilfrid. John Christie of Glyndebourne. New York: Theatre Arts Books, 1968.

SEE: Autobiography by Eugene Goossens (C0416.3).

SEE: Kolodin, Irving. The Musical Life. New York: Alfred A. Knopf, 1958. 266, viii p., index.

SEE: Newton, Ivor. At the Piano: the World of an Accompanist. London: Hamish Hamilton, 1966. viii, 309 p., 21 illus., index.

SEE: O'Donnell, Josephine. Among the Covent Garden Stars. London: Stanley Paul & Co., Ltd., 1936. 295 p., 49 illus., index.

SEE: Charles Reid under Malcolm Sargent (C0973.4).

SEE: Russell, Thomas. Philharmonic Decade. London: Hutchinson & Co., (Publishers) Ltd., n.d. [1944].

C0080.
BEHRENS, JOHAN DIDERIK. b. February 26, 1820, Bergen; d. January 29, 1890, Christiania, Norway.

1. BAKER 7; GROVE 6/2 (Bibliography).

C0081.
van BEINUM, EDUARD. b. September 3, 1900, Arnheim; d. April 13, 1959, Amsterdam, Holland.

1. BAKER 7; GROVE 6/19; MGG/Supp.; PAB-MI/2 (Bibliography); RIEMANN 12.

2. HiFi/MusAm 29/4.

4. Kempers, K. Ph. Bernet & Marius Flothius, eds. Eduard van Beinum. Haarlem: Uitgeverij J.H. Gottmer. 115 p., 29 illus., chronology, discography.

   Paap, Wouter. Eduard van Beinum: vijfentwintig jaar dirigent van het Concertgebouw Orkest. Baarn: Philips' Phonographische Industrie, n.d. [1956]. unpaginated [29 p.], 34 illus., list of recordings with the Concertgebouw.

   Silver jubilee tribute. Van Beinum was appointed assistant conductor and deputy to Willem Mengelberg in 1931. He served as principal conductor beginning with the 1938 season.

5. A0002, A0004, A0008, A0040, A0048.

C0082.
BELLEZZA, VINCENZO. b. February 17, 1888, Botonto, Bari; d. February 8, 1964, Rome, Italy.

1. BAKER 7; EdS 1/2; GROVE 6/2; PAB-MI/2 (Bibliography).

4. Giovine, Alfredo. Vincenzo Bellezza (direttore d'orchestra Bitontino. Bari: Biblioteca dell'archivio delle tradizioni popolari Baresi, 1970. 20 p., 7 illus., 27-item bibliography, discography.

C0083.
BELLUGI, PIERO. b. July 14, 1924, Florence, Italy.

1. BAKER 7; EdS/Supp.; GROVE 6/2; PAB-MI/2 (Bibliography); RIEMANN 12/Supp.

C0084.
von BENDA, HANS. b. November 22, 1888, Strasbourg; d. August 13, 1972, Berlin, Germany.

1. BAKER 7; RIEMANN 12.

C0085.
BENDIX, VICTOR EMANUEL. b. May 17, 1851, Copenhagen; d. January 5, 1926, Copenhagen, Denmark.

1. BAKER 7; GROVE 6/2 (Bibliography); MGG/Supp. (Bibliography); PAB-MI/2 (Bibliography); RIEMANN 12.

C0086.
BENDL, KAREL. b. April 16, 1838, Prague; d. September 20, 1897, Prague.

1. BAKER 7 (Bibliography); EdS 1/2 (Bibliography); GROVE 6/2 (Bibliography); MGG/Supp. (Bibliography); RIEMANN 12.

C0087.
BENEDICT, JULIUS. b. November 27, 1804, Stuttgart; d. June 5, 1885, London, England.

1. BAKER 7; GROVE 6/2 (Bibliography); MGG/Supp. (Bibliography); PAB-MI/2 (Bibliography); RIEMANN 12 + Supp. (Bibliography).

5. B0085.

C0088.
BENEDITO y VIVES, RAFAEL. b. September 3, 1885, Valencia, Spain.

1. BAKER 7 (Bibliography); RIEMANN 12.

C0089.
BENGTSSON, GUSTAF ADOLF. b. April 29, 1886, Vadstena; d. October 5, 1965, Vadstena, Sweden.

1. BAKER 7; GROVE 6/2; RIEMANN 12.

C0090.
BENZI, ROBERTO. b. December 12, 1937, Marseilles, France.

1. BAKER 7; GROVE 6/2; PAB-MI/2 (Bibliography); RIEMANN 12/Supp.

4. Gavoty, Bernard. Roberto Benzi. Genève: Editions René Kister, 1953. 12, [16] p., 24 illus.

C0091.
BERGEL, ERICH. b. June 1, 1930, Rosenau, Romania.

1. BAKER 7; GROVE 6/2 (Bibliography).

C0092.
BERGLUND, PAAVO ALLAN. b. April 14, 1929, Helsinki, Finland.

1. BAKER 7; GROVE 6/2; PAB-MI/2 (Bibliography); RIEMANN 12/Supp.

C0093.
BERGMANN, CARL. b. April 12, 1821, Ebersbach, Saxony; d. August 10, 1876, New York City.

1. BAKER 7; GROVE 6/2 (Bibliography); GROVE-AM 1/1 (Bibliography); PAB-MI/2 (Bibliography); RIEMANN 12.

2. MQ 6/1, 2, 17/2, 18/2, 24/2, 37/2, 39/1.

C0094.
BERLIOZ, (LOUIS-) Hector. b. December 11, 1803, La Côte-Saint-André, Isère; d. March 8, 1869, Paris, France.

According to Jack Westrup in GROVE 6/4, "had Weber lived longer he might have been the true founder of the modern method of conducting. It was left to Wagner and Berlioz to lay down the principles which are still valid and to demonstrate them in practice....Berlioz, in addition to explaining details of time-beating, not all of which are identical with modern practice, stressed the psychological problems of the conductor's art and advocated separate rehearsals for singers and orchestra. He condemned audible time-beating as 'barbarous' but admitted that a single tap might be necessary in the theatre to ensure the entry of the chorus. He also dealt in a practical way with the problem of synchronizing an orchestra or choir behind the scenes with the orchestra in the pit. As conductors Wagner and Berlioz were very different. Wagner indulged in rubato and was impatient, even abusive, at rehearsals. Berlioz preferred a steady tempo and was noted for his consideration to players."

There is a great deal of published material on Berlioz, but most of it has to do with his contributions as a composer. The following sources were chosen because of the light they shed on Berlioz as an artist, a conductor, and a human being.

1. BAKER 7 (Bibliography); EdS 1/2 (Bibliography); GROVE 6/2 (Bibliography); MGG 1/1 (Bibliography); PAB-MI/2 (Bibliography); RIEMANN 12 (Bibliography) + Supp. (Bibliography).

3. Berlioz, Hector. Le chef d'orchestre: théorie de son art. Paris: Schonenberger, 1855 [English edition as The Orchestral Conductor: Theory of his Art. New York: C. Fischer, 1902].

   Neither edition was available.

   Cairns, David, ed. Memoirs of Hector Berlioz, Member of the French Institute: Including His Travels in Italy, Germany, Russia, and England 1803-1865. Translated by David Cairns. London: Victor Gollancz Ltd., 1969. 616 p., 30 illus., comments by contemporaries, glossary, appendix of errors, etc., sources of the Memoirs, 57-item bibliography.

   A brilliant edition of a major contribution to cultural history. Berlioz the artist and the man comes alive in passages such as: "Apart from a few slips due to excitement, I did not do too badly. Yet how far I was from possessing the many varied qualities--precision, flexibility, sensitivity, intensity, presence of mind, combined with an indefinable instinct--that go to make a really good conductor, and how much time and experience and heart-searching have I since put into acquiring two or three of them!"

   "But the audience is arriving, it is time; and shattered in body and mind, you stagger to the conductor's desk, a wreck, weary, stale, flat and unprofitable, scarcely able to stand--until that magical moment when the applause of the audience, the zest of the players, and your own love for the work transform you in an instant into a dynamo of energy, radiating invisible, irresistible rays of light and power. And then the recompense begins. Then, I grant you, the composer-conductor lives on a plane of existence unknown to the virtuoso. With what ecstasy he abandons himself to the delight of 'playing' the orchestra! How he hugs and clasps and sways this immense and fiery instrument! Once more he is all vigilance. His eyes are everywhere. He indicates with a glance each vocal and orchestral entry. His right arm unleashes tremendous chords which go off like explosions. At the pauses he brings the whole accumulated impetus to a sudden halt, rivets every eye, arrests every arm, every breath; listens for an instant to the silence--then gives freer rein than ever to the harnessed whirlwind..."

4. Barzun, Jacques. Berlioz and the Romantic Century. 2 vols. Boston: Little, Brown and Company, 1950. xii, [iii], 573 p., 9 illus.; 511 p., 9 illus., chronology, 1,476-item bibliography, index of misconceptions, index of names and subjects.

   One of the few outstanding biographies of any composer! The massive bibliography is essential to any researcher.

   Davis, Joe, comp. Berlioz and the Romantic Imagination. London: The Arts Council, 1969. xxiv, 146 p., illus., chronology, 43-item bibliography, index of lenders, general index.

   An exhibition of 421 items organized by the Arts Council and the Victoria and Albert Museum on behalf of the Berlioz Centenary Committee in cooperation with the French government.

   Lesure, François. Berlioz. Paris: Imprimerie Centrale Commerciale, 1969. 178 p., 40 illus., chronology.

   Exhibit catalogue of 457 items assembled from major public and private collections.

   Matesky, Michael Paul. Berlioz on Conducting. D.M.A. diss., University of Washington, 1974. 138 p.

5. B0026, B0032, B0080, B0094, B0112.

C0095.
BERNARD, ANTHONY. b. January 25, 1891, London; d. April 6, 1963, London.

1. BAKER 7; GROVE 6/2.

C0096.
BERNARDI, MARIO. b. August 20, 1930, Kirkland Lake, Ontario, Canada.

1. BAKER 7; GROVE 6/2; PAB-MI/2 (Bibliography); RIEMANN 12/Supp.

C0097.
BERNSTEIN, LEONARD. b. August 25, 1918, Lawrence, Massachusetts.

1. BAKER 7 (Bibliography); EdS 1/2 (Bibliography); GROVE 6/2 (Bibliography); GROVE-AM 1/1 (Bibliography); MGG 1/1 (Bibliography);

PAB-MI/2 (Bibliography); RIEMANN 12 + Supp. (Bibliography).

2. GR 48/568, 51/603; HiFi/MusAm 22/2, 24/7, 28/8, 30/4, 30/11; MQ 64, 66; ON 37/3; OW 11/7, 23/1.

3. Bernstein, Leonard. Findings. New York: Simon and Schuster, 1982. 376 p., illus., list of compositions by type.

Bernstein, Leonard. The Infinite Variety of Music. New York: Simon and Schuster, 1966. 286 p., 17 illus.

Bernstein, Leonard. The Joy of Music. New York: Simon and Schuster, 1959. 303 p., 2 illus.

4. Ames, Evelyn. A Wind From the West: Bernstein and the New York Philharmonic Abroad. Boston: Houghton Mifflin Company, 1970. xiv, 169 p., 16 illus.

Ewen, David. Leonard Bernstein: a Biography for Young People. Philadelphia: Chilton Company, 1960. vi, 174 p., 7 illus., list of compositions, discography, 13-item magazine bibliography, index.

Gruen, John. The Private World of Leonard Bernstein. New York: The Ridge Press, Inc., and The Viking Press Inc., 1968. 191 p., 147 family and professional photographs by Ken Heyman.

5. A0007, A0022, A0031, A0048, A0050, B0060, B0067, B0069, B0086, B0092, B0104, B0124, B0138, B0144.

C0098.
BERTINI, GARY. b. May 1, 1927, Briceni, Russia.

1. BAKER 7; GROVE 6/2 (Bibliography); PAB-MI/2 (Bibliography); RIEMANN 12/Supp.

C0099.
BERTON, HENRI-MONTAN. b. September 17, 1767, Paris; d. April 22, 1844, Paris, France.

1. BAKER 7 (Bibliography); EdS 1/2 (Bibliography); GROVE 6/2 (Bibliography); MGG 1/1; RIEMANN 12.

5. B0036.

C0100.
BESLY, MAURICE. b. January 28, 1888, Normanby, Yorkshire; d. March 20, 1945, Horsham, England.

1. BAKER 7; RIEMANN 12.

C0101.
BEVIGNANI, ENRICO. b. September 29, 1841, Naples; d. August 29, 1903, Naples, Italy.

1. BAKER 7; EdS 1/2; GROVE 6/2 (Bibliography).

C0102.
BEYSCHLAG, ADOLF. b. March 22, 1845, Frankfurt/M.; d. August 19, 1914, Mainz, Germany.

1. BAKER 7; RIEMANN 12.

C0103.
BIERDIAJEW, WALERIAN. b. March 7, 1885, Grodno; d. November 28, 1956, Warsaw, Poland.

1. BAKER 7; EdS 1/2 (Bibliography); GROVE 6/2; RIEMANN 12.

C0104.
BIEREY, GOTTLOB BENEDIKT. b. July 25, 1772, Dresden; d. May 5, 1840, Breslau, Germany.

1. BAKER 7; EdS 1/2 (Bibliography); GROVE 6/2; MGG/Supp. (Bibliography); RIEMANN 12.

C0105.
BIGOT, EUGENE. b. February 28, 1888, Rennes; d. July 17, 1965, Paris.

1. BAKER 7; EdS 1/2; GROVE 6/2.

C0106.
BILSE, BENJAMIN. b. August 17, 1816, Liegnitz; d. July 13, 1902, Liegnitz, Germany.

1. BAKER 7; RIEMANN 12.

C0107.
BIRIOTTI, LEON. b. December 1, 1929, Montevideo, Uruguay.

1. BAKER 7; GROVE 6/2 (Bibliography); RIEMANN 12/Supp.

C0108.
BIRNIE, TESSA DAPHNE. b. July 19, 1934, Ashburton, New Zealand.

1. BAKER 7; GROVE 6/2; PAB-MI/2 (Bibliography).

C0109.
BITTNER, ALBERT. b. September 27, 1900, Nuremberg; d. August 7, 1980, Hamburg, Germany.

1. BAKER 7; RIEMANN 12 + Supp.

4. Ullrich, Hermann. Julius Bittner: eine Studie. Wien: Verlag Elisabeth Lafite, 1968. 79, [1] p., 8 illus., list of compositions, 41-item bibliography.

C0110.
BLACK, FRANK J. b. November 29, 1894, Philadelphia, Pennsylvania; d. January 29, 1968, Atlanta, Georgia.

1. BAKER 7; GROVE-AM 1/1 (Bibliography); PAB-MI/2 (Bibliography).

5. A0010.

C0111.
BLATNY, PAVEL. b. September 14, 1931, Brno, Czechoslovakia.

1. BAKER 7; GROVE 6/2 (Bibliography); MGG/Supp. (Bibliography); PAB-MI/2 (Bibliography); RIEMANN 12/Supp. (Bibliography).

C0112.
BLECH, HARRY. b. March 2, 1910, London, England.

1. BAKER 7; GROVE 6/2; PAB-MI/2 (Bibliography); RIEMANN 12.

C0113.
BLECH, LEO. b. April 21, 1871, Aachen; d. August 25, 1958, Berlin.

1. BAKER 7 (Bibliography); GROVE 6/2; MGG 1/1; PAB-MI/2 (Bibliography); RIEMANN 12.

4. Jacob, Walter. _Leo Blech: ein Brevier anlaesslich des 60. Geburtstages_. Hamburg: Prismen-Verlag, 1931. 64 p., 4 illus., list of compositions dedicated to Blech, list of Blech's compositions.

5. B0129, B0138.

C0114.
BLISS, ARTHUR. b. August 2, 1891, London; d. March 27, 1975, London.

1. BAKER 7; EdS 1/2 (Bibliography); GROVE 6/2 (Bibliography); MGG 1/1; PAB-MI/2 (Bibliography); RIEMANN 12 + Supp. (Bibliography).

3. Bliss, Arthur. _As I Remember_. London: Faber and Faber Limited, 1970. 269 p., 25 illus., 2 appendices, index.

C0115.
BLOMSTEDT, HERBERT. b. July 11, 1927, Springfield, Massachusetts.

1. BAKER 7; MGG/Supp. (Bibliography); RIEMANN 12 + Supp.

2. HiFi/MusAm 35/10.

C0116.
BLUMENFELD, FELIX. b. April 19, 1863, Kovalevka, near Kherson, Russia; d. January 21, 1931, Moscow, Russia.

1. BAKER 7; EdS 1/2 (Bibliography); GROVE 6/2 (Bibliography); MGG/Supp. (Bibliography); PAB-MI/2 (Bibliography); RIEMANN 12 + Supp. (Bibliography).

C0117.
BLUMENFELD, HAROLD. b. October 15, 1923, Seattle, Washington.

1. BAKER 7; GROVE-AM 1/1 (Bibliography); PAB-MI/2 (Bibliography).

2. ON 32/26.

C0118.
BLUMER, THEODOR. b. March 24, 1881, Dresden; d. September 21, 1964, Berlin, Germany.

1. BAKER 7; MGG/Supp. (Bibliography); RIEMANN 12.

C0119.
BLUMNER, MARTIN. b. November 21, 1827, Fuerstenberg, Mecklenburg; d. November 16, 1901, Berlin, Germany.

1. BAKER 7 (Bibliography); GROVE 6/2 (Bibliography); RIEMANN 12.

C0120.
BODANZKY, ARTUR. b. December 16, 1877, Vienna; d. November 23, 1939, New York City.

1. BAKER 7; GROVE 6/2; GROVE-AM 1/1; PAB-MI/2 (Bibliography); RIEMANN 12.

2. ON 36/8.

5. B0042, B0051, B0064, B0072, B0088, B0115, B0138.

   SEE: Autobiography of ERICH LEINSDORF (C0663.3).

C0121.
BOEHE, ERNST. b. December 27, 1880, Munich; d. November 16, 1938, Ludwigshafen, Germany.

1. BAKER 7; RIEMANN 12.

C0122.
BOEHM, KARL. b. August 28, 1894, Graz; d. August 14, 1981, Salzburg.

1. BAKER 7 (Bibliography); EdS 1/2; GROVE 6/2 (Bibliography); MGG 1/1 (Bibliography); PAB-MI/2 (Bibliography); RIEMANN 12.

2. GR 50/595; HiFi/MusAm 32/7; ON 25/22, 33/19, 36/20, 39/2, 46/5; OPERA 11/5, 28/12; OW 4/1, 5/8, 11/12, 15/10, 21/8, 22/5; OPER 1976: ein Jarhbuch der Zeitschrift "Opernwelt".

3. Boehm, Karl. Ich erinnere mich ganz genau: Autobiographie. Muenchen: Deutscher Taschenbuch Verlag GmbH & Co. KG, 1979. 196 p., index.

   Boehm, Karl. "Problems in Mozart." In Opera Annual 1955-6 (1955): 46-48.

4. Dostal, Franz Eugen. Karl Boehm: Begegnung mit Richard Strauss. Wien: Verlag Doblinger, 1964. 80 p., 10 illus., discography, list of operas conducted with initial performance.

   Endler, Franz. Karl Boehm ein Dirigentenleben. Forward by Leonard Bernstein. Hamburg: Verlag Hoffmann und Campe, 1981. 287 p., 250+ illus., chronology, discography, filmography, index of names.

Roemer, Margarete. Karl Boehm. Berlin: Rembrandt Verlag, 1966. 64 p., 39 illus., discography.

5. A0002, A0031, A0052, B0055, B0063, B0067, B0069, B0091, B0110, B0125, B0132, B0145, B0164.

C0123.
BOEPPLE, PAUL. b. July 19, 1896, Basel, Switzerland; d. December 21, 1970, Brattleboro, Vermont.

1. BAKER 7; PAB-MI/2 (Bibliography); RIEMANN 12.

C0124.
BOETTCHER, WILFRED. b. August 11, 1929, Bremen, Germany.

1. BAKER 7; GROVE 6/2; PAB-MI/2 (Bibliography).

C0125.
BONAWITZ, JOHANN HEINRICH. b. December 4, 1839, Duerkheim am Rhein, Germany; d. August 15, 1917, London, England.

1. BAKER 7; RIEMANN 12.

C0126.
BOND, VICTORIA. b. May 6, 1945, Los Angeles, California.

1. GROVE-AM 1/1 (Bibliography); PAB-MI/2 (Bibliography).

5. HiFi/MusAm 29/4.

C0127.
BONGARTZ, HEINZ. b. July 31, 1894, Krefeld; d. May 2, 1978, Dresden.

1. BAKER 7; MGG/Supp. (Bibliography); RIEMANN 12 + Supp.

C0128.
BONYNGE, RICHARD. b. September 29, 1930, Sydney, Australia.

1. BAKER 7; GROVE 6/3; PAB-MI/2 (Bibliography); RIEMANN 12/Supp.

2. ON 40/16, 47/6; OPERA 17/6

5. SEE: Adams, Brian. La Stupenda: a Biography of Joan Sutherland. Richmond: Hutchinson Group Pty Ltd, 1980.

   SEE: Braddon, Russell. Joan Sutherland. New York: St, Martin's Press, 1962.

C0129.
BOPP, WILHELM. b. November 4, 1863, Mannheim; d. June 11, 1931, Baden-Baden, Germany.

1. BAKER 7; MGG/Supp.; RIEMANN 12.

C0130.
BORCH, GASTON LOUIS. b. March 8, 1871, Guines, France; d. February 14, 1926, Stockholm, Sweden.

1. BAKER 7; MGG/Supp. (Bibliography); RIEMANN 12.

C0131.
BORDES, CHARLES. b. May 12, 1863, Roche-Corbon, near Vouvray-sur-Loire; d. November 8, 1909, Toulon, France.

1. BAKER 7 (Bibliography); GROVE 6/3 (Bibliography), PAB-MI/2 (Bibliography); RIEMANN 12 (Bibliography) + Supp. (Bibliography).

4. Dowd, Philip M. Charles Bordes and the Schola Cantorum of Paris.... Ph.D. diss., Catholic University of America (Washington, D.C.), 1969. vi, 182 p., bibliography.

C0132.
BOSKOVSKY, WILLI. b. June 16, 1909, Vienna, Austria.

1. BAKER 7; GROVE 6/3 (Bibliography); PAB-MI/2 (Bibliography); RIEMANN 12 + Supp.

C0133.
BOSSI, RENZO. b. April 9, 1883, Como; d. April 2, 1965, Milan, Italy.

1. BAKER 7 (Bibliography); EdS 1/2 (Bibliography); GROVE 6/3 (Bibliography); MGG 1/2; PAB-MI/2 (Bibliography); RIEMANN 12.

C0134.
BOTT, JEAN JOSEPH. b. March 9, 1826, Kassel, Germany; d. April 28, 1895, New York City.

1. BAKER 7; GROVE 6/3 (Bibliography); PAB-MI/2 (Bibliography); RIEMANN 12 + Supp. (Bibliography).

C0135.
BOTTESINI, GIOVANNI. b. December 22, 1821, Crema; d. July 7, 1889, Parma, Italy.

1. BAKER 7 (Bibliography); EdS 1/2 (Bibliography); GROVE 6/3 (Bibliography); PAB-MI/2 (Bibliography); RIEMANN 12 + Supp. (Bibliography).

5. BO007.

C0136.
BOULANGER, NADIA. b. September 16, 1887, Paris; d. October 22, 1979, Paris, France.

1. BAKER 7; GROVE 6/3; GROVE-AM 1/1 (Bibliography); MGG/Supp. (Bibliography); PAB-MI/2 (Bibliography); RIEMANN 12 (Bibliography) + Supp.

4. Kendall, Alan. The Tender Tyrant, Nadia Boulanger: a Life Devoted to Music. Introduction by Yehudi Menuhin. London: Macdonald and Jane's Publishers Limited, 1976. xvi, 144 p., 8 illus., index.

Monsaingeon, Bruno. Mademoiselle: Conversations with Nadia Boulanger. Translated by Robyn Marsack. Manchester: Carcanet Press Limited. 1985 [original: Mademoiselle: entretiens avec Nadia Boulanger. Paris: Editions Van de Velde, 1981]. 141 p., 32 illus., chronology, discography, index.

Nadia Boulanger was the first woman to conduct a symphony orchestra in London (1937).

C0137.
BOULEZ, PIERRE. b. March 26, 1925, Montbrison, France.

1. BAKER 7 (Bibliography); EdS/Supp. (Bibliography); GROVE 6/3 (Bibliography); GROVE-AM 1/1 (Bibliography); MGG/Supp. (Bibliography); PAB-MI/2 (Bibliography); RIEMANN 12 + Supp. (Bibliography).

   A true champion of 20th century music and Wagnerian opera.

2. GR 45/534, 52/614; OPERA 20/11-12, 34/2; OW 9/2, 11/2; OPER 1966/1973/1976: Ein Jahrbuch der Zeitschrift "Opernwelt".

3. Pierre Boulez: Conversations with Célestin Deliège. London: Eugenburg Books, 1976 [original: Par volonté et par hasard: entretiens avec Célestin Deliège. Paris, 1975]. 123 p., notes.

4. Cadieu, Martine. Pierre Boulez. Translated by Felipe Ximénez De Sandoval. Madrid: Espasa-Calpe, S.A., 1977. 126 p., 7 illus., comparative chronology, table of important dates, discography.

   Jameux, Dominique. Pierre Boulez (Musiciens d'aujourd'hui). Paris: Fayard Foundation SACEM, 1984. 486, [6] p., 8 illus., musical examples, catalogue of works, 25-item bibliography, discography, filmography, indexes.

   Peyser, Joan. Boulez: Composer, Conductor, Enigma. New York: Schirmer Books, 1976. 303 p., 28 illus., index.

5. A0031, B0068, B0071, B0092, B0124, B0125, B0144.

C0138.
BOULT, ADRIAN. b. April 8, 1889, Chester; d. February 22, 1983, Tunbridge Wells, England.

1. BAKER 7 (Bibliography); GROVE 6/3 (Bibliography); MGG 1/1 (Bibliography); PAB-MI/2 (Bibliography); RIEMANN 12.

2. GR 46/551, 51/611, 56/671 60/719; OPERA 26/2; RS 42, 48, 77.

3. Boult on Music: Words From a Lifetime's Communication. London: Toccata Press, 1983. 196 p., index.

   Extensive material on Toscanini, Nikisch, Wood, and Walter.

   Boult, Adrian Cedric. My Own Trumpet. London: Hamish Hamilton, 1973. x, 213 p., 23 illus., 3 appendices: first performances from 1931 to

1971; B.B.C. Symphony Orchestra visits 1934-1950; orchestral work out of England 1912-1966, index.

He organized the renowned BBC Symphony which he lead until 1950.

Boult, Adrian Cedric and Walter Emery. The St Matthew Passion: its Preparation and Performance. London: Novello and Co Ltd, n.d. 75 p., 4 appendices including 11-item bibliography.

Boult, Adrian C. Thoughts on Conducting. London: Phoenix House Ltd, 1963. xv, 79 p., 11 illus., 22-item bibliography, index.

Simeone, Nigel and Simon Mundy, eds. Sir Adrian Boult, Companion of Honor: a Tribute. Speldhurst, Tunbridge Wells: Midas Books, 1980. 96 p., discography.

5. A0002, A0003, A0004, A0007, A0022, A0023, A0031, A0045, B0062, B0071, B0096, B0167.

SEE: Northrop, Jerrold. Elgar on Record: the Composer and the Gramophone. London: Oxford University Press, 1974.

C0139.
BOUR, ERNEST. b. April 20, 1913, Thionville, France.

1. BAKER 7; GROVE 6/3; MGG/Supp. (Bibliography); RIEMANN 12 + Supp.

C0140.
BOUSQUET, GEORGES. b. March 12, 1818, Perpignan; d. June 15, 1854, St. Cloud, near Paris, France.

1. BAKER 7; EdS 1/2 (Bibliography); MGG/Supp.; RIEMANN 12.

C0141.
BOUTRY, ROGER. b. February 22, 1932, Paris, France.

1. BAKER 7; GROVE 6/3.

C0142.
BOZZA, EUGENE. b. April 4, 1905, Nice, France.

1. BAKER 7; GROVE 6/3; MGG/Supp.; PAB-MI/2 (Bibliography); RIEMANN 12 + Supp.

C0143.
BRAEIN, EDVARD FLIFLET. b. August 23, 1924, Kristiansund; d. April 30, 1976, Oslo, Norway.

1. BAKER 7; GROVE 6/3.

C0144.
BRAITHWAITE, NICHOLAS. b. August 26, 1939, London, England.

1. BAKER 7; GROVE 6/3; PAB-MI/2 (Bibliography).

C0145.
BRAITHWAITE, WARWICK. b. January 9, 1896, Dunedin, New Zealand; d. January 18, 1971, London, England.

1. BAKER 7; EdS 1/2; GROVE 6/3; PAB-MI/2 (Bibliography); RIEMANN 12/ Supp.

3. Braithwaite, Warwick. The Conductor's Art. London: Williams and Norgate Ltd, 1952. viii, 176 p.

5. A0003.

C0146.
BRANSCOMBE, GENA. b. November 4, 1881, Picton, Ontario, Canada; d. July 26, 1977, New York City.

1. BAKER 7; GROVE 6/3; GROVE-AM 1/1; PAB-MI/2 (Bibliography).

3. BAKER 7 mentions an unpublished autobiography.

4. Marlow, Laurine A.E. Gena Branscombe (1881-1977): American Composer and Conductor. Ph.D. diss., University of Texas/Austin, 1980. 522 p.

C0147.
BRECHER, GUSTAV. b. February 5, 1879, Eichwald, Bohemia; d. May ?, 1940, Ostend, Germany.

1. BAKER 7; EdS 1/2 (Bibliography); MGG/Supp. (Bibliography); RIEMANN 12 + Supp. (Bibliography).

C0148.
BRETON y HERNANDEZ, TOMAS. b. December 29, 1850, Salamanca; d. December 2, 1923, Madrid, Spain.

1. BAKER 7; EdS 1/2 (Bibliography); GROVE 6/3 (Bibliography); MGG 1/2 (Bibliography); RIEMANN 12 (Bibliography).

4. Salcedo, Angel S. Tomas Bretón: su vida y sus obras. Madrid: Imprenta Clásica Española, 1924. 124, [1] p., list of compositions.

C0149.
BRICO, ANTONIA. b. June 26, 1902, Rotterdam, Holland.

1. BAKER 7; GROVE-AM 1/1; PAB-MI/2 (Bibliography); RIEMANN 12 + Supp.

2. NEWSWEEK 12/5; ON 40/14.

5. B0090.

C0150.
BRIDGE, JOHN FREDERICK. b. December 5, 1844, Oldbury; d. March 18, 1924, London, England.

1. BAKER 7; GROVE 6/3 (Bibliography); MGG/Supp. (Bibliography); PAB-MI/2 (Bibliography); RIEMANN 12.

3. Bridge, Frederick. A Westminster Pilgrim: Being a Record of Service in Church, Cathedral, and Abby College, University, and Concert Room with a Few Notes on Sport. London: Novello & Co., Ltd., n.d. [1918]. xiii, [ii], 363 p., 29 illus., appendix of works performed by the Royal Choral Society 1896-1918.

C0151.
BRISTOW, GEORGE F. b. December 19, 1825, Brooklyn, New York; d. December 13, 1898, New York City.

1. BAKER 7 (Bibliography); GROVE 6/3 (Bibliography); GROVE-AM 1/1 (Bibliography); PAB-MI/2 (Bibliography).

C0152.
BROEKMAN, DAVID. b. May 13, 1899, Leiden, Holland; d. April 1, 1958, New York City.

1. BAKER 7; PAB-MI/2 (Bibliography).

C0153.
BROTT, ALEXANDER. b. March 14, 1915, Montreal, Canada.

1. BAKER 7; GROVE 6/3 (Bibliography); PAB-MI/2 (Bibliography); RIEMANN 12/Supp.

His son Boris (b. March 14, 1944, Montreal) is also a conductor.

C0154.
BRUCK, CHARLES. b. May 2, 1911, Timisoara, Romania.

1. BAKER 7; GROVE 6/3; PAB-MI/2 (Bibliography); RIEMANN 12/Supp.

C0155.
BRUN, FRITZ. b. August 18, 1878, Lucerne; d. November 29, 1959, Grosshoechstetten, Switzerland.

1. BAKER 7; GROVE 6/3 (Bibliography); MGG 1/2; RIEMANN 12 (Bibliography) + Supp. (Bibliography).

C0156.
BRUSILOW, ANSHEL. b. August 14, 1928, Philadelphia, Pennsylvania.

1. BAKER 7; GROVE 6/3 (Bibliography); GROVE-AM 1/1 (Bibliography).

C0157.
von BUELOW, HANS. b. January 8, 1830, Dresden, Germany; d. February 12, 1894, Cairo, Egypt.

1. BAKER 7 (Bibliography); EdS 1/2 (Bibliography); GROVE 6/3 (Bibliography); MGG 1/2 (Bibliography); RIEMANN 12 (Bibliography).

2. LS 43; MQ 13/2.

3. von Buelow, Marie, ed. Hans von Buelows Briefe und Schriften. 8 vols. Leipzig: Druck und Verlag Breitkopf und Haertel, 1895-1908.

4. Bollert, Werner. "Hans von Buelow als Dirigent: Marginalien zur kunstlerischen Laufbahn und zum Wesen." Melos/NeueZM I/2 (1975): 88-95.

von Buelow, Marie. *Hans von Buelows Leben dargestellt aus seinen Briefen*. Leipzig: Druck und Verlag von Breitkopf und Haertel, 1919. xxi, 600 p., index.

von Buelow, Marie. *Hans von Buelow in Leben und Wort*. Stuttgart: J. Engelhorns Nachf., 1925. 298 p., 8 illus., 11-item bibliography, index.

Erwiderung an Hans von Buelow von einem Bayreuther. Bayreuth: Druck und Verlag von Th. Burger, 1884. 21 p.

Fischer, Georg. *Hans von Buelow in Hannover*. Hannover: Hahn'sche Buchhandlung, 1902. 64 p.

Hans von Buelow, a Biographical Sketch: His Visit to America. New York: Cushing & Bardua, Printers, 1875. 10 p.

This same pamphlet appears under the imprint of several publishers.

La Mara [pseud. for Ida Maria Lipsius], ed. *Briefwechsel zwischen Franz Liszt und Hans von Buelow*. Leipzig: Druck und Verlag von Breitkopf und Haertel, 1898. viii, 426 p., index of names.

La Mara [pseud. for Ida Maria Lipsius]. *Hans von Buelow*. Leipzig: Druck und Verlag von Breitkopf und Haertel, 1911. 56 p., portrait, list of published compositions.

Laser, Arthur. *Der moderne Dirigent*. Leipzig: Druck und Verlag von Breitkopf und Haertel, 1904. viii, 70 p.

da Motta, Vianna J. *Nachtrag zu Studien bei Hans von Buelow von Theodor Pfeiffer*. Berlin: Verlag von Friedrich Luckhardt, 1896. viii, 84 p., index of names.

Moulin Eckert, Richard Count di. *Letters of Hans von Buelow to Richard Wagner, Cosima Wagner, Daniela & Louise von Buelow, Karl Klindworth and Carl Bechstein*. Translated by Hannah Waller. New York: Vienna House, 1972 [original: Munich, 1927]. xxx, 434, vi p., index.

Moulin Eckert, Richard Count di. *Hans von Buelow*. Muenchen: Roesl & Cie, 1921. 502, [1] p., 3 illus.

Mutzenbecher, Heinrich. *Cecile Mutzenbecher und Hans von Buelow*. Hamburg: Gesellschaft der Buecherfreunde, 1963. 78 p., 3 illus.

Edition of 260 numbered copies plus 90 copies for the editor.

Pfeiffer, Theodor. *Studien bei Hans von Buelow*. 2nd edition. Berlin: Verlag von Friedrich Luckhardt, 1894. vii, 123 p., portrait.

Riemann Heinrich. Hans von Buelow: sein Leben und sein Wirken. Band I: aus Hans von Buelows Lehrzeit. Berlin: "Harmonie" Verlagsgesellschaft fuer Literatur und Kunst, n.d. x, [ii], 295, [2] p., 28 illus., geneology. 2nd revised and enlarged edition subtitled: einer unvollendet gebliebenen Biographie des Kuenstlers. n.d. [1908]. x, 296 p., 16 illus., geneology.

Schemann, Ludwig. Hans von Buelow im Lichte der Wahrheit. Regensburg: Gustav Bosse Verlag, 1935. 97 p., portrait.

Schuh, Willi and Franz Trenner, eds. Hans von Buelow and Richard Strauss: Correspondence. Translated by Anthony Gishford. London: Boosey & Hawkes Limited, 1955. 103, [1] p., 2 illus.

Vogel, Bernhard. Hans von Buelow: sein Leben und sein Entwicklungsgang. Leipzig: Max Hesses Verlag, 1887. vi, 69 p., portrait, index.

Zabel, Eugen. Hans von Buelow: Gedenkblaetter. Hamburg: Verlag von Lucas Graefe & Sillem, 1894. 56 p., 2 illus.

5. A0016, A0050, B0019, B0035, B0076, B0080, B0083, B0112, B0114, B0117, B0156.

SEE: Hanslick, Eduard. Aus dem Tagebuche eines Musikers. Berlin: Allgemeiner Verein fuer Deutsche Litteratur, 1892.

SEE: Hanslick, Eduard. Aus neuer und neuester Zeit: der modernen Oper. Berlin: Allgemeiner Verein fuer Deutsche Litteratur, 1900.

SEE: Newman, Ernest. The Life of Richard Wagner. vols. 2, 3, and 4. New York: Alfred A. Knopf, 1937/1941/1946.

SEE: Autobiography by Siegfried Ochs (C0822.3).

SEE: Autobiography of RICHARD WAGNER (C1175.3).

C0158.
BUNNING, HERBERT. b. May 2, 1863, London; d. November 26, 1937, Thundersley, Essex, England.

1. BAKER 7; RIEMANN 12.

C0159.
BURGHAUSER, JARMIL MICHAEL. b. October 21, 1921, Písek, Czechoslovakia.

1. BAKER 7 (Bibliography); GROVE 6/3 (Bibliography); MGG/Supp.; PAB-MI/2 (Bibliography); RIEMANN 12/Supp.

C0160.
BURKHARD, PAUL. b. December 21, 1911, Zurich; d. September 6, 1977, Toesstal, Switzerland.

1. BAKER 7; EdS 1/2; GROVE 6/3; MGG 1/2; RIEMANN 12 + Supp.

C0161.
BUSCH, CARL. b. March 29, 1862, Bjerre, Denmark; d. December 19, 1943, Kansas City, Kansas.

1. BAKER 7; GROVE-AM 1/1; PAB-MI/2 (Bibliography); RIEMANN 12.

4. Lowe, Donald Robert. Sir Carl Busch: His Life and Work as a Teacher, Conductor, and Composer. D.M.A. diss., University of Missouri/Kansas City, 1972. 456 p., bibliography, list of works.

C0162.
BUSCH, FRITZ. b. March 13, 1890, Siegen, Westphalia, Germany; d. September 14, 1951, London, England.

1. BAKER 7; EdS 1/2 (Bibliography); GROVE 6/3 (Bibliography); GROVE-AM 1/1 (Bibliography); PAB-MI/2 (Bibliography); MGG 1/2; RIEMANN 12 + Supp. (Bibliography).

2. ON 10/4; OPERA 11/3, 36/5; OW 18/8; RS 86.

3. The annotated scores of Fritz Busch are presently housed in the Indiana University School of Music Library. Fritz was the brother of Adolf and Hermann Busch, the former of whom organized the famous Marlboro School of Music in Vermont.

   Busch, Fritz. Aus dem Leben eines Musikers. Zuerich: Rascher & Cie, A.-G., 1949. 222 p., 8 illus., index.

   Translated (London, 1953) by Marjorie Strachey as Pages from a Musician's Life. Comments on Richard Strauss and Toscanini.

4. Burbach, Wolfgang, ed. Im Memoriam Fritz Busch. 2nd edition. Dahlbruch: Brueder-Busch-Gesellschaft e.V., 1968 [1st edition 1964]. 52 p., 26 illus., select discography of historical interest.

   Busch, Grete. Fritz Busch, Dirigent. Frankfurt am Main: S. Fischer Verlag GmbH, 1970. 366, [3] p., portrait, discography by Jacques Delalande, index.

   Dopheide, Bernhard. Fritz Busch: sein Leben und Wirken in Deutschland mit einem Ausblick auf die Zeit seiner Emigration. Tutzing: Hans Schneider, 1970 [original Ph.D. diss., University of Muenster, 1969. 261 p., list of works, bibliography]. 223 p., 5 illus., bibliography.

5. A0010, B0047, B0109, B0167.

   SEE: Wilfrid Blunt under THOMAS BEECHAM (C0079.5).

C0163.
BUSCHKOETTER, WILHELM. b. September 27, 1887, Hoexter, Westphalia; d. May 12, 1967, Berlin, Germany.

1. BAKER 7 (Bibliography); RIEMANN 12 + Supp.

C0164.
BUSSER, (PAUL-) HENRI. b. January 16, 1872, Toulouse; d. December 30, 1973, Paris, France.

1. BAKER 7; GROVE 6/3 (Bibliography); MGG 1/2; PAB-MI/2 (Bibliography); RIEMANN 12 (Bibliography) + Supp. (Bibliography).

3. Busser, Henri. De Pélleas aux indes galantes...de la flûte au tambour. Paris: Librairie Arthème Fayard, 1955. 282, [1] p.

5. A0046, B0133.

C0165.
BUZZOLLA, ANTONIO. b. March 2, 1815, Adria; d. March 20, 1871, Venice.

1. BAKER 7; EdS 1/2 (Bibliography); GROVE 6/3; MGG/Supp.; RIEMANN 12.

C0166.
CAHN-SPEYER, RUDOLF. b. September 1, 1881, Vienna, Austria; d. December 25, 1940, Florence, Italy.

1. BAKER 7; MGG/Supp. (Bibliography); RIEMANN 12.

3. Cahn-Speyer, Rudolf. Handbuch des Dirigierens. Leipzig: Druck und Verlag Breitkopf und Haertel, 1919. viii, 284 p.

C0167.
CALDWELL, SARAH. b. March 6, 1924, Maryville, Missouri.

1. BAKER 7; GROVE 6/3; GROVE-AM 1/1 (Bibliography); PAB-MI/2 (Bibliography.

2. ON 40/14; OW 9/1.

   Caldwell was the first woman to conduct at the Met leading LA Traviata on January 13, 1976. Founder of the Opera Company of Boston, she has had an impact on opera in the United States.

5. B0090, B0124, B0125.

C0168.
CAMERON, BASIL. b. August 18, 1884, Reading; d. June 26, 1975, Leominster, England.

1. BAKER 7; GROVE 6/3; PAB-MI/2 (Bibliography); RIEMANN 12 + Supp. (Bibliography).

5. A0003, A0004.

C0169.
CAMPANARI, LEANDRO. b. October 20, 1857, Rovigo, Italy; d. April 22, 1939, San Francisco, California.

1. BAKER 7; PAB-MI/2 (Bibliography); RIEMANN 12/Supp.

C0170.
CAMPANINI, CLEOFONTE. b. September 1, 1860, Parma, Italy; d. December 19, 1919, Chicago, Illinois.

1. BAKER 7; EdS 1/2; GROVE 6/3 (Bibliography); GROVE-AM 1/1 (Bibliography); PAB-MI/2 (Bibliography).

   Principal conductor of Hammerstein's Manhattan Opera and the Chicago Opera Co., he was one of the finest opera conductors of his time.

5. B0018, B0046, B0049, B0051, B0075, B0151, B0168.

C0171.
CANTELLI, GUIDO. b. April 27, 1920, Novara; d. November 24, 1956, Novara, Italy.

1. BAKER 7; GROVE 6/3 PAB-MI/2 (Bibliography); RIEMANN 12 + Supp. (Bibliography)/

2. GR 34; LGB 3/1; LS 85.

4. Lewis, Laurence. Guido Cantelli: Portrait of a Maestro. San Diego: A.S. Barnes & Company, Inc., 1981. 175 p., illus., appendix of performances 1942-1949, discography, appendix of interviews, 6-item bibliography, index.

5. B0060.

C0172.
CAPE, SAFFORD. b. June 28, 1906, Denver, Colorado; d. March 26, 1973, Brussels, Belgium.

1. BAKER 7; GROVE 6/3; GROVE-AM 1/1.

C0173.
CAPLET, ANDRE. b. November 23, 1878, Le Harve; d. April 22, 1925, Paris.

1. BAKER 7 (Bibliography); EdS 1/2 (Bibliography); GROVE 6/3 (Bibliography); MGG 1/2 (Bibliography); PAB-MI/2 (Bibliography); RIEMANN 12 (Bibliography) + Supp. (Bibliography).

C0174.
CAPUANA, FRANCO. b. September 29, 1894, Fano; d. December 10, 1969, Naples, Italy.

1. BAKER 7; EdS 1/2 + Supp.; GROVE 6/3; PAB-MI/2 (Bibliography); Riemann 12 + Supp.

4. Cagnoli, Bruno. L'art musicale di Franco Capuana. Milano: Electa Editrice, 1983. 286 p., 293 illus., list of compositions, detailed chronological list of operas and concerts 1915-1969, radio broadcasts, discography, 16-item bibliography, repertoire list, index of names.

   This could serve as a model for biographies in this field.

C0175.
CARACCIOLO, FRANCO. b. March 29, 1920, Bari, Italy.

1. BAKER 7; GROVE 6/3; RIEMANN 12/Supp.

C0176.
CARIDIS, MILTIADES. b. May 9, 1923, Gdansk, Poland.

1. BAKER 7; PAB-MI/2 (Bibliography); RIEMANN 12/Supp.

C0177.
CARNER, MOSCO. b. November 15, 1904, Vienna, Austria.

1. BAKER 7 (Bibliography); GROVE 6/3 (Bibliography); RIEMANN 12 (Bibliography) + Supp. (Bibliography).

C0178.
CARRILLO, JULIAN. b. January 28, 1875, Ahualulco, San Luis Potosi; d. September 9, 1965, Mexico City, Mexico.

1. BAKER 7 (Bibliography); GROVE 6/3 (Bibliography); RIEMANN 12 (under Carillo with Bibliography) + Supp. (Bibliography).

3. Carrillo, Julian. Platicas musicales. San Luis Potosi: Linotipografia de la Escuela Industrial Militar, 1914 [vol. 2, 1923]. 196 p., 33 illus.

   BAKER 7 mentions an autobiography, Julian Carrillo: su vida y su obra, but this title is authored by J. Velasco-Urda.

C0179.
de CARVALHO, ELEAZAR. b. July 28, 1912, Iguatú, Ceará, Brazil.

1. BAKER 7; EdS 1/3; GROVE-AM 1/1; RIEMANN 12 + Supp.

2. HiFi/MusAm 28/10.

5. A0022.

C0180.
CASADESUS, FRANCOIS LOUIS. b. December 2, 1870, Paris; d. June 27, 1954, Suresnes, near Paris, France.

1.BAKER 7; EdS 1/3 (Bibliography); GROVE 6/3; MGG 1/2; RIEMANN 12.

C0181.
CASADESUS, JEAN-CLAUDE. b. December 7, 1935, Paris, France.

1. BAKER 7; GROVE 6/3 (Bibliography); RIEMANN 12/Supp.

C0182.
CASALS, PABLO. b. December 29, 1876, Vendrell, Catalonia, Spain; d. October 22, 1973, San Juan, Puerto Rico.

1. BAKER 7 (Bibliography); GROVE 6/3 (Bibliography); GROVE-AM 1/1

(Bibliography); MGG 1/2; PAB-MI/2 (Bibliography); RIEMANN 12 + Supp. (Bibliography).

4. Borras, Jose Garcia. Pablo Casals, peregrino en America: tres semenas con el maestro. México, D.F.: Talleres Gráficos Victoria, 1957. 349, [2] p., 114 illus.

Boult, Adrian Cedric. "Casals as Conductor." Music and Letters IV (1923).

Corredor, J. Ma. Casals: biografia ilustrada. Barcelona: Ediciones Destino, 1967. 149 p., 130 illus., chronology, index.

Kahn, Albert E. Joys and Sorrows: Reflections by Pablo Casals. New York: Simon and Schuster, 1970. 314 p., 67 illus., index.

Kirk, H.L. Pablo Casals. New York: Holt, Reinhart and Winston, 1974. xi, 692 p., 137 illus., list of compositions, discography, notes, 231-item selected bibliography, notes.

Littlehales, Lillian. Pablo Casals. Westport (CT): Greenwood Press, Publishers, 1970 [original: New York: W.W. Norton & Co., Inc., 1929]. 232 p., 19 illus., unrevised list of recordings, index.

Strongin, Theodore. Casals. New York: Paragraphic Books, 1966. unpaginated [106 p.], 82 photographs by Vytas Valaitis.

von Tobel, Rudolf. Pablo Casals. Lisboa: Ramos, Alfonso & Moita, LdA, 1945. 128, [1] p., 9 illus., 13-item bibliography.

5. A0045, B0089, B0096.

C0183.
CASANOVA VICUNA, JUAN. b. December 27, 1894, Santiago de Chile.

1. RIEMANN 12/Supp.

4. Juan Casanova Vicuña y erase un rey.... Santiago de Chile: Ediciones Barcelona, 1975. 103, [2] p., illus.

C0184.
CASSUTO, ALVARO LEON. b. November 17, 1938, Oporto, Portugal.

1. BAKER 7; GROVE 6/3; PAB-MI/2 (Bibliography); RIEMANN 12/Supp.

C0185.
CASTON, SAUL. b. August 22, 1901, New York City.

1. BAKER 7; GROVE-AM 1/1 (Bibliography).

5. A0048.

C0186.
CASTRO, JOSE MARIA. b. December 15, Avellaneda, near Buenos Aires; d. August 2, 1964, Buenos Aires, Argentina.

1. BAKER 7; EdS 1/3; GROVE 6/3 (Bibliography); MGG/Supp.; PAB-MI/2 (Bibliography); RIEMANN 12 + Supp.

C0187.
CASTRO, JUAN JOSE. b. March 7, 1895, Avellaneda, near Buenos Aires; d. September 3, 1968, Buenos Aires, Argentina.

1. BAKER 7; EdS 1/3; GROVE 6/3 (Bibliography); MGG/Supp.; PAB-MI/2 (Bibliography); RIEMANN 12 + Supp.

4. Arizaga, Rodolfo. Juan José Castro. Buenos Aires: Ediciones Culturales Argentinas, 1963. 102, [1] p., 15 illus., repertoire.

C0188.
CECCATO, ALDO. b. February 18, 1934, Milan, Italy.

1. BAKER 7; GROVE 6/4; PAB-MI/2 (Bibliography).

C0189.
CELANSKY, LUDVIK VITEZSLAV. b. July 17, 1870, Vienna, Austria; d. October 27, 1931, Prague, Czechoslovakia.

1. BAKER 7; MGG/Supp. (Bibliography); RIEMANN 12.

C0190.
CELIBIDACHE, SERGIU. b. June 28, 1912, Roman, Romania.

1. BAKER 7; GROVE 6/4; RIEMANN 12 + Supp. (Bibliography).

C0191.
CELLIER, ALFRED. b. December 1, 1844, London; d. December 28, 1891, London, England.

1. BAKER 7; EdS 1/3 (Bibliography); GROVE 6/4 (Bibliography); PAB-MI/2 (Bibliography); RIEMANN 12.

5. B0150, B0151.

C0192.
CHADWICK, GEORGE WHITEFIELD. b. November 13, 1854, Lowell; d. April 4, 1931, Boston, Massachusetts.

1. BAKER 7; GROVE 6/4 (Bibliography); GROVE-AM 1/1 (Bibliography); MGG 1/2 (Bibliography); PAB-MI/2 (Bibliography); RIEMANN 12 (Bibliography) + Supp.

2. MQ 4/3, 6/2, 9/1, 10/3, 16/2, 17/1, 18/1, 19/3, 21/1, 26/3, 31/2, 32/2, 36/2.

4. Campbell, Douglas G. George W. Chadwick: His Life and Works. Ph.D. diss., University of Rochester, 1957. 363 p.

   Yellin, Victor. The Life and Operatic Works of George Whitefield Chadwick. Ph.D. diss., Harvard University, 1957. 308, [113] p.

C0193.
CHALABALA, ZDENEK. b. April 18, 1899, Uherskettradiste; d. March 4, 1962, Prague, Czechoslovakia.

1. BAKER 7; EdS 1/3; GROVE 6/4 (Bibliography); RIEMANN 12 + Supp.

C0194.
CHAVEZ, CARLOS. b. June 13, 1899, Calzada de Tacube; d. August 2, 1978, Mexico City, Mexico.

1. BAKER 7 (Bibliography); EdS 1/3; GROVE 6/4 (Bibliography); MGG/Supp. (Bibliography); PAB-MI/2 (Bibliography).

2. MQ 15/2, 27/2, 31/4, 34/1, 36/1, 39/4.

4. Carmona, Gloria, ed. Homenaje nacional a Carlos Chávez. México, D.F.: Instituto Nacional de Bellas Artes/SEP, 1978. 143 p., chronological catalogue of compositions, discography.

   García Morillo, Roberto. Carlos Chávez: vida y obra. México, D.F.: Fondo de Cultura Económica, 1960. Reprint 1978. 241 p., 20 illus., list of compositions, list of articles, 18-item bibliography, list of 57 musical examples.

C0195.
CHEVILLARD, CAMILE. b. October 14, 1859, Paris; d. May 30, 1923, Chatou, Siene-et-Oise, France.

1. BAKER 7 (Bibliography); GROVE 6/4 (Bibliography); MGG/Supp. (Bibliography); RIEMANN 12.

5. A0046, B0033, B0133, B0140.

C0196.
CHRISTIANSEN, FREDRIK MELIUS. b. April 1, 1871, Eidsvold, Norway; d. June 1, 1955, Northfield, Minnesota.

1. BAKER 7; GROVE-AM 1/1; RIEMANN 12 + Supp.

4. Bergmann, L. N. Music Master of the Middle West: the Story of F. Melius Christiansen and the St. Olaf Choir. Minneapolis, 1944.

   No copy located.

C0197.
CILLARIO, CARLOS FELICE. b. February 7, 1915, San Rafael, Argentina.

1. BAKER 7; EdS 1/3; PAB-MI/2; RIEMANN 12/Supp.

C0198.
CIMARA, PIETRO. b. November 10, 1887, Rome; d. October 1, 1967, Milan, Italy.

1. BAKER 7; RIEMANN 12 + Supp.

C0199.
CLAVE, JOSE ANSELMO. b. April 21, 1824, Barcelona; d. February 24, 1874, Barcelona, Spain.

1. BAKER 7 (Bibliography); GROVE 6/4 (Bibliography); MGG 1/2 (Bibliography); RIEMANN 12.

C0200.
CLEVA, FAUSTO. b. May 17, 1902, Trieste; d. August 6, 1971, Athens.

1. BAKER 7; GROVE 6/4; GROVE-AM 1/1; PAB-MI/2 (Bibliography); RIEMANN 12/Supp.

2. ON 17/19, 20/16, 23/22. 29/23, 30/10.

5. B0101.

C0201.
CLUYTENS, ANDRE. b. March 26, 1905, Antwerp, Belgium; d. June 3, 1967, Neuilly, near Paris, France.

1. BAKER 7; GROVE 6/4 (Bibliography); MGG/Supp.; PAB-MI/2 (Bibliography); RIEMANN 12 + Supp.

4. Gavoty, Bernard. <u>André Cluytens</u>. Translated by A.H. Eichmann. Genf: Verlag R. Kister, 1955. 30, [2] p., 26 illus., discography.

   Cluytens was the first French artist to conduct at Bayreuth leading <u>Tannhaeuser</u> in 1955.

5. A0052, B0145.

C0202.
COATES, ALBERT. b. April 23, 1882, St. Petersburg, Russia; d. December 11, 1953, Milnerton, near Cape Town, South Africa.

1. BAKER 7; EdS 1/3 (Bibliography); GROVE 6/4 (Bibliography); MGG 1/2; PAB-MI/2 (Bibliography); RIEMANN 12 (Bibliography).

2. LGR 17/1; OPERA 5/3; RS 57-58.

5. A0003, A0045, B0006, B0009, B0072.

C0203.
COENEN, JOHANNES MEINARDUS. b. January 28, 1824, The Hague; d. January 9, 1899, Amsterdam, Holland.

1. BAKER 7; GROVE 6/4 (Bibliography); MGG/Supp. (Bibliography); RIEMANN 12.

C0204.
COHN, ARTHUR. b. November 6, 1910, Philadelphia, Pennsylvania.

1. BAKER 7; GROVE 6/4; GROVE-AM 1/1 (Bibliography); PAB-MI/2 (Bibliography); RIEMANN 12 + Supp. (Bibliography).

C0205.
COLLINGWOOD, LAWRANCE A. b. March 14, 1887, London; d. December 19, 1982, near Perthshire, England.

1. BAKER 7; EdS 1/3 (Bibliography); GROVE 6/4; PAB-MI/2 (Bibliography); RIEMANN 12 + Supp.

2. MQ 12/2.

C0206.
COLLINS, ANTHONY. b. September 3, 1893, Hastings, England; d. December 11, 1963, Los Angeles, California.

1. BAKER 7; EdS 1/3; GROVE 6/4; MGG/Supp.; PAB-MI/2 (Bibliography).

C0207.
COLONNE, EDOUARD. b. July 23, 1838, Bordeaux; d. March 28, 1910, Paris.

1. BAKER 7; EdS 1/3; GROVE 6/4 (Bibliography); MGG/Supp. (Bibliography); PAB-MI/2 (Bibliography); RIEMANN 12 + Supp. (Bibliography).

5. B0033, B0112, B0133, B0140.

C0208.
COMBE, EDOUARD. b. September 23, 1866, Aigle; d. November 19, 1942, Lausanne, Switzerland.

1. BAKER 7; GROVE 6/4 (Bibliography); MGG/Supp.; RIEMANN 12.

C0209.
COMISSIONA, SERGIU. b. June 16, 1928, Bucharest, Romania.

1. BAKER 7; GROVE 6/4; GROVE-AM 1/1; PAB-MI/2 (Bibliography).

2. HiFi/MusAm 27/5.

C0210.
CONSTANT, MARIUS. b. February 7, 1925, Bucharest, Romania.

1. BAKER 7; GROVE 6/4; MGG/Supp.; PAB-MI/2 (Bibliography); RIEMANN 12/ Supp.

C0211.
CONZ, BERNHARD. b. June 1, 1906, Karlsruhe, Germany.

1. PAB-MI/2 (Bibliography); RIEMANN 12 + Supp.

3. Conz, Bernhard. Gerettet auf dem Steinway-Fluegel: Bernhard Conz ueber Conz und andere. Herford: Bussesche Verlagshandlung GMBH, 1971. 35, [4] p., 12 illus., list of important dates.

C0212.
COOPER, EMIL. b. December 20, 1877, Kherson, Russia; d. November 16, 1960, New York City.

1. BAKER 7; EdS 1/3; GROVE 6/4; MGG/Supp. (Bibliography); PAB-MI/2 (Bibliography).

C0213.
COPPOLA, PIERO. b. October 11, 1888, Milan; d. March 13, 1971, Lausanne, Switzerland.

1. BAKER 7; GROVE 6/4; RIEMANN 12 + Supp.

2. LGB 10/3-4.

3. Coppola, Piero. Dix-sept ans de musique a Paris 1922-1939. Lausanne: Librairie F. Rouge & Cie S.A., 1944. 253 p., index.

   Promoted the works of Fauré, Debussy, Franck, d'Indy, and Ravel.

C0214.
CORNELIS, EVERT. b. December 5, 1884, Amsterdam; d. November 23, 1931, Bilthoven, Holland.

1. BAKER 7; MGG/Supp. (Bibliography); RIEMANN 12 + Supp. (Bibliography).

4. Papp, W. Gedenkboek Evert Cornelis: 25 jaar na zijn sterfdag. Utrecht: herausgegeben vom Utrechtse Symph. Orkest., 1956.

5. A0008.

C0215.
CORTOLEZIS, FRITZ. b. February 21, 1878, Passau; d. March 13, 1934, Bad Aibling, Bavaria, Germany.

1. BAKER 7; GROVE 6/4 (Bibliography); MGG/Supp.; RIEMANN 12.

C0216.
CORTOT, ALFRED DENIS. b. September 26, 1877, Nyon, Switzerland; d. June 15, 1962, Lausanne, Switzerland.

1. BAKER 7; GROVE 6/4 (Bibliography); MGG 1/2 (Bibliography); PAB-MI/2 (Bibliography); RIEMANN 12 + Supp. (Bibliography).

4. Gavoty, Bernard. Alfred Cortot. Geneva: René Kister, 1955. 30, [2] p., 23 illus.

   Gavoty, Bernard. Alfred Cortot. Paris: Editions Buchet/Chastel, 1978. 316, [1] p., 18 illus., discography.

5. B0033.

C0217.
COSTA, MICHAEL. b. February 4, 1806, Naples, Italy; d. April 29, 1884, Hove, England.

1. BAKER 7; EdS 1/3 (Bibliography); GROVE 6/4 (Bibliography); PAB-MI/2 (Bibliography); RIEMANN 12 + Supp. (Bibliography).

4. Berger, Francesco. 97 [His Age]. London: Elkin Matthews and Marrot, 1931. xii, 180 p., portrait.

5. B0010, B0035, B0075, B0076, B0079, B0085, B0148, B0155.

SEE: Spark, William. Musical Memories. London: Swan Sonnenschein & Co., 1888. viii, 439 p., portrait.

C0218.
COURAUD, MARCEL. b. October 20, 1912, Limoges, France.

1. BAKER 7; GROVE 6/5; RIEMANN 12 + Supp.

C0219.
COURVOISIER, WALTER. b. February 7, 1875, Basel; d. December 27, 1931, Locarno, Switzerland.

1. BAKER 7; GROVE 6/5 (Bibliography); MGG 1/2; RIEMANN 12 + Supp. (Bibliography).

4. Kroyer, Theodore. Walter Courvoisier. Muenchen: Drei Maskenverlag, A.-G., 1929. 108, [1] p., portrait, list of compositions.

C0220.
COWARD, HENRY. b. November 26, 1849, Liverpool; d. June 10, 1944, Sheffield, England.

1. BAKER 7 (Bibliography); GROVE 6/5 (Bibliography); MGG/Supp.; PAB-MI/2 (Bibliography); RIEMANN 12.

3. Coward, Henry. Reminiscences of Henry Coward. London: J. Curwen & Sons, 1919. 326 p., portrait.

C0221.
COWEN, FREDERIC HYMEN. b. January 29, 1852, Kingston, Jamaica; d. October 6, 1935, London, England.

1. BAKER 7 (Bibliography); EdS 1/3 (Bibliography); GROVE 6/5 (Bibliography); MGG 1/2; PAB-MI/2 (Bibliography); RIEMANN 12.

3. Cowen, Frederic Hymen. My Art and My Friends. London: Edward Arnold, 1913. xii, 319 p., index.

5. B0007.

C0222.
CRAFT, ROBERT. b. October 20, 1923, Kingston, New York.

1. BAKER 7 (Bibliography); GROVE 6/5; GROVE-AM 1/1 (Bibliography); PAB-MI/2 (Bibliography); RIEMANN 12/Supp.

C0223.
CRUZ, IVO. b. May 19, 1901, Corumbá, Brazil.

1. BAKER 7; GROVE 6/5; PAB-MI/2 (Bibliography); RIEMANN 12 + Supp.

C0224.
CUNDELL, EDRIC. b. January 29, 1893, London; d. March 19, 1961, Ashwell, Hertfordshire, England.

1. BAKER 7; GROVE 6/5; PAB-MI/2 (Bibliography); RIEMANN 12.

5. A0003.

C0225.
CUSINS, WILLIAM GEORGE. b. October 14, 1833, London, England; d. August 31, 1893, Remouchamps, Ardennes, Belgium.

1. BAKER 7; GROVE 6/5; RIEMANN 12.

5. B0020.

C0226.
CZYZ, HENRYK. b. June 16, 1923, Grudziadz, Poland.

1. BAKER 7; GROVE 6/5; PAB-MI/2 (Bibliography); RIEMANN 12/Supp.

3. Czyz, Henryk. Giocoso ma non troppo: Erinnerungen eines Dirigenten. Translated by Christa Vogel. Berlin: Henschel Verlag, 1974. 205 p.

C0227.
DAMCKE, BERTHOLD. b. February 6, 1812, Hannover, Germany; d. February 15, 1875, Paris, France.

1. BAKER 7 (Bibliography); GROVE 6/5; RIEMANN 12.

C0228.
DAMROSCH, FRANK. b. June 22, 1859, Breslau, Germany; d. October 22, 1937, New York City.

1. BAKER 7; GROVE 6/5; GROVE-AM 1/1 (Bibliography); PAB-MI/2 (Bibliography); RIEMANN 12 + Supp. (Bibliography)

2. MQ 25/2.

4. Stebbins, Lucy Poate and Richard Poate Stebbins. Frank Damrosch: Let the People Sing. Durham: Duke University Press, 1945. xi, 273 p., 17 illus., 56-item bibliographical note.

C0229.
DAMROSCH, LEOPOLD. b. October 22, 1832, Posen, Germany; d. February 15, 1885, New York City.

1. BAKER 7; EdS 1/4; GROVE 6/5; GROVE-AM 1/1 (Bibliography); MGG 1/2; PAB-MI/2 (Bibliography); RIEMANN 12 + Supp. (Bibliography).

2. MQ 28/3.

5. B0007, B0083.

SEE: George Martin under **WALTER DAMROSCH** (C0230.4).

C0230.
DAMROSCH, WALTER J. b. January 30, 1862, Breslau, Germany; d. December 22, 1950, New York City.

1. BAKER 7; EdS 1/4; GROVE 6/5; GROVE-AM 1/1 (Bibliography); MGG 1/2; PAB-MI/2 (Bibliography); RIEMANN 12 + Supp. (Bibliography).

2. MQ 18/1; ON 26/11; OPERA 36/8.

3. There is a comprehensive special collection of Damrosch materials at the Library of Congress in Washington, D.C.

   Damrosch, Walter J. My Musical Life. New York: Charles Scribner's Sons, 1923. Reprint 1972. viii, [i], 376 p., 19 illus., index.

4. Goodell, M. Elaine. Walter Damrosch and His Contributions to Music Education. D.M.A. diss., Catholic University of America, 1973. 590 p., illus., bibliography.

   Martin, George. The Damrosch Dynasty: America's First Family of Music. Boston: Houghton Mifflin Company, 1983. xiii, [ii], 526 p., 31 illus., family table, notes, bibliography, index.

   Perryman, William Ray. Walter Damrosch: an Educational Force in American Music. Ph.D. diss., Indiana University, 1972. 279 p., bibliography, list of works.

5. A0010, B0006, B0079, B0089, B0138, B0159, B0166.

C0231.
DANBE, JULES. b. November 16, 1840, Caen, France; d. November 10, 1905, Vichy, France.

1. BAKER 7; EdS 1/4 (Bibliography); RIEMANN 12.

5. B0033, B0133.

C0232.
DANON, OSKAR. b. February 7, 1913, Sarajevo, Yugoslavia.

1. BAKER 7; GROVE 6/5; PAB-MI/2 (Bibliography); RIEMANN 12/Supp.

2. OPERA 13/8.

C0233.
DASCH, GEORGE. b. May 14, 1877, Cincinnati; d. April 12, 1955, Chicago, Illinois.

1. BAKER 7; PAB-MI/2 (Bibliography); RIEMANN 12.

C0234.
DAVIES, DENNIS RUSSELL. b. April 16, 1944, Toledo, Ohio.

1. BAKER 7; GROVE 6/5; GROVE-AM 1/1 (Bibliography); PAB-MI/2 (Bibliography.

2. HiFi/MusAm 25/8, 35/7; ON 50/1.

C0235.
DAVIES, MEREDITH. b. July 30, 1922, Birkenhead, England.

1. BAKER 7; GROVE 6/5; PAB-MI/2 (Bibliography).

C0236.
DAVIS, ANDREW FRANK. b. February 2, 1944, Ashbridge, England.

1. BAKER 7; GROVE 6/5; PAB-MI/2 (Bibliography).

5. A0017.

C0237.
DAVIS, COLIN. b. September 25, 1927, Weybridge, England.

1. BAKER 7; GROVE 6/5; PAB-MI/2 (Bibliography); RIEMANN 12/Supp.

2. GR 45/535, 53/630, 59/698, 62/736; ON 31/16; OPERA 16/11, 24/9.

4. Blyth, Alan. Colin Davis. New York: Drake Publishers Inc., 1973. 64 p., 66 illus., discography.

5. A0023, A0031.

C0238.
DAVISON, ARCHIBALD THOMPSON. b. October 11, 1883, Boston; d. February 6, 1961, Brant Rock, Cape Cod, Massachusetts.

1. BAKER 7 (Bibliography); GROVE 6/5 (Bibliography); GROVE-AM 1/1 (Bibliography); PAB-MI/2 (Bibliography); RIEMANN 12.

3. Davison, Archibald T. Choral Conducting. Cambridge: Harvard University Press, 1940. 73 p.

4. Tovey, D.G. Archibald Thompson Davison: Harvard Musician and Scholar. Ph.D. diss., University of Michigan/Ann Arbor, 1979.

C0239.
DAWSON, WILLIAM LEVI. b. September 23, 1899, Anniston, Alabama.

1. BAKER 7; GROVE 6/5; GROVE-AM 1/1 (Bibliography); PAB-MI/2 (Bibliography).

4. Malone, M.H. William Levi Dawson: American Music Educator. Ph.D. diss., Florida State University, 1981.

   Spady, J. William L. Dawson: a UmUm Tribute. Philadelphia, 1981.

C0240.
DECKER, FRANZ-PAUL. b. June 23, 1923, Cologne, Germany.

1. BAKER 7; PAB-MI/2 (Bibliography); RIEMANN 12.

C0241.
DeFABRITIIS, OLIVIERO. b. June 13, 1902, Rome; d. August 12, 1982, Rome, Italy.

1. BAKER 7; GROVE 6/5; PAB-MI/2 (Bibliography); RIEMANN/Supp.

5. B0016.

C0242.
DEFAUW, DESIRE. b. September 5, 1885, Ghent, Belgium; d. July 25, 1960, Gary, Indiana.

1. BAKER 7; GROVE 6/5; GROVE-AM 1/1; PAB-MI/2 (Bibliography); RIEMANN 12.

4. Herzberg, Marthe. Désiré Defauw: portraits et souvenirs. Bruxelles: Henri Kumps, 1937. 89 p., 10 illus.

5. A0022, B0167.

C0243.
DEFOSSEZ, RENE. b. October 4, 1905, Spa, Belgium.

1. BAKER 7; GROVE 6/5 (Bibliography); PAB-MI/2 (Bibliography); RIEMANN 12 + Supp.

C0244.
de LACERDA, FRANCISCO. b. May 11, 1869, Ribeira Seca, S. Jorge, Azores; d. July 18, 1934, Lisbon, Portugal.

1. BAKER 7 (under Lacerda); GROVE 6/10 (Bibliography); RIEMANN 12/Supp.

C0245.
De LAMARTER, ERIC. b. February 18, 1880, Lansing, Michigan; d. May 17, 1953, Orlando, Florida.

1. BAKER 7; GROVE-AM 1/1 (Bibliography); PAB-MI/2 (Bibliography).

C0246.
DELDEVEZ, EDOUARD-MARIE. b. May 31, 1817, Paris; d. November 6, 1897, Paris, France.

1. BAKER 7; EdS 1/4 (Bibliography); GROVE 6/5 (Bibliography); MGG 1/3 (Bibliography); PAB-MI/2 (Bibliography); RIEMANN 12.

3. Deldevez, Edouard-Marie. Curiosités musicales: notes, analyses, interprétation de certaines particularités contenues dans les oeuvres des grands maîtres. Paris: Librairie de Firmin Didot Fréres, Fils et Cie, 1873. ix, 272 p., musical examples.

   Deldevez, Edouard-Marie. Le passé a propos du présent: faisant suite a mes mémoires. Paris: Imprimerie Chaix, 1893. viii, 232 p.

   Deldevez, Edouard-Marie. Mes mémoirs. Le Puy: Imprimerie Marchessou Fils, 1890. vi, 312 p., catalogue of MS.

Important works such as L'Art du chef d'orchestre (Paris: Firmin Didot, 1878) and De l'exécution d'ensemble were not available.

5. B0035.

C0247.
DELLINGER, RUDOLF. b. July 8, 1857, Graslitz, Bohemia; d. September 24, 1910, Dresden, Germany.

1. BAKER 7; EdS 1/4 (Bibliography); GROVE 6/5 (Bibliography); MGG/Supp. (Bibliography); RIEMANN 12.

C0248.
DEL MAR, NORMAN. b. July 31, 1919, London, England.

1. BAKER 7; GROVE 6/5; PAB-MI/2 (Bibliography); RIEMANN 12 + Supp.

2. OPERA 4/11

3. Del Mar, Norman. Modern Music and the Conductor. London: John Calder, 1960. Reprint 1970.

   No copy located.

5. A0004.

C0249.
DELOGU, GAETANO. b. April 14, 1934, Messina, Italy.

1. BAKER 7; GROVE 6-AM (Bibliography).

C0250.
DELUNE, LOUIS. b. March 15, 1876, Charleroi; d. January 5, 1940, Paris.

1. BAKER 7; RIEMANN 12.

C0251.
DENZLER, ROBERT. b. March 19, 1892, Zurich; d. August 25, 1972, Zurich, Switzerland.

1. BAKER 7; EdS 1/4; GROVE 6/5 (Bibliography); PAB-MI/2 (Bibliography); RIEMANN 12.

C0252.
DEPPE, LUDWIG. b. November 7, 1828, Alverdissen, Lippe; d. September 5, 1890, Bay Pyramont, Germany.

1. BAKER 7 (Bibliography); GROVE 6/5 (Bibliography); MGG 1/3 (Bibliography); PAB-MI/2 (Bibliography); RIEMANN 12 (Bibliography).

4. Zwei Jahre Kapellmeister an der koeniglichen Oper zu Berlin. Bielefeld: Verlag von H. Selle, 1890. 45, cvii p.

C0253.
DE PRIEST, JAMES. b. November 21, 1936, Philadelphia, Pennsylvania.

1. BAKER 7; GROVE 6/5; GROVE-AM 1/1; PAB-MI/2 (Bibliography).

2. HiFi/MusAm 27/3.

3. De Priest, James. Au fur et à mesure (tel que raconté à Micheline Sinard). Québec, Canada: Les Editions Héritage Inc., 1980. 161, [2] p., 19 illus.

5. B0001.

C0254.
DERVAUX, PIERRE. b. March 3, 1917, Juvisy-sur-Orge, France.

1. BAKER 7; GROVE 6/5; PAB-MI/2 (Bibliography); RIEMANN 12 + Supp.

C0255.
De SABATA, VICTOR. b. April 10, 1892, Trieste; d. December 11, 1967, Santa Margherita Ligure, Italy.

1. BAKER 7; EdS 1/4; GROVE 6/5 (Bibliography); MGG 1/3 (Bibliography); PAB-MI/2 (Bibliography); RIEMANN 12 + Supp. (Bibliography).

2. LS 5; OPERA 19/2; RS 41

4. Celli, Teodoro. L'art di Victor De Sabata. Torino: ERI/Edizioni Rai radiotelevisione italiana, 1978. 173, [2] p., illus., chronology, discography by Luigi Bellingardi, index of names.

   Gatti, Guido M. Victor De Sabata. Milano: G. Ricordi & C., 1958. 30, [2] p., 22 illus., discography.

5. A0004, B0016, B0164.

C0256.
DESARZENS, VICTOR. b. October 27, 1908, Château d'Oex, Switzerland.

1. BAKER 7; GROVE 6/5 (Bibliography); MGG 1/3 (Bibliography); RIEMANN 12 + Supp.

4. Hommage a Victor Desarzens. Lausanne: Orchestre de Chambre de Lausanne et Editions l'Age d'Homme. S.A., 1973. 83, [3] p., 4 illus., 9 appendices.

C0257.
DESORMIERE, ROGER. b. September 13, 1898, Vichy; d. October 25, 1963, Paris, France.

1. BAKER 7; EdS 1/4; GROVE 6/5 (Bibliography); MGG/Supp.; PAB-MI/2 (Bibliography); RIEMANN 12 + Supp.

4. Mayer, Denise and Pierre Souvtchinsky, eds. Roger Désormière et son temps: textes en hommage. Monaco: Editions Du Rocher, 1966. 189 p., list of compositions, discography, programs of Les Concerts de la Pleiade.

C0258.
DESPALJ, PAVLE. b. March 18, 1934, Blato na Korčuli, Yugoslavia.

1. BAKER 7; GROVE 6/5.

C0259.
DESSOFF, FELIX OTTO. b. January 14, 1835, Leipzig; d. October 28, 1892, Frankfurt/M., Germany.

1. BAKER 7; EdS 1/4; MGG/Supp. (Bibliography); RIEMANN 12.

5. B0079.

SEE: Hanslick, Eduard. Geschichte des Concertwesens in Wien. Wien, 1869.

C0260.
DESSOFF, MARGARETHE. b. June 11, 1874, Vienna, Austria; d. November 19, 1944, Locarno, Switzerland.

1. BAKER 7; MGG/Supp. (Bibliography); RIEMANN 12.

C0261.
De VOCHT, LODEWIJK. b. September 21, 1887, Antwerp; d. March 27, 1977, 's Gravenzel, near Antwerp, Belgium.

1. BAKER 7; RIEMANN 12.

C0262.
DEVREESE, FREDERIC. b. June 2, 1929, Amsterdam, Holland.

1. BAKER 7; GROVE 6/5; RIEMANN 12 + Supp. (Bibliography).

C0263.
DEVREESE, GODEFROID. b. January 22, 1893, Kortrijk; d. June 4, 1972, Brussels, Belgium.

1. BAKER 7; GROVE 6/5; RIEMANN 12 + Supp.

C0264.
De WAART, EDO. b. June 1, 1941, Amsterdam, Holland.

1. BAKER 7; GROVE 6/5 (Bibliography); GROVE-AM 1/1 (Bibliography); PAB-MI/2 (Bibliography); RIEMANN 12/Supp.

2. GR 50/596.

5. A0017.

C0265.
Di BONAVENTURA, MARIO. b. February 20, 1924, Follensbee, West Virginia.

1. BAKER 7 (under Bonaventura); GROVE-AM 1/1.

Inaugurated the "Congregation of the Arts" festivals at Dartmouth.

C0266.
DIETRICH, ALBERT HERMANN. b. August 28, 1829, Forsthaus Golk, near Meissen; d. November 19, 1908, Berlin, Germany.

1. BAKER 7; GROVE 6/5 (Bibliography); MGG/Supp. (Bibliography); RIEMANN 12 + Supp. (Bibliography).

C0267.
DIETSCH, PIERRE-LOUIS-PHILIPPE. b. March 17, 1808, Dijon; d. February 20, 1865, Paris, France.

1. BAKER 7; GROVE 6/5 (Bibliography); MGG 1/3 (Bibliography); PAB-MI/2 (Bibliography); RIEMANN 12 (Bibliography).

5. B0036.

SEE: Ernest Newman (vol. 3) under RICHARD WAGNER (C1175.4).

SEE: Autobiography of RICHARD WAGNER (C1175.3).

C0268.
DIXON, DEAN. b. January 10, 1915, New York City; d. November 3, 1976, Zug, near Zurich, Switzerland.

1. BAKER 7 (Bibliography); GROVE 6/5; GROVE-AM 1/1; PAB-MI/2 (Bibliography); RIEMANN 12 + Supp.

2. HiFi/MusAm 20/8, 35/5.

5. A0010, A0040, B0001.

SEE: Hughes, Langston. Famous Negro Music Makers. New York: Dodd, Mead & Company, 1955. 179 p., 23 illus., index.

C0269.
DIXON, JAMES. b. April 26, 1928, Estherville, Iowa.

1. BAKER 7; GROVE-AM 1/1

C0270.
DOBROWEN, ISSAY ALEXANDROVICH. b. February 27, 1891, Nizhny-Novgorod, Russia; d. December 9, 1953, Oslo, Norway.

1. BAKER 7; EdS 1/4; GROVE 6/5; MGG/Supp. (Bibliography); RIEMANN 12.

C0271.
von DOHNANYI, CHRISTOPH. b. September 8, 1929, Berlin, Germany.

1. BAKER 7; GROVE 6/5; PAB-MI/2 (Bibliography); RIEMANN 12/Supp.

2. HiFi/MusAm 34/9; ON 35/4; OPERA 35/1; OW 5/12, 12/7, 13/11, 14/11, 15/12, 19/9, 20/7; OPER 1984: ein Jahrbuch von "Opernwelt".

4. Musiker im Gespraech: Christoph von Dohnányi. Frankfurt: Henry Litolffs Verlag/C. F. Peters, 1976. 16 p.

5. B0063.

The grandson of Ernst von Dohnányi, his father Hans was executed for his role in the abortive attempt on Hitler's life on July 20, 1944.

C0272.
von DOHNANYI, ERNST. b. July 27, 1877, Pressburg, Hungary; d. February 9, 1960, New York City.

1. BAKER 7; EdS 1/4 (Bibliography); GROVE 6/5 (Bibliography); MGG 1/3; PAB-MI/2 (Bibliography); RIEMANN 12 (Bibliography) + Supp. (Bibliography).

3. von Dohnányi, Ernst. Message to Posterity From Ernst von Dohnányi. Translated by Ilona von Dohnányi. Jacksonville (FL): H. & W. B. Drew, 1960. 44 p.

4. Rueth, M.U. The Tallahasse Years of Ernst von Dohnányi. M.A. thesis, Florida State University, 1962.

5. B0114.

C0273.
DONATI, PINO. b. May 9, 1907, Verona; d. February 24, 1975, Rome, Italy.

1. BAKER 7; EdS 1/4; RIEMANN 12 + Supp.

C0274.
DOPPER, CORNELIS. b. February 7, 1870, Stadskanaal, near Groningen; d. September 18, 1939, Amsterdam, Holland.

1. BAKER 7; EdS 1/4; GROVE 6/5 (Bibliography); MGG 1/3 (Bibliography); RIEMANN 12.

C0275.
DOPPLER, ALBERT FRANZ. b. October 16, 1821, Lwow; d. July 27, 1883, Baden, near Vienna, Austria.

1. BAKER 7; EdS 1/4 (Bibliography); GROVE 6/5 (Bibliography); MGG/Supp. (Bibliography); RIEMANN 12.

C0276.
DOPPLER, KARL. b. September 12, 1825, Lwow, Austria; d. March 10, 1900, Stuttgart, Germany.

1. BAKER 7; EdS 1/4 (Bibliography); GROVE 6/5 (Bibliography); MGG/Supp. (Bibliography); RIEMANN 12.

C0277.
DORATI, ANTAL. b. April 9, 1906, Budapest, Hungary.

1. BAKER 7; GROVE 6/5 (Bibliography); GROVE-AM 1/1 (Bibliography); PAB-MI/2 (Bibliography); RIEMANN 12 + Supp.

2. HiFi/MusAm 23/8; OW 17/1, 25/12.

3. Dorati, Antal. Notes of Seven Decades. London: Hodder and Stoughton Limited, 1979. 350 p., 26 illus., index.

   Articulate, frank, and revealing. One of the best autobiographies!

5. A0048, B0071, B0138, B0142, B0152.

C0278.
DORN, HEINRICH LUDWIG. b. November 14, 1800, Koenigsberg; d. January 10, 1892, Berlin, Germany.

1. BAKER 7; EdS 1/4; GROVE 6/5 (Bibliography); MGG 1/3 (Bibliography); RIEMANN 12 + Supp. (Bibliography).

C0279.
DOWNES, EDWARD THOMAS. b. June 17, 1924, Birmingham, England.

1. BAKER 7; GROVE 6/5 (Bibliography).

2. OPERA 19/1.

C0280.
DRANISHNIKOV, VLADIMIR. b. June 10, 1893, St. Petersberg; d. February 6, 1939, Kiev, Russia.

1. BAKER 7; EdS 1/4 (Bibliography); GROVE 6/5 (Bibliography); RIEMANN 12 + Supp. (Bibliography).

C0281.
DREWANZ, HANS. b. December 2, 1929, Dresden, Germany.

1. BAKER 7; PAB-MI/2 (Bibliography); RIEMANN 12/Supp.

2. OW 6/1.

C0282.
DRIGO, RICCARDO. b. June 30, 1846, Padua; d. October 1, 1930, Padua, Italy.

1. BAKER 7 (Bibliography); EdS 1/4 (Bibliography); GROVE 6/5 (Bibliography); PAB-MI/2 (Bibliography); RIEMANN 12.

C0283.
DUBOIS, LEON. b. January 9, 1859, Brussels, Belgium; d. November 19, 1935, Boitsfort, Belgium.

1. BAKER 7; EdS 1/4; MGG/Supp. (Bibliography); PAB-MI/2 (Bibliography); RIEMANN 12.

C0284.
DUCLOUX, WALTER. b. April 17, 1913, Lucerne, Switzerland.

1. BAKER 7; GROVE-AM 1/1; PAB-MI/2 (Bibliography).

C0285.
DUFALLO, RICHARD. b. January 30, 1933, East Chicago, Indiana.

1. BAKER 7; GROVE-AM 1/1.

C0286.
DUNBAR, W. RUDOLF. b. April 5, 1907, Nabaclis, Guyana.

1. BAKER 7; GROVE-AM 1/1 (Bibliography); PAB-MI/2 (Bibliography).

3. His memorabilia are housed in the Yale University Library.

C0287.
DUNN, THOMAS. b. December 21, 1925, Aberdeen, South Dakota.

1. BAKER 7; GROVE 6/5; GROVE-AM 1/1.

C0288.
DUPUIS, SYLVAIN. b. October 9, 1856, Liège, Belgium; d. September 28, 1931, Bruges, Belgium.

1. BAKER 7; EdS 1/4; GROVE 6/5; RIEMANN 12.

C0289.
DUTOIT, CHARLES. b. October 7, 1936, Lausanne, Switzerland.

1. BAKER 7 (Bibliography); GROVE 6/5 (Bibliography); RIEMANN 12/Supp.

2. GR 61/731.

C0290.
EBEL, ARNOLD. b. August 15, 1883, Heide, Holstein; d. March 4, 1963, Berlin, Germany.

1. BAKER 7; RIEMANN 12 + Supp. (Bibliography).

C0291.
ECKERBERG, SIXTEN. b. September 5, 1909, Hjaeltevad, Ingatorp, Sweden.

1. BAKER 7; RIEMANN 12 + Supp.

3. Eckerberg, Sixten. <u>Musiken och mitt liv</u>. Stockholm: Almqvist & Wiksell Foerlag AB, 1970. 155 p., 39 illus.

C0292.
ECKERT, KARL ANTON. b. December 7, 1820, Potsdam; d. September 14, 1879, Berlin, Germany.

1. BAKER 7; EdS 1/4; MGG/Supp. (Bibliography); RIEMANN 12 (Bibliography).

   After serving as principal conductor and music director of the Opera in Vienna and Stuttgart, he succeeded Heinrich Dorn in Berlin.

5. SEE: Autobiography of RICHARD WAGNER (C1175.3).

C0293.
EHLERT, LOUIS. b. January 13, 1825, Koenigsberg; d. January 4, 1884, Wiesbaden, Germany.

1. BAKER 7; MGG/Supp. (Bibliography); RIEMANN 12.

3. Ehlert, Louis. Briefe ueber Musik an eine Freundin. Berlin: Verlag von F. Guttentag, 1868. 156 p.

C0294.
EHRENBERG, CARL EMIL. b. April 6, 1878, Dresden; d. February 26, 1962, Munich, Germany.

1. BAKER 7; GROVE 6/5 (Bibliography); MGG 1/3; RIEMANN 12.

C0295.
EHRLING, SIXTEN. b. April 3, 1918, Malmoe, Sweden.

1. BAKER 7; EdS 1/4; GROVE 6/6; GROVE-AM 1/2; MGG/Supp.; PAB-MI/2 (Bibliography); RIEMANN 12 + Supp.

2. HiFiMusAm 25/3; ON 38/11; OW 16/2, 17/2.

5. B0104, B0124.

C0296.
EIBENSCHUETZ, JOSE. b. January 8, 1872, Frankfurt/M.; d. November 27, 1952, Suelzhayn, Harz, Germany.

1. BAKER 7; RIEMANN 12.

C0297.
EICHHORN, KURT. b. August 4, 1908, Munich, Germany.

1. BAKER 7; RIEMANN 12 + Supp.

C0298.
EISFELD, THEODOR. b. April 11, 1816, Wolfenbuettel; d. September 2, 1882, Wiesbaden, Germany.

1. BAKER 7; GROVE-AM 1/2 (Bibliography); RIEMANN 12.

C0299.
ELDER, MARK PHILIP. b. January 2, 1947, Corbridge, England.

1. BAKER 7; GROVE 6/6; PAB-MI/2 (Bibliography).

2. OPER 1980: ein Jahrbuch der Zeitschrift "Opernwelt".

4. "Sechs Fragen an Mark Elder." Oper Heute: Ein Almanach der Musik-Buehne II (1979): 163-65.

C0300.
ELKAN, HENRI. b. November 23, 1897, Antwerp, Belgium.

1. BAKER 7; GROVE-AM 1/2 (Bibliography); PAB-MI/2 (Bibliography).

C0301.
ELMENDORFF, KARL. b. October 25, 1891, Duesseldorf; d. October 21, 1962, Hofheim am Taunus, Germany.

1. BAKER 7; EdS 1/4; GROVE 6/6; PAB-MI/2 (Bibliography); RIEMANN 12.

5. B0164, B0167.

C0302.
ENDO, AKIRA. b. November 16, 1938, Shido, Japan.

1. BAKER 7; GROVE-AM 1/2.

C0303.
ENGEL, LEHMAN. b. September 14, 1910, Jackson, Mississippi; d. August 29, 1982, New York City.

1. BAKER 7 (Bibliography); GROVE 6/6; GROVE-AM 1/2; MGG/Supp.; PAB-MI/2 (Bibliography); RIEMANN 12/Supp.

3. Engel, Lehman. The Bright Day: an Autobiography. New York: Macmillan Publishing Co., Inc., 1974. xiv, 366 p., illus., index.

C0304.
ENTREMONT, PHILIPPE. b. June 6, 1934, Rheims, France.

1. BAKER 7; GROVE-AM 1/2; PAB-MI/2 (Bibliography).

C0305.
EPPERT, CARL. b. November 5, 1882, Carbon, Indiana; d. October 1, 1961, Milwaukee, Wisconsin.

1. BAKER 7; PAB-MI/2 (Bibliography); RIEMANN 12.

C0306.
EPSTEIN, DAVID MAYER. b. October 3, 1930, New York City.

1. BAKER 7 (Bibliography); GROVE-AM 1/2 (Bibliography); PAB-MI/2 (Bibliography).

2. HiFi/MusAm 26/10, 30/10.

C0307.
ERDELYI, MIKLOS. b. February 9, 1928, Budapest, Hungary.

1. BAKER 7; GROVE 6/6; PAB-MI/2 (Bibliography).

C0308.
von ERDMANNSDOERFER, MAX. b. June 14, 1848, Nuremberg; d. February 14, 1905, Munich, Germany.

1. BAKER 7; MGG/Supp. (Bibliography); RIEMANN 12 (Bibliography).

C0309.
EREDE, ALBERTO. b. November 8, 1908, Genoa, Italy.

1. BAKER 7; EdS 1/4; GROVE 6/6; PAB-MI/2 (Bibliography); RIEMANN 12 + Supp. (Bibliography).

2. ON 18/17, 39/14; OW 4/7.

C0310.
ERICSON, ERIC GUSTAF. b. October 26, 1918, Boras, Sweden.

1. BAKER 7; PAB-MI/2 (Bibliography); RIEMANN 12/Supp.

C0311.
ERKEL, FERENC. b. November 7, 1810, Gyula; d. June 15, 1893, Budapest, Hungary.

1. BAKER 7 (Bibliography); EdS 1/4 (Bibliography); GROVE 6/6 (Bibliography); MGG 1/3 (Bibliography); PAB-MI/2 (Bibliography); RIEMANN 12 + Supp. (Bibliography).

4. Fabó, Bertalan. Erkel Ferencz emlékkönyv: születésének századik évfordulójára írók és tudósok közreműködésével szerkesztette. Budapest: "Pátria" Irodalmi Vállalat Es Nyomdai R.-Társ Nyomása, 1910. 250 p., 244 illus.

   Legány, Dezső. Erkel Ferenc: művei és korabeli történetük. Budapest: Zeneműkiadó, 1975. 138, [5] p.

   Németh, Amadé. Erkel Ferenc: életének krónikája. Budapest: Zeneműkiadó, 1973. 229, [3] p.

C0312.
ESCHENBACH, CHRISTOPH. b. February 20, 1940, Breslau, Germany.

1. BAKER 7; GROVE 6/6; PAB-MI/2 (Bibliography); RIEMANN 12/Supp.

C0313.
ESPINOSA, GUILLERMO. b. January 9, 1905, Cartagena, Columbia.

1. BAKER 7; GROVE 6/6 (Bibliography); RIEMANN 12.

C0314.
ESPOSITO, MICHELE. b. September 29, 1855, Castellammare, near Naples; d. November 23, 1929, Florence, Italy.

1. BAKER 7; GROVE 6/6 (Bibliography); MGG 1/3; PAB-MI/2 (Bibliography); RIEMANN 12 + Supp. (Bibliography).

C0315.
ESSER, HEINRICH. b. July 15, 1818, Mannheim; d. June 3, 1872, Salzburg.

1. BAKER 7 (Bibliography); EdS 1/4; GROVE 6/6 (Bibliography); MGG/Supp. (Bibliography); PAB-MI/2 (Bibliography); RIEMANN 12 + Supp. (Bibliography).

5. SEE: Autobiography of RICHARD WAGNER (C1175.3).

C0316.
ESSER, HERIBERT. b. January 12, 1929, Rheinhausen, Germany.

1. BAKER 7; RIEMANN 12/Supp.

C0317.
ESTRADA, CARLOS. b. September 15, 1909, Montevideo; d. May 7, 1970, Montevideo, Uruguay.

1. BAKER 7 (Bibliography); GROVE 6/6; PAB-MI/2 (Bibliography); RIEMANN 12/Supp.

C0318.
ETTINGER, MAX. b. December 27, 1874, Lemberg; d. July 19, 1951, Basel.

1. BAKER 7; EdS 1/4; GROVE 6/6 (Bibliography); MGG 1/3 (Bibliography); RIEMANN 12.

C0319.
FACCIO, FRANCO. b. March 8, 1840, Verona; d. July 21, 1891, Monza, Italy

1. BAKER 7; EdS 1/4 (Bibliography); GROVE 6/6 (Bibliography); MGG/Supp. (Bibliography); PAB-MI/2 (Bibliography); RIEMANN 12.

4. de Rensis, Raffaello. Franco Faccio e Verdi: carteggi e documenti inediti. Milano: Fratelli Treves Editori, 1934. 268, [3] p., 12 illus.

C0320.
FAERBER, JOERG. b. June 18, 1929, Stuttgart, Germany.

1. BAKER 7; GROVE 6/6.

C0321.
FAGAN, GIDEON. b. November 3, 1904, Somerset West, Cape Province; d. March 21, 1980, Cape Town, South Africa.

1. BAKER 7; GROVE 6/6; RIEMANN 12 + Supp.

5. A0003.

C0322.
FAHRBACH, PHILIPP. b. October 26, 1815, Vienna; d. March 31, 1885, Vienna, Austria.

1. BAKER 7 (Bibliography); GROVE 6/6 (Bibliography); MGG 1/3; RIEMANN 12 + Supp.

C0323.
FAILONI, SERGIO. b. December 18, 1890, Verona; d. July 25, 1948, Verona.

1. BAKER 7; GROVE 6/6 (Bibliography); PAB-MI/2 (Bibliography); RIEMANN/Supp.

3. His autobiography, Senza sordino, was published in Rome in 1946. No copy located.

C0324.
FARBERMAN, HAROLD. b. November 2, 1929, New York City.

1. BAKER 7; GROVE 6/6; GROVE-AM 1/2; PAB-MI/2 (Bibliography); RIEMANN 12/Supp.

2. HiFi/MusAm 29/10.

C0325.
FARNCOMBE, CHARLES. b. July 29, 1919, London, England.

1. BAKER 7; GROVE 6/6; PAB-MI/2 (Bibliography).

C0326.
FASANO, RENATO. b. August 21, 1902, Naples; d. August 3, 1979, Rome.

1. BAKER 7; EdS/Supp.; GROVE 6/6; RIEMANN 12 + Supp.

C0327.
FAYER, YURI F. b. January 17, 1890, Kiev; d. August 3, 1971, Moscow.

1. BAKER 7; GROVE 6/6 (Bibliography).

3. Fayer, Yuri. O sebe, o muzike, o balete. Moscow: Gos. muzykal'noe izd-vo, 1970. 566 p., 95 illus., 31-item bibliography.

C0328.
FELDBRILL, VICTOR. b. April 4, 1924, Toronto, Canada.

1. BAKER 7; GROVE 6/6.

C0329.
FENDLER, EDVARD. b. January 22, 1902, Leipzig, Germany.

1. BAKER 7; GROVE-AM 1/2; PAB-MI/2 (Bibliography).

C0330.
FENNELL, FREDERICK. b. July 2, 1914, Cleveland, Ohio.

1. BAKER 7; GROVE-AM 1/2 (Bibliography); PAB-MI/2 (Bibliography).

   Founder of the Eastman Wind Ensemble (1952) which helped to popularize this repertoire in the United States.

C0331.
FERENCSIK, JANOS. b. January 18, 1907, Budapest; d. June 12, 1984, Budapest, Hungary.

1. BAKER 7; GROVE 6/6; PAB-MI/2 (Bibliography); RIEMANN 12 + Supp. (Bibliography).

2. OW 25/1.

4. Bónis, Ferenc. Tizenbárom talákozás: Ferencsik jánossal. Budapest: Zeneműkiadó, 1984. 225, [4] p., 71 illus., discography, index.

   Várnai, Péter, ed. Ferencsik János. Budapest: Zeneműkiadó, 1972. 24, [24], 81 illus.

5. A0040, B0142.

C0332.
FERNSTROEM, JOHN. b. December 6, 1897, I-Chang, Hupei, China; d. October 19, 1961, Haelsingborg, Sweden.

1. BAKER 7; GROVE 6/6 (Bibliography); MGG/Supp. (Bibliography); RIEMANN 12 + Supp. (Bibliography).

3. BAKER 7 mentions an autobiography, Confessiones, published in Stockholm in 1946, and RIEMANN 12/Supp. mentions another volume published posthumously.

C0333.
FERRARA, FRANCO. b. July 4, 1911, Palermo, Italy.

1. BAKER 7; RIEMANN 12/Supp.

C0334.
FIEDLER, ARTHUR. b. December 17, 1894, Boston; d. July 10, 1979, Brookline, Massachusetts.

1. BAKER 7; GROVE 6/6; GROVE-AM 1/2 (Bibliography); PAB-MI/2 (Bibliography); RIEMANN 12 + Supp.

   Fiedler's collection of scores, papers, and recordings is housed in Special Collections at the Boston University Library.

4. Dickson, Harry Ellis. Arthur Fiedler and the Boston Pops: an Irreverent Memoir. Boston: Houghton Mifflin Company, 1981. 174 p., 30 illus.

   Violinist with the BSO since 1938 and assist. conductor of the Pops.

   Holland, James R. Mr. Pops. Barre (MA): Barre Publishers, 1972. 96 p., 129 illus.

   Moore, Robin. Fiedler, the Colorful Mr. Pops: the Man and His Music. Boston: Little, Brown and Company, 1968. xx, 372 p., 32 illus., discography 1935-1968, index.

   Wilson, Carol Green. Arthur Fiedler, Music for the Millions: the Story of the Conductor of the Boston Pops Orchestra. New York: The Evans Publishing Company, 1968. [vii], 223 p., 13 illus., list of "Current RCA Victor Records".

5. B0116, B0138.

C0335.
FIEDLER, MAX. b. December 31, 1859, Zittau; d. December 1, 1939, Stockholm, Sweden.

1. BAKER 7; GROVE 6/6; MGG 1/4; RIEMANN 12 + Supp. (Bibliography).

4. Dejmet, Gaston. Max Fiedler: Werden und Wirken. Essen: Vulkan-Verlag Dr. W. Classen, 1940. 256 p., 19 illus., works conducted.

5. B0065.

C0336.
von FIELITZ, ALEXANDER. b. December 28, 1860, Leipzig; d. July 29, 1930, Bad Salzungen, Germany.

1. BAKER 7; GROVE 6/6; MGG/Supp.; RIEMANN 12.

C0337.
FINN, WILLIAM JOSEPH. b. September 7, 1881, Boston; d. March 20, 1961, Bronxville, New York.

1. PAB-MI/2 (Bibliography). Dates from The ASCAP Biographical Dictionary of Composers, Authors and Publishers. 1966 edition.

3. Finn, William Joseph. Sharps and Flats in Five Decades: an Autobiography. New York: Harper & Brothers Publishers, 1947. x, 342 p., index.

   Finn, William Joseph. The Art of the Choral Conductor: Choral Technique. Boston: C.C. Birchard and Company, n.d. [1939]. viii, [i], 292 p., index.

   Finn, William Joseph. The Conductor Raises His Baton. New York: Harper & Brothers Publishers, 1944. x, 302 p., index.

C0338.
FISCHER, EDWIN. b. October 8, 1886, Basel; d. January 24, 1960, Zurich.

1. BAKER 7 (Bibliography); GROVE 6/6 (Bibliography); MGG 1/4; PAB-MI/2 (Bibliography); RIEMANN 12 + Supp. (Bibliography).

3. Fischer, Edwin. Musikalische Betrachtungen. St. Gallen: H. Tschudy & Co. AG, 1960 [1st edition 1949. Translated as Reflections on Music. London: Williams and Norgate Ltd., 1951. 47 p.]. 56, [3] p.

C0339.
FISCHER, IRWIN. b. July 5, 1903, Iowa City, Iowa; d. May 7, 1977, Wilmette, Illinois.

1. BAKER 7; GROVE-AM 1/2 (Bibliography); PAB-MI/2 (Bibliography).

C0340.
FISTOULARI, ANATOLE. b. August 20, 1907, Kiev, Russia.

1. BAKER 7; GROVE 6/6; PAB-MI/2 (Bibliography); RIEMANN 12 + Supp.

5. A0003.

C0341.
FITELBERG, GREGOR. b. October 18, 1879, Dvinsk, Latvia; d. June 10, 1953, Katowice, Poland.

1. BAKER 7; GROVE 6/6 (Bibliography); MGG 1/4 (Bibliography); RIEMANN 12.

5. A0050.

C0342.
FJELDSTAD, OIVIN. b. May 2, 1903, Oslo, Norway.

1. BAKER 7; GROVE 6/6; PAB-MI/2 (Bibliography); RIEMANN 12/Supp.

5. B0104.

C0343.
FLAGELLO, NICOLAS. b. March 15, 1928, New York City.

1. BAKER 7; GROVE 6/6; GROVE-AM 1/2 (Bibliography); PAB-MI/2 (Bibliography).

C0344.
FLAMENT, EDOUARD. b. August 27, 1880, Douai; d. December 27, 1958, Bois-Colombes, Seine, France.

1. BAKER 7; MGG 1/4; RIEMANN 12.

C0345.
FLEISCHER, ANTON. b. May 30, 1891, Makó; d. October 30, 1945, Budapest.

1. BAKER 7; RIEMANN 12 + Supp. (Bibliography).

5. B0037.

C0346.
FLEISHER, LEON. b. July 23, 1928, San Francisco, California.

1. BAKER 7; GROVE 6/6; GROVE-AM 1/2 (Bibliography); PAB-MI/2 (Bibliography); RIEMANN 12/Supp.

2. HiFi/MusAm 33/4.

C0347.
FLETCHER, HORACE GRANT. b. October 25, 1913, Hartsburg, Illinois.

1. BAKER 7; GROVE-AM 1/2 (Bibliography); PAB-MI/2 (Bibliography).

C0348.
FLIPSE, EDUARD. b. February 26, 1896, Wissekerke; d. September 11, 1973, Etten-Leur, Holland.

1. BAKER 7; MGG/Supp. (Bibliography); RIEMANN 12/Supp. (Bibliography).

4. Eyl, Ido. Eduard Flipse: zÿn Leven en zÿn Werk. Rotterdam: W.L. & J. Brusse n.v., 1959. 64 p., 55 illus.

5. A0008.

C0349.
FOCH [FOCK], DIRK. b. June 18, 1886, Batavia, Java; d. May 24, 1973, Locarno, Switzerland.

1. BAKER 7; PAB-MI/2 (Bibliography); RIEMANN 12.

C0350.
FORBES, ELLIOT. b. August 30, 1917, Cambridge, Massachusetts.

1. BAKER 7; GROVE 6/6 (Bibliography); PAB-MI/2 (Bibliography); RIEMANN 12/Supp.

C0351.
FORD, ERNEST. b. February 17, 1858, Warminster; d. June 2, 1919, London, England.

1. BAKER 7; GROVE 6/6; RIEMANN 12.

C0352.
FORONI, JACOPO. b. July 25, 1825, Verona, Italy; d. September 8, 1858, Stockholm, Sweden.

1. BAKER 7; RIEMANN 12.

C0353.
FOSS, LUKAS. b. August 15, 1922, Berlin, Germany.

1. BAKER 7 (Bibliography); EdS 1/5 (Bibliography); GROVE 6/6 (Bibliography); GROVE-AM 1/2 (Bibliography); MGG 1/4; PAB-MI/2 (Bibliography); RIEMANN 12 (Bibliography) + Supp. (Bibliography).

2. HiFi/MusAm 31/1.

C0354.
FOSTER, LAWRENCE THOMAS. b. October 23, 1941, Los Angeles, California.

1. BAKER 7; GROVE 6/6 (Bibliography); GROVE-AM 1/2 (Bibliography); PAB-MI/2 (Bibliography).

2. HiFi/MusAm 22/1.

C0355.
FOUGSTEDT, NILS-ERIC. b. May 24, 1910, Raisio, near Turku; d. April 12, 1961, Helsinki, Finland.

1. BAKER 7; GROVE 6/6 (Bibliography); MGG/Supp. (Bibliography); RIEMANN 12.

C0356.
FOURNET, JEAN. b. April 13, 1913, Rouen, France.

1. BAKER 7; GROVE 6/6; PAB-MI/2 (Bibliography); RIEMANN 12 + Supp.

C0357.
FRANCI, CARLO. b. July 18, 1927, Buenos Aires, Argentina.

1. BAKER 7; GROVE 6/6; PAB-MI/2 (Bibliography); RIEMANN 12/Supp.

2. ON 34/26.

C0358.
FRANDSEN, JOHN. b. July 10, 1918, Copenhagen, Denmark.

1. BAKER 7; RIEMANN 12.

C0359.
FRANK, ERNST. b. February 7, 1847, Munich, Germany; d. August 17, 1889, Oberdoebling, near Vienna, Austria.

1. BAKER 7; MGG/Supp. (Bibliography); RIEMANN 12.

C0360.
FRANKO, SAM. b. January 20, 1857, New Orleans, Louisiana; d. May 6, 1937, New York City.

1. BAKER 7; GROVE-AM 1/2; PAB-MI/2 (Bibliography); RIEMANN 12.

3. Franko, Sam. Chords and Dischords: Memoirs and Musings of an American Musician. New York: The Viking Press, 1938. [vi], 186 p., 18 illus., list of published works, index.

C0361.
FRECCIA, MASSIMO. b. September 19, 1906, Florence, Italy.

1. BAKER 7; GROVE-AM 1/2 (Bibliography); PAB-MI/2 (Bibliography); RIEMANN 12/Supp.

5. A0048.

C0362.
FREEMAN, PAUL DOUGLAS. b. January 2, 1936, Richmond, Virginia.

1. BAKER 7; GROVE-AM 1/2; PAB-MI/2 (Bibliography).

2. HiFi/MusAm 24/6.

C0363.
FREMAUX, LOUIS. b. August 13, 1921, Aire-sur-la-lys, France.

1. BAKER 7; GROVE 6/6; PAB-MI/2 (Bibliography).

C0364.
FRESO, TIBOR. b. November 20, 1918, Stiavnik, Czechoslovakia.

1. BAKER 7; GROVE 6/6 (Bibliography); MGG/Supp. (Bibliography); RIEMANN 12/Supp.

C0365.
FREUDENBERG, WILHELM. b. March 11, 1838, Raubacher Huette; d. May 22, 1928, Schweidnitz, Germany.

1. BAKER 7; RIEMANN 12 (Bibliography).

C0366.
FRICSAY, FERENC. b. August 9, 1914, Budapest, Hungary; d. February 20, 1963, Basel, Switzerland.

1. BAKER 7; GROVE 6/6 (Bibliography); MGG/Supp. (Bibliography); PAB-MI/2 (Bibliography); RIEMANN 12 + Supp. (Bibliography).

2. OW 3/5, 4/5, 14/2.

4. Herzfeld, Friedrich. Ferenc Fricsay. Berlin: Rembrandt Verlag, 1964. 116 p., 71 illus, chronology, discography.

5. A0002, A0052, B0063, B0104, B0109, B0110, B0132, B0136.

C0367.
FRIED, OSKAR. b. August 10, 1871, Berlin; d. July 5, 1941, Moscow.

1. BAKER 7; GROVE 6/6 (Bibliography); MGG 1/4 (Bibliography); RIEMANN 12 + Supp. (Bibliography).

4. Bekker, Paul. Oskar Fried: sein Werden und Schaffen. Berlin: "Harmonie" Verlagsgesellschaft fuer Literatur und Kunst, 1907. 47 p., portrait.

   Series included Nikisch, Strauss, Reineke, Mahler, and von Schuch.

   Stefan, Paul. Oskar Fried: das Werden eines Kuenstlers. Berlin: Erich Reiss Verlag, 1911. 46, [1] p., 3 illus., compositions.

C0368.
FROMENT, LOUIS de. b. December 5, 1921, Paris, France.

1. BAKER 7; RIEMANN/Supp.

C0369.
FRUEBECK de BURGOS, RAFAEL. b. September 15, 1933, Burgos, Spain.

1. BAKER 7; GROVE 6/6; RIEMANN 12/Supp.

C0370.
FUCHS, JOHANN NEPOMUK. b. May 5, 1842, Frauenthal, Styria; d. October 5, 1899, Voeslau, near Vienna, Austria.

1. BAKER 7; GROVE 6/7 (Bibliography); MGG 1/4 (Bibliography); RIEMANN 12.

C0371.
FULEIHAN, ANIS. b. April 2, 1900, Kyrenia, Cyprus; d. October 11, 1970, Palo Alto, California.

1. BAKER 7; GROVE-AM 1/2; MGG/Supp. (Bibliography); PAB-MI/2 (Bibliography); RIEMANN 12/Supp.

C0372.
FURTWAENGLER, WILHELM. b. January 25, 1886, Berlin; d. November 30, 1954, Ebersteinburg, Germany.

1. BAKER 7 (Bibliography); EdS 1/5 (Bibliography); GROVE 6/7 (Bibliography); MGG 1/4 (Bibliography); PAB-MI/2 (Bibliography); RIEMANN 12 + Supp. (Bibliography).

   NOTE: Materials are issued from time to time by the Société Wilhelm Furtwaengler in Paris, the Wilhelm Furtwaengler Associates of Urawa City, Japan, and the Wilhelm Furtwaengler Society of Los Angeles.

2. GR 50/592; HiFi/MusAm 22/12, 33/11; LS 6; LGB 2/1; ON 37/7; OPERA 6/2; Opera Quarterly 2/1, 2/2, 2/4, 3/1; OW 15/11; RS 39.

3. Furtwaengler, Wilhelm. Concerning Music. Translated by L.J. Lawrence. London: Boosey & Hawkes Limited, 1953 [original: Zuerich: Atlantis Verlag, 1948]. 96 p.

   Six interviews by Walter Abendroth to which is added a chapter by Furtwaengler in which he discusses tonality and atonality.

   Furtwaengler, Wilhelm. Der Musiker und sein Publicum. Zuerich: Atlantis Verlag, 1955. 37, [1] p., portrait.

   Furtwaengler, Wilhelm. Die Wiener Philharmoniker: Rede gehalten anlaesslich ihrer Hundertjahrfeier. Wien: Herausgegeben von den Wiener Philharmonikern, n.d. [1942]. 31 p., 6 illus.

   Furtwaengler, Wilhelm. Ton und Wort: Aufsaetze und Vortraege 1918 bis 1954. 4th edition. Wiesbaden: F.A. Brockhaus, 1955. 275 p., 3 illus., musical examples, index.

4. Biba, Otto. Wilhelm Furtwaengler: eine Gedaechtnisausstellung. Wien: Gesellschaft der Musikfreunde, 1979. 10, [10] p., illus.

   Furtwaengler, Elisabeth. Ueber Wilhelm Furtwaengler. Wiesbaden: F.A. Brockhaus, 1979 [Translated by Michel Cresta. Paris, 1983. Discography by Henri-Jean Testas]. 168 p., 4 illus., 26-item bibliography, index of names.

   Furtwaengler, Elisabeth. Wilhelm Furtwaengler: Aufzeichnungen 1924-1954. Wiesbaden: F.A. Brockhaus, 1980. 359 p., index.

   Gavoty, Bernard. Furtwaengler. Translated by F.E. Richardson. Geneva: Rene Kister, 1956. 29, [3] p., 23 illus., "Some Recordings by Wilhelm Furtwaengler".

   Gillis, Daniel. Furtwaengler and America. New York: Manyland Books, Inc., 1970. 148 p., 5 illus., index.

   A shallow overview of Furtwaengler's political problems.

Gillis, Daniel, ed. Furtwaengler Recalled. Zuerich: Atlantis Verlag AG, 1965. 224 p., annotated discography by Michael Marcus, publications by Wilhelm Furtwaengler, index of [88] writers.

A collection of testimonials from eighty-eight of the most famous individuals of the era including conductors.

Herzfeld, Friedrich. Wilhelm Furtwaengler: Weg und Wesen. Leipzig: Wilhelm Goldmann Verlag, 1941. 209 p., 57 illus., statistical list of works conducted 1911-1940.

Hoecker, Karla. Begegnung mit Furtwaengler: ein Buch der Erinnerung. Guetersloh: C. Bertelsmann Verlag, 1956. 63, [1] p., 8 illus.

Hoecker, Karla. Sinfonische Reise: Konzerte, Gespraeche, Fahrten mit Wilhelm Furtwaengler und den Berliner Philharmonikern. Guetersloh: C. Bertelsmann Verlag, 1955. 69, [2] p., 8 illus.

Hoecker, Karla. Wilhelm Furtwaengler: Begegnungen und Gespraeche. Berlin: Rembrandt Verlag, 1961. 167, [1] p., 56 illus.

Hoecker, Karla. Die nie vergessenen Klaenge: Erinnerungen an Wilhelm Furtwaengler. Berlin: arani-Verlag GmbH, 1979. 244 p., 57 illus., 11-item bibliography.

Hoecker, Karla. Wilhelm Furtwaengler: Dokumente--Berichte und Bilder --Aufzeichnungen. Berlin: Rembrandt Verlag GmbH, 1968. 151 p., 90 illus., discography, list of published compositions and books, text sources.

Olsen, Henning Smidth. Wilhelm Furtwaengler: a Discography. Copenhagen: Nationaldiskoteket, 1970. 95 p., index of artists and titles.

Olsen, Henning Smidth. Wilhelm Furtwaengler: Konzertprogramme Opern und Vortraege 1947 bis 1954. Wiesbaden: F.A. Brockhaus, 1972. 64 p.

Pirie, Peter. Furtwaengler and the Art of Conducting. London: Gerald Duckworth & Co. Ltd., 1980. 149 p., discography, index.

Riess, Curt. Furtwaengler: Musik und Politik. Bern: Alfred Scherz Verlag, 1953. 319 p., 8 illus., 60-item bibliography.

Riess, Curt. Wilhelm Furtwaengler: a Biography. Translated by Margaret Goldsmith. London: Frederick Muller Ltd, 1955. 240 p., index.

Schrenk, Oswald. Wilhelm Furtwaengler: eine Studie. Berlin: Ed. Bote & G. Bock, 1940. 33 p., portrait.

Seibert, Willy. Furtwaengler: Mensch und Kuenstler. Buenos Aires: Guillermo Kraft Limitada, 1950. 73 p., portrait.

Specht, Richard. Wilhelm Furtwaengler: eine Studie ueber den Dirigenten. Wien: Wiener Literarische Anstalt Gesellschaft m.b.H., 1922. 52, [1] p., portrait.

Thiess, Frank. Wilhelm Furtwaengler Briefe. Wiesbaden: F.A. Brockhaus, 1964. 327 p., notes, index.

Thiess, Frank. In Memoriam Wilhlem Furtwaengler: zwei Gedenkreden. Wien: Paul Zsolnay Verlag, 1955. 15, [1] p.

Wackernagel, Peter. Die Aera Furtwaengler: Vortrag, gehalten aus dem Anlass des 85. Geburtstages des Dirigenten. Berlin: Gesellschaft der Freunde der Berliner Philharmonie e.V., 1971. 18 p.

Wackernagel, Peter, ed. Wilhelm Furtwaengler: die Programme der Konzerte mit dem Berliner Philharmonischen Orchester 1922-1954. 2nd edition. Wiesbaden: F.A. Brockhaus, 1965. 48 p., portrait.

Wessling, Berndt W. Furtwaengler: eine kritische Biographie. Stuttgart: Deutsche Verlags-Anstalt, 1985. 479, [1] p., 15 illus., 52-item bibliography, footnotes, chronology, index.

5. A0002, A0004, A0008, A0016, A0050, A0052, B0015, B0021, B0022, B0031, B0035, B0039, B0047, B0055, B0060, B0063, B0069, B0091, B0092, B0109, B0114, B0117, B0123, B0131, B0132, B0156, B0157, B0159, B0167.

SEE: Robert C. Bachmann under von KARAJAN (C0558.4)

SEE: Dahms, Walter. Der Musikus Almanach. Berlin-Steglitz: Panorama-Verlag, 1927. 160 p.

SEE: Berta Geissmar under THOMAS BEECHAM (C0079.4).

SEE: Peter Haywood under OTTO KLEMPERER (C0590.4).

C0373.
GABRILOWITSCH, OSSIP. b. February 7, 1878, St. Petersburg, Russia; d. September 14, 1936, Detroit, Michigan.

1. BAKER 7; GROVE 6/7; GROVE-AM (Bibliography); MGG 1/4; PAB-MI/2 (Bibliography); RIEMANN 12.

4. Clemens, Clara. My Husband Gabrilowitsch. New York: Harper & Brothers Publishers, 1938. 351 p., 13 illus., index.

5. B0003, B0006, B0038, B0040, B0072, B0089.

SEE: Marie Volpe under ARNOLD VOLPE (C1169.4).

C0374.
GADE, NIELS WILHELM. b. February 22, 1817, Copenhagen; d. December 21, 1890, Copenhagen, Denmark.

1. BAKER 7 (Bibliography); EdS 1/5 (Bibliography); GROVE 6/7 (Bibliography); MGG 1/4 (Bibliography); PAB-MI/2 (Bibliography); RIEMANN 12 (Bibliography) + Supp. (Bibliography).

2. MQ 3/1.

3. Gade, Dagmar, ed. Niels W. Gade: optegnelser og breve. København: Gyldendalske Boghandels Forlag, 1892. [iv], 328, [v] p. + music foldout, portrait, chronological list of compositions.

C0375.
GALES, WESTON SPIES. b. November 5, 1877, Elizabeth, New Jersey; d. October 21, 1939, Portsmouth, New Hampshire.

1. BAKER 7; GROVE-AM 1/2 (Bibliography).

2. MusAm 19/6, 21/13. 59/16.

C0376.
GALKIN, ELLIOTT. b. February 22, 1921, Brooklyn, New York.

1. BAKER 7; GROVE 6/7

3. Galkin, Elliott Washington. The Theory and Practice of Orchestral Conducting Since 1752. Ph.D. diss., Cornell University, 1960. ix, 650 p., 42 illus., 341-item bibliography.

   Also listed as A0014.

C0377.
GALLIERA, ALCEO. b. May 3, 1910, Milan, Italy.

1. BAKER 7; GROVE 6/7; PAB-MI/2 (Bibliography); RIEMANN 12/Supp.

C0378.
GAMBA, PIERO. b. September 16, 1936, Rome, Italy.

1. BAKER 7; GROVE 6/7; PAB-MI/2 (Bibliography).

4. Santos, Isidoro Duarte. Pierino Gamba: o menino-meastro á luz de nova psícologia. Lisboa: Estudos Psiquicos Editora, 1949. 174 p., 6 illus.

5. B0104.

C0379.
GANZ, RUDOLF. b. February 24, 1877, Zurich, Switzerland; d. August 2, 1972, Chicago, Illinois.

1. BAKER 7; GROVE-AM 1/2; PAB-MI/2 (Bibliography); RIEMANN 12 + Supp. (Bibliography).

   His personal papers are in the Newberry Library, Chicago, Illinois.

5. B0166.

C0380.
GANZ, WILHELM. b. November 6, 1833, Mainz, Germany; d. September 12, 1914, London, England.

1. BAKER 7; GROVE 6/7 (Bibliography); RIEMANN 12.

3. Ganz, Wilhelm. Memories of a Musician: Reminiscences of Seventy Years of Musical Life. London: John Murray, 1913. xv, 357 p., 19 illus., index. Also listed as B0049.

C0381.
GARDELLI, LAMBERTO. b. November 8, 1915, Venice, Italy.

1. BAKER 7; GROVE 6/7; PAB-MI/2 (Bibliography); RIEMANN 12/Supp.

C0382.
GARDINER, JOHN ELIOT. b. April 20, 1943, Springhead, Dorset, England.

1. BAKER 7; GROVE 6/7; PAB-MI/2 (Bibliography).

C0383.
GATZ, FELIX MARIA. b. May 15, 1892, Berlin, Germany; d. June 20, 1942, Scranton, Pennsylvania.

1. BAKER 7 (Bibliography).

4. Moissl, Franz. Felix M. Gatz as Bruckner-Conductor. Berlin: AFA-Verlag Hans Duennebeil, 1934. 23 p.

C0384.
GAUBERT, PHILIPPE. b. July 3, 1879, Cahors; d. July 8, 1941, Paris.

1. BAKER 7; PAB-MI/2 (Bibliography); RIEMANN 12 (Bibliography).

4. Fischer, Penelope Ann Peterson. Philippe Gaubert (1879-1941): His Life and Contributions as Flutist, Editor, Teacher, Conductor, and Composer (France). D.M.A. diss., University of Maryland, 1982. 263 p.

5. A0046, B0133.

C0385.
GAVAZZENI, GIANANDREA. b. July 25, 1909, Bergamo, Italy.

1. BAKER 7; GROVE 6/7 (Bibliography); PAB-MI/2 (Bibliography); RIEMANN 12 + Supp. (Bibliography).

3. Gavazzeni, Gianandrea. Diario d'Edinburgo e d'America. Milano: Rusconi e Paolazzi Editori, 1960. 163 p.

   Gavazzeni, Gianandrea. Trent'anni di musica. Milano: G. Ricordi & C., 1958. xv, [i], 313, [1] p.

C0386.
GEDDA, GIULIO. b. April 16, 1899, Turin; d. September 7, 1970, Callegno, near Turin, Italy.

1. BAKER 7; RIEMANN 12 + Supp.

C0387.
GEISLER, PAUL. b. August 10, 1856, Stolp; d. April 3, 1919, Posen.

1. BAKER 7; GROVE 6/7 (Bibliography); MGG 1/4; RIEMANN 12.

C0388.
GEORGE, EARL. b. May 1, 1924, Milwaukee, Wisconsin.

1. BAKER 7; GROVE-AM 1/2; PAB-MI/2 (Bibliography).

2. HiFi/MusAm 26/8.

C0389.
GEORGESCU, GEORGE. b. September 12, 1887, Sulina; d. September 1, 1964, Bucharest, Romania.

1. BAKER 7; GROVE 6/7 (Bibliography); MGG/Supp. (Bibliography); RIEMANN 12 + Supp. (Bibliography).

4. Georgescu, Tutu G. George Georgescu. Bucureşti: Editura Muzicală A Uniunii Compozitorilor, 1971. 452, [1] p., 38 illus.

5. A0050.

C0390.
GERICKE, WILHELM. b. April 18, 1845, Schwanberg, Austria; d. October 27, 1925, Vienna, Austria.

1. BAKER 7; GROVE 6/7 (Bibliography); GROVE-AM 1/2 (Bibliography); PAB-MI/2 (Bibliography); RIEMANN 12.

2. MQ 31/2.

5. B0065, B0121.

C0391.
GERLACH, THEODOR. b. June 25, 1861, Dresden; d. December 11, 1940, Kiel, Germany.

1. BAKER 7; RIEMANN 12.

C0392.
GERLE, ROBERT. b. April 1, 1924, Abbazia, Italy.

1. BAKER 7; PAB-MI/2 (Bibliography); RIEMANN 12/Supp.

C0393.
GERNSHEIM, FRIEDRICH. b. July 17, 1839, Worms; d. September 11, 1916, Berlin, Germany.

1. BAKER 7; GROVE 6/7 (Bibliography); MGG 1/4 (Bibliography); RIEMANN 12 + Supp. (Bibliography).

4. Holl, K. Friedrich Gernsheim: Leben, Erscheinung und Werk. Leipzig, 1928.

C0394.
GHIONE, FRANCO. b. August 28, 1886, Acqui; d. January 19, 1964, Rome.

1. BAKER 7; EdS 1/5; PAB-MI/2 (Bibliography); RIEMANN 12.

C0395.
GIBSON, ALEXANDER. b. February 11, 1926, Motherwell, Scotland.

1. BAKER 7; GROVE 6/7 (Bibliography); PAB-MI/2 (Bibliography); RIEMANN 12/Supp.

2. OPERA 19/8.

C0396.
GIELEN, MICHAEL. b. July 20, 1927, Dresden, Germany.

1. BAKER 7; GROVE 6/7 (Bibliography); GROVE-AM 1/2; MGG/Supp.; PAB-MI/2 (Bibliography); RIEMANN 12 + Supp. (Bibliography).

C0397.
GIERSTER, HANS. b. January 12, 1925, Munich, Germany.

1. BAKER 7; PAB-MI/2 (Bibliography); RIEMANN 12/Supp.

2. OW 2/15, 14/10.

C0398.
GIOVANINETTI, REYNALD JEAN. b. March 11, 1932, Setif, Algeria.

1. BAKER 7; PAB-MI/2 (Bibliography); RIEMANN 12/Supp.

C0399.
GIULINI, CARLO MARIA. b. May 9, 1914, Barletta, Italy.

1. BAKER 7; EdS 1/5; GROVE 6/7 (Bibliography); GROVE-AM 1/2 (Bibliography); PAB-MI/2 (Bibliography); RIEMANN 12/Supp.

2. GR 49/578, 56/672, 59/701, 62/737; HiFi/MusAm 28/4; JCG 2/3; LGB 14/3; OPERA 15/11; OW 25/3.

5. A0031, B0068, B0122.

SEE: William Barry Furlong under GEORG SOLTI (C1070.4).

SEE: Harewood, George, Earl of. The Tongs and the Bones: the Memoirs of Lord Harewood. London: George Weidenfeld and Nicolson Ltd., 1981. xv, 334 p., 55 illus.

C0400.
GLOVER, JOHN WILLIAM. b. June 19, 1815, Dublin; d. December 18, 1889, Dublin, Ireland.

1. BAKER 7; GROVE 6/7 (Bibliography).

C0401.
GLOVER, WILLIAM HOWARD. b. June 6, 1819, London, England; d. October 28, 1875, New York City.

1. BAKER 7; GROVE 6/7.

C0402.
GODFREY, DANIEL EYERS. b. June 20, 1868, London; d. July 20, 1939, Bournemouth, England.

1. BAKER 7; GROVE 6/7; MGG 1/5 (Bibliography); RIEMANN 12.

3. Godfrey, Dan. Memories and Music: Thirty-five years of Conducting. Forward by Charles V. Stanford. London: Hutchinson & Co., 1924. xv, 327 p., 23 illus., 4 appendices including selected works by British composers performed at the Bournemouth Symphony Concerts 1895-1923 and a list of soloists, index.

4. Upton, Stuart. Sir Dan Godfrey and the Bournemouth Municipal Orchestra: a Bibgraphical Discography. West Wickham: Vintage Light Music Society, 1979. 34 p., illus., discography.

C0403.
GOEHLER, KARL GEORG. b. June 29, 1874, Zwickau; d. March 4, 1954, Luebeck, Germany.

1. BAKER 7; GROVE 6/7; MGG 1/5 (Bibliography); RIEMANN 12.

C0404.
GOEHR, WALTER. b. May 28, 1903, Berlin; d. December 4, 1960, Sheffield, England.

1. BAKER 7; GROVE 6/7; RIEMANN 12.

C0405.
GOEPFART, KARL EDUARD. b. March 8, 1859, Weimar; d. February 8, 1942, Weimar, Germany.

1. BAKER 7; RIEMANN 12.

C0406.
GOLDBECK, ROBERT. b. April 19, 1839, Potsdam, Germany; d. May 16, 1908, St. Louis, Missouri.

1. BAKER 7; GROVE-AM 1/2 (Bibliography); PAB-MI/2 (Bibliography); RIEMANN 12.

C0407.
GOLDBERG, SZYMON. b. June 1, 1901, Wloclawek, Poland.

1. BAKER 7 (Bibliography); GROVE 6/7 (Bibliography); GROVE-AM 1/2 (Bibliography); MGG/Supp.; PAB-MI/2 (Bibliography); RIEMANN 12 + Supp.

C0408.
GOLDMAN, EDWIN FRANKO. b. January 1, 1878, Louisville, Kentucky; d. February 21, 1956, New York City.

1. BAKER 7; GROVE 6/7; GROVE-AM 1/2 (Bibliography); MGG 1/5; PAB-MI/2

(Bibliography); RIEMANN 12 + Supp. (Bibliography).

3. Goldman, Edwin Franco. Band Betterment: Suggestions and Advice to Bands, Bandmasters, and Band-Players. New York: Carl Fischer, Inc., 1934. viii, [i], 193 p., 4 illus.

NOTE: His autobiography MS, Facing the Music, is in the library at the University of Maryland, College Park, Maryland.

4. Kirby, R. Jolly. Edwin Franco Goldman and the Goldman Band. Ph.D. diss., New York University, 1971. vii, 169 p., illus.

C0409.
GOLDMAN, RICHARD FRANCO. b. December 7, 1910, New York City; d. January 19, 1980, Baltimore, Maryland.

1. BAKER 7; GROVE-AM 1/2 (Bibliography); PAB-MI/2 (Bibliography).

3. Goldman, Richard Franco. The Band's Music. New York: Pitman Publishing Corporation, 1938. xviii, 442 p., 18-item bibliography.

4. There are two recent dissertations neither of which has been seen:

Stock, P.G. Richard Franco Goldman and the Goldman Band. University of Oregon, 1982.

Lester, N.K. Richard Franco Goldman: His Life and Works. Peabody Conservatory, 1984.

C0410.
GOLDOVSKY, BORIS. b. June 7, 1908, Moscow, Russia.

1. BAKER 7; GROVE 6/7; GROVE-AM 1/2 (Bibliography); PAB-MI/2 (Bibliography); RIEMANN 12 + Supp.

3. Goldovsky, Boris and Curtis Cate. My Road to Opera: the Reflections of Boris Goldovsky. Boston: Houghton Mifflin Company, 1979. x, 401 p., 37 illus., index.

His personal library and memorabilia are in the Northwestern University Music Library.

5. B0138.

C0411.
GOLDSCHMIDT, BERTHOLD. b. January 18, 1903, Hamburg, Germany.

1. BAKER 7; GROVE 6/7; MGG 1/5 (Bibliography); PAB-MI/2 (Bibliography); RIEMANN 12 + Supp.

C0412.
GOLOVANOV, NICOLAI. b. January 21, 1891, Moscow; d. August 28, 1953, Moscow, Russia.

1. BAKER 7; GROVE 6/7 (Bibliography); MGG/Supp. (Bibliography);

RIEMANN 12 + Supp. (Bibliography).

C0413.
GOLSCHMANN, VLADIMIR. b. December 16, 1893, Paris, France; d. March 1, 1972, New York City.

1. BAKER 7; GROVE 6/7; GROVE-AM 1/2 (Bibliography); MGG 1/5 (Bibliography); PAB-MI/2 (Bibliography); RIEMANN 12 + Supp.

5. A0010, A0046, A0048, B0133, B0166.

SEE: Mueller, Richard E. A Century of the Symphony. St. Louis: Knight Publishing Company, 1979.

C0414.
GOODALL, REGINALD. b. July 13, 1901, Lincoln, England.

1. BAKER 7; GROVE 6/7 (Bibliography); PAB-MI/2 (Bibliography).

2. OPERA 22/4.

C0415.
GOODRICH, JOHN WALLACE. b. May 27, 1871, Newton, Massachusetts; d. June 6, 1952, Boston, Massachusetts.

1. BAKER 7; GROVE-AM 1/2; PAB-MI/2 (Bibliography).

C0416.
GOOSSENS, EUGENE. b. May 26, 1893, London; d. June 13, 1962, London.

1. BAKER 7; EdS 1/5 (Bibliography); GROVE 6/7 (Bibliography); GROVE-AM 1/2 (Bibliography); MGG 1/5 (Bibliography); PAB-MI/2 (Bibliography); RIEMANN 12 + Supp. (Bibliography).

3. Goossens, Eugene. Overture and Beginners: a Musical Autobiography. London: Methuen & Co., Ltd., 1951. viii, 327 p., 32 illus., some casts of operas [11], editorial, list of works, quoted statements, index.

   Hired by George Eastman to head the Rochester Philharmonic (1923).

5. A0004, A0010, A0022, A0045, B0006, B0009, B0076, B0095, B0096.

C0417.
GORTER, ALBERT. b. November 23, 1862, Nuremberg; d. March 14, 1936, Munich, Germany.

1. BAKER 7; RIEMANN 12.

C0418.
GOULD, MORTON. b. December 10, 1913, New York City.

1. BAKER 7 (Bibliography); GROVE 6/7; GROVE-AM 1/2 (Bibliography); PAB-MI/2 (Bibliography); RIEMANN 12 (Bibliography) + Supp. (Bibliography.

4. Evans, L. Morton Gould: His Life and Music. Ph.D. diss., Columbia University Teachers College, 1978. 387 p.

C0419.
GRACIS, ETTORE. b. September 24, 1915, La Spezia, Italy.

1. BAKER 7; GROVE 6/7; RIEMANN 12/Supp.

C0420.
GRAM, PEDER. b. November 25, 1881, Copenhagen; d. February 4, 1956, Copenhagen, Denmark.

1. BAKER 7; GROVE 6/7 (Bibliography); MGG 1/5 (Bibliography); RIEMANN 12.

C0421.
GREENBERG, NOAH. b. April 9, 1919, New York City; d. January 9, 1966, New York City.

1. BAKER 7; GROVE 6/7; GROVE-AM 1/2 (Bibliography); PAB-MI/2 (Bibliography).

4. Gaskill, S.J. The Artist as Manager: Noah Greenberg and the New York Pro Musica. Ph.D. diss., American University, 1984.

   No copy seen.

C0422.
GREGOR, BOHUMIL. b. July 14, 1926, Prague, Czechoslovakia.

1. BAKER 7; GROVE 6/7 (Bibliography); PAB-MI/2 (Bibliography); RIEMANN 12/Supp.

C0423.
GREVILLIUS, NILS. b. March 7, 1893, Stockholm; d. August 15, 1970, Mariefred, Sweden.

1. BAKER 7; GROVE 6/7; RIEMANN 12.

C0424.
GRISHKAT, HANS. b. August 29, 1903, Hamburg; d. January 10, 1977, Stuttgart, Germany.

1. BAKER 7; GROVE 6/7 (Bibliography); RIEMANN 12.

C0425.
GRØNDAHL, LAUNY. b. June 30, 1886, Ordrup, near Copenhagen; d. January 21, 1960, Copenhagen, Denmark.

1. BAKER 7; RIEMANN 12.

C0426.
GROSBAYNE, BENJAMIN. b. April 7, 1893, Boston; d. January 24, 1976, Brookline, Massachusetts.

1. BAKER 7; RIEMANN 12.

3. He wrote Techniques of Modern Orchestral Conducting (Cambridge, 1956).

C0427.
GROSSMANN, FERDINAND. b. July 4, 1887, Tulln, Austria; d. December 5, 1970, Vienna, Austria.

1. BAKER 7; RIEMANN 12 + Supp. (Bibliography).

C0428.
GROVES, CHARLES BARNARD. b. March 10, 1915, London, England.

1. BAKER 7; GROVE 6/7; PAB-MI/2 (Bibliography); RIEMANN 12/Supp.

2. GR 49/586.

C0429.
GROVLEZ, GABRIEL MARIE. b. April 4, 1879, Lille, France; d. October 20, 1944, Paris, France.

1. BAKER 7 (Bibliography); GROVE 6/7; MGG 1/5 (Bibliography); PAB-MI/2 (Bibliography); RIEMANN 12.

3. Grovlez, Gabriel. Miniature Essays: Gabriel Grovlez. London: J. & W. Chester Ltd., n.d. 16, [4] p., 2 illus., list of compositions.

C0430.
GRUBER, GEORG. b. July 27, 1904, Vienna, Austria.

1. BAKER 7; RIEMANN 12 + Supp.

C0431.
GRUENER-HEGGE, ODD. b. September 23, 1899, Oslo; d. May 11, 1973, Oslo, Norway.

1. BAKER 7; RIEMANN 12 + Supp.

C0432.
GRUND, FRIEDRICH WILHELM. b. October 7, 1791, Hamburg; d. November 24, 1874, Hamburg, Germany.

1. BAKER 7; RIEMANN 12 (Bibliography).

C0433.
GUADAGNO, ANTON. b. May 2, 1925, Castellammare del Golfo, Grapani, Italy.

1. BAKER 7; GROVE 6/7; PAB-MI/2 (Bibliography).

2. ON 47/11.

C0434.
GUARINO, PIERO. b. June 20, 1919, Alexandria, Egypt.

1. BAKER 7; PAB-MI/2 (Bibliography); RIEMANN 12 + Supp.

C0435.
GUARNIERI, ANTONIO. b. February 1, 1880, Venice; d. November 25, 1952, Milan, Italy.

1. BAKER 7; EdS 1/6; GROVE 6/7; RIEMANN 12.

C0436.
GUI, VITTORIO. b. September 14, 1885, Rome; d. October 16, 1975, Florence, Italy.

1. BAKER 7; EdS 1/6 (Bibliography); GROVE 6/7 (Bibliography); MGG 1/5; PAB-MI/2 (Bibliography); RIEMANN 12.

2, OPERA 3/7, 26/12.

3. Gui, Vittorio. Battute d'aspetto: meditazioni di un musicista militante. Firenze: Casa Editrice Monsalvato, 1944. 278 p., index of names.

5. B0016, B0094.

C0437.
GURLITT, MANFRED. b. September 6, 1890, Berlin, Germany; d. April 29, 1972, Tokyo, Japan.

1. BAKER 7, GROVE 6/7; MGG 1/5 + Supp., RIEMANN 12 + Supp.

C0438.
HAAS, KARL. b. December 27, 1900, Karlsruhe, Germany; d. July 7, 1970, London, England.

1. BAKER 7; GROVE 6/8 (Bibliography).

C0439.
HABENEC, FRANCOIS-ANTOINE. b. January 22, 1781, Mézières; d. February 8, 1849, Paris, France.

1. BAKER 7; EdS 1/6 (Bibliography); GROVE 6/8 (Bibliography); MGG 1/5 (Bibliography); PAB-MI/2 (Bibliography); RIEMANN 12 + Supp.

5. B0035, B0036, B0112.

C0440.
HADLEY, HENRY KIMBALL. b. December 20, 1871, Sommerville, Massachusetts; d. September 6, 1937, New York City.

1. BAKER 7; EdS 1/6; GROVE 6/8 (Bibliography); GROVE-AM 1/2 (Bibliography); MGG 1/5; PAB-MI/2 (Bibliography); RIEMANN 12 + Supp.

4. There are two dissertations neither of which has been seen:

   Boardman, H.R. Henry Hadley: Ambassador of Harmony. Ph.D. diss., Emory University 1932.

Canfield, J. Henry Kimball Hadley (1871-1937): His Life and Works. Ph.D. diss., Florida State University, 1960.

5. B0006.

C0441.
HAGEL, RICHARD. b. July 7, 1872, Erfurt; d. May 1, 1941, Berlin, Germany.

1. BAKER 7; RIEMANN 12.

C0442.
HAGEMANN, RICHARD. b. July 9, 1882, Leeuwarden, Holland; d. March 6, 1966, Beverly Hills, California.

1. BAKER 7; GROBE 6/8; GROVE-AM 1/2; PAB-MI/2 (Bibliography).

C0443.
HAGEN-GROLL, WALTER. b. April 15, 1927, Chemnitz, Germany.

1. BAKER 7; RIEMANN 12/Supp.

C0444.
HAGER, LEOPOLD. b. October 6, 1935, Salzburg, Austria.

1. BAKER 7; PAB-MI/2 (Bibliography); RIEMANN 12/Supp.

C0445.
HAHN, REYNALDO. b. August 9, 1874, Caracas, Venezuela; d. January 28, 1947, Paris, France.

1. BAKER 7; EdS 1/6 (Bibliography); GROVE 6/8 (Bibliography); MGG 1/5 (Bibliography); PAB-MI/2 (Bibliography); RIEMANN 12 + Supp. (Bibliography).

2. RS 21.

3. Hahn, Reynaldo. L'Oreille au guet. Paris: Librairie Gallimard, 1937. 286 p., index.

   Hahn, Reynaldo. Notes: journal d'un musicien. Paris: Librairie Plon, 1933. 293, [2] p.

   Hahn, Reynaldo. Thèmes variés. Paris: J.-B. Janin, Editeur, 1946. 302 p., index.

4. Bendahan, Daniel. Reynaldo Hahn: su vida y su obra. Caracas: Italgrafica, 1973. xvi, 113 p., 49 illus., 70-item bibliography, index of names.

   Gavoty, Bernard. Reynaldo Hahn: le musicien de la Belle Epoque. Paris: Editions Buchet/Chastel, 1976. 314, [29] p., chronology 1874-1947.

5. B0133.

C0446.
HAINL, FRANCOIS. b. November 16, 1807, Issoire; d. June 2, 1873, Paris.

1. BAKER 7; GROVE 6/8 (Bibliography); MGG 1/5 (Bibliography); RIEMANN 12.

5. B0036.

C0447.
HAITINK, BERNARD. b. March 4, 1929, Amsterdam, Holland.

1. BAKER 7; GROVE 6/8 (Bibliography); PAB-MI/2 (Bibliography); RIEMANN 12/Supp.

2. GR 45/537, 51/608, 56/670, 60/713; ON 46/17; OPERA 32/6.

5. A0023, A0031, B0125.

C0448.
HALASZ, LASZLO. b. June 6, 1905, Debrecen, Hungary.

1. BAKER 7; PAB-MI/2 (Bibliography); RIEMANN 12 + Supp.

C0449.
HALFFTER, CRISTOBAL. b. April 24, 1930, Madrid, Spain.

1. BAKER 7; GROVE 6/8; MGG/Supp. (Bibliography); PAB-MI/2 (Bibliography); RIEMANN 12/Supp. (Bibliography).

C0450.
HALLE, CHARLES. b. April 11, 1819, Hagen, Westphalia; d. October 25, 1895, Manchester, England.

1. BAKER 7 (Bibliography); GROVE 6/8 (Bibliography); MGG 1/5; PAB-MI/2 (Bibliography); RIEMANN 12 + Supp. (Bibliography).

3. Hallé, C.E. and Marie Hallé, eds. Life and Letters of Sir Charles Hallé: Being an Autobiography (1819-1860) With Correspondence and Diaries. London: Smith, Elder, & Co., 1896. Reprint 1973. 432 p., 2 illus., 2 appendices, index.

4. Kennedy, Michael. The Hallé Tradition: a Century of Music. Manchester: Manchester University Press, 1960. xiv, 424 p., 44 illus., 6 appendices, 24-item select bibliography, index.

   Especially good for Hallé, Richter, Balling, Beecham, and Harty.

   Rigby, Charles. Sir Charles Hallé: a Portrait for Today. Forward by Sir John Barbirolli. Manchester: The Dolphin Press, 1952. xi, 180 p., 7 illus., index.

   Sir Charles Hallé: a Sketch of His Career as a Musician. Manchester: John Heywood, 1890. 77 p.

5. B0010, B0019, B0049, B0070, B0076, B0126, B0148.

SEE: Dahl, Alice Mangold. Musical Memories. London: Richard Bentley and Son, 1897. xii, 319 p., index.

SEE: Engel, Louis. From Handel to Hallé: Biographical Sketches. New York: Books for Libraries Press, 1972 [original 1890]. viii, 251 p., 13 illus., index.

SEE: Raynor, Henry. Music & Society Since 1875. New York: Schocken Books, 1976. viii, 213 p., 130-item bibliography, index.

C0451.
HAMERIK, ASGER. b. April 8, 1843, Copenhagen; d. July 13, 1923, Copenhagen, Denmark.

1. BAKER 7, GROVE 6/8 (Bibliography); GROVE-AM 1/2 (Bibliography); PAB-MI/2 (Bibliography); RIEMANN 12.

C0452.
HAMM, ADOLF. b. March 9, 1882, Strasbourg; d. October 15, 1938, Basel, Switzerland.

1. BAKER 7; RIEMANN 12.

C0453.
HAMMELBOE, ARNE. b. June 24, 1916, Copenhagen, Denmark.

1. BAKER 7; RIEMANN 12/Supp.

C0454.
HANDLEY, VERNON. b. November 11, 1930, Enfield, Middlesex, England.

1. BAKER 7; GROVE 6/8; Pab-MI/2 (Bibliography).

2. GR 59/698.

C0455.
HANNIKAINEN, PEKKA. b. December 9, 1854, Nurmes; d. September 13, 1924, Helsinki, Finland.

1. BAKER 7; GROVE 6/8 (Bibliography); MGG 1/5 (Bibliography); RIEMANN 12.

C0456.
HANNIKAINEN, TAUNO. b. February 26, 1896, Jyvaesklyae; d. October 12, 1968, Helsinki, Finland.

1. BAKER 6; GROVE 6/8 (Bibliography); MGG 1/5 (Bibliography); PAB-MI/2 (Bibliography); RIEMANN 12 + Supp.

5. A0022, A0040.

C0457.
HANSSENS, CHARLES-LOUIS. b. July 12, 1802, Ghent; d. April 8, 1871, Brussels, Belgium.

1. BAKER 7 (Bibliography); GROVE 6/8; MGG/Supp. (Bibliography); RIEMANN 12.

C0458.
d'HARCOURT, EUGENE. b. May 2, 1859, Paris, France; d. March 4, 1918, Locarno, Switzerland.

1. BAKER 7; RIEMANN 12 (Bibliography).

3. RIEMANN 12 mentions four books on various topics.

5. B0033.

C0459.
HARMATI, SANDOR. b. July 9, 1892, Budapest, Hungary; d. April 4, 1936, Flemington, New Jersey.

1. BAKER 7; GROVE-AM 1/2 (Bibliography); PAB-MI/2 (Bibliography); RIEMANN 12.

5. B0072.

C0460.
HARNONCOURT, NIKOLAUS. b. December 6, 1929, Berlin, Germany.

1. BAKER 7; PAB-MI/2 (Bibliography); RIEMANN 12/Supp. (Bibliography).

5. A0023.

C0461.
HARRIS, WILLIAM VICTOR. b. April 27, 1869, New York City; d. February 15, 1943, New York City.

1. BAKER 7; GROVE-AM 1/2; PAB-MI/2 (Bibliography).

2. MusAm 30/5.

C0462,
HARRISON, GUY FRASER. b. November 6, 1894, Guildford, Surrey, England.

1. BAKER 7; GROVE-AM 1/2 (Bibliography).

5. A0048.

C0463.
HARRISON, JULIUS ALLAN. b. March 26, 1885, Stourport, Worcestershire; d. April 5, 1963, Harpenden, Hertfordshire, England.

1. BAKER 7; GROVE 6/8 (Bibliography); MGG 1/5 (Bibliography); PAB-MI/2 (Bibliography); RIEMANN 12.

5. A0003, A0045, B0058.

C0464.
HART, FRITZ. b. February 11, 1874, London; d. July 9, 1949, Honolulu.

1. BAKER 7; GROVE 6/8; RIEMANN 12.

5. B0108.

C0465.
HARTH, SIDNEY. b. October 5, 1929, Cleveland, Ohio.

1. BAKER 7; GROVE 6/8; GROVE-AM 1/2; PAB-MI/2 (Bibliography); RIEMANN 12/Supp.

C0466.
HARTY, HERBERT HAMILTON. b. December 4, 1879, Hillsborough, County Down, Ireland; d. February 19, 1941, Brighton, England.

1. BAKER 7; GROVE 6/8 (Bibliography); MGG 1/5 (Bibliography); PAB-MI/2 (Bibliography); RIEMANN 12.

2. RS 77.

3. An incomplete and unpublished autobiographical memoir is owned by The Queen's University of Belfast. Harty was conductor of the Halle Orchestra for thirteen years as well as the London Symphony.

4. Greer, David, ed. Hamilton Harty: His Life and Music. Belfast: Blackstaff Press Limited, n.d. [1979]. xi, 161 p., 23 illus., discography by Cyril Ehrlich, list of compositions, documents, 21-item bibliography.

   Greer, David, ed. Hamilton Harty: Early Memories. Belfast: The Queen's University, 1979. 44 p., 11 illus., index.

5. A0045, B0006, B0070, B0126.

   SEE: Szigeti, Joseph. With Strings Attached: Reminiscences and Reflections. New York: Alfred A. Knopf, 1947. xiii, 341, xvii p., 15 illus., discography, index.

C0467.
HASSELMANS, LOUIS. b. July 25, 1878, Paris, France; d. December 27, 1957, San Juan, Puerto Rico.

1. BAKER 7; GROVE 6/8; PAB-MI/2 (Bibliography).

5. B0072.

C0468.
von HAUSEGGER, SIEGMUND. b. August 16, 1872, Graz, Austria; d. October 10, 1948, Munich, Germany.

1. BAKER 7 (Bibliography); RIEMANN 12 (Bibliography).

C0469.
HAWES, WILLIAM. b. June 21, 1785, London; d. February 18, 1846, London.

1. BAKER 7; GROVE 6/8; PAB-MI/2 (Bibliography); RIEMANN 12.

C0470.
HEATH, EDWARD RICHARD GEORGE. b. July 9, 1916, Broadstairs, Kent, England.

1. No music lexicon. Information from Who's Who 1986-87.

2. HiFi/MusAm 22/3.

3. Heath, Edward. Music: a Joy for Life. London: Sidgwick & Jackson, 1974. 204, [4] p., 172 illus., glossary, biographical notes on composers, index.

   How many British prime ministers have been so involved with music including conducting the London Symphony Orchestra? This lavish autobiography is one of six books on a variety of subjects.

C0471.
HEDWALL, LENNART. b. September 16, 1932, Goeteborg, Sweden.

1. BAKER 7; PAB-MI/2 (Bibliography); RIEMANN 12/Supp. (Bibliography).

C0472.
HEGAR, FRIEDRICH. b. October 11, 1841, Basel; d. June 2, 1927, Zurich, Switzerland.

1. BAKER 7; GROVE 6/8 (Bibliography); MGG 1/6 (Bibliography); RIEMANN 12 (Bibliography).

4. Jerg, Werner. Hegar: ein Meister des Maennerchorliedes. Ph.D. diss., University of Zurich, 1946. viii, 96 p.

C0473.
HEGER, ROBERT. b. August 19, 1866, Strasbourg; d. January 14, 1978, Munich, Germany.

1. BAKER 7; GROVE 6/8; PAB-MI/2 (Bibliography); RIEMANN 12 + Supp. (Bibliography).

2. RS 38.

C0474.
HEINZE, BERNARD THOMAS. b. July 1, 1894, Shepparton, near Melbourne; d. June 9, 1982, Sydney, Australia.

1. BAKER 7; GROVE 6/8 (Bibliography); MGG/Supp.; PAB-MI/2 (Bibliography); RIEMANN 12 + Supp.

5. B0053, B0108.

C0475.
HEINZE, GUSTAV ADOLF. b. October 1, 1820, Leipzig, Germany; d. February 20, 1904, Muiderburg, near Amsterdam, Holland.

1. BAKER 7; GROVE 6/8 (Bibliography); RIEMANN 12 + Supp. (Bibliography).

C0476.
HELLMESBERGER, GEORG, Sr. b. April 24, 1800, Vienna; d. August 16, 1873, Neuwaldegg, near Vienna, Austria.

1. BAKER 7 (Bibliography); GROVE 6/8 (Bibliography); MGG 1/6; PAB-MI/2 (Bibliography); RIEMANN 12 + Supp. (Bibliography).

C0477.
HELLMESBERGER, JOSEPH, Jr. b. April 9, 1855, Vienna; d. April 26, 1907, Vienna, Austria.

1. BAKER 7 (Bibliography); GROVE 6/8 (Bibliography); MGG 1/6; PAB-MI/2 (Bibliography); RIEMANN 12 + Supp. (Bibliography).

4. Prosl, Robert Maria. Die Hellmesberger: Hundert Jahre aus dem Leben einer Wiener Musikerfamilie. Wien: Gerlach & Wiedling. 128, [32] p., 32 illus., notes, index of names, list of illustrations.

C0478.
HEMBERG, ESKIL. b. January 19, 1938, Stockholm, Sweden.

1. BAKER 7; GROVE 6/8; PAB-MI/2 (Bibliography).

C0479.
HENDL, WALTER. b. January 12, 1917, West New York, New Jersey.

1. BAKER 7; PAB-MI/2 (Bibliography); RIEMANN 12/Supp.

5. A0048.

C0480.
HENNEBERG, JOHANN BAPTIST. b. December 6, 1768, Vienna; d. November 26, 1882, Vienna, Austria.

1. BAKER 7; GROVE 6/8 (Bibliography); MGG 1/6 (Bibliography); RIEMANN 12.

C0481.
HENSCHEL, ISADOR GEORGE. b. February 18, 1850, Breslau, Germany; d. September 10, 1934, Aviemore, Scotland, England.

1. BAKER 7; GROVE 6/8 (Bibliography); GROVE-AM 1/2; MGG 1/6 (Bibliography); PAB-MI/2 (Bibliography); RIEMANN 12.

3. Henschel, George. Musings and Memories of a Musician. London: Macmillan and Co., Limited, 1918. 400 p., portrait, index.

4. Henschel, Helen. When Soft Voices Die: a Musical Biography. London: John Westhouse Limited, 1944. 216 p., 10 illus., index.

5. B0065, B0085, B0121.

C0482.
HENTSCHEL, THEODOR. b. March 28, 1830, Schirgiswalde; d. December 19, 1892, Hamburg, Germany.

1. BAKER 7; RIEMANN 12.

C0483.
von HERBECK, JOHANN FRANZ. b. December 25, 1831, Vienna; d. October 28, 1877, Vienna, Austria.

1. BAKER 7; GROVE 6/8 (Bibliography); MGG 1/6 (Bibliography) + Supp.; RIEMANN 12 + Supp. (Bibliography).

2. JCG 4/4.

4. Braun, Julius. Johann Ritter von Herbeck und das Wiener Hofoperntheater. Tutzing: Verlegt bei Hans Schneider, 1976 [original: Ph.D. diss., University of Vienna, 1949. 203 p.]. 164 p., list of repertoire, 46-item bibliography.

   Herbeck, Ludwig. Johann Herbeck: ein Lebensbild. Wien: Verlag von Albert J. Gutmann, 1885. xvi, 417 + 172 p., Anhang, portrait.

C0484.
HERBERT, VICTOR. b. February 1, 1859, Dublin, Ireland; d. May 26, 1924, New York City.

1. BAKER 7; EdS 1/6; GROVE 6/8; GROVE-AM 1/2; MGG 1/6; PAB-MI/2 (Bibliography); RIEMANN 12 + Supp. (Bibliography).

4. Kaye, Joseph. Victor Herbert: the Biography of America's Greatest Composer of Romantic Music. New York: G. Howard Watt, 1931. 271 p., 19 illus., appendix of published compositions, index.

   Waters, Edward N. Victor Herbert: a Life in Music. New York: The Macmillan Company, 1955. xvi, 653 p., portrait, list of works, discography, notes, index.

C0485.
HERBIG, GUENTHER. b. November 30, 1931, Usti-Nad-Laben, Czechoslovakia.

1. BAKER 7; GROVE 6/8; GROVE-AM 1/2; PAB-MI/2 (Bibliography).

C0486.
HERMAN, REINHOLD LUDWIG. b. September 21, 1849, Prenzlau, Germany; d. c.1920 probably in New York City.

1. BAKER 7; RIEMANN 12.

C0487.
HERRERA, LUIS de la FUENTE. b. April 26, 1916, Mexico City, Mexico.

1. BAKER 7; RIEMANN 12/Supp.

C0488.
HERRMANN, BERNARD. b. June 29, 1911, New York City; d. December 24, 1975, Los Angeles, California.

1. BAKER 7; EdS 1/6; GROVE 6/8 (Bibliography); MGG/Supp.; PAB-MI/2

(Bibliography); RIEMANN 12 + Supp.

C0489.
den HERTOG, JOHANNES. b. January 20, 1904, Amsterdam, Holland.

1. BAKER 7; RIEMANN 12 + Supp.

C0490.
HERTZ, ALFRED. b. July 15, 1872, Frankfurt/M., Germany; d. April 17, 1942, San Francisco, California.

1. BAKER 7; GROVE 6/8; GROVE-AM 1/2 (Bibliography); PAB-MI/2 (Bibliography); RIEMANN 12.

2. LGB 18/2.

3. His autobiography was published in thirty installments in the San Francisco Chronicle May 3 to July 14, 1942.

5. B0006, B0042, B0051, B0064.

C0491.
HETSCH, KARL LUDWIG. b. April 26, 1806, Stuttgart; d. June 28, 1872, Mannheim, Germany.

1. BAKER 7; GROVE 6/8.

C0492.
HEUBERGER, RICHARD. b. June 28, 1850, Graz; d. October 27, 1914, Vienna, Austria.

1. BAKER 7; GROVE 6/8 (Bibliography); MGG 1/6 (Bibliography); RIEMANN 12.

C0493.
HEWARD, LESLIE. b. December 8, 1897, Littletown, Yorkshire; d. May 3, 1943, Birmingham, England.

1. BAKER 7; GROVE 6/8; MGG 1/6.

2. GR 20/June; LGB 7/5.

4. Blom, Eric, ed. Leslie Heward 1897-1943: a Memorial Volume. Birmingham: Cornish Brothers Ltd., 1946 [original: London, 1944]. 94 p., 3 illus., list of compositions, discography.

   Forty contributors including Ansermet, Barbirolli, and Boult.

5. A0045.

C0494.
HILL, URELI CORELLI. b. c.1802, New York City; d. September 2, 1875, Patterson, New Jersey.

1. BAKER 7; GROVE 6/8 (Bibliography).

C0495.
HILLE, EDUARD. b. May 16, 1822, Wahlhausen; d. December 18, 1891, Goettingen, Germany.

1. BAKER 7; RIEMANN 12

C0496.
HILLER, FERDINAND. b. October 24, 1811, Frankfurt/M.; d. May 10, 1885, Cologne, Germany.

1. BAKER 7 (Bibliography); EdS 1/6 (Bibliography); GROVE 6/8 (Bibliography); MGG 1/6 (Bibliography); PAB-MI/2 (Bibliography); RIEMANN 12 + Supp. (Bibliography).

3. Hiller, Ferdinand. Erinnerungsblaetter. Cologne: Verlag der M. DuMont-Schanberg'schen Buchhandlung, 1884. 257, [2] p.

   Hiller wrote seven other books including Musikalisches und Persoenliches. Leipzig: Breitkopf und Haertel, 1876.

4. Sietz, Reinhold. Aus Ferdinand Hillers Briefwechsel, Band II (1862-1869): Beitraege zu einer Biographie Ferdinand Hillers. Koeln: Arno Volk-Verlag, 1961 [7 vols. 1958-1970]. 161 p., notes, index of names.

C0497.
HILLIS, MARGARET. b. October 1, 1921, Kokomo, Indiana.

1. BAKER 7; GROVE 6/8; GROVE-AM 1/2 (Bibliography); PAB-MI/2 (Bibliography); RIEMANN 12/Supp.

5. B0090, B0134.

C0498.
HINRICHS, GUSTAV. b. December 10, 1850, Ludwigslust, Germany; d. March 26, 1942, Mountain Lake, New Jersey.

1. BAKER 7; GROVE-AM 1/2; PAB-MI/2 (Bibliography).

C0499.
HÖEBERG, GEORG VALDEMAR. b. December 27, 1872, Copenhagen; d. August 3, 1950, Vedboek, Denmark.

1. BAKER 7; RIEMANN 12 (Bibliography).

C0500.
von HOESSLIN, FRANZ. b. December 31, 1885, Munich, Germany; d. September 28, 1946, southern France.

1. BAKER 7; PAB-MI/2 (Bibliography); RIEMANN 12.

C0501.
HOL, RICHARD. b. July 23, 1825, Amsterdam; d. May 14, 1904, Utrecht.

1. BAKER 7; GROVE 6/8; MGG/Supp. (Bibliography); PAB-MI/2 (Bibliog-

raphy); RIEMANN 12.

C0502.
HOLLAENDER, ALEXIS. b. February 25, 1840, Ratibor, Silesia; d. February 5, 1924, Berlin, Germany.

1. BAKER 7 (Bibliography); RIEMANN 12.

5. B0079.

C0503.
HOLLREISER, HEINRICH. b. June 24, 1913, Munich, Germany.

1. BAKER 7; GROVE 6/8; PAB-MI/2 (Bibliography); RIEMANN 12 + Supp.

2. ON 40/10.

5. B0063.

C0504.
HOLOUBEK, LADISLAV. b. July 13, 1913, Prague, Czechoslovakia.

1. BAKER 7; GROVE 6/8 (Bibliography); MGG/Supp. (Bibliography); RIEMANN 12 + Supp. (Bibliography).

C0505.
van **HOOGSTRATEN, WILLEM.** b. March 18, 1884, Utrecht, Holland; d. September 11, 1965, Tutzing, Germany.

1. BAKER 7; RIEMANN 12 + Supp. (Bibliography).

5. B0072.

SEE: Ney, Elly. Erinnerungen und Betrachtungen: mein Leben aus der Musik. Aschaffenburg: Paul Pattloch Verlag, 1957. 386, [1] p., 28 illus.

C0506.
HORENSTEIN, JASCHA. b. May 6, 1898, Kiev, Russia; d. April 2, 1973, London, England.

1. BAKER 7; GROVE 6/8; GROVE-AM 1/2 (Bibliography); MGG/Supp. (Bibliography); PAB-MI/2 (Bibliography); RIEMANN 12 + Supp.

2. GR 48/576; HiFi/MusAm 23/10, 23/16; LGB 13/2.

C0507.
HORN, CHARLES EDWARD. b. June 21, 1786, London, England; d. October 21, 1849, Boston, Massachusetts.

1. BAKER 7; GROVE 6/8 (Bibliography); PAB-MI/2 (Bibliography).

C0508.
van der **HORST, ANTHON.** b. June 20, 1899, Amsterdam; d. March 7, 1965, Hilversum, Holland.

1. BAKER 7; GROVE 6/8; MGG 1/6; RIEMANN 12 + Supp. (Bibliography).

C0509.
HORVAT, MILAN. b. July 28, 1919, Pakrac, Yugoslavia.

1. BAKER 7; GROVE 6/8; RIEMANN 12 + Supp.

C0510.
HOUSELEY, HENRY. b. September 20, 1852, Sutton-in-Ashfield, England; d. March 13, 1925, Denver, Colorado.

1. BAKER 7; GROVE-AM 1/2 (Bibliography); PAB-MI/2 (Bibliography).

5. SEE: Linscome, S.A. A History of Musical Development in Denver, Colorado, 1858-1908. Ph.D. diss., University of Texas, 1970.

C0511.
HOUTMANN, JACQUES. b. March 27, 1935, Mirecourt, France.

1. BAKER 7; PAB-MI/2 (Bibliography); RIEMANN 12/Supp.

C0512.
HOWARTH, ELGAR. b. November 4, 1935, Cannock, Staffordshire, England.

1. BAKER 7; GROVE 6/8; PAB-MI/2 (Bibliography).

C0513.
HUBERT, NICOLAI. b. March 19, 1840, St. Petersburg; d. October 8, 1888, Moscow, Russia.

1. BAKER 7; GROVE 6/7 (under Gubert with Bibliography); RIEMANN 12.

C0514.
HUGHES, ARWEL. b. August 25, 1909, Rhosllanerchrugog, Wales, England.

1. BAKER 7; GROVE 6/8; PAB-MI/2 (Bibliography).

C0515.
HUPPERTS, PAUL. b. January 25, 1919, Gulpen, Holland.

1. BAKER 7; GROVE 6/8; RIEMANN 12.

C0516.
HURST, GEORGE. b. May 20, 1926, Edinburgh, Scotland, England.

1. BAKER 7; GROVE 6/8; PAB-MI/2 (Bibliography).

C0517.
HUSA, KAREL. b. August 7, 1921, Prague, Czechoslovakia.

1. BAKER 7; GROVE 6/8; GROVE-AM 1/2 (Bibliography); MGG/Supp. (Bibliography); PAB-MI/2 (Bibliography); RIEMANN 12 + Supp.

2. MQ 62/1.

C0518.
HUTSCHENRUYTER, WOUTER. b. August 15, 1859, Rotterdam; d. November 14, 1943, The Hague, Holland.

1. BAKER 7; GROVE 6/8 (Bibliography); PAB-MI/2 (Bibliography); RIEMANN 12.

3. He wrote numerous books including Felix Weingartner (1906), De Dirigent (1931), and his memoirs Consonanten en Dessonanten (1930) none of which has been located.

C0519.
HUYBRECHTS, FRANCOIS. b. June 15, 1946, Antwerp, Belgium.

1. BAKER 7; GROVE 6/8; GROVE-AM 1/2.

C0520.
HYE-KNUDSEN, JOHAN. b. May 24, 1896, Nyborg; d. September 28, 1975, Copenhagen, Denmark.

1. BAKER 7; MGG/Supp.; RIEMANN 12 + Supp.

C0521.
ILIEV, KONSTANTIN. b. March 9, 1924, Sofia, Bulgaria.

1. BAKER 7; GROVE 6/9; MGG/Supp. (Bibliography); PAB-MI/2 (Bibliography); RIEMANN 12/Supp. (Bibliography).

C0522.
INBAL, EILAHU. b. February 16, 1936, Jerusalem, Palestine.

1. BAKER 7; GROVE 6/9; PAB-MI/2 (Bibliography); RIEMANN 12/Supp.

C0523.
INGHELBRECHT, DESIRE EMILE. b. September 17, 1880, Paris; d. February 14, 1965, Paris, France.

1. BAKER 7; GROVE 6/9 (Bibliography); MGG/Supp.; PAB-MI/2 (Bibliography); RIEMANN 12 + Supp. (Bibliography).

3. Inghelbrecht, Désiré Emile. Comment on ne doit pas interpréter Carmen, Faust et Pélleas. Paris: Heugel, 1932.

   Inghelbrecht, Désiré Emile. Diabolus in musica: essais sur la musique et ses interprètes. Paris: Etienne Chiron, Editeur, 1933. 220 p.

   Inghelbrecht, Désiré Emile. Le chef d'orchestre et son équipe. Paris: René Julliard, 1949 [The Conductor's World. New York: Library Publishers, 1954]. 239 p.

   Inghelbrecht, Désiré Emile. Le chef d'orchestre: parle au public. Paris: René Julliard, 1957. 227, [2] p., catalogue of works, index of names.

Inghelbrecht, Désiré Emile. Mouvement contraire: souvenirs d'un musician. Paris: Editions Domat, 1947. 337 p., 8 illus.

4. Inghelbrecht, Germaine. D.E. Inghelbrecht et son temps. Neuchâtel: Editions de la Baconnière, 1978. 191 p., 9 illus., discography, list of publications, list of compositions.

5. A0046, B0167.

C0524.
IRVING, ROBERT. b. August 28, 1913, Winchester, England.

1. BAKER 7; GROVE 6/9; GROVE-AM 1/2 (Bibliography); PAB-MI/2 (Bibliography); RIEMANN 12 + Supp.

5. A0003.

C0525.
ITURBI, JOSE. b. November 28, 1895, Valencia, Spain; d. June 28, 1980, Hollywood, California.

1. BAKER 7 (Bibliography); GROVE 6/9; GROVE-AM 1/2; PAB-MI/2 (Bibliography); RIEMANN 12 + Supp.

5. A0010, B0116.

C0526.
JAERNEFELT, ARMAS. b. August 14, 1869, Vyborg, Sweden; d. June 23, 1958, Stockholm, Sweden.

1. BAKER 7; GROVE 6/9; RIEMANN 12 + Supp.

5. A0040.

C0527.
JALAS, JUSSI. b. June 23, 1908, Jyvaeskylae, Finland.

1. BAKER 7; RIEMANN 12 + Supp.

3. Jalas, Jussi. Elaemaeni teemat. Helsinki: Kustannusosakeyhtioe Tammi, 1981. 250, [1] p., 42 illus., index.

C0528.
JAMES, PHILIP. b. May 17, 1890, Jersey City, New Jersey; d. November 1, 1975, Southampton, Long Island, New York.

1. BAKER 7; PAB-MI/2 (Bibliography); RIEMANN 12 + Supp.

C0529.
JANIGRO, ANTONIO. b. January 21, 1918, Milan, Italy.

1. BAKER 7; GROVE 6/9; PAB-MI/2 (Bibliography); RIEMANN 12 + Supp. (Bibliography).

4. Gavoty, Bernard. Antonio Janigro. Geneva: René Kister, 1962. 30,

[2] p., 26 illus., discography as cellist and as conductor.

C0530.
JANSONS, ARVID. b. October 24, 1914, Liepāja, Latvia.

1. GROVE 6/9; REIMANN 12/Supp.

C0531.
JANSSEN, WERNER. b. June 1, 1899, New York City.

1. BAKER 7; GROVE-AM 1/2; PAB-MI/2 (Bibliography); RIEMANN 12 + Supp.

2. New Yorker 10/36, 37.

C0532.
JARECKI, HENRYK. b. December 6, 1846, Warsaw; d December 18, 1918, Warsaw, Poland.

1. BAKER 7; GROVE 6/9 (Bibliography); MGG 1/6 (Bibliography); RIEMANN 12.

C0533.
JARECKI, TADEUSZ. b. December 31, 1888, Lwow, Poland; d. April 29, 1955, New York City.

1. BAKER 7; GROVE 6/9 (Bibliography); GROVE-AM 1/2; MGG 1/6 (Bibliography); PAB-MI/2 (Bibliography); RIEMANN 12.

C0534.
von JAUNER, FRANZ RITTER. b. November 14, 1832, Vienna; d. February 23, 1900, Vienna, Austria.

1. RIEMANN 12.

4. Jauner, Theodor. Fuenf Jahre Wiener Operntheater 1875-1880, Franz Jauner und seine Zeit: eine biographische Erzaehlung seines Neffen. Wien: Herausgegeben im Selbst-Verlag, 1962. [iii], 364 p.

   Jauner, Theodor. '20 Jahre Operette', (1880-1900): Franz Jauner und seine Zeit. Wien: Herausgegeben im Selbst-Verlag, 1966.

C0535.
JENKINS, NEWELL OWEN. b. February 8, 1915, New Haven, Connecticut.

1. BAKER 7; GROVE 6/9; GROVE-AM 1/2; PAB-MI/2 (Bibliography).

C0536.
JEREMIAS, OTAKAR. b. October 17, 1892; Písek; d. March 5, 1962, Prague, Czechoslovakia.

1. BAKER 7; GROVE 6/9 (Bibliography); MGG 1/7 (Bibliography); RIEMANN 12/Supp. (Bibliography).

C0537.
JILEK, FRANTISEK. b. May 22, 1913, Brno, Czechoslovakia.

1. BAKER 7; GROVE 6/9 (Bibliography); PAB-MI/2 (Bibliography); RIEMANN 12/Supp.

C0538.
JIRAK, KAREL BOLESLAV. b. January 28, 1891, Prague, Czechoslovakia; d. January 30, 1972, Chicago, Illinois.

1. BAKER 7; GROVE 6/9 (Bibliography); MGG 1/7 (Bibliography) + Supp.; PAB-MI/2 (Bibliography); RIEMANN 12 + Supp. (Bibliography).

2. MQ 37/2.

5. A0008.

C0539.
JIRASEK, IVO. b. July 16, 1920, Prague, Czechoslovokia.

1. BAKER 7; PAB-MI/2 (Bibliography); RIEMANN 12/Supp.

C0540.
JOACHIM, JOSEPH. b. June 28, 1831, Kittsee, near Pressburg, Germany; d. August 15, 1907, Berlin, Germany.

1. BAKER 7 (Bibliography); GROVE 6/9 (Bibliography); MGG 1/7 (Bibliography); PAB-MI/2 (Bibliography); RIEMANN 12 (Bibliography) + Supp. (Bibliography).

3. Bickley, Nora, ed. Letters from and to Joseph Joachim. Translated by Nora Bickley. London: Macmillan and Co., Limited, 1914. xiii, 470 p., 9 illus., index of names.

   Fuller-Maitland, J.A. Joseph Joachim. London: John Lane, 1905. ix, 63 p., 7 illus.

   Joachim, Johannes and Andreas Moser. Briefe vor und an Joseph Joachim. 3 vols. Berlin: Verlegt von Julius Bard, 1911-1913. Vol. 1 (1842-1857). 476 p., 9 illus.; Vol. 2 (1858-1868). 478 p., 7 illus.; Vol. 3 (1869-1907). 546 p., 9 illus., index.

   Moser, Andreas. Joseph Joachim: ein Lebensbild. Berlin: B. Behr's Verlag (E. Bock), 1898. viii, 301 p., 9 illus.

   Tua, Teresa. Joseph Joachim: ricordi e note. Roma: Nuova Antologia, 1907. 47 p., 5 illus.

C0541.
JOCHUM, EUGEN. b. November 1, 1902, Babenhausen, Bavaria, Germany.

1. BAKER 7; GROVE 6/9; MGG 1/7 (Bibliography); PAB-MI/2 (Bibliography); RIEMANN 12 + Supp.

   The brother of Georg Ludwig and Otto, Eugen Jochum served as the Generalmusikdirektor of the Hamburg Philharmonic (1934-49). His specialty was the music of Bruckner and Mahler.

2. GR 50/591.

5. A0002, A0052, B0110, B0145.

C0542.
JOCHUM, GEORG LUDWIG. b. December 10, 1909, Babenhausen, Bavaria; d. November 1, 1970, Muelheim an der Ruhr, Germany.

1, BAKER 7; GROVE 6/9 (Bibliography); MGG 1/7; RIEMANN 12 + Supp.

C0543.
JOCHUM, OTTO. b. March 18, 1898, Babenhausen, Bavaria; d. November 24, 1969, Bad Reichenhall, Germany.

1. BAKER 7; GROVE 6/9 (Bibliography); MGG 1/7 (Bibliography); RIEMANN 12 + Supp.

C0544.
JOHANOS, DONALD. b. February 10, 1928, Cedar Rapids, Iowa.

1. BAKER 7; GROVE 6/9; GROVE-AM 1/2.

C0545.
JOHNSON, FRANCIS HALL. b. March 12, 1888, Athens, Georgia; d. April 30, 1970, New York City.

1. BAKER 7; GROVE-AM 1/2 (Bibliography); PAB-MI/2 (Bibliography).

5. B0001.

C0546.
JOHNSON, THOR. b. June 10, 1913, Wisconsin Rapids, Wisconsin; d. January 16, 1975, Nashville, Tennessee.

1. BAKER 7; GROVE 6/9; GROVE-AM 1/2 (Bibliography); PAB-MI/2 (Bibliography); RIEMANN 12 + Supp.

5. A0048.

C0547.
JORDA, ENRIQUE. b. March 24, 1911, San Sebastian, Spain.

1. BAKER 7; GROVE 6/9; PAB-MI/2 (Bibliography); RIEMANN 12 + Supp.

3. Jordá, Enrique. El director de orquesta ante la partitura: bosquejo de interpretación de la musica orquestal. Madrid: Editorial Espasa-Calpe, S.A., 1969. 159, [1] p.

   Also listed as A0025.

5. A0040, A0048.

C0548.
JØRGENSEN, POUL. b. October 26, 1934, Copenhagen, Denmark.

1. BAKER 7; PAB-MI/2 (Bibliography); RIEMANN 12/Supp.

C0549.
JOSEPHSON, JACOB AXEL. b. April 27, 1818, Stockholm; d. March 29, 1880, Uppsala, Sweden.

1. BAKER 7; GROVE 6/9 (Bibliography); MGG 1/7 (Bibliography); RIEMANN 12 (Bibliography).

C0550.
JUERGENS, JUERGEN. b. October 5, 1925, Frankfurt/M., Germany.

1. BAKER 7; GROVE 6/9; PAB-MI/2 (Bibliography).

C0551.
JULLIEN, LOUIS ANTOINE. b. April 23, 1812, Sisteron; d. March 14, 1860, Paris, France.

1. BAKER 7 (Bibliography); GROVE 6/9 (Bibliography); PAB-MI/2 (Bibliography).

3. Carse, Adam. *The Life of Jullien: Adventurer, Showman-Conductor and Establisher of the Promenade Concerts in England, Together with a History of Those Concerts up to 1895*. Cambridge: W. Heffer & Sons Ltd., 1951. xi, 136 p., 36 illus., 29-item bibliography, index.

5. B0032, B0085.

SEE: Davison, Henry, ed. *From Mendelssohn to Wagner Being the Memoirs J.W. Davison Forty Years Music Critic of "The Times"*. London: Wm. Reeves, 1912.

SEE: Rivière, Jules. *My Musical Life and Recollections*. London: Marston & Company Limited, 1893. xi, 226 p., portrait.

SEE: Slonimsky, Nicolas. *A Thing or Two about Music*. New York, 1948.

C0552.
KABASTA, OSWALD. b. December 29, 1896, Mistelbach; d. February 6, 1946, Kufstein, Austria.

1. BAKER 7; MGG 1/7 (Bibliography); RIEMANN 12.

C0553.
KAJANUS, ROBERT. b. December 2, 1856, Helsinki; d. July 6, 1933, Helsinki, Finland.

1. BAKER 7; GROVE 6/9 (Bibliography); MGG 1/7 (Bibliography); RIEMANN 12 + Supp. (Bibliography).

4. Suomalainen, Yrjoe. *Robert Kajanus: Haenen Elaemaensae ja toimintansa*. Helsingissae: Kustannusosakeyhitoe Otava, 1952. 284 p., 55 illus., list of compositions, index of names.

5. A0040.

C0554.
KALNINS, JANIS. b. November 2, 1904, Pernav, Latvia.

1. BAKER 7; GROVE 6/9 (Bibliography); PAB-MI/2 (Bibliography).

C0555.
KAMU, OKKO. b. March 7, 1946, Helsinki, Finland.

1. BAKER 7; GROVE 6/9; PAB-MI/2 (Bibliography); RIEMANN 12/Supp.

C0556.
KAPLAN, ABRAHAM. b. May 5, 1931, Tel-Aviv, Palestine.

1. GROVE-AM 1/2; PAB-MI/2 (Bibliography).

C0557.
KARABATCHEVSKY, ISAAC. b. December 27, 1934, São Paulo, Brazil.

1. BAKER 7; REIMANN 12/Supp.

C0558.
von KARAJAN, HERBERT. b. April 5, 1908, Salzburg, Austria.

1. BAKER 7; GROVE 6/9 (Bibliography); MGG 1/7 (Bibliography); PAB-MI/2 (Bibliography); RIEMANN 12 + Supp. (Bibliography).

2. GR 49/582, 55/659, 58/689, 59/701, 60/719, 62/736; HiFi/MusAm 20/3, 22/5, 28/1; ON 26/14, 35/5; OPERA 23/5, 25/6, 29/5, 6; OW 1/1, 3/3, 3/9, 5/1, 8/5, 9/5, 12/5, 13/5, 15/4, 24/4; OPER 1966: ein Jahrbuch der Zeitschrift "Opernwelt".

4. Bachmann, Robert C. Karajan: Anmerkungen zu einer Karriere. Duesseldorf: Econ Verlag GmbH, 1983. 398, [1] p., 11 illus., 381-item bibliography, index of names.

   Fuhrich-Leisler, Edda and Gisela Prossnitz, comps. Herbert von Karajan in Salzburg: Ausstellung 17, Maerz bis 16. April 1978, Salzburg, Schloss Arenberg. Salzburg: Max-Reinhardt-Forschungs- und Gedenkstaette, 1978. 102 p., 45 illus., chronology, catalogue of 581 exhibit items.

   Gavoty, Bernard. Herbert von Karajan. Translated by F.E. Richardson. Geneva: René Kister, 1966. 30, [2] p., 20 illus., list of records.

   Haeusserman, Ernst. Herbert von Karajan: Biographie. Guetersloh: C. Bertelsmann Verlag, 1968. 319, [1] p., 37 illus., discography by Robert Werba, index.

   Haeusserman, Ernst. Herbert von Karajan. Wien: Verlag Fritz Molden, 1978. 311, [1] p., 41 illus., Herbert-von-Karajan Stiftung publications, film and TV productions, discography, index of names.

   Herzfeld, Friedrich. Herbert von Karajan. Berlin: Rembrandt Verlag, 1959. 63 p., 28 illus.

Loebl, Karl. Das Wunder Karajan. Bayreuth: Hestia Verlag GmbH, 1965. 105, [2] p., 37 illus.

Lorcey, Jacques. Herbert von Karajan. Paris: Editions PAC, 1978. 255, [4] p., 52 illus., discography.

Robinson, Paul. Karajan. Toronto: Lester and Orpen Limited, 1975. 154 p., 11 illus., discography by Bruce Surtees, index.

Simon, Walter C., ed. Mensch und Musik: Festschrift fuer Herbert von Karajan. Salzburg: Muller, 1979. 108 p.

Spiel, Christian, comp. Anekdoten um Herbert von Karajan. Muenchen: Bechtle Verlag, 1968. 87, [1] p., chronology.

Vaughan, Roger. Herbert von Karajan: a Biographical Portrait. New York: W.W. Norton & Co., 1986. 274 p., 31-item bibliography, index.

5. A0002, A0004, A0016, A0031, A0040, A0050, A0052, B0016, B0021, B0030, B0063, B0067, B0069, B0091, B0092, B0114, B0117, B0122, B0124, B0125, B0142, B0144, B0157.

SEE: Lipman, Samuel. The House of Music: Art in an Era of Institutions. Boston: David R. Godine, Publisher. 1984.

SEE: Riemann, Victor. Dirigenten, Stars und Buerokraten: Glanz und Abstieg des Wiener Opernensembles. Wien: Hans Deutsch Verlag, A.G., 1961. 283 p., 23 illus.

SEE: WOLFGANG STRESEMAN (C1105.4).

C0559.
KASLIK, VACLAV. b. September 28, 1917, Poličná, Czechoslovakia.

1. BAKER 7; EdS/Supp.; GROVE 6/9; MGG/Supp. (Bibliography); PAB-MI/2 (Bibliography); RIEMANN 12/Supp.

C0560.
KASTALSKY, ALEXANDER DMITRIYEVICH. b. November 28, 1856, Moscow; d. December 17, 1926, Moscow.

1. BAKER 7 (Bibliography); GROVE 6/9 (Bibliography); MGG 1/7 (Bibliography); RIEMANN 12 + Supp. (Bibliography).

2. MQ 11/2.

4. St. Beckwith, Ruth. Alexander Dimitri Kastalsky and the Quest for a Native Russian Choral Style. Ph.D. diss., Cornell University, 1969.

C0561.
KATIMS, MILTON. b. June 24, 1909, New York City.

1. BAKER 7; GROVE 6/9; GROVE-AM 1/2; PAB-MI/2 (Bibliography).

5. B0138.

C0562.
KAUFMANN, WALTER. b. April 1, 1907, Karlsbad, Germany; d. September 9, 1984, Bloomington, Indiana.

1. BAKER 7 (Bibliography); GROVE 6/9; GROVE-AM 1/2; MGG 1/7; PAB-MI/2 (Bibliography); RIEMANN 12 + Supp.

4. Noblitt, Thomas, ed. Music East and West: Essays in Honor of Walter Kaufmann. New York: Pendragon Press, 1980. viii, 403 p., bibliography of Kaufmann's works, index.

C0563.
KAZANDJIEV, VASIL. b. September 10, 1934, Ruse, Bulgaria.

1. BAKER 7; GROVE 6/9; RIEMANN 12/Supp.

C0564.
KEENE, CHRISTOPHER. b. December 21, 1946, Berkeley, California.

1. BAKER 7; GROVE-AM 1/2; PAB-MI/2 (Bibliography).

2. HiFi/MusAm 30/2.

C0565.
KEGEL, HERBERT. b. July 29, 1920, Dresden, Germany.

1. BAKER 7; RIEMANN 12/Supp.

C0566.
KEHR, GUENTER. b. March 16, 1920, Darmstadt, Germany.

1. BAKER 7; RIEMANN 12 + Supp.

C0567.
KEILBERTH, JOSEPH. b. April 19, 1908, Karlsruhe; d. July 20, 1968, Munich, Germany.

1. BAKER 7; GROVE 6/9 (Bibliography); MGG 1/7 (Bibliography) + Supp. (Bibliography); PAB-MI/2 (Bibliography); RIEMANN 12 + Supp. (Bibliography).

2. OPERA 19/10; OW 2/13.

4. von Lewinski, Wolf-Eberhard. Joseph Keilberth. Berlin: Rembrandt Verlag GmbH, 1968. 57, [4] p., 30 illus.

   Trauerfeier fuer Generalmusikdirektor Joseph Keilberth am 28. Juli 1968 im Nationaltheater. Muenchen: Intendanz der Bayrischen Staatsoper Muenchen, 1968. unpaginated [12 p.], 6 illus.

5. A0052, B0063, B0145.

C0568.
KELDORFER, ROBERT. b. August 10, 1901, Vienna; d. September 13, 1980, Klagenfurt, Austria.

1. BAKER 7; MGG 1/7 (Bibliography); PAB-MI/2 (Bibliography); RIEMANN 12 + Supp. (Bibliography).

C0569.
KELDORFER, VIKTOR JOSEF. b. April 14, 1873, Salzburg; d. January 28, 1959, Vienna, Austria.

1. BAKER 7; GROVE 6/9 (Bibliography); MGG 1/7 (Bibliography); RIEMANN 12 + Supp.

C0570.
KEMPE, RUDOLF. b. June 14, 1910, Niederpoyritz, near Dresden, Germany; d. May 11, 1976, Zurich, Switzerland.

1. BAKER 7; GROVE 6/9 (Bibliography); MGG 1/7 (Bibliography); PAB-MI/2 (Bibliography); RIEMANN 12 + Supp.

2. GR 51/609; LGB 15/1-2; ON 19/12; OPERA 10/11; OW 17/6.

4. Kempe-Oettinger, Cordula, comp. Rudolf Kempe: Pictures of a Life. Preface by Dietrich Fischer-Dieskau. Munich: Paul List Verlag, 1979. 180 p., 179 illus., discography by Charles Blyth and Denham Ford.

   Jaeckel, Hildegard and Gottfried Schmiedel. Bildnis des schaffenden Kuenstlers: ein Dirigent bei der Arbeit. Leipzig: VEB Breitkopf & Haertel Musikverlag, 1954. unpaginated [95 p.], 24 portraits, music.

5. A0052, B0063, B0101, B0145.

C0571.
van KEMPEN, PAUL. b. May 16, 1893, Zoeterwonde; d. December 8, 1955, Amsterdam, Holland.

1. BAKER 7 (under Kemper); GROVE 6/9 (Bibliography); MGG 1/7 (Bibliography); RIEMANN 12 + Supp. (Bibliography).

C0572.
KERSJES, ANTON. b. August 17, 1923, Arnhem, Holland.

1. BAKER 7; GROVE 6/10.

C0573.
KERTESZ, ISTVAN. b. August 28, 1929, Budapest, Hungary; d. April 16, 1973, Kfar Saba, Israel.

1. BAKER 7; GROVE 6/10; PAB-MI/2 (Bibliography); RIEMANN 12/Supp.

2. GR 45/536; OW 3/10.

4. Richter, Karl, ed. István Kertész. Augsburg: Schroff-Druck Verlagsgesellschaft mbH, 1974. 180, [1] p., 62 illus., discography, new productions; list of orchestras conducted.

5. A0052.

C0574.
KES, WILLEM. b. February 16, 1856, Dordrecht, Holland; d. February 21, 1934, Munich, Germany.

1. BAKER 7; GROVE 6/10 (Bibliography); MGG 1/7 (Bibliography); PAB-MI/2 (Bibliography); RIEMANN 12.

C0575.
KETTING, PIET. b. November 29, 1905, Haarlem, Holland.

1. BAKER 7; GROVE 6/10 (Bibliography); MGG/Supp.; RIEMANN 12 + Supp.

C0576.
KEURVELS, EDWARD. b. March 8, 1853, Antwerp, Belgium; d. January 29, 1916, Eckeren, near Antwerp, Belgium.

1. BAKER 7; GROVE 6/10 (Bibliography); RIEMANN 12 + Supp. (Bibliography).

C0577.
von KEUSSLER, GERHARD. b. July 5, 1874, Schwanenburg, Latvia; d. August 21, 1949, Niederwartha, near Dresden, Germany.

1. BAKER 7; GROVE 6/10 (Bibliography); MGG 1/7 (Bibliography); RIEMANN 12 (Bibliography) + Supp. (Bibliography).

C0578.
KHAIKIN, BORIS. b. October 26, 1904, Minsk; d. May 10, 1978, Moscow, Russia.

1. BAKER 7; GROVE 6/10 (Bibliography).

C0579.
KIELLAND, OLAV. b. August 16, 1901, Trondheim, Norway.

1. BAKER 7 (Bibliography); PAB-MI/2 (Bibliography); RIEMANN 12 + Supp.

C0580.
KILBURN, NICHOLAS. b. February 7, 1843, Bishop Auckland, Durham; d. December 4, 1923, Bishop Auckland, Durham, England.

1. BAKER 7 (Bibliography); RIEMANN 12.

C0581.
KINDLER, HANS. b. January 8, 1892, Rotterdam, Holland; d. August 30, 1949, Watch Hill, Rhode Island.

1. BAKER 7; GROVE-AM 1/2 (Bibliography); PAB-MI/2 (Bibliography); RIEMANN 12 + Supp. (Bibliography).

3. Materials relating to his life and career are housed in the District of Columbia Public Library.

4. Butkovich, Mary Virginia. Hans Kindler, 1893-1949. Ph.D. diss., Catholic University of America, 1965. xi, 488 p.

5. A0010.

C0582.
KIRBY, PERCIVAL ROBSON. b. April 17, 1887, Aberdeen, Scotland; d. February 7, 1970, Grahamstown, South Africa.

1. GROVE 6/10 (Bibliography); PAB-MI/2 (Bibliography).

3. Kirby, Percival. Wits End: an Unconventional Autobiography. Cape Town: Howard Timmins, 1967. 371 p., 20 illus., index of names, chronology.

C0583.
KITTEL, BRUNO. b. May 26, 1870, Entenbruch, near Posen; d. March 10, 1948, Wasserberg, near Cologne, Germany.

1. BAKER 7; RIEMANN 12.

C0584.
KITZLER, OTTO. b. March 16, 1834, Dresden, Germany; d. September 6, 1915, Graz, Austria.

1. BAKER 7; RIEMANN 12 (Bibliography).

C0585.
KLEE, BERNHARD. b. April 19, 1936, Schleiz, Germany.

1. BAKER 7; PAB-MI/2 (Bibliography); RIEMANN 12/Supp.

C0586.
KLEFFEL, ARNO. b. September 4, 1840, Poessneck; d. July 15, 1913, Nikolassee, near Berlin, Germany.

1. BAKER 7; RIEMANN 12.

C0587.
KLEIBER, CARLOS. b. July 3, 1930, Berlin, Germany.

1. BAKER 7; GROVE 6/10; PAB-MI/2 (Bibliography); RIEMANN 12/Supp.

2. GR 54/640; OW 9/12, 10/11, 13/7, 14/7.

5. A0031, B0063.

C0588.
KLEIBER, ERICH. b. August 5, 1890, Vienna, Austria; d. January 27, 1956, Zurich, Switzerland.

1. BAKER 7; EdS 1/6; GROVE 6/10 (Bibliography); MGG 1/7 (Bibliography); PAB-MI/2 (Bibliography); RIEMANN 12 + Supp. (Bibliography).

2. GR 63/751; OPERA 3/1, 8/10, 11, 12.

4. Freund, Georg. Erich Kleiber: artista luchador. Montevideo: p.p., 1940. 31 p.

Russell, John. Erich Kleiber: a Memoir. London: Andre Deutsch Limited, 1957. 256 p., 5 illus., list of recordings available in Great Britian, index.

Interesting comments on Klemperer, Mahler, and Toscanini.

5. A0002, B0030, B0047, B0109, B0129, B0167.

SEE: Barzun, Jacques. Critical Questions on Music and Letters, Culture and Biography 1940-1980. Chicago: The University of Chicago Press, 1982.

SEE: Haltrecht, Montague. The Quiet Showman: Sir David Webster and the Royal Opera House. London: William Collins Sons and Co Ltd., 1975. 319 p., 26 illus., index.

C0589.
KLEIN, KENNETH. b. September 5, 1939, Los Angeles, California.

1. BAKER 7; GROVE-AM 1/2 (Bibliography); PAB-MI/2 (Bibliography).

C0590.
KLEMPERER, OTTO. b. May 14, 1885, Breslau; d. July 6, 1973, Zurich.

1. BAKER 7; EdS 1/6 (Bibliography); GROVE 6/10; GROVE-AM 1/2 (Bibliography); MGG 1/7 (Bibliography); PAB-MI/2 (Bibliography); RIEMANN 12 + Supp. (Bibliography)

2. GR 47/564, 51/603, 51/607, 608, 62/744; HiFi/MusAm 20/3; ON 35/2; OPERA 12/2, OW 6/5, 10/5.

3. Klemperer, Otto. Meine Erinnerungen an Gustav Mahler und andere autobiographische Skizzen. Zuerich: Atlantis Verlag AG, 1960. 47, [1] p.

   Klemperer, Otto. Minor Recollections. Translated by J. Maxwell Brownjohn. London: Dennis Dobson Books Ltd., 1964. 124 p., 10 illus., discography by F.F. Clough and G.J. Cuming, index.

4. Attila, Boros. Klemperer: magyarországon. Budapest: Zenemuekiadó, 1984. 143, [2] p., 40 illus., list of performances 1947-1950.

   There is an earlier edition of this work published in 1973.

   Heyworth, Peter, ed. Conversations with Klemperer. London: Victor Gollancz Ltd, 1973 [rev. ed. 1985 with expanded and corrected footnotes]. 128 p., 40 illus., discography compiled by Malcolm Walker, index.

   Heyworth, Peter. Otto Klemperer His Life and Times: Volume I, 1885-1933. Cambridge: Cambridge University Press, 1983. xvii, 492 p., 38 illus., notes, biographical glossary of 36 luminaries, discography by Michael H. Gray, index by Frederick Smyth.

   The index is a model of clarity, organization, and helpfulness!

Osborne, Charles and Kenneth Thomson, eds. Klemperer Stories: Anecdotes, Sayings and Impressions of Otto Klemperer. London: Robson Books Ltd, 1980. 96 p., 15 illus., chronology.

Stompor, Stephan, ed. Otto Klemperer ueber Musik und Theater: Erinnerungen--Gespraeche--Skizzen. Berlin: Henschelverlag, 1982. 153, [16] p., 28 illus., chronology, sources, index.

Stompor, Stephan. "'Die Idee kann Man nicht toeten!...' Otto Klemperer und die Berliner Kroll-Oper, 1927-31." Jahrbuch der Komischen Oper Berlin III. Berlin: Henschelverlag, 1963: 145-72.

5. A0002, A0004, A0007, A0016, A0052, B0021, B0022, B0047, B0054, B0069, B0122, B0138, B0157.

SEE: Curjel, Hans. Experiment Krolloper 1927-1931. Muenchen: Prestel-Verlag, 1975.

SEE: George, Earl of Harewood under CARLO MARIA GIULINI (C0399.5).

C0591.
von KLENAU, PAUL AUGUST. b. February 11, 1883, Copenhagen; d. August 31, 1946, Copenhagen, Denmark.

1. BAKER 7; EdS 1/6; GROVE 6/10 (Bibliography); MGG 1/7; PAB-MI/2 (Bibliography); RIEMANN 12.

C0592.
KLENGEL, PAUL. b. May 13, 1854, Leipzig; d. April 24, 1935, Leipzig, Germany.

1. BAKER 7; GROVE 6/10; MGG 1/7 (Bibliography); PAB-MI/2 (Bibliography); RIEMANN 12.

C0593.
KLETZKI, PAUL. b. March 21, 1900, Lodz, Poland; d. March 5, 1973, Liverpool, England.

1. BAKER 7; GROVE 6/10; MGG 1/7; PAB-MI/2 (Bibliography); RIEMANN 12 (under Klecki with bibliography) + Supp.

5. A0002, A0040.

C0594.
KLIMOV, MIKHAIL. b. October 21, 1881, Moscow; d. February 20, 1937, Zavidovo, near Tver, Russia.

1. BAKER 7 (Bibliography); GROVE 6/10 (Bibliography); RIEMANN 12 + Supp.

C0595.
KLITZSCH, KARL EMANUEL. b. October 30, 1812, Schoenhaide; d. March 5, 1889, Zwickau, Germany.

1. BAKER 7; RIEMANN 12.

C0596.
KLOBUCAR, BERISLAV. b. August 28, 1924, Zagreb, Yugoslavia.

1. BAKER 7; PAB-MI/2 (Bibliography); RIEMANN 12/Supp.

2. ON 32/13.

C0597.
KNAPE, WALTER. b. January 14, 1906, Bernburg an der Saale, Germany.

1. BAKER 7; GROVE 6/10 (Bibliography).

C0598.
KNAPPERTSBUSCH, HANS. b. March 12, 1888, Elberfeld; d. October 25, 1965, Munich, Germany.

1. BAKER 7; EdS 1/6; GROVE 6/10 (Bibliography); MGG 1/7 (Bibliography); PAB-MI/2 (Bibliography); RIEMANN 12 + Supp. (Bibliography).

2. OPERA 17/1, OW 1/3, 3/4.

4. Betz, Rudolf and Walter Panofsky. Knappertsbusch. Ingolstadt: Verlag Donau Kurier, n.d. [1958]. unpaginated [67 p.], 44 illus., list of world premieres, first performances at the Bayerischen Staatsoper, repertoire

   Hans Knappertsbusch: Bayreuther Festspieldirigent 1951-1964. Muenchen: Ausstellung der Bayerischen Vereinsbank, 1977. 16 p.

   Knappertsbusch, W.G. Die Knappertsbusch und ihre Vorfahren. Elberfeld: Breitkopf-fraktur, 1943. 385 p., 23 illus., 64-item bibliography, index of names.

5. A0002, A0052, B0030, B0031, B0063, B0069, B0103, B0114.

C0599.
KNIESE, JULIUS. b. December 21, 1848, Roda, near Jena; d. April 22, 1905, Dresden, Germany.

1. BAKER 7; RIEMANN 12.

3. His daughter Julie published his 1883 diary as Der Kampf zweier Welten um das Bayreuther Erbe. Leipzig, 1931.

C0600.
KNITTL, KAREL. b. October 4, 1853, Polna, Bohemia; d. March 17, 1907, Prague, Czechoslovakia.

1. BAKER 7; GROVE 6/10 (Bibliography); RIEMANN 12.

C0601.
KOCH, HELMUT. b. April 5, 1908, Wuppertal-Barmen; d. January 26, 1975, Berlin, Germany.

1. BAKER 7; GROVE 6/10; RIEMANN 12 + Supp. (Bibliography).

C0602.
KOETSIER, JAN. b. August 14, 1911, Amsterdam, Holland.

1. BAKER 7; GROVE 6/10; PAB-MI/2 (Bibliography); RIEMANN 12/Supp.

C0603.
KOGEL, GUSTAV FRIEDRICH. b. January 16, 1849, Leipzig; d. November 13, 1921, Frankfurt/M., Germany.

1. BAKER 7; RIEMANN 12.

C0604.
KOJIAN, VARUJAN. b. March 12, 1935, Beirut, Lebanon.

1. BAKER 7; GROVE-AM 1/2; PAB-MI/2 (Bibliography).

C0605.
KOLAR, VICTOR. b. February 12, 1888, Budapest, Hungary; d. June 16, 1957, Detroit, Michigan.

1. BAKER 7; GROVE-AM 1/2; PAB-MI/2 (Bibliography); RIEMANN 12.

5. A0010.

C0606.
KONDRASHIN, KIRILL. b. March 6, 1914, Moscow, Russia; d. March 7, 1981, Amsterdam, Holland.

1. BAKER 7; GROVE 6/10 (Bibliography); PAB-MI/2 (Bibliography); RIEMANN 12/Supp. (Bibliography).

2. LGB 18/3-4.

3. Kondrashin, Kirill. Mir dirizera: tehnologija vdohnovenija. Leningrad: Muzyka, 1976. 189, [3] p., musical examples.

   Author of a book on the art of conducting (Leningrad, 1970), he was the first Soviet conductor to appear in America (1958).

5. B0142.

C0607.
KONOYE, HIDEMARO. b. November 18, 1898, Tokyo, Japan; d. June 2, 1973, Tokyo, Japan.

1. BAKER 7; PAB-MI/2 (Bibliography); RIEMANN 12 + Supp.

   Principal conductor, New Symphony Orchestra in Tokyo (1926-34).

C0608.
KONTARSKY, BERNHARD. b. April 26, 1937, Westphalia, Germany.

1. BAKER 7; RIEMANN 12/Supp.

C0609.
KONWITSCHNY, FRANZ. b. August 14, 1901, Fulnek, Czechoslovakia; d. July 28, 1962, Belgrade, Yugoslavia.

1. BAKER 7; GROVE 6/10; MGG 1/7 (Bibliography); PAB-MI/2 (Bibliography); RIEMANN 12 + Supp. (Bibliography).

2. OW 2/12.

4. Sanders, H.S., ed. Vermaechtnis und Verpflichtung: Festschrift fuer Franz Konwitschny zum 60. Geburtstag. Leipzig: Deutscher Verlag fuer Musik, 1961. 94, [37] p., 66 illus.

C0610.
KORODI, ANDRAS. b. May 24, 1922, Budapest, Hungary.

1. BAKER 7; GROVE 6/10.

C0611.
KOSLER, ZDENEK. b. March 25, 1928, Prague, Czechoslovakia.

1. BAKER 7; GROVE 6/10 (Bibliography); PAB-MI/2 (Bibliography); RIEMANN 12/Supp.

C0612.
KOSTELANETZ, ANDRE. b. December 22, 1901, St. Petersburg, Russia; d. January 13, 1980, Port-au-Prince, Haiti.

1. BAKER 7; GROVE 6/10; GROVE-AM 1/2; PAB-MI/2 (Bibliography); RIEMANN 12 + Supp.

2. ON 37/25.

3. Kostelanetz, Andre and Gloria Hammond. Echoes: Memoirs of Andre Kostelanetz. New York: Harcourt Brace Jovanovich, Publishers, 1981. 247 p., 79 illus., index.

5. B0138.

C0613.
KOUSSEVITZKY, SERGE. b. July 26, 1874, Vishny-Volochok, Russia; d. June 4, 1951, Boston, Massachusetts.

1. BAKER 7 (Bibliography); GROVE 6/10 (Bibliography); GROVE-AM 1/2 (Bibliography); MGG 1/7 (under Kussewitzky with bibliography); PAB-MI/2 (Bibliography); RIEMANN 12 (under Kussewitzky) + Supp. (Bibliography).

2. HiFi 28/10; MQ 15/4, 16/1, 24/3, 26/1, 29/3, 31/2, 33/2, 34/1, 35/1, 4, 40/4.

3. There is substantial material in the Special Collection at the Library of Congress in Washington, D.C. and also in the Serge Koussevitzky Archive in the Boston Public Library.

4. Leichtentritt, Hugo. Serge Koussevitzky: the Boston Symphony Orchestra and the New American Music. Cambridge: Harvard University Press, 1946. 199 p., portrait, index.

   Lourié, Arthur. Sergei Koussevitzky and His Epoch: a Biographical Chronicle. New York: Alfred A. Knopf, 1931. Reprint 1969, 1971. xiv, 253, v p., 16 illus., index.

   Press Comments on the Retirement of Serge Koussevitzky (Summer of 1949) and the Engagement of Charles Munch (Autumn of 1949) as Conductor of the Boston Symphony Orchestra. Boston: Boston Symphony Orchestra, 1949. Unpaginated mimeo [19 p.].

   Smith, Moses. Koussevitzky. New York: Allen, Towne & Heath, Inc., 1947. x, [ii], 400 p., 12 illus., list of world premieres, compositions by American composers, compositions commissioned by the Koussevitzky Music Foundation, discography, index.

   Koussevitzky filed suit charging invasion of privacy, but lost!

5. A0004, A0010, A0012, A0022, A0045, B0008, B0017, B0038, B0040, B0044, B0048, B0060, B0086, B0116, B0123, B0128, B0138, B0159, B0161, B0166.

   SEE: Autobiography of BORIS GOLDOVSKY (C0410.3).

   SEE: Nabokov, Nicolas. Old Friends and New Music. Boston: Little, Brown and Company, 1951. 294 p., index.

C0614.
KOVAROVIK, KAREL. b. December 9, 1862, Prague; d. December 6, 1920, Prague, Czachoslovakia.

1. BAKER 7; GROVE 6/10; MGG 1/7 (Bibliography); PAB-MI/2 (bibliography); RIEMANN 12 (Bibliography) + Supp. (Bibliography).

C0615.
KRAUSE, THEODOR. b. May 1, 1833, Halle; d. December 12, 1910, Berlin.

1. BAKER 7; RIEMANN 12 (Bibliography).

3. Wrote a book on sight-singing based on the movable "do" as well as Ueber Musik und Musiker. Berlin, 1900.

C0616.
KRAUSS, CLEMENS. b. March 31, 1893, Vienna, Austria; d. May 16, 1954, Mexico City, Mexico.

1. BAKER 7; EdS 1/6; GROVE 6/10 (Bibliography); PAB-MI/2 (Bibliography); MGG 1/7; RIEMANN 12.

2. OPERA 5/2, RS 42/3.

4. Berger, Anton. Clemens Krauss. Graz: Leuschner & Lubensky's Universitaets-Buchhandlung, 1929. 3rd rev. ed. 107, [1] p., 3 illus.

Gregor, Joseph. Clemens Krauss: seine musikalische Sendung. Wien: Walter Krieg Verlag, 1953. 185, [1] p., 28 illus.

Kende, Goetz Klaus. Hoechste Leistung aus begeistertem Herzen: Clemens Krauss als Direktor der Wiener Staatsoper. Salzburg: Residenz Verlag, 1971. 160, [4] p., 41 illus., list of names with biographical information, list of operatic premieres 1929-1934.

von Pander, Oscar. Clemens Krauss in Muenchen. Muenchen: Verlag C.H. Beck, 1955. 132 p., 47 illus., chronology, list of new productions with major artists 1937-1943, concerts in Munich 1937-1944.

5. A0002, A0052, B0063, B0069, B0114.

C0617.
KREJCI, ISA. b. July 10, 1904, Prague; d. March 6, 1968, Prague.

1. BAKER 7; GROVE 6/10 (Bibliography); MGG 1/7 (Bibliography) + Supp.; PAB-MI/2 (Bibliography); RIEMANN 12 + Supp.; (Bibliography).

C0618.
KRENZ, JAN. b. July 14, 1926, Wloclawek, Poland.

1. BAKER 7; GROVE 6/10 (Bibliography); PAB-MI/2 (Bibliography); RIEMANN 12 + Supp. (Bibliography).

4. Kydryński, Lucjan. Jan Krenz. Kraków: Polskie Wydawnictwo Muzyczne, 1960. 42 p., 22 illus., discography.

5. A0050.

C0619.
KREUBE, CHARLES FREDERIC. b. November 5, 1777, Luneville, France; d.1846, near St.-Denis, France.

1. BAKER 7; MGG 1/7 (Bibliography); RIEMANN 12.

C0620.
KREUTZER, RODOLPHE. b. November 16, 1766, Versailles, France; d. January 6, 1831, Geneva, Switzerland.

1. BAKER 7; GROVE 6/10; MGG 1/7 (Bibliography); PAB-MI/2 (Bibliography); RIEMANN 12 (Bibliography) + Supp. (Bibliography).

4. Hardy, Joseph. Rodolphe Kreutzer: sa jeunesse a Versailles 1766-1789. Paris: Librairie Fischbacher, 1910. 70 p., 4 illus.

5. B0036.

C0621.
KRIPS, HENRY. b. February 10, 1912, Vienna, Austria.

1. BAKER 7; GROVE 6/10; PAB-MI/2 (Bibliography); RIEMANN 12 + Supp.

5. B0053.

C0622.
KRIPS, JOSEPH. b. April 8, 1902, Vienna; d. October 13, 1974, Geneva.

1. BAKER 7; EdS 1/6; GROVE 6/10; GROVE-AM 1/2 (Bibliography); PAB-MI/2 (Bibliography); RIEMANN 12 + Supp.

   A major figure in the Viennese musical revival after World War Two.

2. ON 35/21, OW 15/8, 11.

5. A0002, A0048, A0052, B0030, B0069, B0132, B0158.

C0623.
KROMBHOLC, JAROSLAV. b. January 30, 1918, Prague; d. July 16, 1983, Prague, Czechoslovakia.

1. BAKER 7; GROVE 6/10 (Bibliography); RIEMANN 12/Supp.

C0624.
KRUEGER, KARL. b. January 19, 1894, Atchinson, Kansas; d. July 21, 1979, Elgin, Illinois.

1. BAKER 7; GROVE-AM 1/2; PAB-MI/2 (Bibliography); RIEMANN 12 + Supp.

3. Krueger, Karl. The Musical Heritage of the United States: the Unknown Portion. New York: Society for the Preservation of American Musical Heritage, Inc., 1973. 237 p., 28 illus., index of names.

   Krueger was the first American born conductor to serve as permanent head of a major orchestra (Detroit Symphony 1943-49). This volume includes short biographies of Carl Bergmann, F.H. Damrosch, W.J. Damrosch, von Buelow, Wilhelm Gericke, Nikisch, Seidl, Emil Paur, Ernst von Schuch, Mottl, Fritz Scheel, Vassily Safonoff, Mahler, Toscanini, Muck, and Weingartner.

   Krueger, Karl. The Way of the Conductor: His Origins, Purpose, and Procedures. New York: Charles Scribner's Sons, 1958. 250 p., index. Also listed as A0029.

5. A0010.

C0625.
KRUG, WENZEL JOSEF. b. November 8, 1858, Waldsee; d. October 8, 1915, Magdeburg, Germany.

1. BAKER 7; MGG 1/7 (Bibliography); RIEMANN 12.

C0626.
KRUSE, GEORG RICHARD. b. January 17, 1856, Greiffenberg; d. February 23, 1944, Berlin, Germany.

1. BAKER 7; RIEMANN 12.

C0627.
KUBELIK, RAFAEL. b. June 29, 1914, Bychory, near Kolin, Czechoslovakia.

1. BAKER 7; GROVE 6/10 (Bibliography); GROVE-AM 1/2 (Bibliography); MGG 1/7 (Bibliography); PAB-MI/2 (Bibliography); RIEMANN 12 + Supp. (Bibliography).

5. A0040, A0052, B0104, B0145.

SEE: Montague Haltrecht under ERICH KLEIBER (C0588.5).

C0628.
KUECKEN, FRIEDRICH. b. November 16, 1810, Bleckede; d. April 3, 1882, Schwerin, Germany.

1. BAKER 7; GROVE 6/10 (Bibliography); MGG 1/7 (Bibliography); RIEMANN 12 (Bibliography) + Supp. (Bibliography).

C0629.
KULKA, JANOS. b. December 11, 1929, Budapest, Hungary.

1. BAKER 7; PAB-MI/2 (Bibliography); RIEMANN 12/Supp.

C0630.
KUNSEMUELLER, ERNST. b. June 24, 1885, Rehme; d. April 25, 1918, Duesseldorf, Germany.

1. BAKER 7; RIEMANN 12.

C0631.
KUNWALD, ERNST. b. April 14, 1868, Vienna; d. December 12, 1939, Vienna, Austria.

1. BAKER 7; RIEMANN 12.

C0632.
KUNZ, ERNST. b. June 2, 1891, Bern, Switzerland.

1. BAKER 7; GROVE 6/10; MGG 1/7; RIEMANN 12 + Supp.

C0633.
KUNZEL, ERICH. b. March 21, 1935, New York City.

1. BAKER 7; GROVE-AM 1/2.

C0634.
KURTZ, EFREM. b. November 7, 1900, St. Petersburg, Russia.

1. BAKER 7; GROVE 6/10; PAB-MI/2 (Bibliography); RIEMANN 12 + Supp.

C0635.
KURZ, SIEGFRIED. b. July 18, 1930, Dresden, Germany.

1. BAKER 7; GROVE 6/10; PAB-MI/2 (Bibliography); RIEMANN 12/Supp.

C0636.
KUTZSCHBACH, HERMANN LUDWIG. b. August 30, 1875, Meissen; d. February 9, 1938, Dresden, Germany.

1. BAKER 7; RIEMANN 12.

C0637.
KUYPER, ELISABETH. b. September 13, 1877, Amsterdam, Holland; d. February 26, 1953, Lugano, Italy.

1. BAKER 7; RIEMANN 12.

C0638.
LABEY, MARCEL. b. August 6, 1875, Le Vésinet, Seine-et-Oise; d. November 25, 1968, Nancy, France.

1. BAKER 7; GROVE 6/10; MGG 1/8 (Bibliography); RIEMANN 12 (Bibliography).

C0639.
LABITZKY, AUGUST. b. October 22, 1832, Petschau; d. August 28, 1903, Reichenhall, Germany.

1. BAKER 7; GROVE 6/10 (Bibliography); MGG 1/8 (Bibliography); RIEMANN 12.

C0640.
LACHNER, FRANZ PAUL. b. April 2, 1803, Rain-am-Lech; d. January 20, 1890, Munich, Germany.

1. BAKER 7; EdS 1/6; GROVE 6/10; MGG 1/8 (Bibliography); PAB-MI/2 (Bibliography); RIEMANN 12 (Bibliography) + Supp. (Bibliography).

C0641.
LACHNER, IGNAZ. b. September 11, 1807, Rain-am-Lech; d. February 24, 1895, Hannover, Germany.

1. BAKER 7; GROVE 6/10; MGG 1/8; PAB-MI/2 (Bibliography); RIEMANN 12.

C0642.
LACHNER, VINCENZ. b. July 19, 1811, Rain-am-Lech; d. January 22, 1893, Karlsruhe, Germany.

1. BAKER 7; GROVE 6/10 (Bibliography); MGG 1/8; PAB-MI/2 (Bibliography).

C0643.
LAMBERT, CONSTANT. b. August 23, 1905, London; d. August 21, 1951, London, England.

1. BAKER 7 (Bibliography); EdS 1/6 (Bibliography); GROVE 6/10 (Bibliography); MGG 1/8 (Bibliography); PAB-MI/2 (Bibliography); RIEMANN 12 + Supp. (Bibliography).
2. LGB 19/3; OPERA 2/1.
3. Lambert, Constant. <u>Music Ho! A Study of Music in Decline</u>. London: Faber and Faber Ltd., 1934. 324 p., index.

4. Shead, Richard. Constant Lambert. London: Simon Publications, 1973. 208 p., 13 illus., list of compositions, discography, 70-item bibliography, concerts for the BBC, index.

5. A0003.

C0644.
LAMOTE de GRIGNON, JUAN. b. July 7, 1872, Barcelona; d. March 11, 1949, Barcelona, Spain.

1. BAKER 7; GROVE 6/10; MGG 1/8 (Bibliography); RIEMANN 12.

C0645.
LAMOTE de GRIGNON, RICARD. b. September 23, 1899, Barcelona; d. February 5, 1962, Barcelona, Spain.

1. BAKER 7; RIEMANN 12.

C0646.
LAMOUREUX, CHARLES. b. September 28, 1834, Bordeaux; d. December 21, 1899, Paris, France.

1. BAKER 7; GROVE 6/10 (Bibliography); MGG 1/8 (Bibliography); PAB-MI/2 (Bibliography); RIEMANN 12 + Supp. (Bibliography).

5. B0033, B0112, B0140.

SEE: Imbert, Hugues. Portraits et études. Paris, 1894.

SEE: Rolland, Romain. Musiciens d'aujourd'hui. Paris: Librairie Hachette et Cie, 1908. 278, [3] p.

C0647.
LANCHBERY, JOHN. b. May 15, 1923, London, England.

1. BAKER 7; GROVE 6/10; PAB-MI/2 (Bibliography).

C0648.
LANDAU, SIEGFRIED. b. September 4, 1921, Berlin, Germany.

1. BAKER 7; PAB-MI/2 (Bibliography); RIEMANN 12/Supp.

C0649.
LANDSHOFF, LUDWIG. b. June 3, 1874, Stettin, Germany; d. September 20, 1941, New York City.

1. BAKER 7; GROVE 6/10 (Bibliography); MGG 1/8 (Bibliography); PAB-MI/2 (Bibliography); RIEMANN 12.

2. MQ 28/2.

C0650.
LANE, LOUIS. b. December 25, 1923, Eagle Pass, Texas.

1. BAKER 7; GROVE-AM 1/3.

C0651.
LANG, BENJAMIN JOHNSON. b. December 28, 1837, Salem; d. April 3, 1909, Boston, Massachusetts.

1. BAKER 7; GROVE 6/10; GROVE-AM 1/3 (Bibliography); PAB-MI/2 (Bibliography).

C0652.
LANGE, HANS. b. February 17, 1884, Constantinople, Turkey; d. August 13, 1960, Albuquerque, New Mexico.

1. BAKER 7; GROVE-AM 1/3; RIEMANN 12/Supp.

C0653.
La ROSA PARODI, ARMANDO. b. March 14, 1904, Genoa; d. January 21, 1977, Rome, Italy.

1. EdS 1/6; RIEMANN 12/Supp.

C0654.
La ROTELLA, PASQUALE. b. February 26, 1880, Bitonto; d. March 20, 1963, Bari, Italy.

1. BAKER 7; EdS 1/6.

C0655.
L'ARRONGE, ADOLF. b. March 8, 1838, Hamburg; d. May 25, 1908, Berlin.

1. BAKER 7; EdS 1/6 (Bibliography); PAB-MI/2 (Bibliography); RIEMANN 12.

C0656.
LASSEN, EDUARD. b. April 13, 1830, Copenhagen, Denmark; d. January 15, 1904, Weimar, Germany.

1, BAKER 7; GROVE 6/10 (Bibliography); MGG 1/8 (Bibliography); PAB-MI/2 (Bibliography); RIEMANN 12.

C0657.
LAVRANGAS, DENIS. b. October 17, 1864, Argostoli, Cephalonia; d. July 30, 1941, Razata, Cephalonia, Greece.

1. BAKER 7; GROVE 6/10 (Bibliography); MGG 1/8 (Bibliography); RIEMANN 12.

C0658.
LEBRUN, PAUL HENRI. b. April 21, 1863, Ghent; d. November 4, 1920, Louvain, Belgium.

1. BAKER 7; MGG 1/8 (Bibliography); RIEMANN 12.

C0659.
LEDERER, FELIX. b. February 25, 1877, Prague; d. March 26, 1957, Berlin.

1. BAKER 7; RIEMANN 12.

C0660.
LEDGER, PHILIP. b. December 12, 1937, Bexhill-on-Sea, Sussex, England.

1. BAKER; GROVE 6/10; PAB-MI/2 (Bibliography).

C0661.
LEHEL, GYÖRGY. b. February 10, 1926, Budapest, Hungary.

1. BAKER 7; GROVE 6/10; PAB-MI/2 (Bibliography); RIEMANN 12/Supp.

C0662.
LEHMANN, FRITZ. b. May 17, 1904, Mannheim; d. March 30, 1956, Munich.

1. BAKER 7 (Bibliography); RIEMANN 12.

C0663.
LEINSDORF, ERICH. b. February 4, 1912, Vienna, Austria.

1. BAKER 7; GROVE 6/10; GROVE-AM 1/3 (Bibliography); PAB-MI/2 (Bibliography); RIEMANN 12 + Supp. (Bibliography).

2. GR 47/558; ON 25/10, 26/17; OPERA 23/7.

3. Leinsdorf, Erich. Cadenza: a Musical Career. Boston: Houghton Mifflin Company, 1976. x, [iii], 321 p., 29 illus., index.

   Leinsdorf, Erich. The Composer's Advocate: a Radical Orthodoxy for Musicians. New Haven: Yale University Press, 1981. viii, 216 p., index.

   Leinsdorf, Erich. "Toscanini at Salzburg." Opera Annual No. 5. New York: Doubleday & Company, Inc., 1958: 28-31.

5. A0010, B0008, B0042, B0067, B0086, B0099, B0138, B0158.

C0664.
LEITNER, FERDINAND. b. March 4, 1912, Berlin, Germany.

1. BAKER 7; GROVE 6/10; PAB-MI/2 (Bibliography); RIEMANN 12 + Supp. (Bibliography).

2. OW 3/11.

5. B0142.

C0665.
LENAERTS, CONSTANT. b. March 9, 1852, Antwerp; d. March 20, 1931, Antwerp, Belgium.

1. BAKER 7; RIEMANN 12.

C0666.
LENDVAI, ERWIN. b. June 4, 1882, Budapest, Hungary; d. March 31, 1949, Epsom, Surrey, England.

1. BAKER 7; RIEMANN 12 (Bibliography) + Supp. (Bibliography).

C0667.
LEPPARD, RAYMOND. b. August 11, 1927, London, England.

1. BAKER 7; GROVE 6/10; GROVE-AM 1/3 (Bibliography); PAB-MI/2 (Bibliography); RIEMANN 12/Supp. (Bibliography).

2. GR 49/580; HiFi/MusAM 28/9, 32/8; ON 43/21; OPERA 22/11.

C0668.
LERT, RICHARD JOHANNES. b. September 19, 1885, Vienna; d. April 25, 1980, Los Angeles, California.

1. BAKER 7; PAB-MI/2 (Bibliography); RIEMANN 12 + Supp.

2. JCG 3/3, 4, 4/1, 2.

5. B0006.

C0669.
LESLIE, HENRY DAVID. b. June 18, 1822, London; d. February 4, 1896, Llansaintfraid, near Oswestry, England.

1. BAKER 7, GROVE 6/10; PAB-MI/2 (Bibliography); RIEMANN 12 (Bibliography).

C0670.
LEVEY, RICHARD MICHAEL. b. October 25, 1811, Dublin; d. June 28, 1899, Dublin, Ireland.

1. BAKER 7; GROVE 6/10 (Bibliography).

C0671.
LEVEY, WILLIAM CHARLES. b. April 25, 1837, Dublin; d. August 18, 1894, London, England.

1. BAKER 7; GROVE 6/10.

C0672.
LEVI, HERMANN. b. November 7, 1839, Giessen; d. May 13, 1900, Munich, Germany.

1. BAKER 7 (Bibliography); EdS 1/6 (Bibliography); GROVE 6/10 (Bibliography); MGG 1/8 (Bibliography); RIEMANN 12 (Bibliography) + Supp. (Bibliography).

2. ON 38/24.

4. von Possart, Ernst. Hermann Levi: Erinnerungen. Muenchen: C.H. Beck'sche Verlagsbuchhandlung, 1901. 53 p., portrait.

5. B0035, B0062, B0079, B0103, B0114, B0138.

SEE: Ernest Newman under RICHARD WAGNER (C1175.4).

C0673.
LEVINE, JAMES LAWRENCE. b. June 23, 1943, Cincinnati, Ohio.

1. BAKER 7; GROVE 6/10; GROVE-AM 1/3 (Bibliography); PAB-MI/2 (Bibliography); RIEMANN 12/Supp.

2. HiFi/MusAm 24/3, 28/12; ON 36/4, 37/6, 41/4, 45/3; OPERA 28/9; OW 16/2, 16/12, 17/2, 12; TIME (Jan. 17, 1983).

5. A0017, A0023, A0031, B0067, B0092, B0125.

C0674.
LEWIS, ANTHONY CAREY. b. March 2, 1915, Bermuda; d. June 5, 1983, Haslemere, England.

1. BAKER 7; GROVE 6/10 (Bibliography); MGG 1/8; PAB-MI/2 (Bibliography); RIEMANN 12 + Supp.

C0675.
LEWIS, DANIEL. b. May 10, 1925, Flagstaff, Arizona.

1. BAKER 7; GROVE-AM 1/3 (Bibliography); PAB-MI/2 (Bibliography).

C0676.
LEWIS, HENRY. b. October 16, 1932, Los Angeles, California.

1. BAKER 7; GROVE 6/10; GROVE-AM 1/3 (Bibliography); PAB-MI/2 (Bibliography).

2. HiFi/MusAm 20/2; ON 37/11.

5. B0001.

C0677.
LIEBIG, KARL. b. July 25, 1808, Schwedt; d. October 6, 1872, Berlin, Germany.

1. BAKER 7; RIEMANN 12.

C0678.
LILJEFORS, RUBEN. b. September 30, 1871, Uppsala; d. March 4, 1936, Uppsala, Sweden.

1. BAKER 7; GROVE 6/10 (Bibliography); MGG 1/8; RIEMANN 12.

C0679.
LIMANTOUR, JOSE YVES. b. August 9, 1919, Paris, France.

1. BAKER 7; RIEMANN 12/Supp.

C0680.
LIMBERT, FRANK L. b. November 15, 1866, New York City; d. November 19, 1938, Hanau, Germany.

1. BAKER 7; RIEMANN 12.

C0681.
von LINDPAINTER, PETER JOSEF. b. December 9, 1791, Coblenz; d. August 21, 1856, Nonnenhorn, Lake Constance, Germany.

1. BAKER 7; GROVE 6/11 (Bibliography); MGG 1/8 (Bibliography); RIEMANN 12.

C0682.
LIPKIN, SEYMOUR. b. May 14, 1927, Detroit, Michigan.

1. BAKER 7; GROVE-AM 1/3 (Bibliography); PAB-MI/2 (Bibliography); RIEMANN 12/Supp.

C0683.
LISTEMANN, BERNHARD. b. August 28, 1841, Schlotheim, Germany; d. February 11, 1917, Chicago, Illinois.

1. BAKER 7; GROVE-AM 1/3 (Bibliography).

C0684.
LLOYD-JONES, DAVID. b. November 19, 1934, London, England.

1. BAKER 7; GROVE 6/11; PAB-MI/2 (Bibliography).

C0685.
LOCKHART, JAMES LAWRENCE. b. October 16, 1930, Edinburgh, Scotland.

1. BAKER 7; GROVE 6/11; PAB-MI/2 (Bibliography); RIEMANN 12/Supp.

C0686.
LOEWE, FERDINAND. b. February 19, 1865, Vienna; d. January 6, 1925, Vienna, Austria.

BAKER 7; GROVE 6/11.

C0687.
LOEWLEIN, HANS. b. June 24, 1909, Ingolstadt, Germany.

1. BAKER 7; RIEMANN 12 + Supp.

C0688.
LOHSE, OTTO. b. September 21, 1858, Dresden; d. May 5, 1925, Baden-Baden, Germany.

1. BAKER 7; GROVE 6/11; RIEMANN 12 + Supp. (Bibliography).

4. Lert, Ernst. Otto Lohse als Opernleiter. Leipzig: Druck und Verlag von Breitkopf und Haertel, 1918. 79, [1] p., portrait.

C0689.
LOMBARD, ALAIN. b. October 4, 1940, Paris, France.

1. BAKER 7; GROVE 6/11; PAB-MI/2 (Bibliography); RIEMANN 12/Supp.

2. ON 34/25.

C0690.
LONGY, GEORGES. b. August 29, 1868, Abbeville; d. March 29, 1930, Mareuil, Dordogne, France.

1. BAKER 7; GROVE-AM 1/3 (Bibliography).

C0691.
LORENTZ, ALFRED. b. March 7, 1872, Strasbourg; d. April 23, 1931, Karlsruhe, Germany.

1. BAKER 7; RIEMANN 12.

C0692.
LORENZ, ALFRED OTTOKAR. b. July 11, 1868, Vienna, Austria; d. November 20, 1939, Munich, Germany.

1. BAKER 7 (Bibliography); GROVE 6/11 (Bibliography); MGG 1/8 (Bibliography); RIEMANN 12 (Bibliography) + Supp. (Bibliography).

C0693.
LOUGHRAN, JAMES. b. June 30, 1931, Glasgow, Scotland.

1. BAKER 7; GROVE 6/11 (Bibliography); PAB-MI/2 (Bibliography); RIEMANN 12/Supp.

C0694.
LOY, MAX. b. June 18, 1913, Nuremberg; d. February 15, 1977, Nuremberg, Germany.

1. BAKER 7; RIEMANN 12/Supp.

C0695.
LUALDI, ADRIANO. b. March 22, 1885, Larino, Campobasso; d. January 8, 1971, Milan, Italy.

1. BAKER 7 (Bibliography); EdS 1/6 (Bibliography); GROVE 6/11 (Bibliography); MGG 1/8 (Bibliography); PAB-MI/2 (Bibliography); RIEMANN 12 + Supp.

3. Lualdi, Adriano. <u>Il rinnovamento musicale italiano</u>. Milano: Tip. Treves-Tresccani-Tumminelli, 1931. 106, [1] p., list of contemporary composers with works.

   Lualdi, Adriano. <u>L'Arte di dirigere l'orchestra: antologia e guida</u>. Milano: Editore Ulrico Hoepli, 1940. xv, [i], 413 p., 120 musical examples.

   Section two is an anthology of the writings of Berlioz, Saminski, Gui, Gounod, Serafin, Weingartner, and Wagner. Seconda edizione aggiornata e molto acresciuta con nuovi capitoli (1949). xvi, 592 p., 200 musical examples, index. Add Liszt, Schumann, and Wood.

   Lualdi, Adriano. <u>Serate musicali</u>. Milano: Fratelli Treves Editori, 1928. viii, 347, [2], p., 16 illus., index.

Lualdi, Adriano. Viaggio musicale nel Sud-America. Milano: Istituto Editoriale Nazionale, 1934. 245 p., index of names.

4. Confalonieri, Giulio. L'Opera di Adriano Lualdi. Milano: Edizioni "Alpes", 1932. 134, [3] p., 9-item bibliography, list of compositions and publications.

C0696.
LUCAS, LEIGHTON. b. January 5, 1903, London; d. November 1, 1982, London, England.

1. BAKER 7; GROVE 6/11; MGG/Supp. (Bibliography); PAB-MI/2 (Bibliography); RIEMANN 12 + Supp.

C0697.
LUDWIG, LEOPOLD. b. January 12, 1908, Witkowitz; d. April 25, 1979, Lueneburg, Austria.

1. BAKER 7; GROVE 6/11; MGG 1/8 (Bibliography); PAB-MI/2 (Bibliography); RIEMANN 12 + Supp.

2. ON 35/23.

4. Wessling, Berndt W. Leopold Ludwig. Bremen: Carl Schuenemann Verlag, 1968. 133, [16] p., 27 illus., 41-item bibliography, discography, list of operas conducted in Hamburg, sources of illustrations.

C0698.
LUENING, OTTO. b. June 15, 1900, Milwaukee, Wisconsin.

1. BAKER 7; GROVE 6/11 (Bibliography); GROVE-AM 1/3 (Bibliography); MGG/Supp. (Bibliography); PAB-MI/2 (Bibliography); RIEMANN 12 + Supp. (Bibliography).

2. HiFi/MusAm 35/11.

3. He wrote The Odyssey of an American Composer, published in 1980.

C0699.
LUIGINI, ALEXANDRE. b. March 9, 1850, Lyon; d. September 29, 1906, Paris, France.

1. BAKER 7; GROVE 6/11; PAB-MI/2 (Bibliography); RIEMANN 12.

C0700.
LUKACS, MIKLOS. b. February 4, 1905, Gyula, Hungary.

1. BAKER 7; PAB-MI/2 (Bibliography); RIEMANN 12/Supp.

C0701.
LUNSSENS, MARTIN. b. April 16, 1871, Molenbeck-Saint-Jean; d. February 1, 1944, Etterbeck, Belgium.

1. BAKER 7; GROVE 6/11; MGG 1/8 (Bibliography); RIEMANN 12 + Supp. (Bibliography).

C0702.
MAAG, PETER. b. May 10, 1919, St. Gallen, Switzerland.

1. BAKER 7 (Bibliography); GROVE 6/11; PAB-MI/2 (Bibliography); RIEMANN 12 + Supp.

2. OW 4/8.

C0703.
MAAZEL, LORIN. b. March 6, 1930, Neuilly, France.

1. BAKER 7; EdS/Supp.; GROVE 6/11 (Bibliography); GROVE-AM 1/3 (Bibliography); PAB-MI/2 (Bibliography); RIEMANN 12 + Supp.

2. GR 48/574, 51/606; HiFi/MusAm 23/2; ON 33/11, 40/5; OW 7/7; OPER 1984: ein Jahrbuch der Zeitschrift "Opernwelt".

4. Geleng, Ingvelde. Lorin Maazel: Monographie eines Musikers. Berlin: Rembrandt Verlag GmbH, 1971. 135 p., 51 illus., chronology, tours, new opera productions, discography.

5. A0031, A0052, B0067, B0122, B0125.

C0704.
MACAL, ZDENEK. b. January 8, 1936, Brno, Czechoslovakia.

1. BAKER 7; GROVE 6/11 (Bibliography); PAB-MI/2 (Bibliography); RIEMANN 12/Supp.

C0705.
MacCUNN, HAMISH. b. March 22, 1868, Greenock, Scotland; d. August 2, 1916, London, England.

1. BAKER 7; GROVE 6/11 (Bibliography); MGG 1/8; PAB-MI/2 (Bibliography); RIEMANN 12.

3. MGG 1/8 mentions letters and documents in the Glasgow University Library.

C0706.
MACFARREN, GEORGE ALEXANDER. b. March 2, 1813, London; d. October 31, 1887, London, England.

1. BAKER 7; GROVE 6/11; MGG 1/8; PAB-MI/2 (Bibliography); RIEMANN 12.

4. Banister, Henry C. George Alexander Macfarren: His Life, Works, and Influence. London: George Bell & Sons, 1892. xiii, 419 p., portrait, index.

5. B0155.

SEE: Macfarren, Walter Cecil. Memories: an Autobiography. London: The Walter Scott Publishing Co., Ltd., 1905. xiv, 377, [1] p., 36 illus., appendix of published works, list of pupils, index.

C0707.
MACKENZIE, ALEXANDER CAMPBELL. b. August 22, 1847, Edinburgh, Scotland; d. April 28, 1935, London, England.

1. BAKER 7; EdS 1/6; GROVE 6/11 (Bibliography); MGG 1/8; PAB-MI/2 (Bibliography); RIEMANN 12.

2. MQ 13/2.

3. Mackenzie, Alexander Campbell. A Musician's Narrative. London: Cassell and Company, Ltd., 1927. [v], 269, [1] p., 4 illus., index of names.

5. B0007, B0085.

   SEE: O'Connor, T.P., ed. In the Days of My Youth. London: C. Arthur Pearson, Limited, 1901. ix, 318 p., 16 illus.

C0708.
MACKERRAS, CHARLES. b. November 17, 1925, Schenectady, New York.

1. BAKER 7; GROVE 6/11; PAB-MI/2 (Bibliography); RIEMANN 12/Supp.

2. GR 52/622; HiFi/MusAm 29/3; ON 34/24, 38/1; OPERA 14/10, 16/4, 18/10, 21/4, 29/1, 36/2.

5. A0023, A0031, B0071.

C0709.
MacMILLAN, ERNEST. b. August 18, 1893, Mimico, Ontario, Canada; d. May 6, 1973, Toronto, Canada.

1. BAKER 7; GROVE 6/11 (Bibliography); MGG/Supp.; PAB-MI/2 (Bibliography); RIEMANN 12 + Supp.

4. "A Tribute to Sir Ernest MacMillan", Music Across Canada 1 (July-August 1963 [special issue]). 45 p., 46 illus., 48-item bibliography, list of compositions, discography by Richard Johnston.

4. B0166.

C0710.
MADDY, JOSEPH EDGAR. b. October 14, 1891, Wellington, Kansas; d. April 18, 1966, Traverse City, Michigan.

1. BAKER 7; GROVE 6/11; GROVE-AM 1/3; PAB-MI/2 (Bibliography).

   He and T.P. Giddings founded the National Music Camp in 1928 at Interlocken, Michigan.

4. Browning, Norma Lee. Joe Maddy of Interlocken. Forward by Van Cliburn. Chicago: Henry Regnery Company, 1963. xii, [i], 297 p.

C0711.
MADEIRA, FRANCIS. b. February 21, 1917, Jenkintown, Pennsylvania.

1. BAKER 7; RIEMANN 12/Supp.

C0712.
MADERNA, BRUNO. b. April 21, 1920, Venice, Italy; d. November 13, 1973, Darmstadt, Germany.

1. BAKER 7 (Bibliography); EdS/Supp.; GROVE 6/11 (Bibliography); MGG 1/8 + Supp. (Bibliography); PAB-MI/2 (Bibliography); RIEMANN 12 + Supp.

2. MQ 45/2.

C0713.
MADEY, BOGUSLAW. b. May 31, 1932, Sosnowiec, Poland.

1. BAKER 7; PAB-MI/2 (Bibliography); RIEMANN 12/Supp.

C0714.
MAGA, OTMAR. b. June 30, 1929, Brno, Czechoslovakia.

1. BAKER 7; RIEMANN 12/Supp.

C0715.
MAGANINI, QUINTO. b. November 30, 1897, Fairfield, California; d. March 10, 1974, Greenwich, Connecticut.

1. BAKER 7; GROVE 6/11; GROVE-AM 1/3; PAB-MI/2 (Bibliography); RIEMANN 12 + Supp.

C0716.
MAHLER, FRITZ. b. July 16, 1901, Vienna, Austria; d. June 18, 1973, Winston-Salem, North Carolina.

1. BAKER 7; GROVE-AM 1/3; PAB-MI/2 (Bibliography); RIEMANN 12/Supp.

2. MQ 39/2.

C0717.
MAHLER, GUSTAV. b. July 7, 1860, Kalischt, Bohemia; d. May 18, 1911, Vienna, Austria.

Unquestionably one of the leading conductors of his time, Mahler's appointments read like a classic list of the most desirable positions then available. After serving as an assistant to Arthur Nikisch in Leipzig, he was appointed music director of the Royal Opera in Budapest in 1888. A six year stint as conductor at the Hamburg Opera was followed by his appointment as music director of the prestigious Vienna Court Opera. A year later he succeeded Hans Richter as director of the Vienna Philharmonic Concerts. Shortly after his resignation from the Court Opera in 1907, he joined the Metropolitan Opera as principal conductor. In 1909 he was appointed conductor of the New York Philharmonic Society which resulted in the end of his association with the Met. A few short months before his death he fell seriously ill and returned to Vienna. Paul Banks writes in GROVE 6/11: "There can be little but speculation about the actual character of Mahler's conducting, though no doubt at all about the impact it made on his contemporaries. One thing is certain, that his performances of other men's music was re-creative rather than interpretative. That is to say, he approached the works he conducted as if he had composed them himself and labored to achieve the precision, the clarity and the vivid characterization that he insisted on in performance of his own music; this is evident in the elaborate notation of his scores which attempts to find a sign for even the subtlest of nuances. If this primarily re-creative spirit is understood, much else becomes clear, in particular his activities as editor or arranger."

The plethora of published material on Mahler's life and work is rather overwhelming. One needs only to consult Donald Mitchell's outstanding bibliography in GROVE 6/11 to get some idea of available treasures. The Music Division of the Library of Congress has well over one hundred catalogued books and pamphlets devoted to Mahler on the shelves, most of which have to do with his life and his contributions to the evolution of modern music. The selection below, and it is only a selection, is intended as a first step in getting to know Mahler as an artist, a conductor, and a human being.

1. BAKER 7 (Bibliography); EdS 1/6; GROVE 6/11 (193-item Bibliography by Donald Mitchell); MGG 1/8 (Bibliography); PAB-MI/2 (Bibliography); RIEMANN 12 + Supp. (Bibliography).

2. JCG 1/3, 3/2, 4/4; MQ 17/2, 33/2, 45/4, 58/2; ON 11/10, 21/12; OPERA 4/1, 3, 4, 5.

4. Bauer-Lechner, Natalie. Recollections of Gustav Mahler. Translated by Dika Newlin. Edited and annotated by Peter Franklin. Cambridge: Cambridge University Press, 1980 [original: Erinnerungen an Gustav Mahler. Wien: E.P. Tal & Co., Verlag, 1923.]. 250 p., 12-item bibliography, notes, 2 appendices, index.

Blaukopf, Herta. Gustav Mahler Richard Strauss Briefwechsel 1888-1911. Muenchen: R. Piper & Co. Verlag, 1980. 231, [1] p., 14 illus., index of names, index of works.

Blaukopf, Kurt, comp./ed. and Zoltan Roman. Mahler: a Documentary Study. Translated by P.R.J. Ford et al. New York: Oxford University Press, 1976. 280 p., 362 illus., index of names.

Deck, Marvin Lee. Gustav Mahler in New York: His Conducting Activities in New York City, 1908-1911. Ph.D. diss., New York University, 1973. 308 p., bibliography.

de La Grange, Henry Louis. Gustav Mahler: chronique d'une vie. 3 vols. Paris: Librairie Artheme Fayard, 1979/83/84. 1149 p., 20 leaves of plates, 20-page bibliography, index; 1278, [7] p., 16 leaves of plates, 2 appendices, catalogue of works, 57-page bibliography; 1365 p., 16 leaves of plates, 58-page bibliography.

Mahler, Alma Maria, ed. Gustav Mahler Briefe 1879-1911. Berlin: Paul Zsolnay Verlag, 1924. xvi, 492, [1] p., 5 illus.

Mahler, Alma. Gustav Mahler: Erinnerungen und Briefe. Amsterdam: Allert De Lange, 1940. 473 p., portrait.

Mitchell, Donald. Gustav Mahler: the Early Years. revised and edited by Paul Banks and David Matthews. Berkeley: University of California Press, 1980. xxii, 338 p., 19 illus., 54-item bibliography, notes, revised list of early works, index.

Mitchell, Donald. Gustav Mahler the Wunderhorn Years: Chronicles and Commentaries. Boulder: Westview Press, 1976. 461 p., 33 illus., 59-item bibliography, index.

Roller, Alfred, ed. Die Bildnisse von Gustav Mahler. Leipzig: E.P. Tal & Co. Verlag, 1922. 85, [1] p., 96 illus.

Stauber, Paul. Das Wahre Erbe Mahlers, kleine Beitraege zur Geschichte der Wiener Hofoper nebst einem Anhang: Dokumente zum Fall Hirschfeld. Wien: Huber & Lahme Nachfolger, 1909. 67 p.

Stomper, Stephan. "Gustav Mahler als Dirigent und Regisseur: ein Beitrag zur Geschichte der Operninterpretation". Jahrbuch der Komischen Oper Berlin VIII. Berlin: Henschelverlag, 1968: 110-140.

Walter, Bruno. Gustav Mahler. Translated by James Galston. London: Kegan Paul, Trench, Trubner & Co., Ltd., 1937 [original: Wien, 1936.]. ix, 160 p., portrait. Translated by Lotte Walter Lindt. New York: Alfred A. Knopf, 1938. xvii, 175, [1], v, [i] p., portrait, index.

Werfel, Anna Mahler and E.B. Ashton. And the Bridge is Love: Memories of a Lifetime. New York: Harcourt, Brace and Company, 1958. 312 p., 52 illus., index.

Anna married the architect Walter Gropius and then Franz Werfel.

Wiesmann, Sigrid, ed. Gustav Mahler in Vienna. Translated by Anne Shelley. New York: Rizzoli International Publications, 1976. 160, [5] p., illus.

Willnauer, Franz. Gustav Mahler und die Wiener Oper. Wien: Jugend und Volk Verlagsgesellschaft m.b.H., 1979. 314, [1] p., 28 illus., premieres 1897-1907, Vienna repertoire, musical staff with dates, Vienna Philharmonic repertoire, budget 1903-08, contract documents, index of names.

5. B0046, B0055, B0057, B0079, B0080, B0112.

SEE: Foerster, Josef Bohuslav. Der Pilger: Erinnerungen eines Musikers. Prague: Artia, 1955. 762, [3] p., 28 illus., index.

SEE: Autobiography of OTTO KLEMPERER (C0590.3).

SEE: Wouter Paap under WILLEM MENGELBERG (C0751.4).

SEE: Autobiography of BRUNO WALTER (C1182.3).

C0718.
MAJOR, JAKAB GYULA. b. December 13, 1858, Kosice; d. January 30, 1925, Budapest, Hungary.

1. BAKER 7; GROVE 6/11; MGG 1/8 (Bibliography) + Supp. (Bibliography); RIEMANN 12 (Bibliography).

3. His autobiography was published in Musikliterarische Blaetter. Wien, January 1912.

C0719.
MAKSYMIUK, JERZY. b. April 9, 1936, Grodno, Poland.

1. BAKER 7; GROVE 6/11.

C0720.
MALGOIRE, JEAN-CLAUDE. b. November 25, 1940, Avignon, France.

1. BAKER 7; GROVE 6/11; PAB-MI/2 (Bibliography).

C0721.
MALKO, NICOLAI. b. May 4, 1883, Brailov, Russia; d. June 23, 1961, Sydney, Australia.

1. BAKER 7; GROVE 6/11 (Bibliography); PAB-MI/2 (Bibliography); RIEMANN 12 + Supp. (Bibliography).

3. His pedagogical book, The Conductor and His Baton, was published in Copenhagen in 1950. No copy located but see Elizabeth Green entry.

4. Green, Elizabeth A.H. The Modern Conductor. Introduction by Eugene Ormandy. 3rd edition. Englewood Cliffs (NJ): Prentice-Hall, Inc., 1981. xvii, 298 p., 7 appendices including 103-item bibliography.

   "A college text on conducting based on the technical principles of conductor Nicolai Malko as set forth in his The Conductor and His Baton."

   Malko, Berthe, Elizabeth Green and George Malko, eds. Nicolai Malko: a Certain Art. New York: William Morrow & Company, Inc., 1966. 235 p., 17 illus., index.

5. A0004, A0022, B0167.

C0722.
MANCINELLI, LUIGI. b. February 5, 1848, Orvieto; d. February 2, 1921, Rome, Italy.

1. BAKER 7 (Bibliography); EdS 1/7 (Bibliography); GROVE 6/11 (Bibliography); MGG 1/8 (Bibliography); PAB-MI/2 (Bibliography); RIEMANN 12 (Bibliography) + Supp. (Bibliography).

4. Orefice, Giacomo. Luigi Mancinelli. Roma: Ausonia, 1921. 149, [11] p., portrait, list of works, index of names.

C0723.
MANNES, DAVID. b. February 16, 1866, New York City; d. April 25, 1959, New York City.

1. BAKER 7; GROVE 6/11; GROVE-AM 1/3 (Bibliography); PAB-MI/2 (Bibliography); RIEMANN 12.

2. MusAm 15/19.

3. Mannes, David. Music is My Faith: an Autobiography. New York: W.W. Norton & Co., Inc., 1938. 270 p., 8 illus.

C0724.
MANNINO, FRANCO. b. April 25, 1924, Palermo, Italy.

1. BAKER 7; EdS 1/7; GROVE 6/11; PAB-MI/2 (Bibliography); RIEMANN 12/Supp.

C0725.
MANNS, AUGUST. b. March 12, 1825, Stolzenberg, near Stettin, Germany; d. March 1, 1907, London, England.

1. BAKER 7; GROVE 6/11; PAB-MI/2 (Bibliography); RIEMANN 12.

4. Wyndham, H. Saxe. August Manns and the Saturday Concerts: a Memoir and a Retrospect. London: The Walter Scott Publishing Co., Ltd., 1909. xv, [i], 243, [1] p., 6 illus., list of compositions.

5. B0007, B0020, B0056, B0076, B0085.

   SEE: Francesco Berger under MICHAEL COSTA (C0217.4).

C0726.
MANNSTAEDT, FRANZ. b. July 8, 1852, Hagen; d. January 18, 1932, Wiesbaden, Germany.

1. BAKER 7, RIEMANN 12.

C0727.
MARETZEK, MAX. b. June 28, 1821, Bruenn, Moravia; d. May 14, 1897, Staten Island, New York.

1. BAKER 7; GROVE-AM 1/3 (Bibliography); PAB-MI/2 (Bibliography).

3. Maretzek, Max. Crochets and Quavers: or, Revelations of an Opera Manager in America. New York: S. French, 1855. Reprint 1968. viii, 11-346 p.

   For an index see the unabridged Dover Publications reprint which also includes Sharps and Flats. New York, 1890. 87 p.

C0728.
MARIANI, ANGELO. b. October 11, 1821, Ravenna; d. June 13, 1873, Genoa, Italy.

1. BAKER 7 (Bibliography); EdS 1/7 (Bibliography); GROVE 6/11; RIEMANN 12 + Supp. (Bibliography).

4. Martinotti, Sergio. "Angelo Mariani, direttore e musicista, nel suo tempo". U. Cattolica de Milano, StudiM II/2 (1973): 315-39.

   Zoppi, Umberto. Angelo Mariana Giuseppe Verdi e Teresa Stolz in un carteggio inedito. Milano: Garzanti, 1947. 403 p., 27 illus., index of names.

5. SEE: Budden, Julian. The Operas of Verdi 2: From Il Trovatore to La Forza del Destino. New York: Oxford University Press, 1978. ix, 532 p., index.

   SEE: Walker, Frank. The Man Verdi. London: J.M. Dent & Sons Ltd, 1972. xiii, 526 p., 18 illus., index.

C0729.
MARINOV, IVAN. b. October 17, 1928, Sofia, Bulgaria.

1. BAKER 7; GROVE 6/11.

C0730.
MARINUZZI, GINO. b. April 7, 1920, New York City.

1. BAKER 7; EdS 1/7; GROVE 6/11; PAB-MI/2 (Bibliography); RIEMANN 12 + Supp.

C0731.
MARINUZZI, GIUSEPPE (GINO). b. March 24, 1882, Palermo; d. August 17, 1945, Milan, Italy.

1. BAKER 7; EdS 1/7; GROVE 6/11 (Bibliography); MGG 1/8; RIEMANN 12 (Bibliography) + Supp. (Bibliography).

4. Cei, Lia Pierotti. Il signore del golfo mistico Gino Marinuzzi: un artista e un uomo dall'Italia umbertina alla caduta del fascismo. Firenze: G.C. Sansoni Editore Nuova S.p.A., 1982. 446 p., 16 illus., operatic repertoire, compositions.

   Garbelotto, Antonio. Gion Marinuzzi. Ancona: Edizioni Berben, 1965. 62, [9] p., 4 illus., list of works, discography, 28-item bibliography.

C0732.
MARKEVITCH, IGOR. b. July 27, 1912, Kiev, Russia; d. March 7, 1983, Antibes, France.

1. BAKER 7; EdS 1/7 (Bibliography); GROVE 6/11 (Bibliography); MGG/Supp. (Bibliography); PAB-MI/2 (Bibliography); RIEMANN 12 + Supp. (Bibliography).

3. Markevitch, Igor. Être et avoir été. Paris: Editions Gallimard, 1980. 509, [2] p., index of names.

Markevitch, Igor. Made in Italy. Translated by Darina Silone. London: The Harvill Press, 1949. xi, 226 p., 9 illus.

5. A0050, B0142.

C0733.
MARRINER, NEVILLE. b. April 15, 1924, Lincoln, England.

1. BAKER 7; GROVE 6/11; GROVE-AM 1/3 (Bibliography); PAB-MI/2 (Bibliography); RIEMANN 12/Supp.

2. GR 52/617; HiFi/MusAm 29/9.

5. B0134.

C0734.
MARTIN, THOMAS PHILIPP. b. May 28, 1909, Vienna, Austria; d. May 14, 1984, New York City.

1. BAKER 7; GROVE-AM 1/3; PAB-MI/2 (Bibliography).

C0735.
MARTINON, JEAN. b. January 10, 1910, Lyons; d. March 1, 1976, Paris, France.

1. BAKER 7; GROVE 6/11; PAB-MI/2 (Bibliography); RIEMANN 12 + Supp. (Bibliography).

2. GR 50/590.

5. SEE: William Barry Furlong under GEORG SOLTI (C1070.4).

   SEE: Machabey, Armand. Portraits de trente musiciens français. Paris: Richard-Masse Editeurs, 1949.

C0736.
MARTUCCI, GIUSEPPE. b. January 6, 1856, Capua; d. June 1, 1909, Naples, Italy.

1. BAKER 7; EdS 1/7 (Bibliography); GROVE 6/11 (Bibliography); MGG 1/8 (Bibliography); PAB-MI/2 (Bibliography); RIEMANN 12 + Supp. (Bibliography).

4. Fano, Fabio. Giuseppe Martucci: saggio biografico-critico. Milano: Edizioni Curci, 1950. 201 p., 16 illus., 6 appendices, 23-item bibliography, index of names.

   Per Giuseppe Martucci: celebrazione Martucciana pro opere assistenziali del P.N.F. domenica 28 giugno 1931. Napoli: Castello Angioino, 1931. 48 p., 21 illus.

C0737.
MASCAGNI, PIETRO. b. December 7, 1863, Livorno; d. August 2, 1945, Rome, Italy.

1. BAKER 7 (Bibliography); EdS 1/7 (Bibliography); GROVE 6/11 (Bibliography); MGG 1/8 (Bibliography); PAB-MI/2 (Bibliography); RIEMANN 12 + Supp. (Bibliography).

4. de Carlo, Salvatore, comp. Mascagni parla: appunti per le memorie di un grande musicista. Roma: Casa Editrice De Carlo, 1945. 222, [1] p., 12 illus.

   Ricci, Luigi. 34 anni con Pietro Mascagni: cose viste -- sentite -- vissute. Milano: Edizioni Curci, 1976. 168, [6] p., 74 illus.

5. B0089, B0167.

C0738.
MASCHERONI, EDOARDO. b. September 4, 1852, Milan; d. March 4, 1941, Ghirla, near Varese, Italy.

1. BAKER 7; EdS 1/7; GROVE 6/11 (Bibliography); PAB-MI/2 (Bibliography); RIEMANN 12.

2. LS 6.

C0739.
MASUR, KURT. b. July 18, 1927, Brieg, Silesia.

1. GROVE 6/11; RIEMANN 12/Supp.

4. Haertwig, Dieter. Kurt Masur fuer Sie portraetiert. Leipzig: VEB Deutscher Verlag fuer Musik, 1976. 62, [1] p., 31 illus., chronology, select discography.

C0740.
MATA, EDUARDO. b. September 5, 1942, Mexico City, Mexico.

1. BAKER 7; GROVE 6/11; GROVE-AM 1/3 (Bibliography); PAB-MI/2 (Bibliography); RIEMANN 12/Supp.

2. HiFi/MusAm 29/9.

C0741.
von MATACIC, LOVRO. b. February 14, 1899, Sušak, Yugoslavia.

1. BAKER 7; GROVE 6/11; PAB-MI/2 (Bibliography); RIEMANN 12 + Supp.

2. OW 15/9.

C0742.
MAUCERI, JOHN. b. September 12, 1945, New York City.

1. BAKER 7; GROVE-AM 1/3; PAB-MI/2 (Bibliography).

C0743.
MAUERSBERGER, RUDOLF. b. January 29, 1889, Mauersberg, Erzgebirge; d. February 22, 1971, Dresden, Germany.

1. BAKER 7; GROVE 6/11 (Bibliography); MGG/Supp. (Bibliography); RIEMANN 12 + Supp.

C0744.
MAZZOLENI, ETTORE. b. June 18, 1905, Brusio, Switzerland; d. June 1, 1968, Toronto, Canada.

1. BAKER 7; GROVE 6/11; PAB-MI/2 (Bibliography).

C0745.
MEHTA, MEHLI. b. September 25, 1908, Bombay, India.

1. BAKER 7; EdS/Supp.; GROVE-AM 1/3; RIEMANN 12/Supp.

C0746.
MEHTA, ZUBIN. b. April 29, 1936, Bombay, India.

1. BAKER 7; GROVE 6/12; GROVE-AM 1/3 (Bibliography); PAB-MI/2 (Bibliography); RIEMANN 12/Supp.

2. GR 52/615, 58/688; ON 30/9; HiFi/MusAm 27/11, 30/10; OW 18/1; TIME (Jan. 19, 1968).

4. Bookspan, Martin and Ross Yockey. Zubin Mehta. London: Robert Hale Limited, 1978. [vii], 226 p., 33 illus., index.

5. A0017, A0031, A0052, B0092, B0125, B0142.

SEE: William Wordsworth under DANIEL BARENBOIM (C0067.5).

C0747.
MELIK-PASHAYEV, ALEXANDER. b. October 23, 1905, Tiflis, Georgia; d. June 18, 1964, Moscow, Russia.

1. BAKER 7; GROVE 6/12 (Bibliography)

C0748.
MELLES, CARL. b. July 15, 1926, Budapest, Hungary.

1. BAKER 7; PAB-MI/2 (Bibliography); RIEMANN 12/Supp.

2. OPER 1966: ein Jahrbuch der Zeitschrift "Opernwelt".

C0749.
MENDELSSOHN, FELIX. b. February 3, 1809, Hamburg; d. November 4, 1847, Leipzig, Germany.

Mendelssohn is another composer-conductor along with Berlioz, Mahler, and Richard Strauss about whom a wealth of published literature is available. Nicolas Slonimsky in BAKER 7 remarks that "he was still a very young man when, in 1835, he was offered the conductorship of the celebrated Gewandhaus Orch. in Leipzig....Mendelssohn's leadership of the Gewandhaus Orch. was of the greatest significance for the development of German musical culture; he engaged the violin virtuoso Ferdinand

David as concertmaster of the orch., which soon became the most prestigious symph. organization in Germany." Adam Carse (B0024; p. 351), after a marvelous overview of the laudatory comments of his contemporaries, sums it up rather nicely: "Mendelssohn's great musicianship and his attractive personality undoubtedly combined to make him one of the most outstanding conductors of his time. If the adulation of his friends spoilt him a little, it also helped to give him unbounded confidence in his own powers, and helped to make him a leader and figurehead of a school of conducting which was widely accepted as authoritative in Germany and England." There seems to be no basic study of his conducting methods and style similar, for example, to what is available for Mahler (Marvin Lee Deck and Stephan Stomper) and Richard Strauss (see the bibliography in GROVE 6/18), but this is to be expected inasmuch as Mendelssohn was a "founding father" of a discipline which would be greatly refined and exploited for the next one hundred-fifty years! Again our selection, and it is no more than that, brushes the tip of a very large iceberg.

1. BAKER 7 (Bibliography); EdS 1/7; GROVE 6/12 (207-item bibliography by Eveline Bartlitz); MGG 1/9 (Bibliography); PAB-MI/2 (Bibliography); RIEMANN 12 + Supp. (Bibliography).

2. OPERA 5/11, 12.

4. Benedict, Jules. Sketch of the Life and Works of the Late Felix Mendelssohn-Bartholdy: Being the Substance of a Lecture, Delivered at the Camberwell Literary Institution, in December, 1849. London: John Murry, 1850. 61 p.

   Devrient, Eduard. My Recollections of Felix Mendelssohn-Bartholdy, and His Letters to Me. London: Richard Bently, 1869. vii, 307 p., portrait, index.

   Hensel, Sebastian. The Mendelssohn Family (1729-1847) From Letters and Journals. 2nd rev. ed. Translated by Carl Klingemann. New York: Harper & Brothers, 1882 [original: Berlin, 1880/82]. xi, [iv], 340 p., 4 illus.; 359 p., 4 illus., index.

   Marek, George R. Gentle Genius: the Story of Felix Mendelssohn. New York: Funk & Wagnalls, 1972. xiv, 365 p., 25 illus., a Mendelssohn calendar, 133-item bibliography, index.

   Chapter seven deals with Mendelssohn as a conductor. The extensive bibliography is excellent.

   Polko, Elise. Reminiscences of Felix Mendelssohn-Bartholdy: a Social and Artistic Biography. Translated by Lady Wallace. New York: Leypoldt & Holt, 1869. 334 p., portrait.

   Werner, Eric. Mendelssohn: a New Image of the Composer and His Age. Translated by Dika Newlin. New York: The Free Press of Glencoe, 1963. xv, 545 p., 20 illus., appendix, index.

   Werner, Eric. Mendelssohn: Leben und Werk in neuer Sicht. Zuerich: Atlantis Musikbuch-Verlag, 1980. 635 p., 29 illus., notes, 8 page bibliography by chapter, 3 appendices including a complete list of works, index.

5. B0010, B0017, B0026, B0035, B0112, B0155.

SEE: Reinecke, Carl. "Und manche liebe Schatten steigen auf": Gedenkblaetter an beruehmte Musiker. Leipzig: Verlag von Gebrueder Reinecke, 1900: 121-164.

SEE: Wolff, Konrad, ed. Robert Schumann on Music and Musicians. Translated by Paul Rosenfield. New York: Pantheon Books, 1946.

C0750.
MENGELBERG, KAREL. b. July 18, 1902, Utrecht, Holland.

1. BAKER 7; GROVE 6/12; PAB-MI/2 (Bibliography); RIEMANN 12/Supp.

C0751.
MENGELBERG, WILLEM. b. March 28, 1871, Utrecht, Holland; d. March 21, 1951, Chur, Switzerland.

1. BAKER 7 (Bibliography); GROVE 6/12 (Bibliography); MGG 1/9; PAB-MI/2 (Bibliography); RIEMANN 12.

2. HiFi/MusAm 25/8; LGB 8; RS 36.

4. Augsbourg, Georges. Mengelberg. Amsterdam: Andries Blitz, 1937. unpaginated [3 p., + 66 leaves of plates].

van den Boer, Arnoldus. De psychologische Beteekenis van Willem Mengelberg als Dirigent. Amsterdam: L.J. Veen, Uitgever, n.d. [1925]. 132 p., portrait.

Bysterus, Heemskerk E. Over Willem Mengelberg. Amsterdam: Uitgeverij Heuff, 1971. 157 p., illus., chronology, repertoire, discography, tours.

Cronheim, Paul, ed. Willem Mengelberg Gedenkboek 1895-1920. 'S Gravenhage: Martinus Nijhoff, 1920. xiii, 289, [1] p., illus., index of names.

von Gleich, C.C.J., ed. Herdenkingstentoonstelling: Willem Mengelberg (1871-1951). Den Haag: Druk Ando, 1971. 31 p., 16 illus.

Catalogue of 342 items.

Paap, Wouter. Willem Mengelberg. Amsterdam: Elsevier, 1960. 80 p., 68 illus., 45 rpm record.

Sollitt, Edna Richolson. Mengelberg and the Symphonic Epoch. New York: Ives Washburn, Publisher, 1930. 165 p., 8 illus.

5. A0008, A0045, B0038, B0049, B0059, B0072, B0109, B0118, B0164, B0167.

C0752.
MENGES, HERBERT. b. August 27, 1902, Hove; d. February 20, 1972, London, England.

1. BAKER 7; GROVE 6/12; PAB-MI/2 (Bibliography); RIEMANN 12 + Supp.

5. A0003, A0004.

C0753.
MEROLA, GAETANO. b. January 4, 1881, Naples, Italy; d. August 30, 1953, San Francisco, California.

1. BAKER 7; GROVE-AM 1/3 (Bibliography); PAB-MI/2 (Bibliography).

2. ON 37/4.

5. B0042.

C0754.
MESSAGER, ANDRE. b. December 30, 1853, Montlucon, Allier; d. February 24, 1929, Paris, France.

1. BAKER 7 (Bibliography); EdS 1/7 (Bibliography); GROVE 6/12; MGG 1/9 (Bibliography); PAB-MI/2 (Bibliography); RIEMANN 12.

2. MUSICA 72 (September 1908).

4. Fevrier, Henry. <u>André Messager: mon maître, mon ami</u>. Paris: Amiot-Dumont, 1948. 250 p., 8 illus.

5. B0033.

C0755.
MESTER, JORGE. b. April 10, 1935, Mexico City, Mexico.

1. BAKER 7; GROVE 6/12; GROVE-AM 1/3; PAB-MI/2 (Bibliography); RIEMANN 12/Supp. (Bibliography).

C0756.
MEYLAN, JEAN. b. December 22, 1915, Geneva, Switzerland.

1. BAKER 7; PAB-MI/2 (Bibliography); RIEMANN 12 + Supp. (Bibliography).

C0757.
MEYROWITZ, SELMAR. b. April 18, 1875, Bartenstein, East Prussia; d. March 24, 1941, Toulouse, France.

1. BAKER 7; RIEMANN 12.

C0758.
MICHAELIDES, SOLON. b. November 25, 1905, Nicosia, Cyprus; d. September 9, 1979, Athens, Greece.

1. BAKER 7 (Bibliography); GROVE 6/12 (Bibliography); RIEMANN 12/Supp.

C0759.
MIHALY, ANDRAS. b. November 7, 1917, Budapest, Hungary.

1. BAKER 7; GROVE 6/12 (Bibliography); MGG 1/9; PAB-MI/2 (Bibliography); RIEMANN 12/Supp.

C0760.
MIKOREY, FRANZ. b. June 3, 1873, Munich; d. May 11, 1947, Munich, Germany.

1. BAKER 7 (Bibliography); RIEMANN 12.

5. B0084.

C0761.
MILLET, LUIS. b. April 18, 1867, Barcelona; d. December 7, 1941, Barcelona, Spain.

1. BAKER 7 (Bibliography); GROVE 6/12; MGG 1/9 (Bibliography); RIEMANN 12 (Bibliography).

4. <u>Lluís Millet vist per Lluís Millet</u>. Barcelona: Editorial Pòrtic, 1983. 331, [4], 16 p. of plates, 35 illus., index of names.

   Vendrell, Emilio. <u>El mestre Millet i jo: memòries</u>. Barcelona: Ayma, Editors, 1953. 251 p., 26 illus.

C0762.
MIROUZE, MARCEL. b. September 24, 1906, Toulouse; d. August 1, 1957, Aude, France.

1. BAKER 7; RIEMANN 12/Supp.

C0763.
MITCHELL, HOWARD. b. March 11, 1911, Lyons, Nebraska.

1. BAKER 7; GROVE 6/12; GROVE-AM 1/3 (Bibliography); PAB-MI/2 (Bibliography).

5. A0048.

C0764.
MITROPOULOS, DIMITRI. b. March 1, 1896, Athens, Greece; d. November 2, 1960, Milan, Italy.

1. BAKER 7; EdS 1/7; GROVE 6/12 (Bibliography); GROVE-AM 1/3 (Bibliography); MGG 1/9 + Supp.; PAB-MI/2 (Bibliography); RIEMANN 12 + Supp. (Bibliography).

2. GR 33; LS 33, 133; MusAm 80/13; ON 19/9, 25/5.

3. <u>Dimitri Mitropoulos, Katy Katsoyanis: a Correspondence 1930-1960</u>. New York: Martin Dale, 1973. 187 p., 17 illus., notes.

   She published a biography of the years 1929-1960 (Athens, 1966).

4. Christopoulou, Maria. Demetres Mitropoulos: zoe kai ergo. Athens: Yannoukakis, 1971. 248, 16 p. of plates, 56-item bibliography, list of works, discography, index.

5. A0004, A0010, A0022, A0048, A0052, B0052, B0069, B0101, B0110, B0152, B0159, B0161.

C0765.
MLYNARSKI, EMIL. b. July 18, 1870, Kibarty; d. April 5, 1935, Warsaw, Poland.

1. BAKER 7; GROVE 6/12 (Bibliography); MGG 1/9 (Bibliography); RIEMANN 12 + Supp. (Bibliography).

4. Wach, A. Życie i twórczość Emila Mlynarskiego. Ph.D. diss., University of Kraków, 1953.

5. A0050, B0059.

C0766.
MOLINARI, BERNARDINO. b. April 11, 1880, Rome; d. December 25, 1952, Rome, Italy.

1. BAKER 7; GROVE 6/12 (Bibliography); RIEMANN 12.

5. B0006, B0167.

C0767.
MOLINARI PRADELLI, FRANCESCO. b. July 4, 1911, Bologna, Italy.

1. BAKER 7; EdS 1/7; GROVE 6/12; PAB-MI/2 (Bibliography); RIEMANN 12/ Supp.

2. ON 30/15.

C0768.
MOLLENHAUER, EMIL. b. August 4, 1855, Brooklyn, New York; d. December 10, 1927, Boston, Massachusetts.

1. BAKER 7 (Bibliography); GROVE-AM 1/3 (Bibliography); PAB-MI/2 (Bibliography).

C0769.
MONTEUX, CLAUDE. b. October 15, 1920, Brookline, Massachusetts.

1. BAKER 7; GROVE-AM 1/3; PAB-MI/2 (Bibliography).

C0770.
MONTEUX, PIERRE. b. April 4, 1875, Paris, France; d. July 1, 1964, Hancock, Maine.

1. BAKER 7; EdS 1/7; GROVE 6/12 (Bibliography); GROVE-AM 1/3 (Bibliography); MGG 1/9; PAB-MI/2 (Bibliography); RIEMANN 12 + Supp. (Bibliography).

3. Monteux, Fifi [household pet], Doris Gerald Monteux and Pierre Monteux. Everyone is Someone. New York: Farrar, Straus & Cudahy, 1962. 138 p., index of names.

4. Monteux, Doris G. It's All in the Music. New York: Farrar, Straus and Giroux, 1965. 272 p., 19 illus., list of premieres, discography by Erich Kunzel, index of names.

5. A0008, A0010, A0040, A0048, A0050, A0052, B0006, B0008, B0038, B0060, B0095, B0101, B0109, B0116, B0118, B0138, B0167.

C0771.
MONTGOMERY, KENNETH. b. October 28, 1943, Belfast, North Ireland.

1. BAKER 7; GROVE 6/12; PAB-MI/2 (Bibliography).

C0772.
MORALT, RUDOLF. b. February 26, 1902, Munich, Germany; d. December 16, 1958, Vienna, Austria.

1. BAKER 7; GROVE 6/12; RIEMANN 12.

C0773.
MOREL, JEAN. b. January 10, 1903, Abbeville, France; d. April 14, 1975, New York City.

1. BAKER 7; GROVE 6/12; GROVE-AM 1/3 (Bibliography).

2. ON 21/10.

5. B0038.

C0774.
MORLACCHI, FRANCESCO. b. June 14, 1784, Perugia, Italy; d. October 28, 1841, Innsbruck, Austria.

1. BAKER 7 (Bibliography); EdS 1/7; GROVE 6/12 (Bibliography); MGG 1/9 (Bibliography); RIEMANN 12.

4. Ricci des Ferres-Cancani, Gabriella. Francesco Morlacchi (1784-1841): un maestro italiano alla corte di Sassonia. Firenze: Leo S. Olschki-Editore, 1958. viii, 221, [9] p., 13 illus., list of works, 49-item bibliography.

C0775.
MORRIS, WYN. b. February 14, 1929, Triech, Wales, England.

1. BAKER 7; PAB-MI/2 (Bibliography); RIEMANN 12/Supp.

C0776.
MOSCHELES, IGNAZ. b. May 23, 1794, Prague, Czechoslovakia; d. March 10, 1870, Leipzig, Germany.

1. BAKER 7 (Bibliography); GROVE 6/12 (Bibliography); MGG 1/9 (Bibliography); PAB-MI/2 (Bibliography); RIEMANN 12 + Supp. (Bibliography).

3. Moscheles, Felix, ed. Fragments of an Autobiography. New York: Harper & Brothers, Publishers, 1899. viii, 364 p., 3 illus.

4. Moscheles, Charlotte. Aus Moscheles Leben. 2 vols. Leipzig, 1872. Translated by A.D. Coleridge. New York: H. Holt and Company, 1873. xviii, 434 p., illus.

   Moscheles, [Charlotte], ed. Recent Music and Musicians as Described in the Diaries and Correspondence of Ignatz Moscheles. Translated by A.D. Coleridge. New York: Henry Holt and Company, 1874. Reprint 1970. xviii, 434 p., catalogue of compositions, index of names.

C0777.
MOSEL, IGNAZ FRANZ. b. April 1, 1772, Vienna; d. April 8, 1844, Vienna, Austria.

1. BAKER 7 (Bibliography); GROVE 6/12 (Bibliography); MGG 1/9 (Bibliography); RIEMANN 12 (Bibliography) + Supp. (Bibliography).

C0778.
MOSEWIUS, JOHANN THEODOR. b. September 25, 1788, Koenigsberg; d. September 15, 1858, Schaffhausen, Germany.

1. BAKER 7 (Bibliography); GROVE 6/12 (Bibliography); MGG 1/9 (Bibliography); RIEMANN 12 (Bibliography).

C0779.
MOTTL, FELIX. b. August 24, 1856, Unter-St. Veit, near Vienna, Austria; d. July 2, 1911, Munich, Germany.

1. BAKER 7; EdS 1/7 (Bibliography); GROVE 6/12 (Bibliography); MGG 1/9 (Bibliography); PAB-MI/2 (Bibliography); RIEMANN 12 + Supp. (Bibliography).

   Engaged by the Metropolitan Opera in 1903 to conduct "Parsifal" but had to withdraw after protests from Wagner's heirs.

5. B0033, B0035, B0055, B0057, B0062, B0076, B0103, B0112, B0140, B0141, B0148.

   SEE: Berthe Malko under **NICOLAI MALKO** (C0721.4).

   SEE: Autobiography of **FELIX WEINGARTNER** (C1190.3).

C0780.
MRAVINSKY, EVGENY. b. June 4, 1903, St. Petersburg, Russia.

1. BAKER 7 (Bibliography); GROVE 6/12; PAB-MI/2 (Bibliography); RIEMANN 12 + Supp. (Bibliography).

5. A0040, A0052.

   SEE: Lipovsky, Alexander, comp. Lenin Prize Winners: Soviet Stars in the World of Music. Translated by Olga Shartse. Moscow: Progress Publishers, n.d. [c.1966]. 286, [1] p., 12 illus.

C0781.
MUCK, KARL. b. October 22, 1859, Darmstadt; d. March 3, 1940, Stuttgart, Germany.

1. BAKER 7 (Bibliography); EdS 1/7 (Bibliography); GROVE 6/12 (Bibliography); GROVE-AM 1/3 (Bibliography); MGG 1/9 (Bibliography); PAB-MI/2 (Bibliography); RIEMANN 12 + Supp.

2. GR 55/651; HiFi/MusAm 20/10.

4. Hjelle, Eivind Otto, ed. Rolf Nesch: Karl Muck und sein Orchester. Hamburg: Hans Christians Verlag, n.d. [1978]. 55 p., 72 illus.

   Nesch lived and worked in Hamburg (1933-51), and his twenty-four etchings, "Karl Muck und sein Orchester", launched his career as an artist in Hamburg.

5. A0008, A0012, A0015, B0008, B0038, B0065, B0118, B0121, B0156.

C0782.
MUELLER, ADOLF, Sr. b. October 7, 1801, Tolna, Hungary; d. July 29, 1886, Vienna, Austria.

1. BAKER 7; GROVE 6/12 (Bibliography); MGG 1/9 (Bibliography); RIEMANN 12/Supp. (Bibliography).

C0783.
MUELLER, ADOLF, Jr. b. October 15, 1839, Vienna; d. December 14, 1901, Vienna, Austria.

1. BAKER 7; MGG 1/9 (Bibliography); RIEMANN 12/Supp. (Bibliography).

C0784.
MUELLER-KRAY, HANS. b. October 13, 1908, Essen; d. May 30, 1969, Stuttgart, Germany.

1. BAKER 7; RIEMANN 12 + Supp. (Bibliography).

C0785.
MUELLER-REUTER, THEODOR. b. September 1, 1858, Dresden; d. August 11, 1919, Dresden, Germany.

1. BAKER 7; RIEMANN 12.

3. Mueller-Reuter, Theodor. Bilder und Klaenge des Friedens: musikalische Erinnerungen und Aufsaetze. Leipzig: Verlag Wilhelm Hartung, 1919. 208 p., 2 portraits.

C0786.
MUELLER-ZUERICH, PAUL. b. June 19, 1898, Zurich, Switzerland.

1. BAKER 7, GROVE 6/12 (Bibliography); PAB-MI/2 (Bibliography); RIEMANN 12 + Supp. (Bibliography).

C0787.
MUENCH, ERNST. b. December 31, 1859, Niederbronn, Alsatia; d. April 1, 1928, Strasbourg, France.

1. BAKER 7; RIEMANN 12 + Supp. (Bibliography).

C0788.
MUENCH, FRITZ. b. June 2, 1890, Strasbourg; d. March 10, 1970, Niederbronn-les Bains, France.

1. BAKER 7; RIEMANN 12 + Supp. (Bibliography).

C0789.
MUENCH, HANS. b. March 9, 1893, Mulhouse, Alsatia, France.

1. BAKER 7; GROVE 6/12 (Bibliography); MGG 1/9; RIEMANN 12 + Supp.

C0790.
MUENCHINGER, KARL. b. May 29, 1915, Stuttgart, Germany.

1. BAKER 7; GROVE 6/12; PAB-MI/2 (Bibliography); RIEMANN 12 + Supp. (Bibliography).

4. Gavoty, Bernard. Karl Muenchinger. Genève: Editions René Kister, 1959. 30, [2] p., 23 illus., discography.

   Schwarz, Erwin. Weltsprache Musik: Karl Muenchinger und sein Stuttgarter Kammerorchester. Stuttgart: Stuttgarter Kammerorchester, 1975. 52 p.

C0791.
MUGNONE, LEOPOLD. b. September 29, 1858, Naples; d. December 22, 1941, Naples, Italy.

1. BAKER 7; EdS 1/7 (Bibliography); GROVE 6/12 (Bibliography); PAB-MI/2 (Bibliography); RIEMANN 12/Supp.

C0792.
MUNCH, CHARLES. b. September 26, 1891, Strasbourg, France; d. November 6, 1968, Richmond, Virginia.

1. BAKER 7; GROVE 6/12; GROVE-AM 1/3 (Bibliography); MGG 1/9 + Supp.; PAB-MI/2 (Bibliography); RIEMANN 12 + Supp. (Bibliography).

2. Time (December 19, 1949).

3. Munch, Charles. Je suis chef d'orchestre. Paris: Editions du Conquistador, 1954 [Translated by Leonard Barkat as I am a Conductor. New York, 1955]. 107, [2] p.

   The American edition includes the Boston Symphony Orchestra repertoire during the maestro's first five seasons.

5. A0022, A0040, A0048, B0008, B0052, B0086, B0145.

C0793.
MUNCLINGER, MILAN. b. July 3, 1923, Košice, Czechoslovakia.

1. BAKER 7; GROVE 6/12.

C0794.
MUTI, RICCARDO. b. July 28, 1941, Naples, Italy.

1. BAKER 7 (Bibliography); GROVE 6/12 (Bibliography); GROVE-AM 1/3 (Bibliography); PAB-MI/2 (Bibliography); RIEMANN 12/Supp.

2. GR 57/683, 61/725, 63/754; HiFi/MusAm 26/2, 28/3; ON 45/4.

5. A0017, A0031, B0122.

C0795.
NAPRAVNIK, EDUARD. b. August 24, 1839, Býšt, near Hradec Králové, Bohemia; d. November 23, 1916, St. Petersburg, Russia.

1. BAKER 7 (Bibliography); EdS 1/7 (Bibliography); GROVE 6/13 (Bibliography); MGG 1/9 (Bibliography); PAB-MI/2 (Bibliography); RIEMANN 12 + Supp. (Bibliography).

C0796.
NAUMANN, KARL ERNST. b. August 15, 1910, Freiberg, Saxony; d. December 15, 1910, Jena, Germany.

1. BAKER 7; GROVE 6/13 (Bibliography); MGG 1/9; RIEMANN 12.

C0797.
NAUMANN, SIEGFRIED. b. November 27, 1919, Malmoe, Sweden.

1. BAKER 7; GROVE 6/13 (Bibliography); MGG/Supp. (Bibliography); RIEMANN 12/Supp.

C0798.
NAYLOR, BERNARD. b. November 22, 1907, Cambridge, England.

1. BAKER 7; GROVE 6/13 (Bibliography).

C0799.
NEDBAL, KAREL. b. October 28, 1888, Dvurkrálové, near Prague; d. March 20, 1964, Prague, Czechoslovakia.

1. BAKER 7; RIEMANN 12/Supp. (Bibliography).

C0800.
NEDBAL, OSCAR. b. March 26, 1874, Tábor, Bohemia; d. December 24, 1930, Zagreb, Yugoslavia.

1. BAKER 7 (Bibliography); EdS 1/7 (Bibliography); MGG 1/9 (Bibliography); RIEMANN 12/Supp. (Bibliography).

4. Buchner, Alexander. Oskar Nedbal. Praha: Panton, 1976. 359 p., illus., bibliography, list of works, index.

Novák, Ladislav. Oskar Nedbal v mých vzpomínkách: s dvaceti třemi dokumentárními vyobrazenimi. Praha: Vytiskla "Rodina", n.d. [1938]. 99, [2] p., 21 illus.

C0801.
NEEL, LOUIS BOYD. b. July 19, 1905, Blackheath, Kent, England.

1. BAKER 7; GROVE 6/13; PAB-MI/2 (Bibliography); RIEMANN 12 + Supp.

2. GR 50.

3. Neel, Boyd. My Orchestras and Other Adventures: the Memoirs of Boyd Neel. Forward by Sir Peter Peers. Edited by J. David Finch. Toronto: University of Toronto Press, 1985. viii, [i], 230 p., 28 illus., discography 1934-1979, index.

   Neel, Boyd. The Story of an Orchestra. Introduction by Benjamin Britten. London: Vox Mundi Limited, 1950. [viii], 133 p.

5. A0003, A0004.

C0802.
NEF, ALBERT. b. October 20, 1882, St. Gall; d. December 6, 1966, Bern, Switzerland.

1. BAKER 7; GROVE 6/13; MGG 1/9; RIEMANN 12 + Supp.

C0803.
NEIDLINGER, GUENTER. b. October 4, 1930, Heidelberg, Germany.

1. BAKER 7; RIEMANN 12/Supp.

C0804.
NELHYBEL, VACLAV. b. September 24, 1919, Polanka, Czechoslovakia.

1. BAKER 7; GROVE-AM 1/3; PAB-MI/2 (Bibliography).

C0805.
NEUENDORFF, ADOLF. b. June 13, 1843, Hamburg, Germany; d. December 4, 1897, New York City.

1. BAKER 7 (Bibliography); GROVE-AM 1/3 (Bibliography); PAB-MI/2 (Bibliography); RIEMANN 12.

C0806.
NEUHAUS, RUDOLF. b. January 3, 1914, Cologne, Germany.

1. BAKER 7; PAB-MI/2 (Bibliography); RIEMANN 12/Supp.

C0807.
von **NEUKOMM, SIGISMUND.** b. July 10, 1778, Salzburg, Austria; d. April 3, 1858, Paris, France.

1. BAKER 7 (Bibliography); GROVE 6/13 (Bibliography); MGG 1/9 (Bibliography); PAB-MI/2 (Bibliography); RIEMANN 12 + Supp. (Bibliography).

2. MQ 45/4.

3. His autobiography was published in Paris as Esquisses biographiques de Sigismond Neukomm in 1859. No copy located.

C0808.
NEUMANN, FRANZ. b. June 16, 1874, Převov, Moravia; d. February 24, 1929, Brno, Czechoslovakia.

1. BAKER 7; RIEMANN 12.

C0809.
NEUMANN, VACLAV. b. September 29, 1920, Prague, Czechoslovakia.

1. BAKER 7; GROVE 6/13 (Bibliography); MGG/Supp. (Bibliography); PAB-MI/2 (Bibliography); RIEMANN 12/Supp.

C0810.
NICOLAI, CARL OTTO. b. June 9, 1810, Koenigsberg; d. May 11, 1849, Berlin, Germany.

1. BAKER 7 (Bibliography); EdS 1/7 (Bibliography); GROVE 6/13 (Bibliography); MGG 1/9 (Bibliography); PAB-MI/2 (Bibliography); RIEMANN 12 + Supp. (Bibliography).

4. Altmann, Wilhelm. Otto Nicolai: Briefe an seinem Vater. Regensburg: Gustav Bosse Verlag, 1924. 400 p., index.

   Brunsing, Annette. Otto Nicolai als Operndirigent und Opernkomponist. Ph.D. diss., University of Mainz, 1961.

5. B0035.

C0811.
NICOLAU, ANTONIO. b. June 8, 1858, Barcelona; d. February 26, 1933, Barcelona, Spain.

1. BAKER 7 (Bibliography); GROVE 6/13; RIEMANN 12.

4. Mitjana, Rafael. Para musica vamos!...: estudios sobre el arte musical contemporáneo en España. Valencia: F. Sempere y Compañía, Editores, 1909. ix, 229 p.

5. B0007.

C0812.
NIKISCH, ARTHUR. b. October 12, 1855, Szent-Miklos, Hungary; d. January 23, 1922, Leipzig, Germany.

1. BAKER 7 (Bibliography); EdS 1/7; GROVE 6/13 (Bibliography); GROVE-AM 1/3 (Bibliography); MGG 1/9 (Bibliography); PAB-MI/2 (Bibliography); RIEMANN 12 + Supp. (Bibliography).

2. JCG 4/1; LGB 5/2; RS 4.

4. Chevalley, Heinrich, ed. Arthur Nikisch: Leben und Wirken. Berlin: Verlag Ed. Bote & G. Bock, 1922. [ii], 220 p., 29 illus.

Dette, Arthur. Nikisch. Leipzig: Lothar Joachim, 1922. 143 p., portrait.

Pfohl, Ferdinand. Arthur Nikisch als Mensch und Kuenstler. Leipzig: Hermann Seemann Nachfolger, n.d. [1900]. 54 p., 7 illus.

Pfohl, Ferdinand. Arthur Nikisch: sein Leben, seine Kunst, sein Wirken. Hamburg: Alster-Verlag, 1925 [revised and enlarged edition of the above title]. 199 p., 6 illus., index.

Segnitz, Eugen. Arthur Nikisch. Leipzig: Dr. Sally Rabinowitz Verlag, 1920. 47 p.

Wackernagel, Peter. Die Aera Nikisch. Berlin: Gesellschaft der Freunde der Berliner Philharmonie e.V., 1968. 15 p.

Weissmann, Adolf. Arthur Nikisch und die Berliner Philharmonischen Konzerte 1895-1920: ein Rueckblick. Berlin: Buchdruckerei Otto Lange, n.d. [1920]. 67 p., 5 illus., complete programs.

5. A0008, A0012, A0015, A0016, A0050, B0015, B0033, B0035, B0048, B0049, B0057, B0059, B0065, B0112, B0117, B0121, B0127, B0131, B0138, B0140, B0156, B0157.

SEE: Knepler, Hugo. O diese Kuenstler: Indiskretionen eines Managers. Wien: Fiba-Verlag, 1931. 198, [1] p., 28 illus.

C0813.
NILIUS, RUDOLF. b. March 23, 1883, Vienna; d. December 31, Bad Ischl, Austria.

1. BAKER 7; RIEMANN 12.

C0814.
NOBEL, FELIX de. b. May 27, 1907, Haarlem; d. March 25, 1981, Amsterdam, Holland.

1. BAKER 7; GROVE 6/13; RIEMANN 12 + Supp.

C0815.
NORDQUIST, JOHAN CONRAD. b. April 11, 1840, Vaenersborg; d. April 16, 1920, Charlottenlund, Sweden.

1. BAKER 7; GROVE 6/13 (Bibliography); RIEMANN 12.

C0816.
NORMAN, FREDERICK LUDVIG. b. August 28, 1831, Stockholm; d. March 28, 1885, Stockholm, Sweden.

1. BAKER 7; GROVE 6/13 (Bibliography); MGG 1/9 (Bibliography); RIEMANN 12 + Supp.

C0817.
NORTH, ALEX. b. December 4, 1910, Chester, Pennsylvania.

1. BAKER 7; GROVE-AM 1/3 (Bibliography); PAB-MI/2 (Bibliography).

C0818.
von NOSKOWSKI, SIGISMUND. b. May 2, 1846, Warsaw; d. July 23, 1909, Warsaw, Poland.

1. BAKER 7; GROVE 6/13 (Bibliography); MGG 1/9 (Bibliography); PAB-MI/2 (Bibliography); RIEMANN 12 + Supp. (Bibliography).

C0819.
NOVELLO-DAVIES, CLARA. b. April 7, 1861, Cardiff, Wales; d. March 1, 1943, London, England.

1. BAKER 7.

3. Novello-Davies, Clara. The Life I Have Loved. London: William Heinemann Ltd, 1940. x, 323 p., 42 illus.

C0820.
OBERHOFER, EMIL JOHANN. b. August 10, 1861, near Munich, Germany; d. May 22, 1933, San Diego, California.

1. BAKER 7; GROVE-AM 1/3; PAB-MI/2 (Bibliography); RIEMANN 12

5. B0152.

C0821.
OBRIST, ALOIS. b. March 30, 1867, San Remo, Italy; d. June 29, 1910, Stuttgart, Germany.

1. BAKER 7; RIEMANN 12 (Bibliography).

C0822.
OCHS, SIEGFRIED. b. April 19, 1858, Frankfurt/M.; d. February 5, 1929, Berlin, Germany.

1. BAKER 7; GROVE 6/13 (Bibliography); MGG 1/9; RIEMANN 12 (Bibliography) + Supp.

3. Ochs, Siegfried. Der deutsche Gesangsverein fuer gemischten Chor. 4 vols. Berlin: Max Hesses Verlag, 1923/24/26. 147, [1]; 425, [2]; 175, [1]; 151 p.

   Ochs, Siegfried. Geschenes, Gesehenes. Leipzig: Brethlein & Co., n.d. [1922]. 427, [2] p., 12 illus., index of names.

C0823.
O'NEILL, NORMAN. b. March 14, 1875, London; d. March 3, 1934, London, England.

1. BAKER 7 (Bibliography); GROVE 6/13; PAB-MI/2 (Bibliography); RIEMANN 12.

4. Hudson, Derek. Norman O'Neill: a Life of Music. London: Quality Press, Ltd, 1945, 160 p., 15 illus., list of compositions, index.

C0824.
ORCHARD, WILLIAM ARUNDEL. b. April 13, 1867, London, England; d. April 17, 1961, at sea off the coast of South Africa.

1. BAKER 7; RIEMANN 12 + Supp.

3. Orchard, William Arundel. The Distant View. Sydney (Australia): The Curawong Publishers, 1943. 253 p.

5. B0108.

C0825.
ORMANDY, EUGENE. b. November 18, 1899, Budapest, Hungary.

1. BAKER 7; GROVE 6/13 (Bibliography); GROVE-AM 1/3 (Bibliography); MGG 1/10; PAB-MI/2 (Bibliography); RIEMANN 12 + Supp. (Bibliography).

2. GR 47/563, 63/745.

5. A0004, A0010, A0040, A0048, A0052, B0044, B0052, B0116, B0134, B0138, B0152, B0166.

SEE: Kupferberg, Herbert. Those Fabulous Philadelphians: the Life and Times of a Great Orchestra. London: W.H. Allen & Co., Ltd., 1970. x, 257 p., personnel, premieres, discography, index.

C0826.
OSTRCIL, OTAKAR. b. February 25, 1879, Smichov, near Prague; d. August 20, 1935, Prague, Czechoslovakia.

1. BAKER 7; GROVE 6/14 (Bibliography); MGG 1/10 (Bibliography); RIEMANN 12 + Supp. (Bibliography).

4. Bartoš, Josef. Josef Otakar Ostrčil. Praha: Nákladen Ceské Akademie Věd Umèní, 1936. 175 p., portrait, list of works.

Nejedlý, Zdeněk. Otakar Ostrčil: vzrusta a uzrání. Praha: n.p., 1935. 360 p., portrait, index.

C0827.
OTESCU, ION NONNA. b. December 15, 1888, Bucharest; d. March 25, 1940, Bucharest, Romania.

1. BAKER 7; GROVE 6/14 (Bibliography); MGG 1/10; RIEMANN 12 + Supp.

C0828.
van OTTERLOO, JAN WILLEM. b. December 27, 1907, Winterswijk, Holland; d. July 27, 1978, Melbourne, Australia.

1. BAKER 7; GROVE 6/14; MGG 1/10; RIEMANN 12 + Supp.

5. A0008.

C0829.
OTTO, ERNST. b. September 1, 1804, Koenigstein; d. March 5, 1877, Dresden, Germany.

1. BAKER 7; MGG 1/10 (Bibliography); RIEMANN 12 + Supp. (Bibliography).

C0830.
OZAWA, SEIJI. b. September 1, 1935, Hoten, Manchuria.

1. BAKER 7; GROVE 6/14; GROVE-AM 1/3 (Bibliography); PAB-MI/2 (Bibliography); RIEMANN 12/Supp.

5. A0017, A0031, B0008.

C0831.
PAGE, WILLIS. b. September 18, 1918, Rochester, New York.

1. BAKER 7; RIEMANN 12/Supp.

C0832.
PAILLARD, JEAN-FRANÇOIS. b. April 18, 1928, Vitry-le-François, France.

1. BAKER 7; GROVE 6/14; PAB-MI/2 (Bibliography); RIEMANN 12/Supp.

C0833.
PALANGE, LOUIS SALVADOR. b. December 17, 1917, Oakland, California; d. June 8, 1979, Burbank, California.

1. BAKER 7; GROVE-AM 1/3; PAB-MI/2 (Bibliography).

C0834.
PALAU, MANUEL. b. January 4, 1893, Valencia; d. February 18, 1967, Valencia, Spain.

1. BAKER 7; GROVE 6/14 (under Palau Boix with Bibliography); MGG 1/10 (Bibliography); RIEMANN 12 (under Palau-Buix) + Supp.

C0835.
PALSSON, PALL. b. May 9, 1928, Graz, Austria.

1. BAKER 7; GROVE 6/14 (Bibliography); PAB-MI/2 (Bibliography).

C0836.
PANIZZA, ETTORE. b. August 12, 1875, Buenos Aires, Argentina; d. November 27, 1967, Milan, Italy.

1. BAKER 7; EdS 1/7; PAB-MI/2 (Bibliography); RIEMANN 12.

2. ON 38/14.

3. Panizza, Ettore. Medio siglo de vida musical: ensayo autobiografico. Buenos Aires: Ricordi Americana, 1952. 192 p., 29 illus., appendix of compositions.

5. B0168.

C0837.
PANUFNIK, ANDRZEJ. b. September 24, 1914, Warsaw, Poland.

1. BAKER 7; GROVE 6/14 (Bibliography); MGG 1/10 (Bibliography); PAB-MI/2 (Bibliography); RIEMANN 12 + Supp. (Bibliography).

4. His wife Scarlett wrote Out of the City of Fear (London, 1956), a copy of which has not been located.

C0838.
PANULA, JORMA. b. August 10, 1930, Kauhajoki, Finland.

1. BAKER 7; RIEMANN 12/Supp.

C0839.
PAPANDOPULO, BORIS. b. February 25, 1906, Bad Honnef am Rhein, Germany.

1. BAKER 7 (Bibliography); GROVE 6/14 (Bibliography); MGG 1/10; RIEMANN 12.

C0840.
PAPI, GENNARO. b. December 11, 1886, Naples, Italy; d November 29, 1941, New York City.

1. BAKER 7; GROVE-AM 1/3.

5. B0072.

C0841.
PARAY, PAUL. b. May 24, 1886, Le Tréport, Normandy, France; d. October 10, 1979, Monte Carlo, Monaco.

1. BAKER 7; GROVE 6/14 (Bibliography); GROVE-AM 1/3; MGG/Supp. (Bibliography); PAB-MI/2 (Bibliography); RIEMANN 12 + Supp. (Bibliography).

2. HiFi/MusAm 29/3; LGB 17/2.

4. Landowski, W.-L. Paul Paray: musicien de France et de monde. Lyon: Editions et Imprimeries Du Sud-Est, 1956. 94, [1] p., portrait, 10-item bibliography, list of compositions, selected discography.

5. A0004, A0022, A0046, A0048, B0133, B0141.

C0842.
PARELLI, ATTILIO. b. May 31, 1874, Monteleone d'Orvieto, near Perugia; d. December 26, 1944, Perugia, Italy.

1. BAKER 7; RIEMANN 12.

C0843.
PASDELOUP, JULES-ETIENNE. b. September 15, 1819, Paris; d. August 13, 1887, Fountainebleau, France.

1. BAKER 7 (Bibliography); GROVE 6/14 (Bibliography); MGG 1/10 (Bibliography); PAB-MI/2 (Bibliography); RIEMANN 12 + Supp.

5. B0033, B0112.

C0844.
PATANE, GIUSEPPE. b. January 1, 1932, Naples, Italy.

1. BAKER 7; GROVE 6/14; PAB-MI/2 (Bibliography); RIEMANN 12/Supp.

C0845.
PAULLI, HOLGER SIMON. b. February 22, 1810, Copenhagen; d. December 23, 1891, Copenhagen, Denmank.

1. BAKER 7 (Bibliography); EdS 1/7; MGG 1/10 (Bibliography); PAB-MI/2 (Bibliography).

3. MGG mentions a partial autobiography published in K. Hendriksen's <u>Fra billedmagerens kaleidoskop</u>. Copenhagen, 1954.

C0846.
PAULMUELLER, ALEXANDER. b. March 4, 1912, Innsbruck, Austria.

1. BAKER 7; RIEMANN 12/Supp.

C0847.
PAUMGARTNER, BERNHARD. b. November 14, 1887, Vienna; d. July 27, 1971, Salzburg, Austria.

1. BAKER 7; EdS 1/7; GROVE 6/14 (Bibliography); MGG 1/10 + Supp.; RIEMANN 12 + Supp. (Bibliography).

2. OW 4/1.

3. Paumgartner, Bernhard. <u>Erinnerungen</u>. Salzburg: Residenz Verlag, 1969. 209, [2] p., 16 illus., list of publications, list of compositions, index of names.

   Along with important biographies of J.S. Bach (1950), Mozart (1927; 6th expanded ed. 1967), and Schubert (1943; 3rd ed. 1960), he was the author of 140 published articles.

5. A0052, B0069, B0104, B0132, B0145.

C0848.
PAUR, EMIL. b. August 29, 1855, Czernowitz, Bukovina, Austria; d. June 7, 1932, Mistek, Bohemia.

1. BAKER 7; GROVE 6/14 (Bibliography); GROVE-AM 1/3 (Bibliography); MGG 1/10 (Bibliography); PAB-MI/2 (Bibliography); RIEMANN 12.

5. B0065.

C0849.
PEDROTTI, CARLO. b. November 12, 1817, Verona; d. October 16, 1893, Verona, Italy.

1. BAKER 7; EdS 1/7 (Bibliography); GROVE 6/14 (Bibliography); MGG 1/10;

RIEMANN 12.

C0850.
PELLETIER, LOUIS WILFRID. b. June 20, 1896, Montreal, Canada; d. April 9, 1982, New York City.

1. BAKER 7; GROVE 6/14; GROVE-AM 1/3; MGG/Supp.; PAB-MI/2 (Bibliography); RIEMANN 12 + Supp. (Bibliography).

3. Pelletier, Wilfrid. Une symphonie inachevée.... Ottawa: Editions Leméac Inc., 1972. 275 p., 15 illus., index.

4. Hust, C. Evolution de la vie musicale au Québec sous l'influence de Wilfrid Pelletier. Ph.D. diss., Toulouse University, 1973.

5. B0042, B0120.

C0851.
PEMBAUR, KARL MARIA. b. August 24, 1876, Innsbruck, Austria; d. March 6, 1939, Dresden, Germany.

1. BAKER 7; MGG 1/10 (Bibliography); RIEMANN 12.

Son of JOSEPH PEMBAUR, Sr. (b. May 23, 1848, Innsbruck; d. February 19, 1923, Innsbruck, Austria) who published Ueber das Dirigieren.

C0852.
PERESS, MAURICE. b. March 18, 1930, New York City.

1. BAKER 7; GROVE 6/14; GROVE-AM 1/3; RIEMANN 12/Supp.

C0853.
PEREZ CASAS, BARTOLOMEO. b. January 24, 1873, Lorca, near Murcia; d. January 15, 1956, Madrid, Spain.

1. BAKER 7; MGG 1/10 (Bibliography); RIEMANN 12.

C0854.
von PERFALL, KARL. b. January 29, 1824, Munich; d. January 14, 1907, Munich, Germany.

1. BAKER 7; GROVE 6/14 (Bibliography); MGG 1/10 (Bibliography); RIEMANN 12.

4. Oexle, G. Generalintendant Karl von Perfall: ein Beitrag zur Geschichte des Hof- und Nationaltheaters in Muenchen 1867-1892. Ph.D. diss., University of Munich, 1954. 130 p.

5. SEE: Ernest Newman (vol. 4) under RICHARD WAGNER (C1175.4).

SEE: Zenger, Max. Geschichte der Muenchener Oper. Muenchen, 1923.

C0855.
PERGAMENT, MOSES. b. September 21, 1893, Helsinki, Finland; d. March 5, 1977, Gustavsberg, near Stockholm, Sweden.

1. BAKER 7; GROVE 6/14 (Bibliography); MGG 1/10; RIEMANN 12 + Supp. (Bibliography).

C0856.
von PERGER, RICHARD. b. January 10, 1854, Vienna; d. January 11, 1911, Vienna, Austria.

1. BAKER 7; MGG 1/10 (Bibliography).

C0857.
PERISSON, JEAN-MARIE. b. July 6, 1924, Arcachon, France.

1. BAKER 7; PAB-MI/2 (Bibliography); RIEMANN 12/Supp.

C0858.
PERLEA, JONEL. b. December 13, 1900, Ograda, Romania; d. July 29, 1970, New York City.

1. BAKER 7; GROVE 6/14; PAB-MI/2 (Bibliography); RIEMANN 12 + Supp. (Bibliography).

4. Firoiu, V. Un român şi harul său, Ionel Perlea. Bucureşti: Editura Albatros, n.d.

   216, [3] p., 32 illus., 44-item bibliography.

C0859.
PEROSI, DON LORENZO. b. December 21, 1872, Tortona; d. October 12, 1956, Rome, Italy.

1. BAKER 7 (Bibliography); GROVE 6/14 (Bibliography); MGG 1/10 (Bibliography); PAB-MI/2 (Bibliography); RIEMANN 12 + Supp. (Bibliography).

4. Glinski, Matteo. Lorenzo Perosi. Milano: G. Ricordi & C., 1953. 149, [2] p., 17 illus., notes, index of works, index of names.

   Rinaldi, Mario. Lorenzo Perosi. Roma: Edizioni De Santis, 1967. 617 p., 20 illus., compositions, discography, 27-page bibliography.

C0860.
PESKO, ZOLTAN. b. February 15, 1937, Budapest, Hungary.

1. BAKER 7; GROVE 6/14; PAB-MI/2 (Bibliography); RIEMANN 12/Supp.

2. OW 25/4.

C0861.
PETERS, REINHARD. b. April 2, 1926, Magdeburg, Germany.

1. BAKER 7; GROVE 6/14; PAB-MI/2 (Bibliography); RIEMANN 12/Supp.

C0862.
PETKOV, DIMITER. b. May 4, 1919, Smolyan, Bulgaria.

1. BAKER 7; GROVE 6/14.

C0863.
PFITZNER, HANS ERICH. b. May 5, 1869, Moscow, Russia; d. May 22, 1949, Salzburg, Austria.

1. BAKER 7; EdS 1/8; GROVE 6/14 (Bibliography); MGG 1/10 (Bibliography); PAB-MI/2 (Bibliography); RIEMANN 12 + Supp. (Bibliography).

2. RS 45/6.

3. Pfitzner, Hans. Gesammelte Schriften. 3 vols. Augsburg: Dr. Benno Filser Verlag G.m.b.H., 1929. Edited reprint 1969.

   Directly related to this bibliography is the third volume, Werke und Wiedergabe. x, 359 p., index of names.

4. Mueller-Blattau, Josef. Hans Pfitzner. Potsdam: Akademische Verlagsgesellschaft Athenaion, 1940. 128 p., 17 illus., 36 musical examples, list of compositions, 16-item bibliography, index.

   Zorn, Gerhard. Hans Pfitzner als Opern-Regisseur. Ph.D. diss., University of Munich, 1954. 187 p.

C0864.
PFLUEGER, GERHARD. b. April 9, 1907, Dresden, Germany.

1. BAKER 7; RIEMANN 12 + Supp.

C0865.
PIERNE, HENRI-CONSTANT-GABRIEL. b. August 16, 1863, Metz; d. July 17, 1937, Ploujean, near Morlaix, France.

1. BAKER 7 (Bibliography); EdS 1/8 (Bibliography); GROVE 6/14 (Bibliography); MGG 1/10 (Bibliography); PAB-MI/2 (Bibliography); RIEMANN 12 + Supp.

5. A0046.

C0866.
PITT, PERCY. b. January 4, 1870, London; d. November 23, 1932, London, England.

1. BAKER 7; GROVE 6/14; PAB-MI/2 (Bibliography); RIEMANN 12.

4. Chamier, J. Daniel. Percy Pitt of Covent Garden and the B.B.C.. Introduction by Sir Henry J. Wood. London: Edward Arnold & Co., 1938. 248 p., 12 illus., index.

   Pitt was music director of the BBC from 1922 to 1930.

5. B0168.

C0867.
PITZ, WILHELM. b. August 25, 1897, Breinig; d. November 21, 1973, Aachen, Germany.

1. BAKER 7; GROVE 6/14; PAB-MI/2 (Bibliography); RIEMANN 12 + Supp. (Bibliography).

2. OW 3/7-8.

C0868.
POHLIG, KARL. b. February 10, 1858, Teplitz, Bohemia; d. June 17, 1928, Braunschweig, Germany.

1. BAKER 7.

4. Carl Pohlig, Conductor of the Philadelphia Orchestra: Biographical Sketch and Comments of the Foreign Press. n.d. [c.1908]. unpaginated [16 p.], portrait.

C0869.
POLACCO, GIORGIO. b. April 12, 1873, Venice, Italy; d. April 30, 1960, New York City.

1. BAKER 7; GROVE 6/15; GROVE-AM 1/3; PAB-MI/2 (Bibliography); RIEMANN 12.

C0870.
POLLAK, EGON. b. May 3, 1879, Prague; d. June 14, Prague, Czechoslovakia.

1. BAKER 7; RIEMANN 12.

C0871.
PONC, MIROSLAV. b. December 2, 1902, Vysoké Mýto; d. April 1, 1976, Prague, Czechoslovakia.

1. BAKER 7; GROVE 6/15 (Bibliography); MGG 1/10 (Bibliography); RIEMANN 12/Supp.

C0872.
POST, JOSEPH. b. April 10, 1906, Sydney; d. December 27, 1972, Broadbeach, Queensland, Australia.

1. GROVE 6/15; PAB-MI/2 (Bibliography); RIEMANN 12.

C0873.
POULET, GASTON. b. April 10, 1892, Paris; d. April 14, 1974, Draveil, Essonne, France.

1. BAKER 7; GROVE 6/15; RIEMANN 12.

C0874.
PRAUSNITZ, FREDERIK. b. August 26, 1920, Cologne, Germany.

1. BAKER 7; GROVE 6/15; GROVE-AM 1/3; PAB-MI/2 (Bibliography).

3. Prausnitz, Frederik. Score and Podium: a Complete Guide to Conducting. New York: W.W. Norton & Company, Inc., 1983. x, 530 p., index.

C0875.
PRETRE, GEORGES. b. August 14, 1924, Waziers, France.

1. BAKER 7; EdS/Supp.; GROVE 6/15; PAB-MI/2 (Bibliography); RIEMANN 12/Supp.

5. A0052.

C0876.
PREVIN, ANDRE. b. April 6, 1929, Berlin, Germany.

1. BAKER 7; EdS/Supp.; GROVE 6/15; GROVE-AM 1/3; PAB-MI/2 (Bibliography); RIEMANN 12/Supp.

2. GR 47/556, 52/613, 58/695; New Yorker (Jan. 10, 17, 1983); OW 16/6, 17/6.

3. Previn, André and Anthony Hopkins. Music Face to Face. London: Hamish Hamilton Ltd, 1971. ix, 131, [1] p.

   Previn, André, ed. Orchestra. Garden City: Doubleday & Company, Inc., 1979. 224 p., 217 illus., index.

4. Bookspan, Martin and Ross Yockey. André Previn: a Biography. Garden City: Doubleday & Company, Inc., 1981. ix, 398 p., 34 illus., index.

   Greenfield, Edward. André Previn. New York: Drake Publishers Inc., 1973. 96 p., 50 illus., discography by Malcolm Walker.

5. A0031.

   SEE: Smyth, Alan, ed. To Speak for Ourselves: the London Symphony Orchestra. London: William Kimper, 1970.

C0877.
PREVITALI, FERNANDO. b. February 16, 1907, Adria, Italy.

1. BAKER 7; EdS 1/8; GROVE 6/15; PAB-MI/2 (Bibliography); RIEMANN 12 + Supp.

3. Previtali, Fernando. Guida allo studio della direzione d'orchestra. Roma, 1951. No copy located.

C0878.
PREVOST, EUGENE-PROSPER. b. April 23, 1809, Paris, France; d. August 19, 1872, New Orleans, Louisiana.

1. BAKER 7; GROVE 6/15; GROVE-AM 1/3 (Bibliography); MGG 1/10 (Bibliography); PAB-MI/2 (Bibliography).

C0879.
PRIESTMAN, BRIAN. b. February 10, 1927, Birmingham, England.

1. BAKER 7; GROVE 6/15; GROVE-AM 1/3; PAB-MI/2 (Bibliography).

C0880.
PRILL, PAUL. b. October 1, 1860, Berlin; d. December 21, 1930, Bremen, Germany.

1. BAKER 7; RIEMANN 12.

C0881.
PRINGSHEIM, KLAUS. b. July 24, 1883, Feldafing, near Munich, Germany. d. December 7, 1972, Toyko, Japan.

1. BAKER 7; MGG 1/10 (Bibliography); RIEMANN 12 + Supp. (Bibliography).

C0882.
PRITCHARD, JOHN. b. February 5, 1921, London, England.

1. BAKER 7; GROVE 6/15; PAB-MI/2 (Bibliography); RIEMANN 12 + Supp.

2. ON 36/9; OPERA 15/7, 22/10; OW 20/6.

3. Pritchard, John. "Conducting Mozart", Opera Annual 1955-6. London: John Calder, 1955: 26-34.

5. B0071.

C0883.
PROCH, HEINRICH. b. July 22, 1809, Boehmisch-Leipa; d. December 18, 1878, Vienna, Austria.

1. BAKER 7; RIEMANN 12/Supp.

4. Voelker, Inge-Christa. Heinrich Proch: sein Leben und Wirken. Ph.D. diss., University of Vienna, 1949. 410 p.

C0884.
PROHASKA, FELIX. b. May 16, 1912, Vienna, Austria.

1. BAKER 7; GROVE 6/15 (Bibliography); MGG 1/10; PAB-MI/2 (Bibliography); RIEMANN 12 + Supp.

C0885.
PROTHEROE, DANIEL. b. November 5, 1866, Cwmgiedd, near Ystradgynlais, South Wales, England; d. February 24, 1934, Chicago, Illinois.

1. BAKER 7; GROVE 6/15 (Bibliography); PAB-MI/2 (Bibliography).

C0886.
PRUEWER, JULIUS. b. February 20, 1874, Vienna, Austria; d. July 8, 1943, New York City.

1. BAKER 7; RIEMANN 12.

C0887.
QUADRI, AREGO. b. March 23, 1911, Como, Italy.

1. BAKER 7; PAB-MI/2 (Bibliography); RIEMANN 12/Supp.

C0888.
QUELER, EVE. b. January 1, 1936, New York City.

1. BAKER 7; GROVE-AM 1/3 (Bibliography); PAB-MI/2 (Bibliography).

2. ON 36/17, 40/14, 42/20.

5. B0090.

C0889.
QUINET, FERDINAND. b. January 29, 1898, Charleroi, France; d. October 24, 1971, Liège, Belgium.

1. BAKER 7; GROVE 6/15 (Bibliography); MGG 1/10; PAB-MI/2 (Bibliography); RIEMANN 12 + Supp. (Bibliography).

C0890.
QUINTANAR, HECTOR. b. April 15, 1936, Mexico City, Mexico.

1. BAKER 7; GROVE 6/15 (Bibliography); PAB-MI/2 (Bibliography); RIEMANN 12/Supp.

C0891.
RAABE, PETER. b. November 27, 1872, Frankfurt an der Oder; d. April 12, 1945. Weimar, Germany.

1. BAKER 7; GROVE 6/15 (Bibliography); MGG 1/10 (Bibliography); RIEMANN 12.

C0892.
van **RAALTE, ALBERT.** b. May 21, 1890, Amsterdam, Holland; d. November 23, 1952, Amsterdam, Holland.

1. BAKER 7; RIEMANN 12.

C0893.
RABAUD, HENRI. b. November 10, 1873, Paris, France; d. September 11, 1949, Paris, France.

1. BAKER 7; EdS 1/8 (Bibliography); GROVE 6/15 (Bibliography); MGG 1/10 (Bibliography); PAB-MI/2 (Bibliography); RIEMANN 12 (Bibliography).

5. B0033, B0121.

C0894.
RACHMANINOFF, SERGEI. b. April 1, 1873, Oneg, Novgorod, Russia; d. March 28, 1943, Beverly Hills, California.

1. BAKER 7 (Bibliography); EdS 1/8 (Bibliography); GROVE 6/15 (under Rakhmaninov with Bibliography); GROVE-AM 1/4 (Bibliography); MGG 1/10 (Bibliography); PAB-MI/2 (Bibliography); RIEMANN 12 (Bibliography) + Supp. (Bibliography).

   Conductor/Bolshoi Opera/Moscow (1904-06), Rachmaninoff was twice offered the permanent conductorship of the Boston Symphony Orchestra.

2. MQ 13/3, 30/1, 2 (Two installments of his personal reminiscences).

3. SEE: MQ 30/1, 2 (1944).

4. Seroff, Victor I. Rachmaninoff. New York: Simon and Schuster, 1950. Forward by Virgil Thompson. xiv, [xiv], 269 p., 21 illus., list of compositions, 201-item bibliography, index.

C0895.
RADECKE, ROBERT. b. October 31, 1830, Dittmannsdorf; d. June 21, 1911, Wernigerode, Germany.

1. BAKER 7; RIEMANN 12.

C0896.
RADECKE, RUDOLF. b. September 6, 1829, Dittmannsdorf; d. April 15, 1893, Berlin, Germany.

1. BAKER 7; RIEMANN 12.

C0897.
RAHLWES, ALFRED. b. October 23, 1878, Wesel; d. April 20, 1946, Halle, Germany.

1. BAKER 7 (Bibliography); RIEMANN 12 + Supp. (Bibliography).

C0898.
RAJTER, LUDOVIT. b. July 30, 1906, Pezinok, Czechoslovakia.

1. BAKER 7; GROVE 6/15; MGG/Supp. (Bibliography); RIEMANN 12 + Supp.

C0899.
RANDEGGER, ALBERTO. b. April 13, 1832, Trieste, Italy; d. December 18, 1911, London, England.

1. BAKER 7; GROVE 6/15 (Bibliography); MGG 1/10 (Bibliography).

5. B0007.

C0900.
RANKL, KARL. b. October 1, 1898, Vienna; d. September 6, Salzburg, Austria.

1. BAKER 7; GROVE 6/15; MGG/Supp.; PAB-MI/2 (Bibliography); RIEMANN 12 + Supp. (Bibliography).

2. OPERA 1/2, 19/11.

5. A0004.

SEE: Montague Haltrecht under **ERICH KLEIBER** (C0588.5).

C0901.
RAPEE, ERNO. b. June 4, 1891, Budapest, Hungary; d. June 26, 1945, New York City.

1. BAKER 7; GROVE-AM 1/4 (Bibliography); PAB-MI/2 (Bibliography); RIEMANN 12/Supp.

2. New Yorker 19 (Feb. 5, 1944).

5. A0010.

C0902.
RASTRELLI, JOSEPH. b. April 13, 1799, Dresden; d. November 15, 1842, Dresden, Germany.

1. BAKER 7; GROVE 6/15 (Bibliography); MGG 1/11 (Bibliography); RIEMANN 12.

C0903.
RATTLE, SIMON DENIS. b. January 19, 1955, Liverpool, England.

1. BAKER 7; GROVE 1/15; PAB-MI/2 (Bibliography).

2. HiFi/MusAm 31/12; GR 60/719.

5. A0031.

C0904.
REDEL, KURT. b. October 8, 1918, Breslau, Germany.

1. BAKER 7; GROVE 6/15; RIEMANN 12 + Supp.

C0905.
REICHWEIN, LEOPOLD. b. May 16, 1878, Breslau, Germany; d. April 8, 1945, Vienna, Austria.

1. BAKER 7; RIEMANN 12.

C0906.
REINECKE, CARL HEINRICH. b. June 23, 1824, Altona; d. March 10, 1910, Leipzig, Germany.

1. BAKER 7; EdS 1/8; GROVE 6/15 (Bibliography); MGG 1/11 (Bibliography); PAB-MI/2 (Bibliography); RIEMANN 12 + Supp. (Bibliography).

   Conductor of the Gewandhaus Concerts in Leipzig for thirty-five years (1860-95), Reinecke was a musical leader in Germany.

4. Topusov, Nikolai. Carl Reinecke: Beitraege zu seinem Leben und seiner Symphonik. Ph.D. diss., University of Berlin, 1943. iii, 461, vii p.

C0907.
REINER, FRITZ. b. December 19, 1888, Budapest, Hungary; d. November 15, 1963, New York City.

1. BAKER 7; EdS 1/8; GROVE 6/15 (Bibliography); GROVE-AM 1/4 (Bibliography); PAB-MI/2 (Bibliography); RIEMANN 12.

2. HiFi 14/4; ON 13/17.

3. His personal library and memorabilia are housed in the Northwestern University Music Library.

4. Potter, R.R. Fritz Reiner: Conductor, Teacher, Musical Innovator. Ph.D. diss., Northwestern University, 1980.

   No copy seen.

   The Podium: Magazine of the Fritz Reiner Society. Vol. 1, No. 1/1976. 16 p., 1 illus.

   This appears to be the only number issued.

5. A0010, A0022, A0048, B0042, B0072, B0088, B0138, B0163.

   SEE: William Barry Furlong under GEORG SOLTI (C1070.4).

   SEE: Autobiography of BORIS GOLDOVSKY (C0410.3).

C0908.
van REMOORTEL, EDOUARD. b. May 30, 1926, Brussels, Belgium; d. May 16, 1977, Paris, France.

1. BAKER 7; GROVE 6/15; RIEMANN 12 (under Van Remoortel) + Supp.

C0909.
RENNER, JOSEPH. b. April 25, 1832, Schmatzhausen, near Landshut, Bavaria; d. August 11, 1895, Regensburg, Germany.

1. BAKER 7; RIEMANN 12.

C0910.
RETTICH, WILHELM. b. July 3, 1892, Leipzig, Germany.

1. BAKER 7; GROVE 6/15 (Bibliography); PAB-MI/2 (Bibliography); RIEMANN 12 + Supp. (Bibliography).

C0911.
REY, JEAN-BAPTISTE. b. December 18, 1734, Tarn-et-Garonne; d. July 15, 1810, Paris, France.

1. BAKER 7; GROVE 6/15; MGG 1/11 (Bibliography).

5. B0036.

C0912.
RHENE-BATON [real name, René Baton]. b. September 5, 1879, Courseulles-sur-Mer, Calvados; d. September 23, 1940, Le Mans, France.

1. BAKER 7; RIEMANN 12; PAB-MI/2 (Bibliography).

5. A0008, A0046, B0133.

C0913.
RHODES, WILLARD. b. May 12, 1901, Dashler, Ohio.

1. BAKER 7; GROVE 6/15 (Bibliography); PAB-MI/2 (Bibliography).

C0914.
RIBERA y MANEJA, ANTONIO. b. May 3, 1873, Barcelona; d. March 4, 1956, Madrid, Spain.

1. BAKER 7; RIEMANN 12.

C0915.
RICHTER, HANS. b. April 4, 1843, Raab, Hungary; d. December 5, 1916, Bayreuth, Germany.

1. BAKER 7 (Bibliography); EdS 1/8 (Bibliography); GROVE 6/15 (Bibliography); MGG 1/11 (Bibliography); PAB-MI/2 (Bibliography); RIEMANN 12 + Supp. (Bibliography).

   He was selected by Wagner to conduct the _Ring_ at Bayreuth in 1876.

4. Kufferath, Maurice. _L'Art de diriger: Richard Wagner et la "Neuvième Symphonie" de Beethoven. Hans Richter et la Symphonie en "ut" mineur. L'Idylle de Siegfried.--Interprétation et tradition_. 3rd edition. Paris: Librairie Fischbacher, 1909. [iv], 265 p.

5. B0033, B0035, B0049, B0054, B0055, B0057, B0062, B0070, B0075, B0076, B0077, B0085, B0112, B0126, B0148, B0168.

   SEE: J. Daniel Chamier under PERCY PITT (C0866.4).

   SEE: Graves, C.L. _The Diversions of a Music-Lover_. London: Macmillan and Co., Limited, 1904.

   SEE: Ernest Newman under RICHARD WAGNER (C1175.4).

   SEE: Reece, Henry and Oliver Elton, eds. _Musical Criticisms by Arthur Johnstone_. Manchester: at the University Press, 1905. xiv, 225 p., portrait.

   SEE: Young, Percy M. _Elgar O.M.: a Study of a Musician_. London: Collins Clear-Type Press, 1955. 447 p., 18 illus., index of works including literary works, 62-item bibliography, index.

C0916.
RICHTER, KARL. b. October 15, 1926, Plauen; d. February 15, 1981, Munich, Germany.

1. BAKER 7; GROVE 6/15; PAB-MI/2 (Bibliography); RIEMANN 12 + Supp.

2. LGB 18/1.

C0917.
RIEDEL, KARL. b. October 6, 1827, Kronenberg, near Elberfeld; d. June 3, 1888, Leipzig, Germany.

1. BAKER 7; GROVE 6/15 (Bibliography); RIEMANN 12 + Supp.

C0918.
RIEGER, FRITZ. b. June 28, 1910, Oberalstadt; d. September 29, 1978, Bonn, Germany.

1. BAKER 7; PAB-MI/2 (Bibliography); RIEMANN 12 + Supp.

4. Kriem, Werner F. "Dirigent in einer mass-stablosen Zeit: zur Problematik des gesellschaftlichen Verstaendnisses des heutigen Dirigententums. Gleichzeitig ein Beitrag zu Fritz Riegers 65. Geburtstag", Hans Pfitzner Gesellschaft 34 (1975): 3-22.

C0919.
RIETZ, JULIUS. b. December 28, 1812, Berlin; d. September 12, 1877, Dresden, Germany.

1. BAKER 7; GROVE 6/16 (Bibliography); MGG 1/11 (Bibliography); RIEMANN 12 + Supp.

2. MQ 1/3, 2/1.

4. Zimmer, Herbert. Julius Rietz. Ph.D. diss., Humboldt University, Berlin, 1943. 168 p.

C0920.
RIFKIN, JOSHUA. b. April 22, 1944, New York City.

1. BAKER 7; GROVE 6/16 (Bibliography); GROVE-AM 1/4; PAB-MI/2 (Bibliography).

C0921.
RIGNOLD, HUGO HENRY. b. May 15, 1905, Kingston-on-Thames; d. May 30, 1976, London, England.

1. BAKER 7; GROVE 6/16; PAB-MI/2 (Bibliography).

5. A0004.

C0922.
RILLING, HELMUTH. b. May 29, 1933, Stuttgart, Germany.

1. BAKER 7; GROVE 6/16; PAB-MI/2 (Bibliography); RIEMANN 12/Supp.

C0923.
RIOTTE, PHILIPP JAKOB. b. August 16, 1776, St. Wendel, Saar; d. August 20, 1856, Vienna, Austria.

1. BAKER 7; GROVE 6/16 (Bibliography); MGG 1/11 (Bibliography); RIEMANN 12 + Supp.

3. MGG 1/11 lists a manuscript autobiography (1826) owned by the Gesellschaft der Musikfreunde in Vienna.

4. Spengler, Gernot. Der Komponist Philipp Jakob Riotte aus St. Wendel: sein Leben und seine Instrumentalmusik. Ph.D. diss., University of Saarbruecken, 1973.

C0924.
RISTENPART, KARL. b. January 26, 1900, Kiel, Germany; d. December 24, 1967, Lisbon, Portugal.

1. BAKER 7; GROVE 6/16; RIEMANN 12 + Supp. (Bibliography).

C0925.
RITTER, FREDERIC LOUIS. b. June 22, 1824, Strasbourg, France; d. July 4, 1891, Antwerp, Belgium.

1. BAKER 7; GROVE-AM 1/4 (Bibliography); PAB-MI/2 (Bibliography).

C0926.
ROBINSON, STANFORD. b. July 5, 1904, Leeds, England.

1. BAKER 7; GROVE 6/16; PAB-MI/2 (Bibliography); RIEMANN 12/Supp.

5. A0003, A0004.

C0927.
RODAN, MENDI. b. April 17, 1929, Isai, Romania.

1. BAKER 7; GROVE 6/16; PAB-MI/2 (Bibliography).

C0928.
RODZINSKI, ARTUR. b. January 1, 1892, Spalato, Dalmatia, Poland; d. November 27, 1958, Boston, Massachusetts.

1. BAKER 7; EdS 1/8 (Bibliography); GROVE 6/16; GROVE-AM 1/4; MGG 1/11 (Bibliography); PAB-MI/2 (Bibliography); RIEMANN 12 + Supp. (Bibliography).

   Noted for his elaborate concert performances of operas.

2. RS 42/3, 73.

4. Rodzinski, Halina. Our Two Lives. New York: Charles Scribner's Sons, 1976. ix, 403 p., 77 illus., discography by Michael Gray, index.

5. A0004, A0010, B0006, B0044, B0099, B0138.

C0929.
ROEGNER, HEINZ. b. January 16, 1929, Leipzig, Germany.

1. BAKER 7; RIEMANN 12/Supp.

C0930.
ROEHR, HUGO. b. February 13, 1866, Dresden; d. June 7, 1937, Munich, Germany.

1. BAKER 7; RIEMANN 12.

C0931.
ROGALSKI, THEODOR. b. April 11, 1901, Bucharest, Romania; d. February 2, 1954, Zurich, Switzerland.

1. BAKER 7; GROVE 6/16 (Bibliography); MGG 1/11 (Bibliography); RIEMANN 12/Supp. (Bibliography).

C0932.
RONALD, LANDON. b. June 7, 1873, London; d. August 14, 1938, London, England.

1. BAKER 7; GROVE 6/16; MGG 1/11; PAB-MI/2 (Bibliography); RIEMANN 12.

2. GR 51/601.

3. Ronald, Landon. Myself and Others: Written, Lest I Forget. London: Sampson Low, Marston & Co., Ltd., n.d. vii, [iv], 13-226 p., 22 illus., index.

   Ronald, Landon. Variations on a Personal Theme. London: Hodder and Stoughton Ltd., 1922. 177 p., 20 illus.

5. B0048, B0058, B0059, B0096, B0107, B0138.

   SEE: Jerrold Northrop under **ADRIAN BOULT** (C0138.5).

C0933.
RONNENFELD, PETER. b. January 26, 1935, Dresden; d. August 6, 1965, Kiel, Germany.

1. BAKER 7; GROVE 6/16; RIEMANN 12/Supp.

2. OW 6/3.

C0934.
ROSA, CARL. b. March 22, 1842, Hamburg, Germany; d. April 30, 1889, Paris, France.

1. BAKER 7; EdS 1/8 (Bibliography); GROVE 6/16 (Bibliography); MGG 1/11 (Bibliography); PAB-MI/2 (Bibliography); RIEMANN 12 (under Rose, Karl with Bibliography) + Supp. (Bibliography).

2. OPERA 9/6, 18/4, 6, 7, 9.

4. Phillips, Annette. "The Opera Companies of Great Britain: Carl Rosa", Opera Annual 1954-55 (London, 1954): 34-36.

5. B0007, B0010, B0018, B0075, B0085.

C0935.
ROSBAUD, HANS. b. July 22, 1895, Graz, Austria; d. December 29, 1962, Lugano, Switzerland.

1. BAKER 7; GROVE 6/16 (Bibliography); MGG 1/11 (Bibliography); PAB-MI/2 (Bibliography); RIEMANN 12 + Supp. (Bibliography).

   His personal library is at Washington State University in Pullman, Washington.

5. B0109, B0110.

C0936.
ROSENSTOCK, JOSEPH. b. January 27, 1895, Cracow, Poland.

1. BAKER 7; PAB-MI/2 (Bibliography); RIEMANN 12 + Supp.

2. ON 28/5.

C0937.
ROSENTHAL, MANUEL. b. June 18, 1904, Paris, France.

1. BAKER 7; GROVE 6/16; GROVE-AM 1/4; MGG 1/11; PAB-MI/2 (Bibliography); RIEMANN 12 + Supp. (Bibliography).

C0938.
ROSS, HUGH. b. August 21, 1898, Langport, England.

1. BAKER 7; GROVE-AM 1/4.

C0939.
ROSSI, MARIO. b. March 29, 1902, Rome, Italy.

1. BAKER 7; EdS 1/8; GROVE 6/16; MGG 1/11; PAB-MI/2 (Bibliography); RIEMANN 12 + Supp.

5. A0052.

C0940.
ROSTROPOVICH, MSTISLAV. b. March 27, 1927, Baku, Russia.

1. BAKER 7; GROVE 6/16 (Bibliography); GROVE-AM 1/4 (Bibliography); MGG/ Supp. (Bibliography); PAB-MI/2 (Bibliography); RIEMANN 12 + Supp. (Bibliography).

   An excellent pianist, brilliant cellist and very independent thinker.

2. GR 54/646; HiFi/MusAm 25/10, 28/2; ON 40/3; OPER 1970: ein Jarhbuch der Zeitschrift "Opernwelt"; Time (Oct. 24, 1977).

3. Rostropowitsch, Mstislaw & Galina. Die Musik und unser Leben. Bern: Scherz Verlag, 1985 [1st edition Paris, 1983]. 223 p., notes, discography, index of names.

5. A0031.

   SEE: Vishnevskaya, Galina. Galina: a Russian Story. Translated by Guy Daniels. New York: Harcourt Brace Jovanovich, Publishers, 1984. xiii, 519 p., 71 illus., repertoire, discography, index.

C0941.
ROTHER, ARTUR. b. October 12, 1885, Stettin; d. September 22, 1972, Aschau, Germany.

1. BAKER 7; GROVE 6/16; RIEMANN 12 + Supp.

C0942.
ROTHWELL, WALTER HENRY. b. September 22, 1872, London, England; d. March 12, 1927, Los Angeles, California.

1. BAKER 7; GROVE-AM 1/4 (Bibliography); PAB-MI/2 (Bibliography).

C0943.
ROTTENBERG, LUDWIG. b. October 11, 1864, Czernowitz, Bukovina; d. May 6, 1932, Frankfurt/M., Germany.

1. BAKER 7; RIEMANN 12.

C0944.
ROTZSCHE, HANS-JOACHIM. b. April 25, 1929, Leipzig, Germany.

1. BAKER 7; RIEMANN 12/Supp.

C0945.
ROWICKI, WITOLD. b. February 26, 1914, Taganrog, Russia.

1. BAKER 7 (Bibliography); GROVE 6/16; PAB-MI/2 (Bibliography); RIEMANN 12 + Supp. (Bibliography).

4. Terpilowski, Lech. Witold Rowicki. Kraków: Polskie Wydawnictwo Muzyczne, 1961. 43 p., 27 illus.

C0946.
ROZHDESTVENSKY, GENNADI. b. May 4, 1931, Moscow, Russia.

1. BAKER 7 (Bibliography); GROVE 6/16 (Bibliography); PAB-MI/2 (Bibliography).

5. B0071.

C0947.
RUDEL, JULIUS. b. March 6, 1921, Vienna, Austria.

1. BAKER 7 (Bibliography); GROVE 6/16 (Bibliography); GROVE-AM 1/4 (Bibliography); PAB-MI/2 (Bibliography); RIEMANN 12/Supp.

   Championed American opera and moved NY City Opera to Lincoln Center.

2. HiFi/MusAm 29/8; ON 25/15, 28/16, 38/2; OPERA 16/10.

5. B0124.

C0948.
RUDNICKI, MARIAN TOEFIL. b. March 7, 1888, Cracow; d. December 31, 1944, Warsaw, Poland.

1. BAKER 7; RIEMANN 12.

C0949.
RUDNYTSKY, ANTIN. b. February 7, 1902, Luka, Galicia, Poland; d. November 30, 1975, Toms River, New Jersey.

BAKER 7; PAB-MI/2 (Bibliography); RIEMANN 12.

C0950.
RUDOLF, MAX. b. June 15, 1902, Frankfurt/M., Germany.

1. BAKER 7; GROVE 6/16; GROVE-AM 1/4; PAB-MI/2 (Bibliography); RIEMANN 12 + Supp. (Bibliography).

2. JCG 2/2, 2/4; ON 20/11, 30/12, 38/12, 39/13.

3. Rudolf, Max. The Grammar of Conducting: a Practical Guide to Baton Technique and Orchestral Interpretation. 2nd edition. 1980 [1st edition 1950 with Forward by George Szell]. xviii, 471 p., 3 appendices, list of diagrams, index of music.

5. B0101, B0158.

C0951.
RUEDEL, HUGO. b. February 7, 1868, Havelberg; d. November 27, 1934, Berlin, Germany.

1. BAKER 7; RIEMANN 12.

C0952.
RUEHLMANN, FRANS. b. January 11, 1868, Brussels, Belgium; d. June 8, 1948, Paris, France.

1. BAKER 7; EdS 1/8.

5. A0046, B0033, B0133.

C0953.
RUMMEL, CHRISTIAN. b. November 27, 1787, Brichsenstadt; d. February 13, 1849, Wiesbaden, Germany.

1. BAKER 7; GROVE 6/16; MGG 1/11.

C0954.
RUNG, FREDERIK. b. January 14, 1854, Copenhagen; d. January 22, 1914, Copenhagen, Denmark.

1. BAKER 7; GROVE 6/16 (Bibliography); MGG 1/11 (Bibliography).

C0955.
RUNG, HENRIK. b. March 3, 1807, Copenhagen; d. December 13, 1871, Copenhagen, Denmark.

1. BAKER 7 (Bibliography); MGG 1/11.

C0956.
RUNGENHAGEN, CARL FRIEDRICH. b. September 27, 1778, Berlin; d. December 21, 1851, Berlin, Germany.

1. BAKER 7; MGG 1/11 (Bibliography); RIEMANN 12 (Bibliography) + Supp. (Bibliography).

C0957.
RYBNER, PETER MARTIN CORNELIUS. b. October 26, 1855, Copenhagen, Denmark; d. January 21, 1929, New York City.

BAKER 7; PAB-MI/2 (Bibliography); RIEMANN 12 (under Ruebner).

C0958.
SACHER, PAUL. b. April 28, 1906, Basel, Switzerland.

1. BAKER 7 (Bibliography); GROVE 6/16 (Bibliography); MGG 1/11 (Bibliography); PAB-MI/2 (Bibliography); RIEMANN 12 + Supp. (Bibliography).

5. A0002.

C0959.
SAFONOV, VASILI. b. February 6, 1852, Ishcherskaya, Caucasus; d. February 27, 1918, Kislovodsk, Russia.

1. BAKER 7; GROVE 6/16 (Bibliography); MGG 1/11; RIEMANN 12 + Supp. (Bibliography).

5. B0059.

C0960.
SAINT-REQUIER, LEON. b. August 8, 1872, Rouen; d. October 1, 1964, Paris, France.

1. BAKER 7; RIEMANN 12.

C0961.
SAITO, HIDEO. b. May 23, 1902, Tokyo; d. September 18, 1974, Tokyo, Japan.

1. BAKER 7; RIEMANN 12/Supp.

C0962.
SALTER, LIONEL PAUL. b. September 8, 1914, London, England.

1. BAKER 7; GROVE 6/16 (Bibliography); PAB-MI/2 (Bibliography).

C0963.
SAMINSKY, LAZARE. b. November 8, 1882, Valegotsulova, near Odessa, Russia; d. June 30, 1959, Port Chester, New York.

1. BAKER 7 (Bibliography); GROVE 6/16 (Bibliography); GROVE-AM 1/4 (Bibliography); PAB-MI/2 (Bibliography); RIEMANN 12 (Bibliography) + Supp. (Bibliography).

   Co-founder of the League of Composers in New York City.

3. He published Essentials of Conducting in New York in 1958, and GROVE 6/16 mentions a manuscript autobiography, Third Leonardo.

5. B0094.

C0964.
SAMOSUD, SAMUEL. b. May 14, 1884, Odessa; d. November 6, 1964, Moscow, Russia.

1. BAKER 7; GROVE 6/16 (Bibliography); RIEMANN 12/Supp.

C0965.
SAMPSON, GEORGE. b. July 24, 1861, Clifton, England; d. December 23, 1949, Brisbane, Australia.

1. BAKER 7; RIEMANN 12.

C0966.
SAMUEL, GERHARD. b. April 20, 1924, Bonn, Germany.

1. BAKER 7; GROVE 6/16; GROVE-AM 1/4; PAB-MI/2 (Bibliography); RIEMANN 12/Supp.

C0967.
SANDERLING, KURT. b. September 9, 1912, Arys, Germany.

1. BAKER 7; GROVE 6/16; RIEMANN 12/Supp.

2. GR 51/611.

5. SEE: Krause, Ernst. Schreiben ueber Musik: Essays - Kritiken - Berichte. Berlin: Henschelverlag Kunst und Gesellschaft, 1981. 384 p., 60-item bibliography.

   Conductors included are Blech, Walter, Abendroth, Fritz Busch, Erich Kleiber, Eugen Jochum, Koch, von Karajan, Keilberth, Kempe, Fricsay, Konwitschny, Furtwaengler, and Karl Boehm.

C0968.
SANJUAN, PEDRO. b. November 15, 1886, San Sebastian, Spain; d. October 18, 1976, Washington, D.C.

1. BAKER 7; PAB-MI/2 (Bibliography); RIEMANN 12/Supp.

C0969.
SANTI, NELLO. b. September 22, 1931, Adria, Italy.

1. BAKER 7; PAB-MI/2 (Bibliography); RIEMANN 12/Supp.

2. ON 27/10.

C0970.
SANTINI, GABRIELE. b. January 20, 1886, Perugia; d. November 13, 1964, Rome, Italy.

1. BAKER 7; EdS 1/8; GROVE 6/16; PAB-MI/2 (Bibliography); RIEMANN 12/Supp.

C0971.
SANTORO, CLAUDIO. b. November 23, 1919, Manáos, Brazil.

1. BAKER 7; GROVE 6/16 (Bibliography); MGG 1/11; PAB-MI/2 (Bibliography); RIEMANN 12 + Supp.

C0972.
SANZONO, NINO. b. April 13, 1911, Venice; d. May 4, 1983, Milan, Italy.

1. BAKER 7; EdS 1/8; GROVE 6/16; PAB-MI/2 (Bibliography); RIEMANN 12 + Supp.

C0973.
SARGENT, HAROLD MALCOLM. b. April 29, 1895, Stamford, Lincolnshire, d. October 3, 1967, London, England.

1. BAKER 7; GROVE 6/16 (Bibliography); MGG 1/11 (Bibliography); PAB-MI/2 (Bibliography); RIEMANN 12 + Supp. (Bibliography).

2. GR 45/534.

4. Reid, Charles. Malcolm Sargent: a Biography. London: Hamish Hamilton, 1968. xiv, 491 p., 19 illus., 5 appendices including a short survey of programs, index.

5. A0002, A0003, A0004, A0040, A0045, B0009, B0060, B0071, B0096, B0167.

C0974.
SAVINE, ALEXANDER. b. April 26, 1881, Belgrade, Yugoslavia; d. January 19, 1949, Chicago, Illinois.

1. BAKER 7; RIEMANN 12.

C0975.
SAWALLISCH, WOLFGANG. b. August 23, 1923, Munich, Germany.

1. BAKER 7; EdS/Supp.; GROVE 6/16; PAB-MI/2 (Bibliography); RIEMANN 12 + Supp. (Bibliography).

2. OW 1/7, 16/7, 17/7, 23/12.

4. Krellmann, Hanspeter, ed. Stationen eines Dirigenten: Wolfgang Swallisch. Muenchen: Verlag F. Bruckmann KG, 1983. 232 p., 58 illus., chronology, discography, biographies of forty contributors, index of names.

5. A0052, B0145.

C0976.
SCHAEFFER, JULIUS. b. September 28, 1823, Krevese, near Osterburg; d. February 10, 1902, Breslau, Germany.

1. BAKER 7 (Bibliography); RIEMANN 12 (Bibliography).

C0977.
SCHALK, FRANZ. b. May 27, 1863, Vienna; d. September 2, 1931, Edlach, Austria.

1. BAKER 7; EdS 1/8 (Bibliography); GROVE 6/16 (Bibliography); MGG 1/11; PAB-MI/2 (Bibliography); RIEMANN 12 + Supp. (Bibliography).

2. RS 38.

4. Schalk, Lili, ed. Franz Schalk: Briefe und Betrachtungen mit einem Lebensabriss von Victor Junk. Leipzig: Musikwissenschaftlicher Verlag, 1935. 91, [1] p., portrait.

5. A0015, B0069.

C0978.
SCHARRER, AUGUST. b. August 18, 1866, Strasbourg; d. October 24, 1936, Weiherhof, near Fuerth, Germany.

1. BAKER 7; MGG 1/11 (Bibliography); RIEMANN 12/Supp.

C0979.
SCHEEL, FRITZ. b. November 7, 1852, Luebeck, Germany; d. March 13, 1907, Philadelphia, Pennsylvania.

1. BAKER 7 (Bibliography); GROVE-AM 1/4 (Bibliography); PAB-MI/2 (Bibliography); RIEMANN 12 (Bibliography) + Supp. (Bibliography).

5. B0089.

SEE: Wister, Frances A. 25 Years of the Philadelphia Orchestra 1900-1925. Philadelphia, 1925.

C0980.
SCHEINPFLUG, PAUL. b. September 10, 1875, Loschwitz, near Dresden; d. March 11, 1937, Memel, Germany.

1. BAKER 7 (Bibliography); GROVE 6/16 (Bibliography); MGG 1/11; RIEMANN 12 + Supp. (Bibliography).

C0981.
SCHELLING, ERNEST HENRY. b. July 26, 1876, Belvidere, New Jersey; d. December 8, 1939, New York City.

1. BAKER 7 (Bibliography); GROVE 6/16; GROVE-AM 1/4 (Bibliography); PAB-MI/2 (Bibliography); RIEMANN 12.

4. Hill, T.H. Ernest Schelling (1876-1939): His Life and Contributions to Music Education Through Education Concerts. Ph.D. diss., Catholic University of America, 1970.

C0982.
SCHERCHEN, HERMANN. b. June 21, 1891, Berlin, Germany; d. June 12, 1966, Florence, Italy.

1. BAKER 7 (Bibliography); EdS 1/8 (Bibliography); GROVE 6/16 (Bibliography); MGG 1/11 + Supp. (Bibliography); PAB-MI/2 (Bibliography); RIEMANN 12 + Supp. (Bibliography).

2. RS 60.

3. Klemm, Eberhardt, comp. ...alles hoerbar machen: Briefe eines Dirigenten 1920 bis 1939. Berlin: Henschelverlag Kunst und Gesellschaft, 1976. 391, [1] p., 13 illus., notes, chronology, index of names.

   Scherchen, Hermann. Handbook of Conducting. Translated by M.D. Calvocoressi. London: Oxford University Press, 1933 [original: Lehrbuch des Dirigierens. Leipzig, 1929]. xiii, 243 p.

4. Curjel, Hans. Gedenkrede fuer Hermann Scherchen 1891-1966. Zuerich: Kommissionsverlag Hugt Co., n.d. [1967]. 35 p., 3 illus.

5. A0002, B0167.

C0983.
SCHERMAN, THOMAS KIELTY. b. February 12, 1917, New York City; d. May 14, 1979, New York City.

1. BAKER 7; GROVE 6/16; GROVE-AM 1/4 (Bibliography); RIEMANN 12.

C0984.
SCHERMERHORN, KENNETH DeWitt. b. November 20, 1929, Schenectady, New York.

1. BAKER 7; GROVE 6/16; GROVE-AM 1/4; PAB-MI/2 (Bibliography); RIEMANN 12/Supp.

C0985.
SCHICK, GEORGE. b. April 5, 1908, Prague, Czechoslovakia; d. March 7, 1985, New York City.

1. BAKER 7; GROVE-AM 1/4.

2. HiFi/MusAm 20/3.

C0986.
SCHILHAWSKY, PAUL. b. November 9, 1918, Salzburg, Austria.

1. BAKER 7; RIEMANN 12/Supp.

C0987.
von SCHILLINGS, MAX. b. April 19, 1868, Dueren; d. July 24, 1933, Berlin, Germany.

1. BAKER 7 (Bibliography); EdS 1/8 (Bibliography); GROVE 6/16 (Bibliography); MGG 1/11; PAB-MI/2 (Bibliography); RIEMANN 12 + Supp. (Bibliography).

   Intendant of the Berlin State Opera from 1919 to 1925.

4. Raupp, Wilhelm. Max von Schillings: der Kampf eines deutschen Kuenstlers. Hamburg: Hanseatischen Verlagsanstalt, Aktiengesellschaft, 1935. 310 p., 13, illus., index of names.

Richard, August. Max Schillings. Muenchen: Drei Masken Verlag A.-G., 1922. 67, [1] p., portrait, list of published compositions.

NOTE: The series indicates future books on Leo Blech, Mahler, Pfitzner, and Weingartner.

5. B0129.

C0988.
SCHINDLER, ANTON FELIX. b. June 13, 1795, Meedl, Moravia; d. January 16, 1864, Bokenheim, near Frankfurt/M., Germany.

1. BAKER 7 (Bibliography); GROVE 6/16 (Bibliography); MGG 1/11; PAB-MI/2 (Bibliography); RIEMANN 12 + Supp. (Bibliography).

C0989.
SCHINDLER, KURT. b. February 17, 1882, Berlin, Germany; d. November 16, 1935, New York City.

1. BAKER 7; GROVE-AM 1/4 (Bibliography); PAB-MI/2 (Bibliography).

C0990.
SCHIPPERS, THOMAS. b. March 9, 1930, Kalamazoo, Michigan; d. December 16, 1977, New York City.

1. BAKER 7; EdS/Supp.; GROVE 6/16; GROVE-AM 1/4; PAB-MI/2 (Bibliography); RIEMANN 12 + Supp.

2. HiFi/MusAm 28/4; ON 20/14, 27/4, 39/12.

The youngest musician ever to conduct the New York Philharmonic, his great potential ended in tragedy.

C0991.
SCHLETTERER, HANS MICHEL. b. May 29, 1824, Ansbach; d. June 4, 1893, Ausgburg, Germany.

1. BAKER 7 (Bibliography); RIEMANN 12.

C0992.
SCHMID, ERICH. b. January 1, 1907, Balsthal, Switzerland.

1. BAKER 7; GROVE 6/16; MGG 1/11; PAB-MI/2 (Bibliography); RIEMANN 12 + Supp. (Bibliography).

C0993.
SCHMIDT, GUSTAV. b. September 1, 1816, Weimar; d. February 11, 1882, Darmstadt, Germany.

1. BAKER 7; GROVE 6/16; MGG 1/11 (Bibliography).

C0994.
SCHMIDT, OLE. b. July 14, 1928, Copenhagen, Denmark.

1. BAKER 7; GROVE 6/16; PAB-MI/2 (Bibliography).

C0995.
SCHMIDT-ISSERSTEDT, HANS. b. May 5, 1900, Berlin; d. May 28, 1973, Holm, near Hamburg, Germany.

1. BAKER 7; GROVE 6/16; MGG 1/11 + Supp. (Bibliography); PAB-MI/2 (Bibliography); RIEMANN 12 + Supp.

2. GR 45/540.

5. B0110.

C0996.
SCHMITT, GEORG ALOYS. b. February 2, 1827, Hannover; d. October 15, 1902, Dresden, Germany.

1. BAKER 7; MGG 1/11 (Bibliography); RIEMANN 12 + Supp.

C0997.
SCHNEEVOIGT, GEORG LENNART. b. November 8, 1872, Viborg; d. November 28, 1947, Malmoe, Finland.

1. BAKER 7; GROVE 6/16 (Bibliography); MGG 1/11 (Bibliography); RIEMANN 12 + Supp. (Bibliography).

5. A0008, A0040, B0040, B0072.

C0998.
SCHNEIDER, ABRAHAM ALEXANDER. b. October 21, 1908, Vilna, Lithuania.

1. BAKER 7; GROVE-AM 1/4 (Bibliography); PAB-MI/2 (Bibliography).

C0999.
SCHNEIDT, HANNS-MARTIN. b. December 6, 1930, Kitzingen-am-Main, Germany.

1. BAKER 7; RIEMANN 12 + Supp. (Bibliography).

C1000.
SCHOEK, OTHMAR. b. September 1, 1886, Brunnen; d. March 8, 1957, Zurich, Switzerland.

1. BAKER 7 (Bibliography); GROVE 6/16 (Bibliography); MGG 1/12 (Bibliography); RIEMANN 12 + Supp. (Bibliography).

4. Vogel, Werner, ed. Othmar Schoeck im Gespraech. Zuerich: Atlantis Verlag, 1965. 192 p., portrait, list of works, index of names.

   Vogel, Werner, ed. Othmar Schoeck: Leben und Schaffen im Spiegel von Selbstzeugnissen und Zeitgenossenberichten. Zuerich: Altlantis Musikbuch-Verlag, 1976. 367 p., 63 illus., chronology, list of works, discography, bibliography, index of names.

C1001.
SCHOENZELER, HANS-HUBERT. b. June 22, 1925, Leipzig, Germany

1. BAKER 7; PAB-MI/2 (Bibliography); RIEMANN 12/Supp.

C1002.
SCHOLZ, BERNARD E. b. March 30, 1835, Mainz; d. December 26, 1916, Munich, Germany.

1. BAKER 7; GROVE 6/16 (Bibliography); MGG 1/12 (Bibliography); RIEMANN 12 + Supp.

C1003.
SCHREKER, FRANZ. b. March 23, 1878, Monaco; d. March 21, 1934, Berlin, Germany.

1. BAKER 7; GROVE 6/16 (Bibliography); MGG 1/12 (Bibliography); PAB-MI/2 (Bibliography); RIEMANN 12 + Supp. (Bibliography).

4. Neuwirth, Goesta. Franz Schreker. Wien: Bergland Verlag, 1959. 96 p., 24 illus., list of compositions, arrangements, librettos, list of students.

   Schreker-Bures, Haidy, H.H. Stuckenschmidt, and Werner Oehlmann. Franz Schreker. Wien: Oesterreichischer Bundesverlag fuer Unterricht, Wissenschaft und Kunst, 1970. 96 p., 10 illus., list of compositions, 22-item bibliography.

   St. Hoffmann, Rudolf. Franz Schreker. Wien: E.P. Tal & Co. Verlag, 1921. 170, [3] p., portrait.

C1004.
SCHREMS, JOSEPH. b. October 5, 1815, Warmensteinach; d. October 25, 1872, Regensburg, Germany.

1. BAKER 7; RIEMANN 12.

C1005.
von SCHUCH, ERNST. b. November 23, 1846, Graz, Austria; d. May 10, 1914, Koetzschenbroda, near Dresden, Germany.

1. BAKER 7; EdS 1/8; GROVE 6/16 (Bibliography); MGG 1/12; PAB-MI/2 (Bibliography); RIEMANN 12 + Supp.

4. Sakolowski, Paul. Ernst von Schuch. Leipzig: Hermann Seemann Nachfolger, 1901. 31 p., 2 illus.

   The series includes monographs on Nikisch, Strauss, Reinecke, and Mahler.

5. B0127.

   SEE: Kohut, Adolf. Das Dresdner Hoftheater in der Gegenwart. Dresden: E. Pierson's Verlag, 1888.

C1006.
SCHUECHTER, WILHELM. b. December 15, 1911, Bonn; d. May 27, 1974, Dortmund, Germany.

1. BAKER 7; GROVE 6/16 (Bibliography); RIEMANN 12/Supp.

C1007.
SCHUELER, JOHANNES. b. June 21, 1894, Vietz, Neumark; d. October 3, 1966, Berlin, Germany.

1. BAKER 7; PAB-MI/2 (Bibliography); RIEMANN 12 + Supp.

C1008.
SCHULLER, GUNTHER ALEXANDER. b. November 22, 1925, New York City.

1. BAKER 7 (Bibliography); GROVE-AM 1/4 (Bibliography); PAB-MI/2 (Bibliography).

   A very significant performer (horn), composer, educator, and writer.

2. HiFi/MusAm 26/4.

C1009.
SCHULTHESS, WALTER. b. July 24, 1894, Zurich; d. June 23, 1971, Zurich, Switzerland.

1. BAKER 7; GROVE 6/16 (Bibliography); MGG 1/12 + Supp. (Bibliography); RIEMANN 12 + Supp.

C1010.
SCHULTZ, SVEND. b. December 30, 1913, Nykøbing, Denmark.

1. BAKER 7; GROVE 6/16; MGG 1/12; PAB-MI/2 (Bibliography); RIEMANN 12/Supp.

C1011.
SCHULZ, JOHANN PHILIPP CHRISTIAN. b. February 1, 1773 [GROVE 6/16 and RIEMANN 12/Supp. September 24, 1773], Langensalza; d. January 30, 1827, Leipzig, Germany.

1. BAKER 7; GROVE 6/16 (Bibliography); MGG 1/12 (Bibliography); RIEMANN 12 (Bibliography) + Supp. (Bibliography).

C1012.
SCHULZ-DORNBURG, RUDOLF. b. March 31, 1891, Wuerzburg; d. August 16, 1949, Gmund-am-Tegernsee, Germany.

1. BAKER 7; RIEMANN 12.

C1013.
SCHUMANN, GEORG ALFRED. b. October 25, 1866, Koenigstein; d. May 23, 1952, Berlin, Germany.

1. BAKER 7; GROVE 6/16; MGG 1/12 (Bibliography); RIEMANN 12.

C1014.
SCHURICHT, CARL. b. July 3, 1880, Danzig, Germany; d. January 7, 1967, Corseaux-sur-Vevey, Switzerland.

1. BAKER 7; GROVE 6/16 (Bibliography); MGG 1/12 (Bibliography) + Supp. (Bibliography); PAB-MI/2; RIEMANN 12 + Supp. (Biblioggraphy).

4. Gavoty, Bernard. Carl Schuricht. Geneva: Rene Kister, 1956. 30, [2] p., 26 illus., list of recordings.

5. A0008, A0052, B0045, B0164.

C1015.
SCHWARZ, BORIS. b. March 26, 1906, St. Petersburg, Russia; d. December 31, 1983, New York City.

1. BAKER 7; GROVE 6/17 (Bibliography); MGG 1/12 (Bibliography); PAB-MI/2 (Bibliography); RIEMANN 12/Supp.

A fine violinist, he wrote Great Masters of the Violin (1983).

C1016.
SCHWARZ, GERARD. b. July 19, 1947, Weehawken, New Jersey.

1. BAKER 7; GROVE 6/17 (Bibliography); GROVE-AM 1/4 (Bibliography).

2. HiFi/MusAm 32/12.

C1017.
SCHWARZ, RUDOLF. b. April 29, 1905, Vienna, Austria.

1. BAKER 7; GROVE 6/17; PAB-MI/2 (Bibliography); RIEMANN 12 + Supp. (Bibliography).

5. A0004, B0071.

C1018.
SCHWIEGER, HANS. b. June 15, 1906, Cologne, Germany.

1. BAKER 7; GROVE-AM 1/4; RIEMANN 12 + Supp.

5. A0048.

C1019.
SCIMONE, CLAUDIO. b. December 23, 1934, Padua, Italy.

1. BAKER 7; GROVE 6/17.

C1020.
SCOTT, CHARLES KENNEDY. b. November 16, 1876, Romsey; d. July 2, 1965, London, England.

1. BAKER 7 (Bibliography); GROVE 6/17 (Bibliography); PAB-MI/2 (Bibliography); RIEMANN 12 + Supp. (Bibliography).

C1021.
SCRIBNER, NORMAN ORVILLE. b. February 25, 1936, Washington, D.C.

1. BAKER 7; GROVE-AM 1/4.

C1022.
SEBASTIAN, GEORGES. b. August 17, 1903, Budapest, Hungary.

1. BAKER 7; GROVE 6/17; PAB-MI/2 (Bibliography); RIEMANN 12 + Supp.

C1023.
SEBOR, KARL. b. August 13, 1843, Brandeis, Bohemia; d May 17, 1903, Prague, Czechoslovakia.

1. BAKER 7; MGG 1/12 (Bibliography); RIEMANN 12.

C1024.
SEGAL, URI. b. March 7, 1944, Jerusalem, Palestine.

1. BAKER 7; GROVE 6/17 (Bibliography); PAB-MI/2 (Bibliography).

C1025.
SEGERSTAM, LEIF SELIM. b. March 2, 1944, Vaasa, Finland.

1. BAKER 7; GROVE 6/17; PAB-MI/2 (Bibliography); RIEMANN 12/Supp.

C1026.
SEIDL, ANTON. b. May 7, 1850, Pest, Hungary; d. March 28, 1898, New York City.

1. BAKER 7; EdS 1/8 (Bibliography); GROVE 6/17 (Bibliography); GROVE-AM 1/4 (Bibliography); MGG 1/12 (Bibliography); PAB-MI/2 (Bibliography); RIEMANN 12.

   His personal library and memorabilia are housed in the Music Library at Columbia University. A protege of Hans Richter and a favorite of Richard Wagner, Seidl established orchestral standards in America.

3. Seidl, Anton. The Music of the Modern World Illustrated in the Lives and Works of the Greatest Modern Musicians and in Reproductions of Famous Paintings, etc. vol. 1 Text; vol. 2 Music. New York: D. Appleton and Company, 1895. xi, 236 p., 52 illus.; vii, 348 p., 27 illus. [Originally issued in twenty-five fasciles in 1895].

4. Finck, Henry T., ed. Anton Seidl: a Memorial by His Friends. New York: Charles Scribner's Sons, 1899. xiii, 259, [31] p., 22 illus.

5. B0035, B0046, B0075, B0077, B0083, B0089.

   SEE: Arthur Laser under **HANS von BUELOW** (C0157.4).

   SEE: Angelo Neumann. Erinnerungen an Richard Wagner. Leipzig, 1907.

   SEE: Ernest Newman under **RICHARD WAGNER** (C1175.4).

C1027.
SEJNA, KAREL. b. November 1, 1896, Zálezly, Czechoslovakia.

1. BAKER 7; GROVE 6/17 (Bibliography).

C1028.
SEKLES, BERNHARD. b. March 20, 1872, Frankfurt/M.; d. December 8, 1934, Frankfurt/M., Germany.

1. BAKER 7; GROVE 6/17 (Bibliography); MGG 1/12 (Bibliography); PAB-MI/2 (Bibliography); RIEMANN 12 + Supp.

C1029.
SEMKOW, JERZY. b. October 12, 1928, Radomsko, Poland.

1. BAKER 7; GROVE 6/17; PAB-MI/2 (Bibliography); RIEMANN 12/Supp.

C1030.
SERAFIN, TULLIO. b. September 1, 1878, Rottanova de Cavarzere, Venice; d. February 2, 1968, Rome, Italy.

1. BAKER 7; EdS 1/8; GROVE 6/17; GROVE-AM 1/4; PAB-MI/2 (Bibliography); RIEMANN 12 + Supp. (Bibliography).

2. ON 25/24; OPERA 19/4.

3. Serafin, Tullio. "A Triptych of Singers", Opera Annual 8 (1962): 93-96.

   Serafin, Tullio and Alceo Toni. Stile, tradizioni e convenzioni del melodramma italiano del Settecento e del'Ottocento. 2 vols. Milano: G. Ricordi & C., 1958/1964. xi, [i], 166, [1] p.; 322, [1] p.

4. Celli, Teodoro and Giuseppe Pugliese. Tullio Serafin: il patriarca del melodramma. Venezia: Corbo e Fiore Editore, 1985. 235, [2] p., 10 illus., chronology, repertoire, list of singers, discography.

   Rubboli, Daniele. Tullio Serafin: vita carriera scriti inediti. Cavarzere: Edizione Tiengo, 1979. 82 p., 12 illus., discography, index of names.

5. B0016, B0072, B0088, B0094.

C1031.
SEREBRIER, JOSE. b. December 3, 1938, Montevideo, Uruguay.

1. BAKER 7; GROVE 6/17; GROVE-AM 1/4; PAB-MI/2 (Bibliography); RIEMANN 12/Supp.

2. HiFi/MusAm 34/10.

5. A0023.

C1032.
SERENDERO-PROUST, DAVID. b. July 28, 1934, Santiago, Chile.

1. BAKER 7; RIEMANN 12/Supp. (Bibliography).

C1033.
SERVAIS, FRANCOIS. b. c.1847, St. Petersburg, Russia; d. January 14, 1901, Asnières, Near Paris, France.

1. BAKER 7; GROVE 6/17 (Bibliography); MGG 1/12 (Bibliography); RIEMANN 12.

C1034.
SEVITZKY, FABIEN. b. September 29, 1891, Vishny Volochok, Russia; d. February 2, 1967, Athens, Greece.

1. BAKER 7; GROVE-AM 1/4; PAB-MI/2 (Bibliography); RIEMANN 12 + Supp.

5. A0004, A0010, A0022.

C1035.
SHANET, HOWARD. b. November 9, 1918, Brooklyn, New York.

1. BAKER 7; GROVE 6/17; GROVE-AM 1/4; PAB-MI/2 (Bibliography).

3. Shanet, Howard. Philharmonic: a History of New York's Orchestra. Garden City: Doubleday & Company, Inc., 1975. xxi, 788 p. + 24 leaves of plates, 74 illus., repertoire of the New York Philharmonic 1842-1970, 17 p. comprehensive bibliography, 8 appendices, index.

   Also listed as B0147. Shanet edited a series of reprints of early histories of the New York Philharmonic published in 1978.

C1036.
SHAPEY, RALPH. b. March 12, 1921, Philadelphia, Pennsylvania.

1. BAKER 7; GROVE 6/17; GROVE-AM 1/4; PAB-MI/2 (Bibliography); RIEMANN 12/Supp.

2. New Yorker 55 (July 9, 1979).

C1037.
SHAW, ROBERT. b. April 30, 1916, Red Bluff, California.

1. BAKER 7; GROVE 6/17; GROVE-AM 1/4 (Bibliography); PAB-MI/2 (Bibliography); RIEMANN 12 + Supp.

4. Mussulman, Joseph A. Dear People. . .Robert Shaw: a Biography. Bloomington: Indiana University Press, 1979. x, 267 p., 13 illus., selected discography, index.

C1038.
SHEPPHERD, ARTHUR. b. February 19, 1880, Paris, Idaho; d. January 12, 1958, Cleveland, Ohio.

1. BAKER 7; GROVE-AM 1/4 (Bibliography); PAB-MI/2 (Bibliography).

2. MQ 11/2, 14/3, 21/1, 23/2, 30/3.

C1039.
SHOSTAKOVICH, MAXIM. b. May 10, 1939, Leningrad, Russia.

1. BAKER 7; GROVE 6/17; PAB-MI/2 (Bibliography); RIEMANN 12/Supp. (under Schostakowitsch).

2. US News & World Report (Nov. 9, 1981).

C1040.
SIDLIN, MURRY. b. May 6, 1940, Baltimore, Maryland.

1. BAKER 7; GROVE-AM 1/4 (Bibliography).

2. HiFi/MusAm 28/2.

C1041.
SIEGEL, RUDOLF. b. April 12, 1878, Berlin; d. December 4, 1948, Bayreuth, Germany.

1. BAKER 7; MGG 1/12; RIEMANN 12.

C1042.
SIEGL, OTTO. b. October 6, 1896, Graz; d. November 9, 1978, Vienna, Austria.

1. BAKER 7 (Bibliography); GROVE 6/17 (Bibliography); MGG 1/12 (Bibliography); PAB-MI/2 (Bibliography); RIEMANN 12 + Supp.

C1043.
SILOTI, ALEXANDER. b. October 9, 1863, near Kharkov, Russia; d. December 8, 1945, New York City.

1. BAKER 7; MGG 1/12 (Bibliography); PAB-MI/2 (Bibliography); RIEMANN 12 + Supp. (Bibliography).

   A student of Liszt (1883-86), he published a book of reminiscences about his teacher in 1911; translated in English, Edinburgh, 1913.

C1044.
SILVERSTEIN, JOSEPH. b. March 21, 1932, Detroit, Michigan.

1. BAKER 7; GROVE 6/17; GROVE-AM 1/4 (Bibliography).

C1045.
SILVESTRI, CONSTANTIN. b. June 13, 1913, Bucharest, Romania; d. February 23, 1969, London, England.

1. BAKER 7; GROVE 6/17 (Bibliography); RIEMANN 12 + Supp. (Bibliography).

4. Pricope, Eugen. Constantin Silvestri: intre străluciri si ... cîniece de pustiu. Bucureşti: Editura Muzicala, 1975. 318, [1] p., 28 illus.

C1046.
SIMEONOV, KONSTANTIN. b. June 20, 1910, Koznakovo, Russia.

1. BAKER 7; GROVE 6/17 (Bibliography); RIEMANN 12.

C1047.
SIMILAE, MARTTI. b. April 9, 1898, Oulu; d. January 9, 1958, Lahti, Finland.

1. BAKER 7; RIEMANN 12.

C1048.
SIMMONS, CALVIN. b. April 27, 1950, San Francisco, California; d. August 21, 1982, Connery Pond, east of Lake Placid, New York.

1. BAKER 7; GROVE-AM 1/4 (Bibliography); PAB-MI/2 (Bibliography).

2. HiFi/MusAm 29/3; ON 43/9.

C1049.
SIMON, STEPHEN. b. May 3, 1937, New York City.

1. BAKER 7; GROVE 6/17; GROVE-AM 1/4; PAB-MI/2 (Bibliography).

C1050.
SIMONOV, YURI. b. March 4, 1941, Saratov, Russia.

1. BAKER 7; GROVE 6/17; PAB-MI/2 (Bibliography); RIEMANN 12/Supp.

2. ON 39/23.

C1051.
SINGER, JACQUES. b. May 9, 1911, Przemyśl, Poland; d. August 11, 1980 New York City.

1. BAKER 7; RIEMANN 12/Supp.

C1052.
SINOPOLI, GIUSEPPE. b. November 2, 1946, Venice, Italy.

1. BAKER 7; GROVE 6/17; RIEMANN 12/Supp.

C1053.
SIQUEIRA, JOSE de LIMA. b. June 24, 1907, Conceicão, Brazil.

1. BAKER 7; GROVE 6/17 (Bibliography); RIEMANN 12/Supp.

C1054.
SKROUP, FRANZ (FRANTISEK). b. June 3, 1801, Osice, near Pardubice, Czechoslovakia; d. February 7, 1862, Rotterdam, Holland.

1. BAKER 7; GROVE 6/17 (Bibliography); MGG 1/12 (Bibliography); RIEMANN 12 + Supp. (Bibliography).

4. Plavec, Josef. <u>František Skroup</u>. Melantrich: n.p., 1941. 658, [1] p., 36 illus., chronology, index of names.

C1055.
SKROWACZEWSKI, STANISLAW. b. October 3, 1923, Lwow, Poland.

1. BAKER 7; GROVE 6/17 (Bibliography); GROVE-AM 1/4 (Bibliography); MGG 1/12 (Bibliography); PAB-MI/2 (Bibliography); RIEMANN 12 + Supp.

C1056.
SLATKIN, FELIX. b. December 22, 1915, St. Louis, Missouri; d. February 8, 1963, Los Angeles, California.

1. BAKER 7; GROVE 6/7; GROVE-AM 1/4; PAB-MI/2 (Bibliography).

C1057.
SLATKIN, LEONARD. b. September 1, 1944, Los Angeles, California.

1. BAKER 7; GROVE-AM 1/4 (Bibliography).

2. HiFi/MusAm 30/1.

C1058.
SLOVAK, LADISLAW. b. September 9, 1919, Bratislava, Czechoslovakia.

1. BAKER 7; GROVE 6/17; RIEMANN 12/Supp.

C1059.
SMALLENS, ALEXANDER. b. January 1, 1889, St. Petersburg, Russia; d. November 24, 1972, Tucson, Arizona.

1. BAKER 7; GROVE 6/17; GROVE-AM 1/4; PAB-MI/2 (Bibliography).

2. ON 33/10.

5. A0010, B0006, B0072, B0138.

C1060.
SMART, GEORGE THOMAS. b. May 10, 1776, London; d. February 23, 1867, London, England.

1. BAKER 7 (Bibliography); GROVE 6/17 (Bibliography); MGG 1/12; PAB-MI/2 (Bibliography); RIEMANN 12 + Supp. (Bibliography).

3. Bertram, H. and C.L. Cox, eds. Leaves From the Journals of Sir George Smart. London: Longmans, Green, and Co., 1907. x, 355 p., 2 illus.

5. B0007.

C1061.
SMETACEK, VACLAV. b. September 30, 1906, Brno, Czechoslovakia.

1. BAKER 7; GROVE 6/17 (Bibliography); PAB-MI/2 (Bibliography); RIEMANN 12 + Supp. (Bibliography).

C1062.
SMETANA, BEDRICH. b. March 2, 1824, Leitomischl, Bohemia; d. May 12, 1884, Prague, Czechoslovakia.

1. BAKER 7 (Bibliography); EdS 1/9 (Bibliography); GROVE 6/17 (103-item bibliography); MGG 1/12 (Bibliography); PAB-MI/2 (Bibliography); RIEMANN 12 + Supp. (Bibliography).

4. The basic study is that of Zdenek Nejedly: Bedřich Smetana. 4 vols. Prague, 1924-33; 2nd edition. 7 vols. Prague, 1950-54.

   Bartoš, František. Bedřich Smetana: Letters and Reminiscences. Translated by D. Rusbridge. Prague: Artia, 1953. 293 p., 37 illus.

Large, Brian. Smetana. London: Gerald Duckworth & Company Limited, 1970. xvii, 473 p., 29 illus., 9 appendices including a genealogical table, chronological list of works, premiere cast lists, and opera synopses, index, 31-item select bibliography.

Reznicek, L., ed. Smetana. Oslo: Biblioscandia, 1974. [iii], 32, [2] p., 25 illus.

Documents from Goeteborg 1856-1860.

C1063.
SMITH, DAVID STANLEY. b. July 6, 1877, Toledo, Ohio; d. December 17, 1949, New Haven, Connecticut.

1. BAKER 7; GROVE-AM 1/4; PAB-MI/2 (Bibliography).

2. MQ 9/1, 10/4, 16/2.

4. Goode, E.A. David Stanley Smith and His Music. Ph.D. diss., University of Cincinnati, 1978.

C1064.
SMITH, LAWRENCE LEIGHTON. b. April 8, 1936, Portland, Oregon.

1. BAKER 7; GROVE-AM 1/4.

C1065.
SMOLA, EMMERICH. b. July 8, 1922, Bergreichenstein, Germany.

1. BAKER 7; RIEMANN 12/Supp.

C1066.
SOBOLEWSKI, FRIEDRICH EDUARD de. b. October 1, 1808, Koenigsberg, Germany; d. May 17, 1872, St. Louis, Missouri.

1. BAKER 7 (Bibliography); GROVE-AM 1/4 (Bibliography); PAB-MI/2 (Bibliography).

C1067.
SOKOLOFF, NICOLAI. b. May 28, 1886, Kiev, Russia; d. September 25, 1965, La Jolla, California.

1. BAKER 7; GROVE-AM 1/4; PAB-MI/2 (Bibliography).

5. B0072, B0099.

C1068.
SOLLBERGER, HARVEY. b. May 11, 1938, Cedar Rapids, Iowa.

1. BAKER 7; GROVE 6/17; GROVE-AM 1/4 (Bibliography).

C1069.
SOLOMON, IZLER. b. January 11, 1910, St. Paul, Minnesota.

1. BAKER 7; PAB-MI/2 (Bibliography); RIEMANN 12/Supp.

5. A0010, A0048.

C1070.
SOLTI, GEORG. b. October 21, 1912, Budapest, Hungary.

1. BAKER 7; GROVE 6/17 (Bibliography); GROVE-AM 1/4 (Bibliography); MGG 1/12; PAB-MI/2 (Bibliography); RIEMANN 12 + Supp.

2. GR 45/539, 50/593, 59/699, 60/713; HiFi/MusAm 17/1, 26/12, 31/5; ON 25/16, 41/3; OPERA 12/8, 15/3, 19/7, 22/7, 8, 28/2, 35/12; OW 4/9, 8/7, 12/9, 19/2, 24/7.

4. Furlong, William Barry. Season with Solti: a Year in the Life of the Chicago Symphony. New York: Macmillan Publishing Co., Inc., 1974. 372 p., 68 illus., index.

   Robinson, Paul. Solti. Toronto: Vanguard Press, Inc., 1979. 168 p., 11 illus., discography by Bruce Surtees, 6-item bibliography, index.

5. A0031, A0052, B0030, B0031, B0067, B0091, B0092, B0124, B0125, B0144.

   SEE: Montague Haltrecht under ERICH KLEIBER (C0588.5).

   SEE: Lawrence, Robert. A Rage for Opera. New York, 1971.

C1071.
SOMARY, JOHANNES. b. April 7, 1935, Zurich, Switzerland.

1. BAKER 7; GROVE-AM 1/4.

C1072.
SOMOGI, JUDITH. b. May 13, 1937, Brooklyn, New York.

1. BAKER 7; GROVE-AM 1/4; PAB-MI/2 (Bibliography).

2. ON 40/14.

C1073.
SOPKIN, HENRY. b. October 20, 1903, Brooklyn, New York.

1. BAKER 7; GROVE-AM 1/4 (Bibliography); PAB-MI/2 (Bibliography).

5. A0048.

C1074.
SOUSA, JOHN PHILIP. b. November 6, 1854, Washington, D.C.; d. March 6, 1932, Reading, Pennsylvania.

1. BAKER 7 (Bibliography); EdS 1/9; GROVE 6/17 (Bibliography); GROVE-AM 1/4 (Bibliography); MGG 1/12; PAB-MI/2 (Bibliography); RIEMANN 12 + Supp. (Bibliography).

   GROVE 6/17 claims that "he was unquestionably one of the finest conductors of his era."

3. Sousa, John Philip. Marching Along: Recollections of Men Women and Music. Boston: Hale, Cushman & Flint, 1928. xiv, 384 p., 41 illus.

4. Bierley, Paul E. John Philip Sousa: American Phenomenon. Forward by Arthur Fiedler. Englewood Cliffs (NJ): Prentice-Hall, Inc., 1973. xxiii, 261 p., 101 illus., 4 appendices (works, genealogy, residences, and military career), 81-item bibliography, index.

   Newsom, Jon, ed. Perspectives on John Philip Sousa. Washington: Library of Congress Music Division Research Services, 1983. viii, 144 p., 46 illus., notes.

5. B0089.

C1075.
SPIEGELMAN, JOEL. b. January 23, 1933, Buffalo, New York.

1. BAKER 7; PAB-MI/2 (Bibliography); RIEMANN 12/Supp.

C1076.
SPIERING, THEODORE. b. September 5, 1871, St. Louis, Missouri; d. August 11, 1925, Munich, Germany.

1. BAKER 7; PAB-MI/2 (Bibliography); RIEMANN 12.

C1077.
SPOHR, LUDWIG. b. April 5, 1784, Braunschweig; d. October 22, 1859, Kassel, Germany.

1. BAKER 7 (Bibliography); EdS 1/9 (Bibliography); GROVE 6/18 (66-item Bibliography); MGG 1/12 (Bibliography); PAB-MI/2 (Bibliography); RIEMANN 12 + Supp. (Bibliography).

   The Spohr Society originally located in Kassel (1908-1934) was reconstituted in 1952.

3. Spohr, Ludwig. Louis Spohr's Autobiography. 2 vols. London: Reeves & Turner, 1878 [original published posthumously as Louis Spohrs Selbstbiographie. Kassel, 1860/61]. vii, 327; 342 p.

   There is an earlier English edition published in 1865. Ludwig Spohr bridged the gap from the old Kapellmeister who sat at the harpsichord to the modern conductor who used a baton and who established discipline and a comprehensive unified interpretation of the score.

5. B0035, B0085, B0155.

   SEE: Rellstab, Ludwig. Ueber mein Verhaeltniss als Critiker zu Herrn Spontini als Componisten und General-Musikdirector in Berlin, nebst einem vergnueglichen Anhang. Berlin, 1927.

   Another of his famous satirical pamphlets, this one against catering to virtuosity.

   SEE: William Spark under MICHAEL COSTA (C0217.5).

C1078.
SPONTINI, GASPARE. b. November 14, 1774, Majolati, Ancona; d. January 24, 1851, Majolati, Ancona, Italy.

1. BAKER 7 (Bibliography); EdS 1/9 (Bibliography); GROVE 6/18 (Bibliography); MGG 1/12 (Bibliography); PAB-MI/2 (Bibliography); RIEMANN 12 (Bibliography) + Supp. (Bibliography).

4. Bouvet, Charles. Spontini. Paris: Les Editions Rieder, 1930. 99, [61] p., 91 illus., chronological list of works with date and place of the premiere, 24-item bibliography.

   Ghislanzoni, Alberto. Gaspare Spontini: studio storico-critico. Roma: Edizioni Dell'Ateneo, 1951. 283 p., 51 illus., list of compositions, iconography, 57-item bibliography, index of names.

   Traglia, Gustavo. Monsieur Spontini a Parigi. Ancona: Stabilimento Tipografico S.E.V.A., 1951. 199 p.

5. B0083.

   SEE: Ludwig Rellstab under LUDWIG SPOHR (C1077.5).

C1079.
SPRINGER, ALOIS. b. December 20, 1935, Gross Olkowitz, Germany.

1. BAKER 7; RIEMANN 12/Supp.

C1080.
STADLMAIR, HANS. b. May 3, 1929, Neuhofen an der Krems, Austria.

1. BAKER 7; RIEMANN 12 + Supp. (Bibliography).

C1081.
STANFORD, CHARLES VILLIERS. b. September 30, 1852, Dublin, Ireland; d. March 29, 1924, London, England.

1. BAKER 7 (Bibliography); EdS 1/9 (Bibliography); GROVE 6/18 (Bibliography); MGG 1/12 (Bibliography); PAB-MI/2 (Bibliography); RIEMANN 12 + Supp.

3. Stanford, Charles V. Interludes: Records and Reflections. London: John Murray, 1922. xi, 212 p., 8 illus., index.

   Stanford, Charles V. Studies and Memories. London: Archibald Constable and Co. Ltd., 1908. xi, 212 p., 7 illus., index.

4. Greene, Harry Plunket. Charles Villiers Stanford. London: Edward Arnold & Co., 1935. 287 p., 9 illus., index of names.

5. B0007.

C1082.
STEFANI, JAN. b. c.1746, Prague, Bohemia; d. February 24, 1829, Warsaw, Poland.

1. BAKER 7; EdS 1/9; GROVE 6/18; MGG 1/12; RIEMANN 12.

C1083.
STEFANI, JOZEF. b. April 16, 1800, Warsaw; d. March 19, 1867, Warsaw, Poland.

1. BAKER 7; GROVE 6/18; MGG 1/12 (Bibliography); RIEMANN 12 + Supp. (Bibliography).

C1084.
STEIN, ERWIN. b. November 7, 1885, Vienna, Austria; d. July 19, 1958, London, England.

1. BAKER 7; GROVE 6/18; MGG/Supp. (Bibliography); RIEMANN 12 + Supp. (Bibliography).

C1085.
STEIN, HORST. b. May 2, 1928, Elberfeld, Germany.

1. BAKER 7; GROVE 6/18; PAB-MI/2 (Bibliography); RIEMANN 12/Supp.

2. OPER 1982: ein Jahrbuch der Zeitschrift "Opernwelt".

C1086.
STEIN, LEON. b. September 18, 1910, Chicago, Illinois.

1. BAKER 7 (Bibliography); GROVE 6/18; PAB-MI/2 (Bibliography); RIEMANN 12/Supp.

C1087.
STEINBACH, FRITZ. b. June 17, 1855, Gruensfeld; d. August 13, 1916, Munich, Germany.

1. BAKER 7 (Bibliography); GROVE 6/18 (Bibliography); MGG 1/12 (Bibliography); RIEMANN 12.

C1088.
STEINBERG, WILLIAM. b. August 1, 1899, Cologne, Germany; d. May 16, 1978, New York City.

1. BAKER 7; GROVE 6/18; GROVE-AM 1/4 (Bibliography); PAB-MI/2 (Bibliography); RIEMANN 12 + Supp.

2. ON 29/19.

5. A0048, B0138.

C1089.
STEINITZ, CHARLES PAUL. b. August 25, 1909, Chichester, England.

1. BAKER 7; GROVE 6/18 (Bibliography); PAB-MI/2 (Bibliography).

C1090.
STENHAMMER, WILHELM. b. February 7, 1871, Stockholm; d November 20, 1927, Stockholm, Sweden.

1. BAKER 7; GROVE 6/18 (Bibliography); MGG 1/12; PAB-MI/2 (Bibliography); RIEMANN 12 + Supp.

C1091.
STERN, JULIUS. b. August 8, 1820, Breslau; d. February 27, 1883, Berlin, Germany.

1. BAKER 7; GROVE 6/18; MGG 1/12 (Bibliography); RIEMANN 12.

4. Stern, Richard. Erinnerungsblaetter an Julius Stern. Leipzig: Druck und Verlag von Breitkopf und Haertel, 1886. x, 262 p.

5. B0079.

C1092.
STERNEFELD, DANIEL. b. November 27, 1905, Antwerp, Belgium.

1. BAKER 7; GROVE 6/18; PAB-MI/2 (Bibliography); RIEMANN 12 + Supp.

C1093.
STEVENS, DENIS WILLIAM. b. March 2, 1922, High Wycombe, Buckinghamshire, England.

1. BAKER 7; GROVE 6/18 (Bibliography); MGG 1/12; PAB-MI/2 (Bibliography); RIEMANN 12 + Supp. (Bibliography).

C1094.
STIEDRY, FRITZ. b. October 11, 1883, Vienna, Austria; d. August 9, 1968, Zurich, Switzerland.

1. BAKER 7; GROVE 6/18; GROVE-AM 1/4; PAB-MI/2 (Bibliography); RIEMANN 12 + Supp. (Bibliography).

2. ON 11/12.

5. B0138.

C1095.
STOCK, DAVID FREDERICK. b. June 3, 1939, Pittsburgh, Pennsylvania.

1. BAKER 7; GROVE-AM 1/4; PAB-MI/2 (Bibliography).

C1096.
STOCK, FREDERICK A. b. November 11, 1872, Juelich, Rheinland, Germany; d. October 20, 1942, Chicago, Illinois.

1. BAKER 7; GROVE 6/18; GROVE-AM 1/4; MGG 1/12 (Bibliography); PAB-MI/2 (Bibliography); RIEMANN 12.

   A large collection of his memorabilia is housed at the Chicago Historical Society.

2. LGB 6/2.

5. A0010, B0006, B0118, B0166.

SEE: Otis, Philo Adams. The Chicago Symphony Orchestra: Its Organization Growth and Development 1891-1924. Freeport: Books For Libraries Press, 1972 [original 1924].

C1097.
STOCKHAUSEN, FRANZ, Jr. b. January 30, 1839, Gebweiler, Alsace; d. January 4, 1926, Strasbourg, Germany.

1. BAKER 7; GROVE 6/18 (Bibliography); PAB-MI/2 (Bibliography); RIEMANN 12.

C1098.
STOESSEL, ALBERT. b. October 11, 1894, St. Louis, Missouri; d. May 12, 1943, New York City.

1. BAKER 7; GROVE 6/18; GROVE-AM 1/4 (Bibliography); MGG 1/12; PAB-MI/2 (Bibliography); RIEMANN 12.

3. Stoessel, Albert. The Technique of the Baton. Preface by Walter Damrosch. New York: Carl Fischer, 1920 (rev. 1928). v, 88 p.

4. McNaughton, C.D. Albert Stoessel, American Musician. Ph.D. diss., New York University, 1957.

5. B0072.

   SEE: Cowden, Robert H. The Chautauqua Opera Association 1929-1958: an Interpretative History. New York: Natl. Opera Assn., 1974.

C1099.
STOKOWSKI, LEOPOLD. b. April 18, 1882, London; d. September 13, 1977, Nether Wallop, Hampshire, England.

1. BAKER 7; GROVE 6/18 (Bibliography); GROVE-AM 1/4 (Bibliography); MGG 1/12 + Supp. (Bibliography); PAB-MI/2 (Bibliography); RIEMANN 12 + Supp. (Bibliography).

   1,500+ orchestral scores and parts annotated by Stokowski are in the library collection at the Curtis Institute of Music in Philadelphia.

2. GR 47/561; HiFi/MusAm 32/4; ON 26/15.

3. Stokowski, Leopold. Music for All of Us. New York: Simon and Schuster, 1943. vii, 340 p., portrait, index.

4. Chasins, Abram. Leopold Stokowski: a Profile. New York: Hawthorn Books, Inc., 1979. xvii, 313 p., 35 illus., 25-item bibliography, selective discography by Robert Bragalini, index.

   Daniel, Oliver. Stokowski: a Counterpoint of View. New York: Dodd, Mead & Company, 1982. xxviii, 1090 p., 107 illus., chapter notes, 88-item selected bibliography, discography by Edward Johnson, various first performances, orchestral transcriptions, compositions, index.

Johnson, Edward, ed. Stokowski: Essays in Analysis of His Art. London: Triad, 1973. 116 p., illus., list of works, discography.

Opperby, Preben. Leopold Stokowski. Tunbridge Wells (England): Midas Books, 1982. 288 p., 90 illus., 25-item bibliography, discography, list of first performances, index.

Robinson, Paul. Stokowski. Toronto: The Vanguard Press, Inc., 1977. 154 p., 11 illus., 13-item selected bibliography, discography by Bruce Surtees, index of names.

5. A0002, A0004, A0007, A0008, A0010, A0012, A0022, A0040, A0048, A0050, B0017, B0044, B0060, B0068, B0116, B0118, B0128, B0136, B0158, B0159, B0161.

SEE: Armitage, Merle. Accents on America. New York: E. Weyhe, 1944.

SEE: Armitage, Merle. Accents on Life. Ames: The Iowa State University Press, 1964. xv, 386 p., 53 illus.

SEE: Herbert Kupferberg under EUGENE ORMANDY (C0825.5).

SEE: Cheslock, Louis, ed. H.L Mencken on Music. New York: Alfred A. Knopf, 1961.

SEE: Joseph Szigeti under HAMILTON HARTY (C0466.5).

C1100.
STOUTZ, EDMOND de. b. December 18, 1920, Zurich, Switzerland.

1. BAKER 7; GROVE 6/18; RIEMANN 12/Supp.

C1101.
STRANSKY, JOSEF. b. September 9, 1872, Humpoletz, near Deutschbrod, Bohemia; d. March 6, 1936, New York City.

1. BAKER 7; GROVE 6/18; GROVE-AM 1/4; PAB-MI/2 (Bibliography); RIEMANN 12.

C1102.
STRARAM, WALTER. b. July 9, 1876, London, England; d. November 24, 1933, Paris, France.

1. BAKER 7; RIEMANN 12/Supp.

C1103.
STRAUSS, EDUARD. b. March 15, 1835, Vienna; d. December 28, 1916, Vienna, Austria.

1. BAKER 7; GROVE 6/18 (Bibliography); MGG 1/12 (Bibliography); PAB-MI/2 (Bibliography); RIEMANN 12 (Bibliography) + Supp. (Bibliography).

Eduard was the younger brother of Johann Strauss, Jr. (b. October 25, 1825, Vienna; d. June 3, 1899, Vienna) who conducted the royal court balls from 1863 to 1871; Eduard conducted from 1872 to 1878. Their father, Johann Strauss, Sr. (b. March 14, 1804, Vienna; d. September 25, 1849, Vienna), conducted the court orchestra between 1845 and 1849. The family orchestra, a national institution, was in existence for seventy-five years until Eduard disbanded it in 1901.

3. Strauss, Eduard. Erinnerungen. Leipzig: Franz Deuticke, 1906. 175, [39] p., 20 illus.

C1104.
STRAUSS, RICHARD. b. June 11, 1864, Munich; d. September 8, 1949, Garmisch-Partenkirchen, Germany.

Another of the towering composer-conductor giants, Richard Strauss had, by the time he was 20, an American premiere (Symphony in F-minor performed by the New York Philharmonic under Theodore Thomas on Dec. 13, 1884) to go along with Hans von Buelow's invitation to join his orchestra in Meiningen as an assistant conductor. Both successes were to prove prophetic of parallel major careers. Again, the shelves in the Music Division at the Library of Congress in Washington, D.C. hold well over one hundred titles of books and pamphlets on Strauss. GROVE 6/18 mentions a study, Richard Strauss als Dirigent (Amsterdam, 1907) by J.C. Mannifarges, which is not in the collection, but the available riches are overwhelming. The titles listed here are only the most obvious candidates from those which were available for annotation. Oswald Ortner's definitive bibliography is critical to any research effort: Richard Strauss-Bibliographie, Teil I (1882-1944). Wien, 1964; Teil II (1944-64), Guenter Brosche, ed. Wien, 1973. This important research effort remains in progress.

1. BAKER 7 (Bibliography); EdS 1/9 (Bibliography); GROVE 6/18 (188-item Bibliography); MGG 1/12 (Bibliography); PAB-MI/2 (Bibliography); RIEMANN 12 (Bibliography) + Supp. (Bibliography).

2. JCG 3/2; RS 24.

4. Del Mar, Norman. Richard Strauss: a Critical Commentary on His Life and Works. 3 vols. London: Barrie & Rockliff, 1962/1969/1972. xv, 462 p., 7 illus., 4 appendices of works, 74-item bibliography, chronology, index; xi, 452 p., 10 illus., index; xxi, 552 p., 10 illus., alphabetical list of songs, 5 appendices of works, discography of Strauss as a conductor and pianist, 69-item bibliography, index to all three volumes.

Grasberger, Franz. Richard Strauss und die Wiener Oper. Tutzing: Verlegt bei Hans Schneider, 1969. 247 p., 30 illus., 16-item bibliography, index of names.

Krause, Ernst. Richard Strauss: the Man and His Work. Boston: Crescendo Publishing Company, n.d. 587, [1] p., illus., chronology, list of works, discography, 40-item bibliography, index.

Mann, William. Richard Strauss: a Critical Study of the Operas. London: Cassell & Company Ltd, 1964. xiv, 402 p., 40 illus. 74-item bibliography, index.

von Schuch, Friedrich. Richard Strauss Ernst von Schuch und Dresdens Oper. Dresden: VEB Verlag der Kunst, n.d. [c.1952]. 151 p., 6 illus., 17-item bibliography.

Schuh, Willi. Richard Strauss: a Chronicle of the Early Years 1864-1898. Translated by Mary Whittal. Cambridge: Cambridge University Press, 1982 [original: Zuerich, 1976]. xvii, 555 p., 40 illus., 3 appendices, chronological summary 1864-98, list of works, notes, 16-item bibliography, index.

Schuh, Willi, ed. Richard Strauss: Recollections and Reflections. Translated by L.J. Lawrence. London: Boosey & Hawkes Limited, 1953 [original: Zuerich, 1949]. 173 p., notes, 33-item bibliography.

5. A0016, B0015, B0057, B0080, B0112, B0132, B0141, B0156, B0157, B0167.

SEE: Franz Eugen Dostal under KARL BOEHM (C0122.4).

SEE: Peter Heyworth under OTTO KLEMPERER (C0590.4).

SEE: Huneker, James. Overtones: a Book of Temperaments. New York: Charles Scribner's Sons, 1906: 1-63.

SEE: Wouter Paap under WILLEM MENGELBERG (C0751.4).

C1105.
STRESEMANN, WOLFGANG. b. July 20, 1904, Dresden, Germany.

1. BAKER 7; RIEMANN 12/Supp.

4. Stresemann, Wolfgang. ...und Abends in die Philharmonie: Erinnerungen an grosse Dirigenten. Muenchen: Georg Mueller Verlag GmbH, 1981. 280 p., 29 illus.

Also listed as B0157.

Stresemann, Wolfgang. The Berlin Philharmonic From Buelow to Karajan: Home and History of a World-Famous Orchestra. Berlin, 1979.

No copy located.

C1106.
STRICKLAND, WILLIAM. b. January 25, 1914, Defiance, Ohio.

1. BAKER 7; GROVE-AM 1/4.

C1107.
STRIEGLER, KURT. b. January 7, 1886, Dresden; d. August 4, 1958, Wildthurn, near Landau, Germany.

1. BAKER 7; GROVE 6/18; MGG 1/12 (Bibliography); RIEMANN 12.

C1108.
STRINGFIELD, LAMAR. b. October 10, 1897, Raleigh; d. January 21, 1959, Asheville, North Carolina.

1. BAKER 7; PAB-MI/2 (Bibliography); RIEMANN 12.

4. Nelson, D. The Life and Works of Lamar Stringfield (1897-1959). Ph.D. diss., University of North Carolina/Chapel Hill, 1971.

C1109.
STRUBE, GUSTAV. b. March 3, 1867, Ballenstedt, Germany; d. February 2, 1953, Baltimore, Maryland.

1. BAKER 7; GROVE-AM 1/4; PAB-MI/2 (Bibliography).

2. MQ 9/2, 28/3.

C1110.
STUNTZ, JOSEPH HARTMANN. b. July 23, 1793, Arlesheim, near Basel, Switzerland; d. June 18, 1859, Munich, Germany.

1. BAKER 7; GROVE 6/18; MGG 1/12 (Bibiography); RIEMANN 12.

4. Gross, Rolf. Joseph Hartmann Stuntz als Opernkomponist. Ph.D. diss., University of Munich, 1936. 104 p.

C1111.
STUPKA, FRANTISEK. b. January 18, 1879, Tedrazice; d. November 24, 1965, Prague, Czechoslovakia.

1. BAKER 7; RIEMANN 12/Supp.

C1112.
SUCHER, JOSEPH. b. November 23, 1843, Doeboer, Hungary; d. April 4, 1908, Berlin, Germany.

1. BAKER 7; GROVE 6/18 (Bibliography); MGG 1/12 (Bibliography); RIEMANN 12.

5. SEE: Sucher, Rosa [wife]. Aus meinem Leben. Leipzig: Breitkopf und Haertel, 1914. 95 p., 4 illus.

C1113.
SUESS, CHRISTIAN. b. October 8, 1937, Leipzig, Germany.

1. BAKER 7; RIEMANN 12/Supp.

C1114.
SUITNER, OTMAR. b. May 16, 1922, Innsbruck, Austria.

1. BAKER 7; GROVE 6/18; PAB-MI/2 (Bibliography); RIEMANN 12/Supp.

C1115.
SUK, VASA. b. November 16, 1861, Kladno, Czechoslovakia; d. January 12, 1933, Moscow, Russia.

1. BAKER 7; GROVE 6/18 (Bibliography); MGG 1/12 (Bibliography); RIEMANN 12 + Supp. (Bibliography).

4. REMEZOV, I. V.I. Suk. Moscow: Iskusstvo, 1951. 61, [1] p., portrait.

   Uherek, Zdeněk. Kladenský rodák: Váša Suk, národní umělec RSFSR. Praha: Orbis, 1963. 94, [1] p., 13 illus.

C1116.
SULLIVAN, ARTHUR SEYMOUR. b. May 13, 1842, Lambeth; d. November 22, 1900, London, England.

1. BAKER 7 (Bibliography); EdS 1/9 (Bibliography); GROVE 6/18 (Bibliography); MGG 1/12 (Bibliography); PAB-MI/2 (Bibliography); RIEMANN 12 + Supp. (Bibliography).

4. Allen, Reginald and Gale R. D'Luhy. Presenting in Word & Song, Score & Deed the Life and Work of Sir Arthur Sullivan: Composer for Victorian England from "Onward Christian Soldiers" to Gilbert & Sullivan Opera. New York: The Pierpont Morgan Library and David R. Godine, Publisher, 1975. xiii, 215 p., 207 illus., 22-item bibliography, index.

   Annotated exhibit catalog of the 1975 centennial salute to Gilbert, Sullivan, and D'Oyly Catre held at the Morgan Library in New York City 13 February to 20 April.

   Goldberg, Isaac. The Story of Gilbert and Sullivan or the 'Compleat' Savoyard. New York: Simon and Schuster, 1928. xviii, 588 p., 47 illus., annotated list of 38 books, index.

   Sullivan, Herbert and Newman Flower. Sir Arthur Sullivan: His Life, Letters & Diaries. New York: George H. Doran Company, 1927. xii, 393 p., 31 illus., list of works, 97-item bibliography compiled by William C. Smith, index.

5. B0009, B0010, B0049, B0062, B0075, B0076, B0085.

   SEE: Louis Engel under CHARLES HALLE (C0450.5).

   SEE: Alice Mangold Dahl under CHARLES HALLE (C0450.5).

   SEE: O'Connor, T.P., ed. In the Days of My Youth. London: C. Arthur Pearson, Limited. 1901. ix, 318 p., 16 illus.

C1117.
SURINACH, CARLOS. b. March 4, 1915, Barcelona, Spain.

1. BAKER 7; GROVE 6/18; GROVE-AM 1/4; PAB-MI/2 (Bibliography); RIEMANN 12/Supp.

C1118.
SUSSKIND, JAN WALTER. b. May 1, 1913, Prague, Czechoslovakia; d. March 25, 1980, Berkeley, California.

1. BAKER 7 (Bibliography); GROVE 6/18; GROVE-AM 1/4 (Bibliography); PAB-MI/2 (Bibliography); RIEMANN 12 + Supp.

2. GR 49; HiFi/MusAm 24/8.

5. A0004.

C1119.
SUTER, HERMANN. b. April 28, 1870, Kaiserstuhl; d. June 22, Basel, Switzerland.

1. BAKER 7; GROVE 6/18 (Bibliography); MGG 1/12; RIEMANN 12 + Supp.

4. Merian, W. Hermann Suter: der Dirigent und der Komponist. 2 vols. Basel, 1936/37.

   No copy located.

C1120.
SVETLANOV, EVGENY. b. September 6, 1928, Moscow, Russia.

1. BAKER 7; GROVE 6/18 (Bibliography).

2. GR 47/562.

C1121.
SWAROWSKY, HANS. b. September 16, 1899, Budapest, Hungary; d. September 10, 1975, Salzburg, Austria.

1. BAKER 7; GROVE 6/18 (Bibliography); MGG 1/12; RIEMANN 12 + Supp. (Bibliography).

3. Huss, Manfred, ed. Hans Swarowsky, Wahrung der Gestalt: Schriften ueber Werk und Wiedergabe, Stil und Interpretation in der Musik. Wien: Universal Edition A.G., 1979. 303 p., 13 illus., list of unpublished material, notes, 41-item bibliography, list of musical examples, discography, list of conducting students, index.

C1122.
SZELL, GEORGE. b. June 7, 1897, Budapest, Hungary; d. July 30, 1970, Cleveland, Ohio.

1. BAKER 7; GROVE 6/18; GROVE-AM 1/4 (Bibliography); MGG/Supp.; PAB-MI/2 (Bibliography); RIEMANN 12.

2. GR 47/555, 48/568, 569, 573; LGB 4/4, 9/1-2; New Yorker 41 (November 6, 1965).

5. A0022, A0040, A0048, A0052, B0030, B0069, B0092, B0099, B0110, B0120, B0138, B0144.

C1123.
SZENDREI, ALADAR [SENDRY, ALFRED]. b. February 29, 1884, Budapest, Hungary; d. March 3, 1976, Los Angeles, California.

1. BAKER 7 (Bibliography); GROVE-AM 1/4 (Bibliography); RIEMANN 12 + Supp. (Bibliography).

3. Szendrei, Aladar. Dirigierkunde. Leipzig, 1932. 2nd edition 1952.

   No copy located.

C1124.
SZENKAR, EUGEN. b. April 9, 1891, Budapest, Hungary.

1. BAKER 7; PAB-MI/2 (Bibliography); RIEMANN 12 + Supp.

   His brother Alexander Michael (b. October 24, 1896, Budapest; d. August 27, 1971, Buenos Aires, Argentina) was also a condcutor. SEE: RIEMANN 12/Supp.

5. B0163.

C1125.
TABACHNIK, MICHEL. b. November 10, 1942, Geneva, Switzerland.

1. BAKER 7; GROVE 6/18; PAB-MI/2 (Bibliography); RIEMANN 12/Supp.

C1126.
TAFFANEL, CLAUDE-PAUL. b. September 16, 1844, Bordeaux; d. November 22, 1908, Paris, France.

1. BAKER 7; GROVE 6/18; MGG 1/13; PAB-MI/2 (Bibliography).

3. MGG 1/13 mentions an unpublished MS, Carnets intimes.

5. B0033, B0133.

C1127.
TALICH, VACLAV. b. May 28, 1883, Kroměříž; d March 16, 1961, Beroun, Czechoslovakia.

1. BAKER 7; GROVE 6/18 (Bibliography); MGG 1/13 (Bibliography); PAB-MI/2 (Bibliography); RIEMANN 12 + Supp. (Bibliography).

4. Kuna, Milan. Vaclav Talich. Praha: Panton, 1980. 423 p., 214 illus.

   Masaryková, Herberta, ed. Václav Talich: dokument života a díla. Praha: Státní Hudební Vydavatelství, 1967. 491, [2] p., 65 illus., chronology, index of names.

   Pospíšil, Vilém. Václav Talich: několik kapitol o díle a životě: ceskeho umelce. Praha: Panton, 1961. 144. [1] p.

   Vaclav Talich a gramofonová deska. Praha: Gramofonové Závody, 1960. 29 p., 7 illus., discography.

5. A0050, B0167.

C1128.
TANGO, EGISTO. b. November 13, 1873, Rome, Italy; d. October 5, 1951, Copenhagen, Denmark.

1. BAKER 7; EdS 1/9.

4. Flor, Kai. Egisto Tango. Kobenhavn: NYT Nordisk Forlag, 1948. 63 p., 5 illus.

C1129.
TAUBMANN, OTTO. b. March 8, 1859, Hamburg; d. July 4, 1929, Berlin.

1. BAKER 7; GROVE 6/18 (Bibliography); MGG 1/13 (Bibliography); RIEMANN 12/Supp.

C1130.
TAUSCH, JULIUS. b. April 15, 1827, Dessau; d. November 11, 1895, Bonn, Germany.

1. BAKER 7; GROVE 6/18 (Bibliography); MGG 1/13 (Bibliography); PAB-MI/2 (Bibliography); RIEMANN 12 + Supp. (Bibliography).

C1131.
TEMIANKA, HENRI. b. November 19, 1906, Greenock, Scotland.

1. BAKER 7; GROVE 6/18 (Bibliography); GROVE-AM 1/4 (Bibliography); PAB-MI/2 (Bibliography).

3. Temianka, Henri. Facing the Music: an Irreverent Close-up of the Real Concert World. Preface by Yehudi Menuhin. New York: David McKay Company, Inc., 1973. x, 272 p., 16 illus., index.

C1132.
TENNSTEDT, KLAUS. b. June 6, 1926, Merseburg, Germany.

1. BAKER 7; GROVE 6/18; GROVE-AM 1/4 (Bibliography); PAB-MI/2 (Bibliography); RIEMANN 12/Supp.

2. GR 59/708.

5. A0031.

C1133.
THOMAS, MICHAEL TILSON. b. December 21, 1944, Hollywood, California.

1. BAKER 7; GROVE 6/18; GROVE-AM 1/4 (Bibliography); PAB-MI/2 (Bibliography); RIEMANN 12/Supp.

2. GR 49/577, 58/692, 63/745; HiFi/MusAm 22/6; ON 40/1.

5. B0068, B0134.

C1134.
THOMAS, THEODORE. b. October 11, 1835, Esens, East Friesland, Germany; d. January 4, 1905, Chicago, Illinois.

1. BAKER 7; GROVE 6/18 (Bibliography); GROVE-AM 1/4 (Bibliography); MGG 1/13 (Bibliography); PAB-MI/2 (Bibliography); RIEMANN 12 + Supp. (Bibliography).

There is a substantial collection of his materials at the Chicago Historical Society, in the Newberry Library, Chicago, at the Library of Congress, Washington, D.C., and at the New York Public Library.

2. MQ 26/2, 37/2.

3. Upton, George P., ed. Theodore Thomas: a Musical Autobiography. 2 vols. Chicago: A.C. McClurg & Co., 1905. 327 p., 21 illus., index; 382 p., list of premieres, Chicago Orchestra personnel. Reprint 1964. New York: Da Capo Press. 69, 1-378 p., 37 illus.

4. Logan, Margaret Ann. The Musical Life of Theodore Thomas and His Young People's Concerts. M.M. thesis, Catholic University of America, 1973. 96 p.

Russell, Charles Edward. The American Orchestra and Theodore Thomas. New York: Doubleday, Page & Company, 1927. xx, 344 p., 33 illus., 7 appendices, index.

Russell, T.C. Theodore Thomas: His Role in the Development of Musical Culture in the United States, 1835-1905. Ph.D. diss., University of Minnesota, 1969. ii, 228 p., bibliography.

Thomas, Rose Fay. Memoirs of Theodore Thomas. New York: Moffat, Yard and Company, 1911. Reprint 1971. xviii, 569 p., 31 illus.

Whistler, H.S. The Life and Work of Theodore Thomas. Ph.D. diss., Ohio State University, 1942.

5. B0007, B0046, B0083, B0089.

SEE: Philo Adams Otis under FREDERICK STOCK (C1096.5).

C1135.
TIESSEN, HEINZ. b. April 10, 1887, Koenigsberg; d. November 29, 1921, Berlin, Germany.

1. BAKER 7 (Bibliography); GROVE 6/18 (Bibliography); MGG 1/13; PAB-MI/2 (Bibliography); RIEMANN 12 + Supp.

3. BAKER 7 mentions an autobiography.

C1136.
TIETJEN, HEINZ. b. June 24, 1881, Tangier; d. November 30, 1967, Baden-Baden, Germany.

1. BAKER 7; PAB-MI/2 (Bibliography); RIEMANN 12/Supp.

5. B0063, B0164.

SEE: Peter Heyworth under OTTO KLEMPERER (C0590.4).

C1137.
TILMANT, THEOPHILE. b. July 8, 1799, Valenciennes; d. May 7, 1878, Asnières, France.

1. BAKER 7; GROVE 6/18.

C1138.
TITL, ANTON EMIL. b. October 2, 1809, Pernstein, Bohemia; d. January 21, 1882, Vienna, Austria.

1. BAKER 7; GROVE 6/19; MGG 1/13 (Bibliography).

C1139.
TOLDRA, EDUARDO. b. April 7, 1895, Villaneuva y Geltrú, Catalonia; d. May 31, 1962, Barcelona, Spain.

1. BAKER 7; GROVE 6/19; MGG 1/13 (Bibliography); RIEMANN 12 + Supp.

4. Capdevila Massana, Manuel. <u>Eduardo Toldrá, músic</u>. Barcelona: Editorial Aedos, 1964. 423, [1] p., 15 illus., 5 appendices.

   Fernández-Cid, Antonio. <u>Eduardo Toldrá</u>. Bilbao: Graficas Ellacuria-Erandio, n.d. [1984]. 119 p., 16 illus., chronology.

5. B0045.

C1140.
TOSCANINI, ARTURO. b. March 25, 1867, Parma, Italy; d. January 16, 1957, New York City.

1. BAKER 7; EdS 1/9; GROVE 6/19 (Bibliography); GROVE-AM 1/4 (Bibliography); MGG 1/13; PAB-MI/2 (Bibliography); RIEMANN 12 + Supp. (Bibliography).

   Substantial material in the Toscanini Memorial Archives at the New York Public Library Music Division.

2. GR 34, 44/526; JCG 2/4, 3/2; LGB 2/2, 4/2-3; LS 37, 62, 88, 98, 100, 102, 132; MQ 24/4, 33/2; ON 21/20, 25/19, 28/3, 30/11, 31/22; OPERA 5/5, 6, 8, 9, 10, 11, 12, 8/3, 18/7, 8, 34/1; OW 23/1.

4. Allodi, Carlo, ed. <u>Arturo Toscanini: Parma nel centenario della nascita -- (1867-1967)</u>. Parma: Edito Dal Comitato Delle Celebrazioni, 1967. 136, [1] p., 78 illus.

   Antek, Samuel. <u>This was Toscanini</u>. Forward by Marcia Davenport. New York: The Vanguard Press, 1963. 192 p., recorded repertoire, 84 photographs by Robert Hupka.

   Barblan, Guglielmo. <u>Toscanini e La Scala: testimonianze e confessioni</u>. Edited by Eugenio Gara. Milano: Edizioni Della Scala, 1972. 400 p., 56 illus., index of names and works.

   Bonardi, Dino. <u>Toscanini</u>. Milano: Libreria Editrice Milanese, 1929. 125 p., 3 illus.

   Chotzinoff, Samuel. <u>On Tour with Toscanini and RCA Victor</u>. New York: National Broadcasting Company, n.d. [c.1950]. unpaginated [20 p.], illus.

Chotzinoff, Samuel. Toscanini: an Intimate Portrait. New York: Alfred A. Knopf, 1956. 148 p., 8 illus.

Ciampelli, Giulio Mario. Toscanini: impressioni, ricordi...e null' altro. Milano: "La Modernissima", 1923. 44 p.

Della Corte, Andrea. Toscanini: visto da un critico. Torino: Industria Libraria Tipografica Editrice, 1958. 513 p., 77 illus., 111-item bibliography, index of names, discography. The 1981 edition published by Edizioni Studio Tesi has a discography by Raffaele Vegeto.

Della Corte, Andrea. Toscanini. Vicenza: Casa Editrice "Il Pellicano", 1945. 145 p.

Escher, Rudolf. Toscanini en Debussy: magie der werkelijkheid. Rotterdam: Uitgave D. van Sijn & Zonen, 1938. 55 p., 2 illus., folding plate.

Ewen, David. The Story of Arturo Toscanini. New York: Henry Holt and Company, 1951. xviii, 142 p., portrait, chronology, selected world premieres, 13-item bibliography, discography, index.

Fiorda, Nuccio. Arte beghe e bizze di Toscanini. Roma: Fratelli Palombi Editori, 1969. 187 p., 72 illus., index of names.

Frassati, Luciana. Il maestro Arturo Toscanini e il suo mondo. Lucerne: H.F. Kammermann, 1967. 276 [7] p., over 200 mostly rare illus. and photographs, index of names.

Folio size monumental record of the most famous conductor of the 20th century.

Gilman, Lawrence. Toscanini and Great Music. New York: Farrar & Rinehart, 1938. xiv, 202 p., portrait, index.

Haggin, Bernard H. Conversations with Toscanini. Garden City: Doubleday & Company, Inc., 1959. 261 p., portrait, discography, index.

Haggin, B.H. The Toscanini Musicians Knew. New York: Horizon Press, 1967. 245 p., 8 illus., notes.

Hoeller, Susanne Winternitz. Arturo Toscanini: a Photobiography. New York: Island Workshop Press Co-op., Inc., 1943. 56 p., 53 illus.

The two printings include a special edition of 300 numbered copies.

Hughes, Spike. The Toscanini Legacy: a Critical Study of Arturo Toscanini's Performances of Beethoven, Verdi and Other Composers. London: Putnam and Company Ltd, 1959. 346 p., portrait, 192 musical illus., index. 2nd enlarged edition. New York: Dover Publications, Inc., 1969. 346 p. Includes a helpful table of original and current record numbers.

Lezuo-Pandolfi, Amina. Toscanini: ein Leben fuer die Musik. Translated by Margot Frey. Zuerich: Apollo-Verlag, 1957. 80 p., 20 illus., discography.

Marek, George R. Toscanini. New York: Atheneum, 1975. xiv, 321 p., 24 illus., chronology, 54-item bibliography, index.

Marsh, Robert Charles. Toscanini and the Art of Orchestral Performance. Philadelphia: J.B. Lippincott Company, 1956 [new revised edition 1962]. Reprint 1973. 252 p., repertoire, chronology, discography. German edition Stuttgart: Pan-Verlag, 1958.

Matthews, Denis. Arturo Toscanini. New York: Hippocrene Books Inc, 1982. 176 p., 49 references, selected annotated discography by Ray Burford, index.

Medici, Mario, ed. Parma a Toscanini: onoranze a Toscanini, Parma -- Teatro Regio -- 1958. Parma: Edito dal Comitato Onoranze, 1958. 92, [12] p., 20 illus.

Nello Vetro, Gaspare. Arturo Toscanini alla ra scuola del carmine in Parma (1876-1885). Parma: Editrice tipolito la ducale, n.d. 219 p., 11 illus., 29-item bibliography.

Nello Vetro, Gaspare with Vittorio Vaccaro. Il giovane Toscanini. Parma: Grafiche STEP editrice, 1983. 148, [8] p., 141 illus., index of names, 9-item bibliography.

Nicotra, Tobia. Arturo Toscanini. Translated by Irma Brandeis and H.D. Kahn. New York: Alfred A. Knopf, 1929. 235, [1] p., 5 illus., list of works performed at the Turin Exposition, Italian premieres and first performances at La Scala.

Paap, Wouter. Toscanini. Amsterdam: Bigot En Van Rossum N.V., 1938. 83 p.

Paumgartner, Rosana, ed. La lezione di Toscanini: atti del convengo di studi toscaniniani al XXX Maggio Musicale Fiorentino. Firenze: Vallecchi editore, 1970. x, 387 p., chronology of operas directed, discography by Raffaele Vegeto, index.

Includes contributions from performers, critics, and conductors.

Sacchi, Filippo. Toscanini. Verona: Arnoldo Mondadori Editore, 1951. 382, [5] p., 17 illus. Translated, revised and abridged as: The Magic Baton: Toscanini's Life for Music. London: Putnam, 1957.

Sachs, Harvey. Toscanini. Philadelphia: J.B. Lippincott Company, 1978. [vi], 380 p., 31 illus., notes, orchestral seating, repertoire, 226-item bibliography, index.

Stefan, Paul. Arturo Toscanini. Introduction by Stefan Zweig. Wien: Herbert Reichner Verlag, 1936. 77, [33] p., 54 illus., 13-item bibliography. Translated by Eden and Cedar Paul. New York: Blue Ribbon Books, 1936.

Steiner, Lilly and Henry Prunieres. Seize attitudes de Toscanini. Paris: Editions Paul de Montaignac, n.d. [c.1935]. unpaginated [4, 16 p. plates].

Sixteen signed lithographs with brief commentary in a limited folio edition.

Tarozzi, Giuseppe. Non muore la musica: la vita e l'opera di Arturo Toscanini. Milano: SugarCo Edizioni S.M.1., 1977. 296, [4] p., 18 illus., index of names.

Taubman, Howard. The Maestro: the Life of Arturo Toscanini. New York: Simon and Schuster, 1951. viii, 342 p., index.

"The Maestro" published by the Arturo Toscanini Society. Vol. 1, Nos. 1 and 2 (January-July, 1969) through Vol. 7 (1975).

Valdengo, Giuseppe. Ho canto con Toscanini. Como: Pietro Cairoli Editore, 1962. 163 p., 15 illus., discography, 29-item bibliography, index of names.

Vergani, Orio, Emilio Radius and Waldemar George. Toscanini nella pittura di Caselli Bergamo. Bergamo: Istituto Italiano D'Arti Grafiche Editore, 1953. 88, [11] p., 23 plates, 8 portraits.

Wessling, Berndt W. Toscanini in Bayreuth. Muenchen: Verlag Kurt Desch Edition GmbH, 1976. 143, [1] p., 29-item bibliography, notes, 153-item NBC Orchestra discography.

Winfrey, Dorman H. Arturo Toscanini in Texas: the 1950 NBC Symphony Orchestra Tour. Austin: The Encino Press, 1967. ix, 30 p., illus.

Limited to 750 copies. Concerts in Houston, Austin, and Dallas on the legendary 1950 transcontinental tour.

Zweig, Stefan. Arturo Toscanini: ein Bildnis. Wien: Herbert Reichner Verlag, 1935. 14 p.

5. A0002, A0004, A0008, A0010, A0012, A0015, A0045, A0050, B0006, B0015, B0016, B0017, B0035, B0038, B0044, B0046, B0048, B0051, B0052, B0054, B0055, B0060, B0064, B0069, B0088, B0092, B0107, B0116, B0118, B0131, B0152, B0157, B0159, B0161, B0167.

SEE: Teodoro Celli under VICTOR De SABATA (C0255.4).

SEE: Clara Clemens under OSSIP GABRILOWITSCH (C0373.4).

SEE: Eby, Gordon M. From the Beauty of Embers: a Musical Aftermath. New York: Robert Speller & Sons, Publishers, Inc., 1961.

SEE: The North Texas State Music Library collection includes the personal papers of composer Don Gillis from the period 1944-54 when he produced and directed Toscanini's radio programs.

SEE: Autobiography of EUGENE GOOSSENS (C0416.3).

SEE: Hahn, Reynaldo. Thèmes variés. Paris: J.-B. Janin Editeur, 1945.

SEE: Robert C. Bachmann under HERBERT von KARAJAN (C0558.4).

SEE: Autobiography of ERICH LEINSDORF (C0663.3).

SEE: Laurence Lewis under GUIDO CANTELLI (C0171.4).

SEE: Leinsdorf, Erich. "Toscanini at Salzburg", Opera Annual No. 5. New York: Doubleday & Company, Inc., 1958: 28-31.

SEE: Autobiography of WILFRID PELLETIER (C0850.3).

SEE: Sargeant, Winthrop. Geniuses, Goddesses and People. New York: E. P. Dutton & Company, 1949.

SEE: Serate musicali under ADRIANO LUALDI (C0695.3).

SEE: William Barry Furlong under GEORG SOLTI (C1070.4).

C1141.
TOYE, EDWARD GEOFFREY. b. February 17, 1889, Winchester, England; d. June 11, 1942, London, England.

1. BAKER 7; GROVE 6/19; PAB-MI/2 (Bibliography); RIEMANN 12.

C1142.
TROMMER, WOLFGANG. b. July 10, 1927, Wuppertal, Germany.

1. BAKER 7; RIEMANN 12/Supp.

C1143.
TRUNK, RICHARD. b. February 10, 1879, Tauberbischopsheim, Baden; d. June 2, 1968, Herrsching-am-Ammersee, Germany.

1. BAKER 7; GROVE 6/19; MGG 1/13; RIEMANN 12 + Supp. (Bibliography).

4. Ott, Alfons. Richard Trunk: Leben und Werk. Muenchen: Verlag Walter Ricke, 1964. 92 p., portrait, chronology, publishers, works, index.

C1144.
TSCHIRCH, FRIEDRICH WILHELM. b. June 8, 1818, Lichtenau; d. January 6, 1892, Gera, Germany.

1. BAKER 7; MGG 1/13 (Bibliography); RIEMANN 12.

C1145.
TURNOVSKY, MARTIN. b. September 29, 1928, Prague, Czechoslovakia.

1. BAKER 7; GROVE 6/19 (Bibliography); PAB-MI/2 (Bibliography); RIEMANN 12/Supp.

C1146.
TUTHILL, BURNET CORWIN. b. November 16, 1888, New York City; d. January 18, 1982, Knoxville, Tennessee.

1. BAKER 7; GROVE 6/19; GROVE-AM 1/4; PAB-MI/2 (Bibliography).

3. Tuthill, Burnet Corwin. Recollections of a Musical Life. Memphis: privately printed for the author, 1974.

No copy located.

4. Raines, J.L. Burnet C. Tuthill: His Life and Music. Ph.D. diss., Michigan State University, 1979.

C1147.
TUUKKANEN, KALERVO. b. October 14, 1909, Mikkeli; d. July 12, 1979, Helsinki, Finland.

1. BAKER 7; GROVE 6/19; PAB-MI/2 (Bibliography); RIEMANN 12/Supp.

C1148.
TUXEN, ERIK. b. July 4, 1902, Mannheim, Germany; d. August 28, 1957, Copenhagen, Denmark.

1. BAKER 7; GROVE 6/19; RIEMANN 12.

C1149.
TZIPINE, GEORGES. b. June 22, 1907, Paris, France.

1. BAKER 7; GROVE 6/19.

C1150.
UNGER, HEINZ. b. December 14, 1895, Berlin; d. February 25, 1965, Berlin, Germany.

1. BAKER 7; GROVE 6/19; RIEMANN 12 + Supp.

3. Unger, Heinz and Naomi Walford. Hammer, Sickle, and Baton: the Soviet Memoirs of a Musician. London: The Cresset Press Ltd, 1939. ix, 275 p.

Covers his life in Russia between 1924 and 1937.

C1151.
USIGLIO, EMILIO. b. January 8, 1841, Parma, Italy; d. July 7, 1910, Milan, Italy.

1. BAKER 7; EdS 1/9; GROVE 6/19 (Bibliography); MGG 1/13 (Bibliography).

C1152.
VACH, FERDINAND. b. February 25, 1860, Jažlovice, Moravia; d. February 16, 1939, Brno, Czechoslovakia.

1. BAKER 7; MGG 1/13 (Bibliography); RIEMANN 12 + Supp. (Bibliography).

C1153.
VALENTINO, HENRI-JUSTIN-ARMAND-JOSEPH. b. October 4, 1785, Lille; d. January 20, 1865, Versailles, France.

1. BAKER 7; GROVE 6/19 (Bibliography).

C1154.
Van der STUCKEN, FRANK VALENTIN. b. October 15, 1858, Fredericksburg, Texas; d. August 16, 1929, Hamburg, Germany.

1. BAKER 7; GROVE-AM 1/4; PAB-MI/2 (Bibliography); RIEMANN 12.

C1155.
Van VACTOR, DAVID. b. May 8, 1906, Plymouth, Indiana.

1. BAKER 7 (Bibliography); GROVE-AM 1/4 (Bibliography); PAB-MI/2 (Bibliography); RIEMANN 12/Supp.

C1156.
VARVISO, SILVIO. b. February 26, 1924, Zurich, Switzerland.

1. BAKER 7; GROVE 6/19 (birthdate given as June 20, 1924; Bibliography); PAB-MI/2 (Bibliography); RIEMANN 12/Supp.

2. ON 27/21.

C1157.
VASARY, TAMAS. b. August 11, 1933, Debrecen, Hungary.

1. BAKER 7; GROVE 6/19; PAB-MI/2 (Bibliography); RIEMANN 12/Supp.

C1158.
VAUGHAN, DENIS EDWARD. b. June 6, 1926, Melbourne, Australia.

1. BAKER 7; GROVE 6/19 (Bibliography); PAB-MI/2 (Bibliography); RIEMANN 12/Supp. (Bibliography).

C1159.
VELASCO MAIDANA, JOSE MARIA. b. July 4, 1899, Sucre, Bolivia.

1. BAKER 7; GROVE 6/19; RIEMANN 12/Supp.

C1160.
VENTH, CARL. b. February 16, 1860, Cologne, Germany; d. January 29, 1938, San Antonio, Texas.

1. BAKER 7; RIEMANN 12.

3. Venth, Carl. My Memories. San Antonio (TX): privately printed for Mrs. C. Venth, 1959. 130 p.

C1161.
VERBRUGGHEN, HENRI. b. August 1, 1873, Brussels, Belgium; d. November 12, 1934, Northfield, Minnesota.

1. BAKER 7; GROVE 6/19.

5. B0108, B0152.

C1162.
VERHULST, JOHANNES. b. March 19, 1816, The Hague; d. January 17, 1891, The Hague, Holland.

1. BAKER 7; GROVE 6/19 (Bibliography); MGG 1/13 (Bibliography); PAB-MI/2 (Bibliography); RIEMANN 12 + Supp.

C1163.
VIANESI, AUGUST-CHARLES-LEONARD-FRANCOIS. b. November 2, 1837, Livorno, Italy; d. November 4, 1908, New York City.

1. BAKER 7; GROVE 6/19 (Bibliography).

C1164.
VILLA, RICARDO. b. October 23, 1873, Madrid; d. April 10, 1935, Madrid, Spain.

1. BAKER 7; RIEMANN 12/Supp.

C1165.
VIOTTA, HENRI. b. July 16, 1848, Amsterdam, Holland; d. February 17, 1933, Montreux, Switzerland.

1. BAKER 7; GROVE 6/19 (Bibliography); MGG 1/13 (Bibliography); RIEMANN 12.

   Viotta authored the Lexicon der toonkunst (Amsterdam, 1883-85).

C1166.
VOGEL, JAROSLAV. b. January 11, 1894, Pilsen; d. February 2, 1970, Prague, Czechoslovakia.

1. GROVE 6/20 (Bibliography); MGG 1/13 (Bibliography); RIEMANN 12 + Supp. (Bibliography).

C1167.
VOGT, AUGUSTUS STEPHEN. b. August 14, 1861, Elmira, Ontario; d. September 17, 1926, Toronto, Canada.

1. BAKER 7 (Bibliography); GROVE 6/20 (Bibliography); PAB-MI/2 (Bibliography).

C1168.
VOLBACH, FRITZ. b. December 17, 1861, Wipperfuerth, near Cologne; d. November 30, 1940, Wiesbaden, Germany.

1. BAKER 7 (Bibliography); GROVE 6/20 (Bibliography); MGG 1/13; RIEMANN 12 + Supp.

3. BAKER 7 mentions a posthumous volume of memoirs, Erlebtes und Erstrebtes, published 1956 in Mainz.

C1169.
VOLLERTHUN, GEORG. b. September 29, 1876, Fuerstenau; d. September 15, 1945, Strausberg, near Berlin, Germany.

1. BAKER 7 (Bibliography); RIEMANN 12.

C1170.
VOLPE, ARNOLD. b. July 9, 1869, Kovno, Lithuania; d. February 2, 1940, Miami, Florida.

1. BAKER 7; GROVE-AM 1/4; PAB-MI/2 (Bibliography); RIEMANN 12.

4. Volpe, Marie. Arnold Volpe: Bridge between Two Musical Worlds. Forward by Olin Downes. Coral Gables (Florida): University of Miami Press, 1950. [iii], v, 15-223, [7] p., 51 illus., list of works performed at Lewisohn Stadium 1918-19, index.

5. SEE: Volpe, Marie. Marie Volpe for "Music for Miami": an Autobiography. Miami: Hurricane House Publishers, Inc., 1967. ix, 126 p., 55 illus., index of names.

C1171.
VOSTRAK, ZBYNEK. b. June 10, 1920, Prague, Czechoslovakia.

1. BAKER 7; GROVE 6/20 (Bibliography); PAB-MI/2 (Bibliography); RIEMANN 12/Supp. (Bibliography).

C1172.
VOTTO, ANTONIO. b. October 30, 1896, Piacenza, Italy.

1. BAKER 7; EdS 1/9; GROVE 6/20, PAB-MI/2 (Bibliography); RIEMANN 12/ Supp.

C1173.
WAGHALTER, IGNATZ. b. March 15, 1882, Warsaw, Poland; d. April 7, 1949, New York City.

1. BAKER 7; RIEMANN 12.

C1174.
WAGNER, JOSEPH FREDERICK. b. January 9, 1900, Springfield, Massachusetts; d. October 12, 1974, Los Angeles, California.

1. BAKER 7; GROVE-AM 1/4; PAB-MI/2 (Bibliography); RIEMANN 12 + Supp.

4. Bowling, Lance. Joseph Wagner: a Retrospective of a Composer-Conductor. Lomita (California), 1976.

   No copy located.

C1175.
WAGNER, RICHARD. b. May 22, 1813, Leipzig, Germany; d. February 13, 1883, Venice, Italy.

1. BAKER 7 (Bibliography); EdS 1/9; GROVE 6/20 (Bibliography); MGG 1/14 (Bibliography); PAB-MI/2 (Bibliography); RIEMANN 12 (Bibliography) + Supp. (Bibliography).

   There is an excellent brief summary of Wagner's autobiography, the

"Brown Book", and his collected writings in the new BAKER 7. There exist a number of basic biographies of Wagner's work which focus primarily on his contributions as a composer. There is more written by and about Richard Wagner than any other composer in history, and most of this material has been assembled by Kastner, Oesterlein, Silege, Frankenstein, and Barth. The reader is referred to the excellent bibliographies mentioned above as useful guides.

3. Wagner, Richard. My Life. Authorized translation. New York: Tudor Publishing Company, 1936 (originally published 1911). vii, [i], 911 p., portrait, index.

This is an abridged version of his autobiography which was privately published in four parts between 1870 and 1881. Intended only for his close friends, numerous passages were suppressed in later editions. M. Gregor-Dellin edited a definitive edition based upon Wagner's original MS which was published in Munich in 1963.

Wagner, Richard. Ueber das Dirigiren. Leipzig: Verlag von C.F. Kahnt, n.d. [1869]. 86 p.

4. Bobbington, Warren Arthur. The Orchestral Conducting Practice of Richard Wagner. Ph.D. diss., City University of New York, 1984. 561 p.

Newman, Ernest. The Life of Richard Wagner. 4 vols. New York: Alfred A. Knopf, 1933/1937/1941/1946. xxvii, 512, xxxi p., 12 illus., sources, index; xx, 619, xxviii p., 13 illus., additional sources and references, index; xvi, 569, xxxvi p., 12 illus., additional sources and references, 3 appendices, index; xv, 729, lvi p., 12 illus., additional sources and references, 2 appendices, index.

5. B0017, B0032, B0080, B0083, B0085, B0094, B0112.

SEE: Maurice Kufferath under HANS RICHTER (C0915.4).

C1176.
WAGNER, ROBERT. b. April 20, 1915, Vienna, Austria.

1. BAKER 7; PAB-MI/2 (Bibliography); RIEMANN 12 + Supp. (Bibliography).

C1177.
WAGNER, ROGER. b. January 16, 1914, Le Puy, France.

1. BAKER 7; GROVE 6/20; GROVE-AM 1/4 (Bibliography); PAB-MI/2 (Bibliography).

C1178.
WALLAT, HANS. b. October 18, 1929, Berlin, Germany.

1. BAKER 7; PAB-MI/2 (Bibliography); RIEMANN 12/Supp.

C1179.
WALLBERG, HEINZ. b. March 16, 1923, Herringen-Hamm, Germany.

1. BAKER 7; PAB-MI/2 (Bibliography); RIEMANN 12 + Supp. (Bibliography).

C1180.
WALLENSTEIN, ALFRED. b. October 7, 1898, Chicago, Illinois; d. February 8, 1983, New York City.

1. BAKER 7; GROVE 6/20; GROVE-AM 1/4 (Bibliography); PAB-MI/2 (Bibliography); RIEMANN 12 + Supp.

5. A0010, A0048.

C1181.
WALLERSTEIN, LOTHAR. b. November 6, 1882, Prague, Czechoslovakia; d. November 13, 1949, New Orleans, Louisiana.

1.BAKER 7; PAB-MI/2 (Bibliography); RIEMANN 12/Supp. (Bibliography).

C1182.
WALTER, BRUNO. b. September 15, 1876, Berlin, Germany; d. February 17, 1962, Beverly Hills, California.

1. BAKER 7; EdS 1/9; GROVE 6/20 (Bibliography); GROVE-AM 1/4 (Bibliography); MGG 1/14; PAB-MI/2 (Bibliography); RIEMANN 12 + Supp. (Bibliography).

2. HiFi 14/1; LS 84; MQ 12/2, 32/4; ON 10/15, 15/22, 20/17, 26/19, 40/13; OPERA 13/4; OW 14/4; RS 40.

3. Lindt, Lotte Walter, ed. Bruno Walter Briefe 1894-1962. Frankfurt am Main: Fischer Verlag GmbH, 1969. xv, [i], 461, [2] p., notes, list of recipients, index.

   Walter, Bruno. Gustav Mahler. Complete citation under C0717.4.

   Bruno Walter's correspondence with Gustav Mahler is housed in the Music Division of the Library and Museum of the Performing Arts at Lincoln Center, New York City.

   Walter, Bruno. Of Music and Music-Making. Translated by Paul Hamburger. London: Faber and Faber Limited, 1961 [originally published in Frankfurt/M., 1957]. 222 p., index.

   Walter, Bruno. Theme and Variations: an Autobiography. Translated by James A. Galston. New York: Alfred A. Knopf, 1946. xi, 344, xx p., 15 illus., index.

4. Bruno Walter: Schallplattenverzeichnis. Frankfurt/M.: Deutsches-Rundfunkarchiv, 1972. 5 p.

   Gavoty, Bernard. Bruno Walter. Geneva: René Kister, 1956. 30, [2] p., 24 illus., discography.

   Komorn-Rebhan, Mary. Was wir von Bruno Walter lernten: Erinnerungen eines ausuebenden Mitgliedes der Wiener Singakademie. Leipzig: Universal-Edition A.-G., n.d. [c.1913]. 111, [1] p., portrait.

Stefan, Paul. Bruno Walter. Wien: Herbert Reichner Verlag, 1936. 76 p., 8 illus.

5. A0002, A0004, A0007, A0008, A0010, A0016, A0022, A0048, A0052, B0006, B0015, B0035, B0039, B0047, B0048, B0052, B0054, B0055, B0060, B0063, B0069, B0088, B0103, B0104, B0107, B0109, B0110, B0120, B0123, B0131, B0138, B0150, B0156, B0157, B0167.

C1183.
WAND, GUENTER. b. January 7, 1912, Elberfeld, Germany.

1. BAKER 7; GROVE 6/20; RIEMANN 12 + Supp.

4. Berger, Friedrich. Guenter Wand: Guerzenichkapellmeister 1947-1974. Koeln: Wienand Verlag, 1974. 55 p., 7 illus., repertoire, discography.

C1184.
WANGENHEIM, VOLKER. b. July 1, 1928, Berlin, Germany.

1. BAKER 7; GROVE 6/20 (Bibliography); PAB-MI/2 (Bibliography); RIEMANN 12 + Supp.

C1185.
WASSERMANN, HEINRICH JOSEPH. b. March 3, 1791, Schwarzbach, near Fulda, Germany; d. September 3, 1838, Riehen, near Basel, Switzerland.

1. BAKER 7; MGG 1/14.

C1186.
WATANABE, AKEO. b. June 5, 1919, Tokyo, Japan.

1. BAKER 7; RIEMANN 12/Supp.

C1187.
von WEBER, CARL MARIA. b. November 18, 1786, Eutin, Oldenburg, Germany; d. June 5, 1826, London, England.

1. BAKER 7 (Bibliography); EdS 1/9; GROVE 6/20 (Bibliography); MGG 1/14 (Bibliography); PAB-MI/2 (Bibliography); RIEMANN 12 + Supp. (Bibliography).

2. MQ 11/1, 14/3, 19/2, 20/1.

3. Kaiser, G. Saemtliche Schriften von Carl Maria von Weber. Berlin: Schuster & Loeffler, 1908. cxxiv, 585 p., portrait.

4. Benedict, Julius. Weber. New York: Charles Scribner's Sons, 1913. [iii], 176 p., descriptive catalogue of works.

Schnoor, Hans. Weber auf dem Welttheater: ein Freischuetzbuch. 3rd edition. Dresden: Deutscher Literatur-Verlag, 1943. 329, [6] p., 77 illus., index of names.

The first edition was a "Geschenk-ausgabe" published January 1943.

von Weber, Baron Max Maria [son]. Carl Maria von Weber: the Life of an Artist. Translated by J. Palgrave Simpson. 2 vols. London: Chapman and Hall, 1865. ix, [ii], 404 p.; 483 p.

This was compiled in part from von Weber's personal diary.

C1188.
WEBER, FRANZ. b. August 26, 1805, Cologne; d. September 18, 1876, Cologne, Germany.

1. BAKER 7; MGG 1/14 (Bibliography).

C1189.
WEIKERT, RALF. b. November 10, 1940, St. Florian, near Linz, Austria.

1. BAKER 7; PAB-MI/2 (Bibliography); RIEMANN 12/Supp.

C1190.
WEINGARTNER, FELIX, EDLER von MUENZBERG. b. June 2, 1863, Zara, Dalmatia; d. May 7, 1942, Winterthur, Switzerland.

1. BAKER 7 (Bibliography); EdS 1/9 (Bibliography); GROVE 6/20 (Bibliography); MGG 1/14 (Bibliography); PAB-MI/2 (Bibliography); RIEMANN 12 (Bibliography) + Supp. (Bibliography).

2. RS 55/56.

3. Weingartner, Felix. Akkorde: gesammelte Aufsaetze. Leipzig: Druck und Verlag von Breitkopf und Haertel, 1912. 295 p.

   Weingartner, Felix. Buffets and Rewards: a Musician's Reminiscences. Translated by Marguerite Wolff. London: Hutchinson & Co., 1937. 383 p., 17 illus., list of musical and literary works, index of names.

   Weingartner was a prodigious writer, and this is a version of his Lebenserinnerungen (vol. 1. Zurich: Orell Fussli Verlag, 1923. 377 p., 24 illus.; vol. 2, 1929 has not been seen.

   Weingartner, Felix. Eine Kuenstlerfahrt nach Suedamerika: Tagebuch Juni-November 1920. Wien: Hugo Heller & Cie, 1921. 154 p., portrait.

   Weingartner, Felix. Erlebnisse eines "Koeniglichen Kapellmeisters" in Berlin. Berlin: Verlegt bei Paul Cassirer, 1912. 87 p.

   This is an open attack on the cultural administration. There is a spirited rebuttal, Der Fall Weingartner (Berlin, 1912), by A. Wolff.

   Weingartner, Felix. On the Performance of Beethoven's Symphonies. Translated by Jessie Crosland. New York: E.F. Kalmus Orchestra Scores, Inc., n.d. x, 195 p.

   This was originally published as Ratschlaege fuer Auffuhrung der Sinfonien Beethoven (Berlin, 1906), and it was followed by similar treatments of Schubert and Schumann (Berlin, 1918), and Mozart (Berlin, 1923).

Weingartner, Felix. The Symphony Writers Since Beethoven. Translated by Arthur Bles. London: William Reeves Bookseller Limited, n.d. [1904; original Berlin, 1897]. vii, 168 p., 12 illus., index, appendix.

Weingartner, Felix. Ueber das Dirigieren. 3rd rev. ed. Leipzig: Druck und Verlag von Breitkopf & Haertel, 1905 [1st edition 1896]. 61 p.

Weingartner on Music and Conducting. New York: Dover Publications, Inc., 1969. vii, 304 p., musical examples.

This volume includes three important essays: Ernest Newman's translation of the third edition of Ueber das Dirigieren; Jessie Crosland's translation of the first edition of ...der Sinfonien Beethoven; H.M. Schott's new translation of Die Symphonie nach Beethoven.

Weingartner, Felix. Unwirkliches und Wirkliches: Maerchen - Essays - Vortraege. Wien: Saturn-Verlag, 1936. 207 p.

4. Dyment, Christopher. Felix Weingartner: Recollections & Recordings. Forward by Josef Krips. Rickmansworth: Triad Press, 1976. 114 p., 46 illus., discography, appendix, index.

The appendix is a translated and edited version of Weingartner's essay on Bayreuth which was published in Berlin in 1897.

Festschrift fuer Dr. Felix Weingartner zu seinem siebzigsten Geburtstag. Basel: Allgemeinen Musikgesellschaft, 2. Juni 1933. 167 p., 20 illus.

Hutschenruijter, Wouter. Felix Weingartner. Haarlem: H.D. Tjeenk & Zoon, 1906. 48 p., portrait.

Krause, Emil. Felix Weingartner als schaffender Kuenstler. Berlin: Gose & Tetzlaff Verlagsbuchhandlung, 1904. 70 p., portrait, list of works, index of names.

Lusztig, J.C. Felix Weingartner. Berlin: Virgil Verlag, n.d. 29 p.

Stefan, Paul. Gustav Mahlers Erbe: ein Beitrag zur neusten Geschichte des deutschen Theaters und des Herrn Felix von Weingartner. Muenchen: Hans von Weber Verlag, 1908. 72 p.

This is a polemic against Weingartner who succeeded Mahler in Vienna.

5. A0012, B0015, B0033, B0035, B0054, B0055, B0057, B0059, B0062, B0094, B0112, B0127, B0140, B0156, B0167.

SEE: Graça, Fernando Lopes. Reflexões sôbre a música. Lisboa: Seara Nova, 1941. 150 p.

C1191.
WEINWURM, RUDOLF. b. March 3, 1835, Schaidldorf-am-Thaja; d. May 26, 1911, Vienna, Austria.

1. BAKER 7; MGG 1/14 (Bibliography).

C1192.
von **WEINZIERL, MAX**. b. September 16, 1841, Bergstadtl, Bohemia; d. July 10, 1898 Moedling, near Vienna, Austria.

1. BAKER 7; MGG 1/14 (Bibliography).

C1193.
WEIS, KAREL. b. February 13, 1862, Prague; d. April 4, 1944, Prague, Czechoslovakia.

1. BAKER 7; GROVE 6/20 (Bibliography); MGG 1/14 (Bibliography); PAB-MI/2 (Bibliography); RIEMANN 12.

4. Firkusny, Leos. Karel Weis. Prague: Nakladem ceske akademie ved a umeni, 1949. 62 p., 4 illus., list of works.

C1194.
WEISBACH, HANS. b. July 19, 1885, Golgau; d. April 23, 1961, Wuppertal, Germany.

1. BAKER 7 (Bibliography); RIEMANN 12 + Supp. (Bibliography).

C1195.
WEISBERG, ARTHUR. b. April 4, 1931, New York City.

1. BAKER 7; GROVE 6/20.

C1196.
WEISSENBAECK, FRANZ ANDREAS. b. November 26, 1880, St. Lorenzen, Styria; d. March 14, 1960, Vienna, Austria.

1. BAKER 7; RIEMANN 12 + Supp. (Bibliography).

C1197.
WEISSENBORN, GUENTHER. b. June 2, 1911, Coburg, Germany.

1. BAKER 7; RIEMANN 12 + Supp.

C1198.
WEISSHEIMER, WENDELIN. b. February 26, 1838, Osthofen, Alsace; d. June 16, 1910, Nuremberg, Germany.

1. BAKER 7; GROVE 6/20; MGG 1/14 (Bibliography); RIEMANN 12 (Bibliography) + Supp. (Bibliography).

C1199.
WELDON, GEORGE. b. June 5, 1906, Chichester, England; d. August 16, 1963, Cape Town, South Africa.

1. BAKER 7; GROVE 6/20.

5. A0003, A0004.

C1200.
WELLER, WALTER. b. November 30, 1939, Vienna, Austria.

1. BAKER 7; GROVE 6/20; PAB-MI/2 (Bibliography); RIEMANN 12/Supp.

C1201.
WESTERBERG, STIG. b. November 26, 1918, Malmoe, Sweden.

1. BAKER 7; GROVE 6/20; RIEMANN 12/Supp.

C1202.
WETZLER, HERMANN HANS. b. September 8, 1870, Frankfurt-am-Main, Germany. d. May 29, 1943, New York City.

1. BAKER 7; GROVE 6/20; GROVE-AM 1/4; PAB-MI/2 (Bibliography); RIEMANN 12 (Bibliography).

C1203.
WHITNEY, ROBERT SUTTON. b. July 9, 1904, Newcastle upon Tyne, England.

1. BAKER 7; GROVE 6/20; GROVE-AM 1/4 (Bibliography); PAB-MI/2.

2. HiFi/MusAm 25/4.

5. A0048.

C1204.
WHITTAKER, WILLIAM GILLIES. b. July 23, 1876, Newcastle upon Tyne, England; d. July 5, 1944, Orkney Islands.

1. BAKER 7; GROVE 6/20; MGG 1/14 (Bibliography); PAB-MI/2 (Bibliography); RIEMANN 12 + Supp. (Bibliography).

C1205.
WICH, GUENTHER. b. May 23, 1928, Bamberg, Germany.

1. BAKER 7; GROVE 6/20; PAB-MI/2 (Bibliography); RIEMANN 12 + Supp.

C1206.
WIEDEBEIN, GOTTLOB. b. July 27, 1779, Eilenstadt; d. April 17, 1854, Braunschweig, Germany.

1. BAKER 7; GROVE 6/20 (Bibliography); MGG 1/14 (Bibliography).

C1207.
WIKLUND, ADOLF. b. June 5, 1879, Langserud; d. April 2, 1950 Stockholm, Sweden.

1. BAKER 7; GROVE 6/20; MGG 1/14; RIEMANN 12 + Supp. (Bibliography).

C1208.
WILKOMIRSKI, KAZIMIERZ. b. September 1, 1900, Moscow, Russia.

1. BAKER 7; GROVE 6/20; MGG 1/14; PAB-MI/2 (Bibliography); RIEMANN 12 + Supp. (Bibliography).

3. RIEMANN 12/Supp. mentions a volume of memoirs (Moscow, 1971).

C1209.
WILLCOCKS, DAVID VALENTINE. b. December 30, 1919, Newquay, England.

1. BAKER 7; GROVE 6/20 (Bibliography); PAB-MI/2 (Bibliography).

C1210.
WILLIAMSON, JOHN FINLEY. b. June 23, 1887, Canton; d. May 28, 1964, Toledo, Ohio.

1. BAKER 7; GROVE-AM 1/4 (Bibliography).

4. Wehr, D.A. John Finley Williamson (1887-1964): His Life and Contribution to Choral Music. Ph.D. diss., Miami University, 1971.

C1211.
WINDINGSTAD, OLE. b. May 18, 1886, Sandefjord, Norway; d. June 3, 1959, Kingston, New York.

1. BAKER 7; GROVE-AM 1/4; PAB-MI/2 (Bibliography).

C1212.
WINOGRAD, ARTHUR. b. April 22, 1920, New York City.

1. BAKER 7; GROVE-AM 1/4.

C1213.
WISKE, CHARLES MORTIMER. b. January 12, 1853, Bennington, Vermont; d. July 9, 1934, Lewiston, Maine.

1. BAKER 7; PAB-MI/2 (Bibliography); RIEMANN 12.

C1214.
WISLOCKI, STANISLAW. b. July 7, 1921, Rzeszów, Poland.

1. BAKER 7; GROVE 6/20; RIEMANN 12 + Supp.

C1215.
WODELL, FREDERICK WILLIAM. b. December 17, 1859, London, England; d. February 13, 1938, St. Petersburg, Florida.

2. BAKER 6.

3. Wodell, Frederick W. Choir and Chorus Conducting: a Treatise on the Organization, Management, Training, and Conducting of Choirs and Choral Societies. Philadelphia: Theodore Presser, 1901. 177 p., 56-item bibliography.

C1216.
WODICZKO, BOHDAN. b. July 5, 1912, Warsaw, Poland.

1. RIEMANN 12/Supp.

4. Pociej, Bohdan. Bohdan Wodiczko. Kraków: Polskie Wydawnictwo Muzyczne, 1964. 43 p., 21 illus.

5. A0050.

C1217.
WOELDIKE, MOGENS. b. July 5, 1897, Copenhagen, Denmark.

1. BAKER 7; GROVE 6/20; MGG 1/14; PAB-MI/2 (Bibliography); RIEMANN 12 (Bibliography) + Supp. (Bibliography).

C1218.
WOESS, KURT. b. May 2, 1914, Linz, Austria.

1. BAKER 7; PAB-MI/2 (Bibliography); RIEMANN 12 + Supp.

C1219.
WOHLGEMUTH, GUSTAV. b. December 2, 1863, Leipzig; d. March 2, 1937, Leipzig, Germany.

1. BAKER 7; MGG 1/14 (Bibliography); RIEMANN 12.

C1220.
WOLFES, FELIX. b. September 2, 1892, Hannover, Germany; d. March 28, 1971, Boston, Massachusetts.

1. BAKER 7; GROVE 6/20; GROVE-AM 1/4.

C1221.
WOLFF, ALBERT LOUIS. b. January 19, 1884, Paris; d. February 20, 1970, Paris, France.

1. BAKER 7 (Bibliography); EdS 1/9 (Bibliography); GROVE 6/20 (Bibliography); MGG 1/14; PAB-MI/2 (Bibliography); RIEMANN 12 + Supp.

5. A0040, A0046, B0167.

C1222.
WOOD, HENRY JOSEPH. b. March 3, 1869, London; d. August 19, 1944, Hitchin, Hertfordshire, England.

1. BAKER 7; GROVE 6/20 (Bibliography); MGG 1/14 (Bibliography); PAB-MI/2 (Bibliography); RIEMANN 12 + Supp. (Bibliography).

2. RS 53.

3. Wood, Henry Joseph. About Conducting. Prefatory note by Hubert Foss. London: Sylvan Press, 1945. Reprint 1972. 124, [3] p., portrait.

   Wood, Henry Joseph. My Life of Music. London: Victor Gollancz Ltd, 1938. 495 p., appendix of "novelties" conducted between 1895 and 1937, index.

4. Hill, Ralph & C.B. Rees, eds. Sir Henry Wood: Fifty Years of the Proms. London: The BBC, n.d. [1944]. 63, [1] p., 22 illus.

The BBC's tribute on the occasion of the Jubilee Year of the Promenade Concerts and Sir Henry's seventy-fifth birthday. Articles by twelve associates and friends.

Newmarch, Rosa. Henry J. Wood. London: John Lane. The Bodley Head, 1904. 100 p., 6 illus., list of first performances with the Queen's Hall Orchestra 1895-1903.

Pound, Reginald. Sir Henry Wood: a Biography. London: Cassell & Company Ltd, 1969. x, 346 p., 30 illus., 34-item bibliography, index.

Wood, Jessie. The Last Days of Henry J. Wood. Forward by Sir Malcolm Sargent. London: Victor Gollancz Ltd, 1954. 192 p., 7 illus.

5. A0003, A0045, B0010, B0015, B0054, B0058, B0059, B0062, B0075, B0094, B0167.

SEE: Cox, David. The Henry Wood Proms. London: British Broadcasting Company, 1980.

SEE: Mackenzie, Compton. My Record of Music. New York: G.P. Putnam's Sons, 1955?

SEE: Orga, Artes. The Proms. London: David & Charles, 1974.

SEE: Charles Reid under THOMAS BEECHAM (C0079.4).

C1223.
WOODWORTH, GEORGE WALLACE. b. November 6, 1902, Boston; d. July 18, 1969, Cambridge, Massachusetts.

1. BAKER 7; GROVE 6/20 (Bibliography); GROVE-AM 1/4; RIEMANN 12/Supp. (Bibliography).

5. B0158.

C1224.
WOOLDRIDGE, DAVID. b. August 24, 1927, Deal, Kent, England.

1. BAKER 7.

3. Wooldridge, David. Conductor's World. New York: Praeger Publishers, 1970. xiv, 379 p., orchestral layouts under various conductors, table of six major American orchestras with the terms of office of the respective permanent condcutors, select discography, index. Also listed as A0053.

Also authored a basic biography of Charles Ives (New York, 1974).

C1225.
von WOYRSCH, FELIX. b. October 8, 1860, Troppau, Silesia; d. March 20, 1944, Altona-Hamburg, Germany.

1. BAKER 7; GROVE 6/20; MGG 1/14 (Bibliography); RIEMANN 12 (Bibliography).

C1226.
WUELLNER, FRANZ. b. January 28, 1832, Muenster; d. September 7, 1902, Braunfels-an-der-Lahn, Germany.

1. BAKER 7 (Bibliography); GROVE 6/20 (Bibliography); MGG 1/14 (Bibliography); RIEMANN 12 + Supp. (Bibliography).

C1227.
WUEST, PHILIPP. b. May 3, 1894, Oppau; d. November 1, 1975, Saarbruecken, Germany.

1. BAKER 7; RIEMANN 12 + Supp.

C1228.
WYLDE, HENRY. b. May 22, 1822, Bushey, Herts; d. March 13, 1890, London, England.

1. BAKER 7; GROVE 6/20; MGG 1/14.

C1229.
YAMADA, KOSAKU. b. June 9, 1886, Tokyo; d. December 29, 1965, Tokyo, Japan.

1. BAKER 7; GROVE 6/20; MGG 1/14; RIEMANN 12 + Supp.

C1230.
YSAYE, EUGENE. b. July 16, 1858, Liège; d. May 12, 1931, Brussels, Belgium.

1. BAKER 7; GROVE 6/20 (Bibliography); GROVE-AM 1/4 (Bibliography); MGG 1/14 (Bibliography); PAB-MI/2 (Bibliography); RIEMANN 12 + Supp. (Bibliography).

4. Axelrod, H.R., ed. Prof. Lev Ginsburg's Ysaÿe. Translated by X.M. Danko. Neptune City (New Jersey): Paganiniana Publications, Inc., 1980. 572 p., numerous illus., discography, index.

   Ysaÿe, Antoine [son]. Eugene Ysaÿe: sa vie - son oeuvre - son influence d'après les documents receuillis par son fils. Preface by Yehudi Menuhin. Bruxelles: Editions L'Ecran Du Monde, n.d. [1947]. 550 p., 78 illus., list of works dedicated to Ysaye, 61-item bibliography, iconography, list of outstanding students.

   There is an abridged translation published the same year in London by William Heinemann Ltd.

C1231.
ZACH, MAX WILHELM. b. August 31, 1864, Lwow, Austria; d. February 3, 1921, St. Louis, Missouri.

1. BAKER 7; GROVE-AM 1/4 (Bibliography); PAB-MI/2 (Bibliography).

C1232.
ZAFRED, MARIO. b. February 21, 1922, Trieste, Italy.

1. BAKER 7; EdS 1/9; GROVE 6/20 (Bibliography); PAB-MI/2 (Bibliography); RIEMANN 12/Supp. (Bibliography).

C1233.
von ZALLINGER, MEINHARD. b. February 25, 1897, Vienna, Austria.

1. BAKER 7; RIEMANN 12 + Supp.

C1234.
ZANOTELLI, HANS. b. August 23, 1927, Wuppertal, Germany.

1. BAKER 7; PAB-MI/2 (Bibliography); RIEMANN 12 + Supp.

C1235.
ZAUN, FRITZ. b. June 19, 1893, Cologne; d. January 17, 1966, Duesseldorf, Germany.

1. BAKER 7; RIEMANN 12 + Supp.

C1236.
ZDRAVKOVIC, ZIVOJIN. b. November 24, 1914, Belgrade, Yugoslavia.

1. BAKER 7; RIEMANN 12/Supp.

C1237.
ZECCHI, ADONE. b. July 23, 1904, Bologna, Italy.

1. BAKER 7; GROVE 6/20 (Bibliography); MGG 1/14; RIEMANN 12 + Supp. (Bibliography).

C1238.
ZEDDA, ALBERTO. b. January 2, 1928, Milan, Italy.

1. BAKER 7; GROVE 6/20; PAB-MI/2 (Bibliography).

C1239.
von ZEMLINSKY, ALEXANDER. b. October 14, 1871, Vienna, Austria; d. March 15, 1942, Larchmont, New York.

1. BAKER 7 (Bibliography); EdS 1/9 (Bibliography); GROVE 6/20 (Bibliography); MGG 1/14; PAB-MI/2 (Bibliography); RIEMANN 12 + Supp. (Bibliography).

   There is a special collection of his memorabilia at the Library of Congress, Washington, D.C. He was assistant conductor under Otto Klemperer at the Kroll Opera in Berlin.

4. Kolleritsch, Otto, ed. Alexander Zemlinsky: Tradition im Umkreis der Wiener Schule. Gratz: Institut fuer Wertungsforschung, 1976. 154 p.

C1240.
ZENDER, HANS. b. November 22, 1936, Wiesbaden, Germany.

1. BAKER 7; GROVE 6/20; MGG 1/14; RIEMANN 12/Supp. (Bibliography).

C1241.
ZENGER, MAX. b. February 2, 1837, Munich; d. November 18, 1911, Munich, Germany.

1. BAKER 7; MGG 1/14 (Bibliography).

C1242.
ZILLIG, WINFRIED. b. April 1, 1905, Wuerzburg; d. December 17, 1963, Hamburg, Germany.

1. BAKER 7; GROVE 6/20 (Bibliography); MGG 1/14 (Bibliography); RIEMANN 12 + Supp. (Bibliography).

C1243.
ZINMAN, DAVID JOEL. b. July 9, 1936, New York City.

1. BAKER 7; GROVE-AM 1/4; RIEMANN 12/Supp.

C1244.
ZOELLNER, CARL FRIEDRICH. b. March 17, 1800, Mittelhausen; d. September 25, 1860, Leipzig, Germany.

1. BAKER 7; GROVE 6/20 (Bibliography); MGG 1/14 (Bibliography); RIEMANN 12.

C1245.
ZORAS, LEONIDAS. b. March 8, 1905, Sparta, Greece.

1. BAKER 7; GROVE 6/20 (birthdate as February 23, 1905 with Bibliography); MGG 1/14; RIEMANN 12/Supp.

C1246.
ZULAUF, ERNST. b. February 15, 1876, Kassel; d. January 28, 1963, Wiesbaden, Germany.

1. BAKER 7; RIEMANN 12 + Supp.

C1247.
ZUMPE, HERMAN. b. April 9, 1850, Oppach; d. September 4, 1903, Munich, Germany.

1. BAKER 7; GROVE 6/20; MGG 1/14 (Bibliography); RIEMANN 12 + Supp. (Bibliography).

3. Zumpe, Herman. Persoenliche Erinnerungen nebst Mitteilungen aus seinen Tagebuchblaettern und Briefen. Muenchen: C.H. Beck'sche Verlagsbuchhandlung, 1905. xv, 176 p., portrait, work with Wagner, aphorisms, list of compositions.

C1248.
ZUSCHNEID, KARL. b. May 29, 1854, Oberglogau, Silesia; d. August 1, 1926, Weimar, Germany.

1. BAKER 7; MGG 1/14 (Bibliography); RIEMANN 12.

C1249.
ZWEIG, FRITZ. b. September 8, 1893, Olmuetz, Bohemia; d. February 28, 1984, Los Angeles, California.

1. BAKER 7; PAB-MI/2 (Bibliography); RIEMANN 12 + Supp.

APPENDIX I:
Reference Material

Apart from the standard encyclopedia entries (EdS 1/4 under "Direzione e concertazione"; GROVE 6/4 under "Conducting"; HARVARD 3 under "Conducting"; MENDEL 1/3 under "Direction"; and MGG 1/3 under "Dirigenten" and "Dirigieren"), there exist a limited number of other sources which are often helpful in tracking down titles by and about concert and opera conductors. Most of these are titles which would be familiar to the serious researcher but not, perhaps, to the collector or afficionado. Please note that these authors and editors are not listed in the Index.

D0001. Adams, John L. Musicians' Autobiographies: an Annotated Bibliography of Writings Available in English 1800 to 1980. Jefferson (NC): McFarland & Company, Inc., 1982. x, 11-126 p., chronological index, title index, subject index.

800+ titles not including reprints. The chronological index is most helpful for pinpointing related material. Not in DUCKLES 3 (D0009).

D0002. Angelis, Alberto de. L'Italia musicale d'oggi: Dizionario dei musicisti: compositori, direttori d'orchestra, concertisti, insegnanti, liutae, cantanti, scrittori musicali, librettisti, editori musicali ecc. 3rd ed., corredate di una appendice. Roma: Ausonia, 1928. 523, 211 p.

D0003. Basso, Alberto, ed. Dizionario enciclopedico universale della musica e dei musicisti. Le biografie. Torino: Unione Tipografico, 1985.

Two volumes (A-BUR; BUS-FOX) have appeared to date in a major work which promises to replace Carlo Schmidl's standard dictionary. Not in DUCKLES 3 (D0009).

D0004. Bernsdorf, Eduard. Neues Universal-Lexikon der Tonkunst: fuer Kuenstler, Kunst-Freunde und alle Gebildeten. 3 vols. Dresden: (vols. 1/2) Verlag von Robert Schaefer, 1856/57; Offenbach: (vol. 3) Verlag von Johann Andre, 1861. 878 p.; 1084 p.; 912, [2] p., supp. 1865.

Helpful for obscure artists. Not in DUCKLES 3 (D0009).

D0005. Bertz-Dostal, Helga. Oper im Fernsehen. 2 vols. Wien: Verlag und Druck Minor. Herausgegeben mit Foerderung der Gesellschaft fuer Musiktheater. 1970. 623 p., 110 illus.; 629-1123 p., index of names.

Production details including conductors of 1,646 television productions (1936-1970). Not in DUCKLES 3 (D0009).

D0006. Blyth, Alan, ed. Opera on Record. 3 vols. New York: (vol. 1) Harper Colophon Books, 1982; New York: (vol. 2) Beaufort Books, Inc., 1983; Dover (NH): (vol. 3) Longwood Press, 1984. 663 p., index; 399 p., index; 375 p., index.

Full of comments on conductors. Not in DUCKLES 3 (D0009).

D0007. Cowden, Robert H. Concert and Opera Singers: a Bibliography of Biographical Materials. Westport (CT): Greenwood Press, 1985. xviii, 278 p., 2 appendices including an index to singers in GROVE 6, index of authors.

A wealth of references which relate directly to many conductors. For example, included in the entry for Marilyn Horne (C0293.5) is Harvey E. Phillips' book about the rehearsals, performances, and recording sessions of CARMEN which was to have been the late Goeran Gentele's Metropolitan Opera opening night. Leonard Bernstein was the conductor, and there is a great deal of material about him. Not in DUCKLES 3 (D0009).

D0008. Current Biography. New York: H.W. Wilson, 1940-

This monthly journal which has an annual accumulation gathers biographies of 100+ individuals including musicians each year. The occupation index makes it easy to use.

D0009. Duckles, Vincent. Music Reference and Research Materials: an Annotated Bibliography. 3rd edition. New York: The Free Press, 1974. xvi, 526 p.

The standard reference for music research materials in all languages, DUCKLES 3 is most valuable for the international and national biography sections. There are 130 titles, many of which include material related to concert and opera conductors.

D0010. Eisenberg, Ludwig. Grosses biographisches Lexikon der deutschen Buehne im XIX. Jahrhundert. Leipzig: Verlagsbuchhandlung Paul List, 1903. [iii], 1180, [1] p., frontispiece, 182-item bibliography, index of cross-referenced artists, errata.

Very important period source. Not in DUCKLES 3 (D0009).

D0011. Eitner, Robert. Biographisch-bibliographisches Quellen-Lexikon der Musiker und Musikgelehrten der christlichen Zeitrechnung bis zur Mitte des 19. Jahrhumderts.... 10 vols. Leipzig: Breitkopf & Haertel, 1898-1904. Miscellanea Musicae Bio-bibliographica; Musikgeschichtliche Quellennachweise als Nachtraege und Verbesserungen zu Eitners Quellen-lexikon. Leipzig: Breitkopf & Haertel, 1912-1914.

D0012. Ewen, David, ed. Living Musicians. New York: The H.W. Wilson Company, 1940. 390 p., photo of each musician, classified list by type of musician.

Includes 123 conductors from Hermann Abendroth to Sir Henry Wood.

D0013. Ewen, David, ed. Living Musicians. First Supplement. New York: The H.W. Wilson Company, 1957. 178 p., necrology [2nd printing 1964], list of new biographies, classified list of new biographies.

Thirty-five additions from Victor Alessandro to Georg Solti plus updates of material included in the 1940 edition.

D0014. Fétis, Francois J. Biographie universelle des musiciens et bibliographie générale de la music. 8 vols. 2me éd. Paris: Firmin Didot Fréres, 1866-70. Supplément et complément. pub. sous la direction de M. Arthur Pougin. 2 vols. Paris, 1878-80.

D0015. Kosch, Wilhelm. Deutsches Theater-Lexikon: biographisches und bibliographisches Handbuch. 2 vols. Klagenfurt: Verlag Ferd. Kleinmayr, 1953/1960. [iii], 864 p.; 865-1728 p. fortgefuehrt von Hanspeter Bennwitz.

The valuable work of Kosch/Bennwitz needs to be completed. Excellent for obscure artists. Helpful bibliographical citations. Not in DUCKLES 3 (D0009).

D0016. Marco, Guy A. Opera: a Research and Information Guide. New York: Garland Publishing, Inc., 1984. xxvi, 373 p., appendix, author-title index, subject index.

There is a short supplement in the second printing. Not in DUCKLES 3 (D0009).

D0017. Mendel, Hermann. Musikalisches Conversations-Lexikon: eine Encyklopaedie der gesammten musikalischen Wissenschaften: fuer Gebildete aller Staende, unter Mitwirkung der Literarischen Commission des Berliner Tonkuenstlervereins.... 11 vols. Berlin: L. Heimann, 1870-79.

D0018. Mixter, Keith E. General Bibliography for Music Research. second edition. Detroit: Information Coordinators, Inc. 1975. 135 p.

The section on national and international biographical dictionaries is particularly helpful.

D0019. Schmidl, Carlo. Dizionario universale dei musicisti. 2 vols. Milano: Sonzogno, 1928-29. Supplemento. Milano, 1938.

Readers should consult Alberto Basso (D0003) for current information.

APPENDIX II:

Index to Conductors in BAKER 7

This index lists the sixteen hundred fifteen conductors who are accorded an individual entry in the monumental Baker's Biographical Dictionary of Musicians (seventh edition, 1984) edited by the justly legendary Nicolas Slonimsky. THE outstanding work of its kind presently available, BAKER 7 is one of the few standard reference works consulted by those seeking correct information on past and present performers. A cross-referenced list should prove helpful to those seeking to track down information concerning their favorite conductors. Some 1,249 artists are accorded entries in the main body of this bibliography, and any commonality with BAKER 7 is indicated by the appropriate code number preceding the name, e.g. C0001 (the entry number in the INDIVIDUAL SINGERS, A-Z, p. 37) before CLAUDIO ABBADO who is the first conductor listed in BAKER 7.

Several things should be kept in mind when utilizing this compilation: all names are not spelled as they are in BAKER 7; the order is not always the same; and the nationality designation, which has been abbreviated, depends primarily but not exclusively on Slonimsky. Maps change, dates are elusive and little, if anything, in life is absolute; however, a sincere attempt has been made to be consistent.

C0001. Abbado, Claudio ITA
C0002. Abbado, Marcello ITA
C0003. Abendroth, Hermann GER
Ábrányi, Emil HUN
C0004. Abravanel, Maurice USA
Abt, Franz GER
C0005. Ackermann, Otto RUM
C0006. Adam, Jeno HUN
Adler, Charles F. ENG
C0007. Adler, Kurt AUS-USA
C0008. Adler, Kurt H. AUS-USA
C0009. Adler, Peter Herman CZE
C0010. Aeschbacher, Niklaus SWZ
Aeschbacher, Walter SWZ
C0011. Ahronovich, Yuri RUS
C0012. Aiblinger, Johann K. GER
Aigner, Engelbert AUS
Ajmone-Marsan, Guido ITA
Akiyama, Kazuyoshi JAP
C0013. Albert, Herbert GER
Albert, Rudolf GER
Albini, Srecko CRO
C0014. Albrecht, George A. GER
C0015. Albrecht, Gerd GER
C0016. Albrecht, Karl GER-RUS
C0017. Albrecht, Max GER
Alcantara, Theo SPA
Alessandrescu, Alfred RUM
Alessandro, Victor USA
C0018. Not in BAKER 7
C0019. Alldis, John ENG
C0020. Not in BAKER 7
Allen, Nathan H. USA
C0021. Allers, Franz CZE
C0022. Almeida, Antonio de POR
Alpaerts, Jef BEL
C0023. Altschuler, Modest RUS
C0024. Alwin, Karl Oskar GER

Alwyn, Kenneth ENG
Amaducci, Bruno ITA
Ameln, Konrad GER
Amfiteatrov, Daniele RUS
C0025. Ammann, Benno SWZ
C0026. Amy, Gilbert FRA
C0027. Ančerl, Karel CZE
Andersen, Karsten NOR
Andrae, Marc SWZ
C0028. André, Franz BEL
C0029. Andreae, Volkmar SWZ
Andreoli, Carlo ITA
Andreoli, Guglielmo ITA
C0030. Angerer, Paul AUS
C0031. Anrooy, Peter van DUT
C0032. Anschuetz, Karl GER
C0033. Ansermet, Ernest SWZ
C0034. Anton, Max GER
Antonini, Alfredo ITA-USA
Appia, Edmond SWZ
C0035. Arámbarri y Garate, J. SPA
C0036. Arbós, Enrique F. SPA
C0037. Archangelsky, Alex. RUS
C0038. Archer, Frederick ENG-USA
C0039. Arditi, Luigi ITA
C0040. Argenta, Ataulfo SPA
C0041. Argenta, Pietro ITA
C0042. Armbruster, Karl GER
Armstrong, Richard ENG
C0043. Arndt, Guenther GER
C0044. Arnold, Gustav SWZ
Arnold, Karl GER
Arthur, Alfred USA
C0045. Ashkenazy, Vladimir RUS
C0046. Atherton, David ENG
C0047. Attenhofer, Karl SWZ
C0048. Atzmon, Moshe ISR
C0049. Auberson, Jean-Marie SWZ
C0050. Auriacombe, Louis FRA
Autori, Franco ITA-USA
C0051. Averkamp, Anton DUT
Azmayparashvili, S. RUS

-B-

Badea, Christian RUM
Bahner, Gert GER
C0052. Not in BAKER 7
C0053. Bakala, Břetislav CZE
C0054. Balatka, Hans CZE
Bales, Richard USA
C0055. Balfe, Michael William IRE
C0056. Balkwill, Bryan ENG
C0057. Balling, Michael GER
C0058. Balmer, Luc SWZ
C0059. Bamberger, Carl AUS
C0060. Bamboschek, Giuseppe ITA
Bamert, Matthias SWZ
C0061. Band, Erich GER
C0062. Barati, George HUN-USA
C0063. Barbieri, Carlo E. ITA
C0064. Barbirolli, John ENG
C0065. Barcewicz, Stanislaw POL
Barclay, Arthur ENG
C0066. Bardos, Lajos HUN
C0067. Barenboim, Daniel ARG
Barkel, Charles SWE
C0068. Barlow, Howard USA
C0069. Barnby, Joseph ENG
Barnes, Milton CAN
Barnett, John USA
C0070. Not in BAKER 7
Baron, Maurice FRA
Baron, Samuel USA
C0071. Barshai, Rudolf RUS
Bartholomew, Marshall USA
C0072. Bartoletti, Bruno ITA
C0073. Barzin, Leon E. BEL-USA
Batiz, Enrique MEX
C0074. Baudo, Serge FRA
C0075. Bauer-Theussl, Franz AUS
Baumbach, Friedrich GER
Baumgartner, Rudolf SWZ
Baur, Juerg GER
C0076. Bayer, Josef AUS
C0077. Beck, Johann Heinrich USA
Beck, Karl GER-USA
Beckett, Wheeler USA
C0078. Bedford, Stuart ENG
C0079. Beecham, Thomas ENG
C0080. Behrens, Johan Diderik NOR
C0081. Beinum, Eduard van DUT
Beissel, Heribert GER
C0082. Bellezza, Vincenzo ITA
Bellini, Renato ITA
C0083. Bellugi, Piero ITA
Bělohlávek, Jiří CZE
C0084. Benda, Hans von GER
Bendix, Max USA
C0085. Bendix, Victor Emanuel DAN
C0086. Bendl, Karel CZE
C0087. Benedict, Julius GER-ENG
C0088. Benedito y Vives, R. SPA
C0089. Bengtsson, Gustaf A. SWE
C0090. Benzi, Roberto FRA
C0091. Bergel, Erich ROM
Berger, Jean GER-USA
Bergh, Arthur USA
C0092. Berglund, Paavo Allan FIN
C0093. Bergmann, Carl GER
C0094. Berlioz, Hector FRA
C0095. Bernard, Anthony ENG

Bernardi, Enrico ITA
C0096. Bernardi, Mario CAN
Bernet, Dietfried AUS
C0097. Bernstein, Leonard USA
Bernuth, Julius von GER
C0098. Bertini, Gary RUS-ISR
C0099. Berton, Henri-Montan FRA
C0100. Besly, Maurice ENG
C0101. Bevignani, Enrico ITA
C0102. Beyschlag, Adolf GER
Bial, Rudolf SIL
C0103. Bierdiajew, Walerian POL
C0104. Bierey, Gottlob B. GER
C0105. Bigot, Eugène FRA
C0106. Bilse, Benjamin GER
C0107. Biriotti, León URG
C0108. Birnie, Tessa Daphne NZL
C0109. Bittner, Albert GER
Bjoerlin, Ulf SWE
C0110. Black, Frank USA
Black, Stanley ENG
Blank, Hubert de DUT
C0111. Blatný, Pavel CZE
Blazhkov, Igor RUS
C0112. Blech, Harry ENG
C0113. Blech, Leo GER
C0114. Bliss, Arthur ENG
Bloch, Alexander USA
C0115. Blomstedt, Herbert SWE
Bloomfield, Theodore USA
C0116. Blumenfeld, Felix RUS
C0117. Blumenfeld, Harold USA
Blumenschein, Wm. GER-USA
C0118. Blumer, Theodor GER
C0119. Blumner, Martin GER
Boatwright, Howard USA
C0120. Bodanzky, Artur AUS
C0121. Boehe, Ernst GER
C0122. Boehm, Karl AUS
C0123. Boepple, Paul SWZ-USA
C0124. Boettcher, Wilfred GER
Bombardelli, Silvije CRO
Bon, Willem Frederik DUT
C0265. Bonaventura, M. di USA
C0125. Bonawitz, Johann H. GER
C0126. Not in BAKER 7
C0127. Bongartz, Heinz GER
C0128. Bonynge, Richard AST
C0129. Bopp, Wilhelm GER
C0130. Borch, Gaston Louis FRA
C0131. Bordes, Charles FRA
C0132. Boskovsky, Willi AUS
C0133. Bossi, Renzo ITA
C0134. Bott, Jean Joseph GER
C0135. Bottesini, Giovanni ITA
Boudreau, Robert A. USA
C0136. Boulanger, Nadia FRA
C0137. Boulez, Pierre FRA
C0138. Boult, Adrian ENG
C0139. Bour, Ernest FRA
C0140. Bousquet, Georges FRA
C0141. Boutry, Roger FRA
C0142. Bozza, Eugène FRA
C0143. Braein, Edvard F. NOR
C0144. Braithwaite, Nicholas ENG
C0145. Braithwaite, Warwick ENG
C0146. Branscombe, Gena USA
C0147. Brecher, Gustav GER
C0148. Bretón y Hernández, T. SPA
Briccetti, Thomas USA
C0149. Brico, Antonia USA
C0150. Bridge, John Frederick ENG
C0151. Bristow, George F. USA
C0152. Broekman, David DUT-USA
C0153. Brott, Alexander CAN
Brott, Boris CAN
Brounoff, Planton RUS
Brown, Iona ENG
C0154. Bruck, Charles ROM-FRA
Brueckner-Rueggeberg, GER
C0155. Brun, Fritz SWZ
C0156. Brusilow, Anshel USA
Buckley, Emerson USA
C0157. Buelow, Hans von GER
Buketoff, Igor USA
C0158. Bunning, Herbert ENG
Burco, Ferruccio ITA
Burgess, Russell ENG
C0159. Burghauser, Jarmil M. CZE
Burgin, Richard POL-USA
C0160. Burkhard, Paul SWZ
Bury, Edward POL
C0161. Busch, Carl DEN-USA
C0162. Busch, Fritz GER
C0163. Buschkoetter, Wilhelm GER
C0164. Busser, Paul-Henri FRA
C0165. Buzzolla, Antonio ITA
Bychkov, Semyon RUS
-C-
Caduff, Sylvia SWZ
C0166. Cahn-Speyer, Rudolf AUS
Calabro, Louis USA
C0167. Caldwell, Sarah USA
Cambreling, Sylvain FRA
C0168. Cameron, Basil ENG
C0169. Campanari, Leandro ITA
C0170. Campanini, Cleofonte ITA
C0171. Cantelli, Guido ITA
C0172. Cape, Safford USA-BEL
C0173. Caplet, André FRA

C0174. Capuana, Franco ITA
C0175. Caracciolo, Franco ITA
Carey, Bruce CAN
C0176. Caridis, Miltiades GRE
C0177. Carner, Mosco AUS-ENG
Carr, Howard ENG
C0178. Carrillo, Julián MEX
C0179. Carvalho, Eleazar de BRA
C0180. Casadesus, Francois L. FRA
C0181. Casadesus, Jean-Claude FRA
C0182. Casals, Pablo SPA
C0183. Not in BAKER 7
C0184. Cassuto, Alvaro Leon POR
C0185. Caston, Saul USA
C0186. Castro, José María ARG
C0187. Castro, Juan José ARG
Castro, Washington ARG
C0188. Çeccato, Aldo ITA
C0189. Čelansky, Ludvík V. CZE
C0190. Celibidache, Sergiu ROM
Celis, Fritz BEL
C0191. Cellier, Alfred ENG
C0192. Chadwick, George W. USA
Chailly, Riccardo ITA
C0193. Chalabala, Zdenek CZE
Chapman, William R. USA
Chapple, Stanley ENG
C0194. Chávez, Carlos MEX
C0195. Chevillard, Camile FRA
C0196. Christiansen, F. NOR-USA
Christiansen, Olaf USA
C0197. Cillario, Carlo F. ITA
C0198. Cimara, Pietro ITA
Claassen, Arthur USA
Clark, Edward ENG
C0199. Clavé, José Anselmo SPA
C0200. Cleva, Fausto ITA
Clifton, Chalmers USA
Clippinger, David A. USA
C0201. Cluytens, André BEL
C0202. Coates, Albert ENG
C0203. Coenen, Johannes M. DUT
C0204. Cohn, Arthur USA
C0205. Collingwood, Lawrence ENG
C0206. Collins, Anthony ENG
C0207. Colonne, Edouard FRA
C0208. Combe, Edouard SWZ
C0209. Comissiona, Sergiu ROM
Conlon, James USA
C0210. Constant, Marius ROM
C0211. Not in BAKER 7
C0212. Cooper, Emil RUS
C0213. Coppola, Piero ITA
Corboz, Michel-Jules SWZ
C0214. Cornelis, Evert DUT
C0215. Cortolezis, Fritz GER
C0216. Cortot, Alfred Denis SWZ
Costa, Dan USA
C0217. Costa, Michael ITA-ENG
C0218. Couraud, Marcel FRA
C0219. Courvoisier, Walter SWZ
C0220. Coward, Henry ENG
C0221. Cowen, Frederic Hymen ENG
C0222. Craft, Robert USA
Crawford, Robert M. USA
Crouch, Frederick N. ENG
C0223. Cruz, Ivo POR
C0224. Cundell, Edric ENG
C0225. Cusins, William George ENG
C0226. Czyź, Henryk POL

-D-

C0227. Damcke, Berthold GER
C0228. Damrosch, Frank GER-USA
C0229. Damrosch, Leopold GER-USA
C0230. Damrosch, Walter GER-USA
C0231. Danbé, Jules FRA
C0232. Danon, Oskar YUG
C0233. Dasch, George USA
C0234. Davies, Dennis Russell USA
C0235. Davies, Meredith ENG
C0236. Davis, Andrew Frank ENG
C0237. Davis, Colin ENG
C0238. Davison, Archibald T. USA
C0239. Dawson, William Levi USA
C0240. Decker, Franz-Paul GER
C0241. DeFabritiis, Oliviero ITA
C0242. Defauw, Désiré BEL
C0243. Defossez, Rene GEL
Delacôte, Jacques FRA
C0245. De Lamarter, Eric USA
C0246. Deldevez, Edouard-M. FRA
C0247. Dellinger, Rudolf GER
C0248. Del Mar, Norman ENG
C0249. Delogu, Gaetano ITA
C0250. Delune, Louis BEL
De Main, John USA
Demian, Wilhelm RUM
Dendrino, Gherase ROM
C0251. Denzler, Robert SWZ
C0252. Deppe, Ludwig GER
C0253. De Priest, James USA
C0254. Dervaux, Pierre FRA
C0255. De Sabata, Victor ITA
C0256. Desarzens, Victor SWZ
C0257. Desormière, Roger FRA
C0258. Dešpalj, Pavle YUG
C0259. Dessoff, Felix Otto GER
C0260. Dessoff, Margarethe AUS
C0261. De Vocht, Lodewijk BEL
C0262. Devreese, Frédéric BEL

C0263. Devreese, Godefroid BEL
C0264. De Waart, Edo DUT
C0266. Dietrich, Albert H. GER
C0267. Dietsch, Pierre-Louis FRA
C0268. Dixon, Dean USA
C0269. Dixon, James USA
C0270. Dobrowen, Issay A. RUS
C0271. Dohnányi, Ch. von GER
C0272. Dohnányi, Ernst von HUN
Doire, René FRA
C0273. Donati, Pino ITA
C0274. Dopper, Cornelis DUT
C0275. Doppler, Albert Franz AUS
C0276. Doppler, Karl AUS
C0277. Dorati, Antal HUN-USA
C0278. Dorn, Heinrich Ludwig GER
C0279. Downes, Edward Thomas ENG
C0280. Dranishnikov, Vladimir RUS
Dregert, Alfred GER
Dreier, Per NOR
C0281. Drewanz, Hans GER
C0282. Drigo, Riccardo ITA
C0283. Dubois, Léon BEL
C0284. Ducloux, Walter SWZ-USA
Dudarova, Veronica RUS
Duerrner, Ruprecht GER
C0285. Dufallo, Richard USA
Dumbraveanu, Corneliu RUM
C0286. Dunbar, W. Rudolf BRG
C0287. Dunn, Thomas USA
C0288. Dupuis, Sylvain BEL
C0289. Dutoit, Charles SWZ
-E-
C0290. Ebel, Arnold GER
C0291. Eckerberg, Sixten SWE
C0292. Eckert, Karl Anton GER
C0293. Ehlert, Louis GER
C0294. Ehrenberg, Carl Emil GER
C0295. Ehrling, Sixten SWE
C0296. Eibenschuetz, Jose GER
C0297. Eichhorn, Kurt GER
C0298. Eisfeld, Theodor GER
Eisler, Louis AUS
Ekman, Karl FIN
C0299. Elder, Mark Philip ENG
C0300. Elkan, Henri BEL-USA
C0301. Elmendorff, Karl GER
Emerson, Luther USA
C0302. Endo, Akira JAP
C0303. Engel, Lehman USA
C0304. Entremont, Philippe FRA
C0305. Eppert, Carl USA
C0306. Epstein, David Mayer USA
C0307. Erdélyi, Miklós HUN
C0308. Erdmannsdoerfer von GER
C0309. Erede, Alberto ITA
C0310. Ericson, Eric Gustaf SWE
C0311. Erkel, Ferenc HUN
Eroes, Peter HUN
C0312. Eschenbach, Christoph GER
C0313. Espinosa, Guillermo COL
C0314. Esposito, Michele ITA
C0315. Esser, Heinrich GER
C0316. Esser, Heribert GER
C0317. Estrada, Carlos URU
C0318. Ettinger, Max GER
-F-
C0319. Faccio, Franco ITA
C0320. Faerber, Joerg GER
C0321. Fagan, Gideon SOA
C0322. Fahrbach, Philipp AUS
C0323. Failoni, Sergio ITA
Falk, Richard GER
Fall, Fritz GER
Faller, Nikola CRO
Fanciulli, Francesco ITA
Faning, Eaton ENG
C0324. Farberman, Harold USA
C0325. Farncombe, Charles ENG
C0326. Fasano, Renato ITA
C0327. Fayer, Yuri F. RUS
C0328. Feldbrill, Victor CAN
C0329. Fendler, Edvard GER-USA
C0330. Fennell, Frederick USA
C0331. Ferencsik, János HUN
C0332. Fernstroem, John SWE
C0333. Ferrara, Franco ITA
Ferrer, Rafael SPA
Ferrero, Willy ITA
Ferris, William USA
C0334. Fiedler, Arthur USA
C0335. Fiedler, Max GER
C0336. Fielitz, Alexander von GER
Filev, Ivan BUL
Finko, David RUS
C0337. Not in BAKER 7
C0338. Fischer, Edwin SWZ
Fischer, Frederick GER
C0339. Fischer, Irwin USA
Fischer, Ivan HUN
C0340. Fistoulari, A. RUS-ENG
C0341. Fitelberg, Gregor POL
C0342. Fjeldstad, Oivin, NOR
C0343. Flagello, Nicolas USA
C0344. Flament, Edouard FRA
C0345. Fleischer, Anton HUN
C0346. Fleischer, Leon USA
C0347. Fletcher, Horace Grant USA
C0348. Flipse, Eduard DUT
Flummerfelt, Joseph USA

C0349. Foch, Dirk DUT
C0350. Forbes, Elliot USA
C0351. Ford, Ernest ENG
C0352. Foroni, Jacopo ITA
C0353. Foss, Lukas GER-USA
C0354. Foster, Lawrence Th. USA
C0355. Fougstedt, Nils-Eric FIN
Fourestier, Louis FRA
C0356. Fournet, Jean FRA
C0357. Franci, Carlo ITA
C0358. Frandsen, John DEN
C0359. Frank, Ernst GER
Franko, Nathan USA
C0360. Franko, Sam USA
C0361. Freccia, Massimo ITA
C0362. Freeman, Paul Douglas USA
C0363. Fremaux, Louis FRA
C0364. Frešo, Tibor CZE
C0365. Freudenberg, Wilhelm GER
C0366. Fricsay, Ferenc HUN
C0367. Fried, Oskar GER
C0368. Froment, Louis de FRA
C0369. Fruebeck de Burgos, R. SPA
C0370. Fuchs, Johann Nepomuk AUS
Fuchs, Peter Paul AUS-USA
C0371. Fuleihan, Anis USA
Fumi, Vinceslao ITA
C0372. Furtwaengler, Wilhelm GER

-G-

C0373. Gabrilowitsch, Ossip RUS
C0374. Gade, Niels Wilhelm DEN
C0375. Gales, Weston Spies USA
C0376. Galkin, Elliott W. USA
C0377. Galliera, Alceo ITA
C0378. Gamba, Piero ITA
C0379. Ganz, Rudolf SWZ
C0380. Ganz, Wilhelm GER
C0381. Gardelli, Lamberto ITA
C0382. Gardiner, John Eliot ENG
Gati, Laszlo RUM
C0383. Gatz, Felix Maria GER
C0384. Gaubert, Philippe FRA
Gauk, Alexander RUS
Gaul, Harvey B. USA
C0385. Gavazzeni, Gianandrea ITA
C0386. Gedda, Giulio ITA
C0387. Geisler, Paul GER
C0388. George, Earl USA
C0389. Georgescu, Georges ROM
Gerelli, Ennio ITA
C0390. Gericke, Wilhelm AUS
C0391. Gerlach, Theodor GER
C0392. Gerle, Robert HUN
C0393. Gernsheim, Friedrich GER
Gershkovitch, Jacques RUS
C0394. Ghione, Franco ITA
Gialdini, Gialdino ITA
C0395. Gibson, Alexander ENG
C0396. Gielen, Michael GER
C0397. Gierster, Hans GER
C0398. Giovaninetti, R. J. FRA
C0399. Giulini, Carlo Maria ITA
Glover, Jane Allison ENG
C0400. Glover, John William IRE
C0401. Glover, William Howard ENG
C0402. Godfrey, Daniel Eyers ENG
Godfrey, Isidore ENG
C0403. Goehler, Karl George GER
C0404. Goehr, Walter GER
Goennenwein, Wolfgang GER
C0405. Goepfart, Karl Eduard GER
C0406. Goldbeck, Robert GER
C0407. Goldberg, Szymon POL
C0408. Goldman, Edwin Franko USA
C0409. Goldman, Richard F. USA
C0410. Goldovsky, Boris RUS-USA
C0411. Goldschmidt, Berthold GER
C0412. Golovanov, Nicolai RUS
C0413. Golschmann, Vladimir FRA
Gomez Martínez, Miguel SPA
C0414. Goodall, Reginald ENG
C0415. Goodrich, John W. USA
C0416. Goossens, Eugene ENG
C0417. Gorter, Albert GER
Gosling, John USA
C0418. Gould, Morton USA
C0419. Gracis, Ettore ITA
C0420. Gram, Peder DEN
Green, John USA
C0421. Greenberg, Noah USA
C0422. Gregor, Bohumil CZE
C0423. Grevillius, Nils SWE
C0424. Grishkat, Hans GER
C0425. Grøndahl, Launy DEN
C0426. Grosbayne, Benjamin USA
C0427. Grossmann, Ferdinand AUS
C0428. Groves, Charles B. ENG
C0429. Grovlez, Gabriel M. FRA
C0430. Gruber, Georg AUS
C0431. Gruener-Hegge, Odd NOR
C0432. Grund, Friedrich W. GER
C0433. Guadagno, Anton ITA
C0434. Guarino, Piero ITA
C0435. Guarnieri, Antonio ITA
C0436. Gui, Vittorio ITA
C0437. Gurlitt, Manfred GER
Guschlbauer, Theodor AUS

-H-

C0438. Haas, Karl GER-ENG
C0439. Habenec, Francois-A. FRA

C0440. Hadley, Henry Kimball USA
C0441. Hagel, Richard GER
C0442. Hagemann, Richard DUT-USA
C0443. Hagen-Groll, Walter GER
C0444. Hager, Leopold AUS
Hahn, Carl USA
C0445. Hahn, Reynaldo FRA
C0446. Hainl, Francois FRA
C0447. Haitink, Bernard DUT
C0448. Halász, László HUN
C0449. Halffter, Cristobal SPA
C0450. Halle, Charles GER-ENG
C0451. Hamerik, Asger DEN
C0452. Hamm, Adolf SWZ
C0453. Hammelboe, Arne DEN
Handford, Maurice ENG
C0454. Handley, Vernon ENG
C0455. Hannikainen, Pekka FIN
C0456. Hannikainen, Tauno FIN
C0457. Hanssens, Charles-L. BEL
C0458. d'Harcourt, Eugène FRA
C0459. Harmati, Sándor HUN-USA
C0460. Harnoncourt, Nikolaus GER
C0461. Harris, William V. USA
C0462. Harrison, Guy F. ENG-USA
C0463. Harrison, Julius A. ENG
C0464. Hart, Fritz ENG
C0465. Harth, Sidney USA
Hartmann, Pater GER
C0466. Harty, H. Hamilton ENG
C0467. Hasselmans, Louis FRA
C0468. Hausegger, Sieg. von AUS
C0469. Hawes, William ENG
Hayman, Richard USA
C0470. Heath, Edward R. ENG
C0471. Hedwall, Lennart SWE
C0472. Hegar, Friedrich SWZ
C0473. Heger, Robert GER
Hein, Carl GER-USA
C0474. Heinze, Bernard T. AST
C0475. Heinze, Gustav A. GER
Helfman, Max AUS
C0476. Hellmesberger, Georg AUS
C0477. Hellmesberger, Joseph AUS
C0478. Hemberg, Eskil SWE
C0479. Hendl, Walter USA
C0480. Henneberg, Johann B. AUS
Henriques, Robert DEN
Henry, Leigh Vaughan ENG
C0481. Henschel, Isador G. GER
Hentschel, Franz GER
C0482. Hentschel, Theodor GER
C0483. Herbeck, Johann F. von AUS
C0484. Herbert, Victor IRE-USA
C0485. Herbig, Guenther CZE
C0486. Herman, Reinhold L. GER
C0487. Herrera, Luis de la F. MEX
C0488. Herrmann, Bernard USA
Herrmann, Eduard GER-USA
C0489. Hertog, Johannes den DUT
C0490. Hertz, Alfred GER-USA
C0491. Hetsch, Ludwig F. GER
Hetu, Pierre CAN
C0492. Heuberger, Richard AUS
C0493. Heward, Leslie ENG
Hickox, Richard ENG
C0494. Hill, Ureli Corelli USA
C0495. Hille, Eduard GER
C0496. Hiller, Ferdinand GER
C0497. Hillis, Margaret USA
Hilsberg, Alexander USA
C0498. Hinrichs, Gustav GER-USA
C0499. Hoeberg, Georg V. DEN
C0500. Hoesslin, Franz von GER
Hoffman, Irwin USA
C0501. Hol, Richard DUT
C0502. Hollaender, Alexis GER
Hollingsworth, John ENG
C0503. Hollreiser, Heinrich GER
C0504. Holoubek, Ladislaw CZE
Holt, Henry USA
C0505. Hoogstraten, Willem van DUT
C0506. Horenstein, Jascha RUS-USA
C0507. Horn, Charles Edward ENG
Horner, Ralph Joseph ENG
C0508. Horst, Anthon van der DUT
C0509. Horvat, Milan YUG
C0510. Houseley, Henry ENG-USA
C0511. Houtmann, Jacques FRA
C0512. Howarth, Elgar ENG
Hubbell, Frank Allen USA
C0513. Hubert, Nicolai RUS
C0514. Hughes, Owain Arwel ENG
C0515. Hupperts, Paul DUT
C0516. Hurst, George ENG
C0517. Husa, Karel CZE
C0518. Hutschenruyter, Wouter DUT
C0519. Huybrechts, Francois BEL
C0520. Hye-Knudsen, Johan DEN
-I-
C0521. Iliev, Konstantin BUL
C0522. Inbal, Eilahu ISR
C0523. Inghelbrecht, Desire FRA
C0524. Irving, Robert ENG
Iseler, Elmer CAN
C0525. Iturbi, José SPA
Ivanov, Konstantin RUS
Iwaki, Hiroyuki JAP
-J-
Jacchia, Agide ITA

Jacquillat, Jean-P. FRA
Jadin, Louis E. FRA
C0526. Jaernefelt, Armas SWE
Jaervi, Neeme EST
Jahn, Wilhelm AUS
C0527. Jalas, Jussi FIN
C0528. James, Philip USA
C0529. Janigro, Antonio ITA
Janowski, Marek POL
C0530. Not in BAKER 7
Jansons, Mariss LAT
C0531. Janssen, Werner USA
C0532. Jarecki, Henryk POL
C0533. Jarecki, Tadeusz POL
Jarov, Sergei RUS
C0534. Not in BAKER 7
C0535. Jenkins, Newell Owen USA
C0536. Jeremias, Otakar CZE
C0537. Jílek, František CZE
C0538. Jirák, Karel Boleslav CZE
C0539. Jirásek, Ivo CZE
C0540. Joachim, Joseph GER
C0541. Jochum, Eugen GER
C0542. Jochum, Georg Ludwig GER
C0543. Jochum, Otto GER
C0544. Johanos, Donald USA
C0545. Johnson, Francis Hall USA
C0546. Johnson, Thor USA
C0547. Jordá, Enrique SPA
C0548. Jorgensen, Poul DEN
C0549. Josephson, Jacob Axel SWE
Juengst, Hugo GER
C0550. Juergens, Juergen GER
C0551. Jullien, Louis Antoine FRA

-K-

C0552. Kabasta, Oswald AUS
Kacinkas, Jeronimas LIT
Kaehler, Willibald GER
C0553. Kajanus, Robert FIN
C0554. Kalnins, Janis RUS
C0555. Kamu, Okko FIN
C0556. Not in BAKER 7
Kapp, Richard USA
C0557. Karabatchevsky, Isaac BRA
C0558. Karajan, Herbert von AUS
C0559. Kašlík, Václav CZE
C0560. Kastalsky, Alex. D. RUS
C0561. Katims, Milton USA
Katlewicz, Jerzy POL
C0562. Kaufmann, Walter GER-USA
C0563. Kazandjiev, Vasil BUL
C0564. Keene, Christopher USA
C0565. Kegel, Herbert GER
C0566. Kehr, Guenter GER
C0567. Keilberth, Joseph GER
Kelbe, Theodore GER
C0568. Keldorfer, Robert AUS
C0569. Keldorfer, Viktor J. AUS
C0570. Kempe, Rudolf GER
C0571. Kempen, Paul van DUT
C0572. Kersjes, Anton DUT
C0573. Kertész, István HUN
C0574. Kes, Willem DUT
C0575. Ketting, Piet DUT
C0576. Keurvels, Edward BEL
C0577. Keussler, Gerhard von GER
C0578. Khaikin, Boris RUS
C0579. Kielland, Olav NOR
Kiesewetter, Tomasz POL
C0580. Kilburn, Nicholas ENG
C0581. Kindler, Hans DUT-USA
C0582. Not in BAKER 7
Kitayenko, Dimitri RUS
C0583. Kittel, Bruno GER
Kitzinger, Fritz GER
C0584. Kitzler, Otto GER
Kjellsby, Erling NOR
C0585. Klee, Bernhard GER
Klee, Eugen GER
C0586. Kleffel, Arno GER
C0587. Kleiber, Carlos GER
C0588. Kleiber, Erich AUS
C0589. Klein, Kenneth USA
C0590. Klemperer, Otto GER
C0591. Klenau, Paul von DEN
C0592. Klengel, Paul GER
C0593. Kletzki, Paul POL
Klima, Alois CZE
C0594. Klimov, Mikhail RUS
C0595. Klitzsch, Karl E. GER
C0596. Klobučar, Berislav YUG
C0597. Knape, Walter GER
C0598. Knappertsbusch, Hans GER
C0599. Kniese, Julius GER
C0600. Knittl, Karel CZE
Knoch, Ernst GER
Knyvett, William ENG
C0601. Koch, Helmut GER
Koemmerich, Louis GER-USA
Koenig, Gustav GER
Koenigsloew, Otto GER
C0602. Koetsier, Jan DUT
C0603. Kogel, Gustav F. GER
Kohler, Franz USA
Koizumi, Kazuhiro JAP
C0604. Kojian, Varujan LEB
C0605. Kolar, Victor HUN-USA
Kolchinskaya, Camilla RUS
C0606. Kondrashin, Kirill RUS
C0607. Konoye, Hidemaro JAP

C0608. Kontarsky, Bernhard GER
C0609. Konwitschny, Franz GER
Kord, Kazimierz POL
C0610. Korodi, Andras HUN
Kortschak, Hugo AUS
C0611. Košler, Zdeněk CZE
C0612. Kostelanetz, Andre RUS-USA
C0613. Koussevitzky, Serge RUS
C0614. Kovařovik, Karel CZE
Krasnapolsky, Yuri USA
Krause, Anton GER
C0615. Krause, Theodor GER
C0616. Krauss, Clemens AUS
C0617. Krejčí, Iša CZE
C0618. Krenz, Jan POL
C0619. Kreubé, Charles F. FRA
C0620. Kreutzer, Rodolphe FRA
C0621. Krips, Henry AUS
C0622. Krips, Joseph AUS
Krohn, Felix FIN
C0623. Krombholc, Jaroslav CZE
C0624. Krueger, Karl USA
C0625. Krug, Wenzel Josef GER
C0626. Kruse, Georg Richard GER
C0627. Kubelík, Rafael CZE
C0628. Kuecken, Friedrich GER
Kuhn, Gustav AUS
C0629. Kulka, János HUN
C0630. Kunsemueller, Ernst GER
C0631. Kunwald, Ernst AUS
C0632. Kunz, Ernst SWZ
C0633. Kunzel, Erich USA
C0634. Kurtz, Efrem RUS-USA
C0635. Kurz, Siegfried GER
Kutev, Filip BUL
C0636. Kutzschbach, H. L. GER
C0637. Kuyper, Elisabeth DUT

-L-

C0638. Labey, Marcel FRA
C0639. Labitzky, August GER
C0244. Lacerda, F. de POR
C0640. Lachner, Franz Paul GER
C0641. Lachner, Ignaz GER
C0642. Lachner, Vincenz GER
LaMarchina, Robert USA
C0643. Lambert, Constant ENG
Lambeth, Henry A. ENG
C0644. Lamote de Grignon, J. SPA
C0645. Lamote de Grignon, R. SPA
C0646. Lamoureux, Charles FRA
C0647. Lanchbery, John ENG
C0648. Landau, Siegfried GER-USA
C0649. Landshoff, Ludwig GER
C0650. Lane, Louis USA
C0651. Lang, Benjamin J. USA
C0652. Lange, Hans GER-USA
C0653. La Rosa Parodi, A. ITA
C0654. La Rotella, Pasquale ITA
C0655. L'Arronge, Adolf GER
C0656. Lassen, Eduard DAN
C0657. Lavrangas, Denis GRE
C0658. Lebrun, Paul Henri BEL
C0659. Lederer, Felix GER
C0660. Ledger, Philip ENG
C0661. Lehel, György HUN
C0662. Lehmann, Fritz GER
C0663. Leinsdorf, Erich AUS-USA
C0664. Leitner, Ferdinand GER
Lemoyne, Jean B. FRA
C0665. Lenaerts, Constant DUT
C0666. Lendvai, Erwin HUN
C0667. Leppard, Raymond ENG
Leps, Wassili RUS
C0668. Lert, Richard J. AUS-USA
C0669. Leslie, Henry David ENG
Levenson, Boris RUS
C0670. Levey, Richard M. IRE
C0671. Levey, William C. IRE
C0672. Levi, Hermann GER
C0673. Levine, James L. USA
C0674. Lewis, Anthony C. ENG
C0675. Lewis, Daniel USA
C0676. Lewis, Henry USA
Leyden, Norman USA
Liadov, Konstantin RUS
C0677. Liebig, Karl GER
C0678. Liljefors, Ruben SWE
C0679. Limantour, Jose Yves FRA
C0680. Limbert, Frank L. USA-GER
C0681. Lindpainter, Peter von GER
C0682. Lipkin, Seymour USA
C0683. Listemann, B. GER-USA
C0684. Lloyd-Jones, David ENG
C0685. Lockhart, James L. ENG
C0686. Loewe, Ferdinand AUS
C0687. Loewlein, Hans GER
C0688. Lohse, Otto GER
C0689. Lombard, Alain FRA
C0690. Longy, Georges FRA
Lopez-Cobos, Jesús SPA
C0691. Lorentz, Alfred GER
C0692. Lorenz, Alfred O. AUS
C0693. Loughran, James ENG
C0694. Loy, Max GER
C0695. Lualdi, Adriano ITA
C0696. Lucas, Leighton ENG
C0697. Ludwig, Leopold AUS
C0698. Luening, Otto USA
C0699. Luigini, Alexandre FRA
C0700. Lukács, Miklós HUN

Luke, Ray USA
C0701. Lunssens, Martin BEL
Lynn, George USA

-M-

C0702. Maag, Peter SWZ
C0703. Maazel, Lorin USA
C0704. Macal, Zdenek CZE
C0705. MacCunn, Hamish ENG
C0706. Macfarren, George A. ENG
C0707. Mackenzie, Alex. C. ENG
C0708. Mackerras, Charles AST
Maclean, Alexander M. ENG
C0709. MacMillan, Ernest CAN
C0710. Maddy, Joseph Edgar USA
C0711. Madeira, Francis USA
C0712. Maderna, Bruno ITA-GER
C0713. Madey, Boguslaw POL
Maerzendorfer, Ernst AUS
C0714. Mága, Otmar CZE
C0715. Maganini, Quinto USA
C0716. Mahler, Fritz AUS-USA
C0717. Mahler, Gustav AUS
C0718. Major, Jakab Gyula HUN
C0719. Maksymiuk, Jerzy POL
C0720. Malgoire, Jean-Clause FRA
C0721. Malko, Nicolai RUS
C0722. Mancinelli, Luigi ITA
C0723. Mannes, David USA
C0724. Mannino, Franco ITA
C0725. Manns, August GER-ENG
C0726. Mannstaedt, Franz GER
Marcelli, Nino CHI
C0727. Maretzek, Max AUS-USA
C0728. Mariani, Angelo ITA
Marino, Amerigo USA
C0729. Marinov, Ivan BUL
C0730. Marinuzzi, Gino ITA
C0731. Marinuzzi, Giuseppe ITA
C0732. Markevitch, Igor RUS
C0733. Marriner, Neville ENG
C0734. Martin, Thomas P. AUS-USA
C0735. Martinon, Jean FRA
C0736. Martucci, Giuseppe ITA
Marx, Burle BRA
C0737. Mascagni, Pietro ITA
C0738. Mascheroni, Edoardo ITA
C0739. Not in BAKER 7
C0740. Mata, Eduardo MEX
C0741. Matačić, Lovro von YUG
C0742. Mauceri, John USA
C0743. Mauersberger, Rudolf GER
C0744. Mazzoleni, Ettore SWZ-CAN
McCutchen, Robert Guy USA
Mees, Arthur USA
Mehrkens, Friedrich GER
C0745. Mehta, Mehli IND
C0746. Mehta, Zubin IND
C0747. Melik-Pashayev, A. RUS
C0748. Melles, Carl HUN
C0749. Mendelssohn, Felix GER
C0750. Mengelberg, Karel DUT
C0751. Mengelberg, Willem DUT
C0752. Menges, Herbert ENG
C0753. Merola, Gaetano ITA-USA
C0754. Messager, André FRA
C0755. Mester, Jorge USA
C0756. Meylan, Jean SWZ
C0757. Meyrowitz, Selmar GER
Mézeray, L.-Charles FRA
C0758. Michaelides, Solon GRE
Michalak, Thomas POL
Miedél, Rainer GER
C0759. Mihály, András HUN
C0760. Mikorey, Franz GER
Miles, Maurice ENG
C0761. Millet, Luis SPA
C0762. Mirouze, Marcel FRA
C0763. Mitchell, Howard USA
C0764. Mitropoulos, Dimitri GRE
C0765. Mlynarski, Emil POL
Molina, Antonio J. PHI
C0766. Molinari, Bernardino ITA
C0767. Molinari Pradelli, F. ITA
C0768. Mollenhauer, Emil USA
Montani, Nicola A. USA
C0769. Monteux, Claude USA
C0770. Monteux, Pierre FRA
C0771. Montgomery, Kenneth ENG
C0772. Moralt, Rudolf GER
C0773. Morel, Jean FRA
Morelli, Giuseppe ITA
C0774. Morlacchi, Francesco ITA
C0775. Morris, Wyn ENG
C0776. Moscheles, Ignaz GER
C0777. Mosel, Ignaz F. von AUS
C0778. Mosewius, Johann GER
C0779. Mottl, Felix AUS
C0780. Mravinsky, Evgeny RUS
C0781. Muck, Karl GER
C0782. Mueller, Adolf, Sr., HUN
C0783. Mueller, Adolf, Jr., AUS
Mueller, Friedrich GER
Mueller, Heinrich F. GER
C0784. Mueller-Kray, Hans GER
C0785. Mueller-Reuter, Th. GER
C0786. Mueller-Zuerich, Paul SWZ
C0787. Muench, Ernst ALS
C0788. Muench, Fritz FRA
C0789. Muench, Hans ALS
C0790. Muenchinger, Karl GER

C0791. Mugnone, Leopold ITA
C0792. Munch, Charles FRA
C0793. Munclinger, Milan CZE
Muti, Lorenzo ITA
C0794. Muti, Riccardo ITA
-N-
C0795. Napravnik, Eduard RUS
C0796. Naumann, Karl Ernst GER
C0797. Naumann, Siegfried SWE
Navarro, García SPA
C0798. Naylor, Bernard ENG-CAN
C0799. Nedbal, Karel CZE
C0800. Nedbal, Oscar CZE
C0801. Neel, Louis Boyd ENG
C0802. Nef, Albert SWZ
Negri, Vittorio ITA
C0803. Neidlinger, Guenter GER
C0804. Nelhybel, Vaclav CZE
Nelson, John USA
C0805. Neuendorff, Adolf GER
C0806. Neuhaus, Rudolf GER
C0807. Neukomm, Sigismund von AUS
C0808. Neumann, Franz CZE
C0809. Neumann, Václav CZE
C0810. Nicolai, Carl Otto GER
C0811. Nicolau, Antonio SPA
C0812. Nikisch, Arthur HUN
C0813. Nilius, Rudolf AUS
Niyazi [Khadzhibekov] RUS
C0814. Nobel, Felix de DUT
C0815. Nordquist, Johan C. SWE
C0816. Norman, Frederick L. SWE
C0817. North, Alex USA
C0818. Noskowski, S. von POL
C0819. Novello-Davies, Clara ENG
-O-
C0820. Oberhofer, Emil Johann GER
C0821. Obrist, Alois ITA
C0822. Ochs, Siegfried GER
O'Connell, Charles USA
O'Dwyer, Robert ENG
Oetvos, Gabor HUN
Oliver, John USA
C0823. O'Neill, Norman ENG
C0824. Orchard, William A. ENG
Orem, Preston Ware USA
C0825. Ormandy, Eugene HUN-USA
C0826. Ostrcil, Otakar CZE
C0827. Otescu, Ion Nonna ROM
C0828. Otterloo, Willem van DUT
C0829. Otto, Ernst GER
Ovchinnikov, V. RUS
C0830. Ozawa, Seiji JAP
-P-
Pacchierotti, Ubaldo ITA
Pache, Joseph GER
Page, Robert USA
C0831. Page, Willis USA
C0832. Paillard, Jean-F. FRA
Paita, Carlos ARG
C0833. Palange, Louis S. USA
C0834. Palau, Manuel SPA
Pallo, Imre HUN
C0835. Palsson, Pall P. ICE
C0836. Panizza, Ettore ARG
C0837. Panufnik, Andrzej POL
C0838. Panula, Jorma FIN
Panzner, Karl GER
C0839. Papandopulo, Boris YUG
C0840. Papi, Gennaro ITA
Paranov, Moshe USA
C0841. Paray, Paul FRA
C0842. Parelli, Attilio ITA
Parrott, Andrew ENG
C0843. Pasdeloup, Jules-E. FRA
Pasternack, Josef A. POL
C0844. Patane, Giuseppe ITA
C0845. Paulli, Holger Simon DEN
C0846. Paulmueller, A. AUS
C0847. Paumgartner, Bernhard AUS
C0848. Paur, Emil AUS
C0849. Pedrotti, Carlo ITA
C0850. Pelletier, L. Wilfrid CAN
C0851. Pembaur, Karl Maria AUS
C0852. Peress, Maurice USA
C0853. Pérez Casas, B. SPA
C0854. Perfall, Karl von GER
C0855. Pergament, Moses FIN-SWE
C0856. Perger, Richard von AUS
C0857. Perisson, Jean-Marie FRA
C0858. Perlea, Jonel RUM-USA
C0859. Perosi, Don Lorenzo ITA
C0860. Pesko, Zoltan HUN
C0861. Peters, Reinhard GER
C0862. Petkov, Dimiter BUL
C0863. Pfitzner, Hans GER
C0864. Pflueger, Gerhard GER
Picka, František CZE
C0865. Pierné, Gabriel H.-C. FRA
C0866. Pitt, Percy ENG
C0867. Pitz, Wilhelm GER
Plasson, Michel FRA
Plotnikov, Eugene RUS
C0868. Pohlig, Karl GER
C0869. Polacco, Giorgio ITA
Polgar, Tibor HUN-CAN
C0870. Pollak, Egon CZE-AUS
Pollikoff, Max USA
C0871. Ponc, Miroslav CZE
Pone, Gundaris LAT-USA

C0872. Not in BAKER 7
C0873. Poulet, Gaston FRA
Powell, Laurence ENG-USA
C0874. Prausnitz, F. GER-USA
C0875. Prêtre, Georges FRA
C0876. Previn, André USA
C0877. Previtali, Fernando ITA
C0878. Prévost, Eugène-Pros. FRA
Price, Enrique ENG
C0879. Priestman, Brian ENG
C0880. Prill, Paul GER
C0881. Pringsheim, Klaus GER
C0882. Pritchard, John ENG
C0883. Proch, Heinrich AUS
C0884. Prohaska, Felix AUS
C0885. Protheroe, Daniel ENG-USA
C0886. Pruewer, Julius AUS

-Q-

C0887. Quadri, Arego ITA
C0888. Queler, Eve USA
C0889. Quinet, Ferdinand FRA
C0890. Quintanar, Hector MEX

-R-

C0891. Raabe, Peter GER
C0892. Raalte, Albert van DUT
C0893. Rabaud, Henri FRA
Rabich, Ernst GER
Rabl, Walter AUS
C0894. Rachmaninoff, Sergei RUS
Rachmilovich, Jacques RUS
C0895. Radecke, Robert GER
C0896. Radecke, Rudolf GER
C0897. Rahlwes, Alfred GER
C0898. Rajter, Ludovít CZE
C0899. Randegger, Alberto ITA
Randolph, David USA
C0900. Rankl, Karl AUS
C0901. Rapee, Erno HUN
C0902. Rastrelli, Joseph GER
C0903. Rattle, Simon Denis ENG
Raudenbush, George USA
Ray, Don Brandon USA
Řebiček, Josef CZE
C0904. Redel, Kurt GER
Reichert, Johannes GER
C0905. Reichwein, Leopold AUS
C0906. Reinecke, Carl H. GER
C0907. Reiner, Fritz HUN
C0908. Remoortel, Edouard van BEL
C0909. Renner, Joseph GER
C0910. Rettich, Wilhelm GER
Reuling, Wilhelm GER
Reuss, Wilhelm F. GER
Reuter, Rolf GER
C0911. Rey, Jean-Baptiste FRA
C0912. Rhené-Baton, FRA
C0913. Rhodes, Willard USA
C0914. Ribera y Maneja, A. SPA
Riccius, Karl A. GER
C0915. Richter, Hans GER
C0916. Richter, Karl GER
Rickenbacher, Karl A. SWZ
C0917. Riedel, Karl GER
C0918. Rieger, Fritz GER
C0919. Rietz, Julius GER
C0920. Rifkin, Joshua USA
C0921. Rignold, Hugo Henry ENG
C0922. Rilling, Helmuth GER
Ringwall, Rudolph USA
C0923. Riotte, Philipp J. GER
Riseley, George ENG
C0924. Ristenpart, Karl GER
C0925. Ritter, Frederic GER-USA
C0926. Robinson, Stanford ENG
C0927. Rodan, Mendi ROM
C0928. Rodzinski, Artur POL
C0929. Roegner, Heinz GER
C0930. Roehr, Hugo GER
C0931. Rogalski, Theodor ROM
Roig, Gonzalo CUB
Roland, Claude-Robert BEL
C0932. Ronald, Landon ENG
C0933. Ronnenfeld, Peter GER
C0934. Rosa, Carl GER-ENG
C0935. Rosbaud, Hans AUS
C0936. Rosenstock, Joseph POL-USA
C0937. Rosenthal, Manuel FRA
Ros-Marbá, Antonio SPA
C0938. Ross, Hugh ENG
C0939. Rossi, Mario ITA
C0940. Rostropovich, Mstislav RUS
C0941. Rother, Artur GER
C0942. Rothwell, Walter H. ENG
C0943. Rottenberg, Ludwig AUS
C0944. Rotzsche, Hans-Joachim GER
C0945. Rowicki, Witold POL
C0946. Rozhdestvensky, G. RUS
Rozsnyai, Zoltán HUN
C0947. Rudel, Julius AUS-USA
C0948. Rudnicki, Marian T. POL
C0949. Rudnytsky, Antin POL
C0950. Rudolf, Max GER
C0951. Ruedel, Hugo GER
C0952. Ruehlmann, Frans BEL
C0953. Rummel, Christian GER
C0954. Rung, Frederik DEN
C0955. Rung, Henrik DEN
C0956. Rungenhagen, Carl F. GER
Ruygrok, Leo DUT

C0957. Rybner, Cornelius DEN-USA
-S-
C0958. Sacher, Paul SWZ
C0959. Safonov, Vasili RUS
C0960. Saint-Requier, Leon FRA
C0961. Saito, Hideo JAP
Salonen, Esa-Pekka FIN
C0962. Salter, Lionel Paul ENG
C0963. Saminsky, Lazare RUS-USA
C0964. Samosud, Samuel RUS
C0965. Sampson, George ENG
C0966. Samuel, Gerhard GER-USA
C0967. Sanderling, Kurt GER
Sandoval, Miguel GUA-USA
Sanford, Harold B. USA
C0968. Sanjuán, Pedro SPA-USA
C0969. Santi, Nello ITA
C0970. Santini, Gabirele ITA
C0971. Santoro, Caludio BRA
C0972. Sanzono, Nino ITA
C0973. Sargent, Malcolm ENG
Savín, Francisco MEX
C0974. Savine, Alexander YUG-USA
C0975. Sawallisch, Wolfgang GER
Scarmolin, Louis USA
C0976. Schaeffer, Julius GER
C0977. Schalk, Franz AUS
C0978. Scharrer, August GER
Schaub, Hans F. GER
C0979. Scheel, Fritz GER
C0980. Scheinpflug, Paul GER
C0981. Schelling, Ernest H. USA
C0982. Scherchen, Hermann GER
C0983. Scherman, Thomas K. USA
C0984. Schermerhorn, Kenneth USA
C0985. Schick, George CZE-USA
C0986. Schilhawsky, Paul AUS
C0987. Schillings, Max von GER
C0988. Schindler, Anton Felix AUS
C0989. Schindler, Kurt GER
C0990. Schippers, Thomas USA
C0991. Schletterer, Hans M. GER
Schmid, Adolf AUS
C0992. Schmid, Erich SWZ
C0993. Schmidt, Gustav GER
C0994. Schmidt, Ole DEN
C0995. Schmidt-Isserstedt, H. GER
C0996. Schmitt, Georg Aloys GER
C0997. Schneevoigt, Georg L. FIN
C0998. Schneider, Abraham A. LIT
Schneider, Theodor GER
C0999. Schneidt, Hanns-Martin GER
C1000. Schoek, Othmar SWZ
C1001. Schoenzeler, Hans-H. GER
C1002. Scholz, Bernard E. GER
Schondorf, Johannes GER
C1003. Schreker, Franz GER
C1004. Schrems, Joseph GER
Schrøder, Jens POL
Schryock, Buren USA
C1005. Schuch, Ernst von AUS
C1006. Schuechter, Wilhelm GER
C1007. Schueler, Johannes GER
C1008. Schuller, Gunther USA
C1009. Schulthess, Walter SWZ
C1010. Schultz, Svend DEN
Schulz, August GER
Schulz, Ferdinand GER
C1011. Schulz, Johann P. GER
C1012. Schulz-Dornburg, R. GER
C1013. Schumann, Georg A. GER
C1014. Schuricht, Carl GER
Schurmann, Gerard DUT-ENG
C1015. Schwarz, Boris RUS-USA
C1016. Schwarz, Gerard USA
C1017. Schwarz, Rudolf AUS
C1018. Schwieger, Hans GER
C1019. Scimone, Claudio ITA
C1020. Scott, Charles K. ENG
C1021. Scribner, Norman O. USA
Seaman, Christopher ENG
C1022. Şebastian, Georges HUN
C1023. Šebor, Karl CZE
C1024. Segal, Uri ISR
C1025. Segerstam, Leif S. FIN
C1026. Şeidl, Anton HUN
C1027. Šejna, Karel CZE
C1028. Sekles, Bernhard GER
C1029. Semkow, Jerzy POL
C1030. Serafin, Tullio ITA
C1031. Serebrier, José URU
C1032. Serendero-Proust, D. CHI
Serly, Tibor HUN-USA
C1033. Servais, François FRA
C1034. Sevitzky, Fabien RUS
Seyffardt, Ernst H. GER
C1035. Shanet, Howard USA
C1036. Shapey, Ralph USA
Shavitch, Vladimir RUS
C1037. Shaw, Robert USA
C1038. Sheppherd, Arthur USA
Shilket, Nathaniel USA
Shira, Francesco ITA
C1039. Shostakovich, Maxim RUS
C1040. Sidlin, Murry USA
C1041. Siegel, Rudolf GER
C1042. Siegl, Otto AUS
C1043. Siloti, Alexander RUS
C1044. Silverstein, Joseph USA
C1045. Silvestri, Constantin ROM

C1046. Simeonov, Konstantin RUS
C1047. Similae, Martti FIN
C1048. Simmons, Calvin USA
C1049. Simon, Stephen USA
C1050. Simonov, Yuri RUS
C1051. Singer, Jacques POL-USA
Sinico, Francesco ITA
C1052. Sinopoli, Giuseppe ITA
C1053. Siqueira, José de Lima BRA
Sjoeberg, Svante SWE
C1054. Škroup, Franz CZE
C1055. Skrowaczewski, Stan. POL
C1056. Slatkin, Felix USA
C1057. Slatkin, Leonard USA
C1058. Slovák, Ladislaw CZE
C1059. Smallens, Alexander USA
C1060. Smart, George Thomas ENG
C1061. Smetáček, Václav CZE
C1062. Smetana, Bedřich CZE
C1063. Smith, David Stanley USA
C1064. Smith, Lawrence L. USA
C1065. Smola, Emmerich GER
Smolian, Arthur GER
C1066. Sobolewski, E. de GER-USA
Sodero, Cesare ITA
Soederblom, Ulf FIN
C1067. Sokoloff, Nicolai RUS-USA
C1068. Sollberger, Harvey USA
C1069. Solomon, Izler USA
C1070. Solti, Georg HUN-ENG
C1071. Somary, Johannes SWZ
C1072. Somogi, Judith USA
Somogyi, László HUN
C1073. Sopkin, Henry USA
Soudant, Hubert DUT
C1074. Sousa, John Philip USA
Spialek, Hans AUS-USA
Spicker, Max GER-USA
C1075. Spiegelman, Joel USA
C1076. Spiering, Theodore USA
C1077. Spohr, Ludwig GER
C1078. Spontini, Gaspare ITA
C1079. Springer, Alois GER
C1080. Stadlmair, Hans AUS
C1081. Stanford, Charles V. ENG
C1082. Stefani, Jan POL
C1083. Stefani, Józef POL
Stegmayer, Ferdinand AUS
C1084. Stein, Erwin AUS
C1085. Stein, Horst GER
C1086. Stein, Leon USA
C1087. Steinbach, Fritz GER
C1088. Steinberg, Wm. GER-USA
Steiner, Emma USA
Steinert, Alexander USA
C1089. Steinitz, Charles P. ENG
Steinitz, Paul ENG
C1090. Stenhammer, Wilhelm SWE
C1091. Stern, Julius GER
C1092. Sternefeld, Daniel BEL
C1093. Stevens, Denis W. ENG
Stewart, Reginald ENG-USA
C1094. Stiedry, Fritz AUS
C1095. Stock, David F. USA
C1096. Stock, Frederick GER-USA
C1097. Stockhausen, Franz GER
C1098. Stoessel, Albert USA
C1099. Stokowski, Leopold ENG-USA
Storch, M. Anton AUS
C1100. Stoutz, Edmond de SWZ
C1101. Stransky, Josef CZE
C1102. Straram, Walter FRA
C1103. Strauss, Eduard AUS
Strauss, Paul USA
C1104. Strauss, Richard GER
C1105. Stresemann, Wolfgang GER
C1106. Strickland, William USA
C1107. Striegler, Kurt GER
C1108. Stringfield, Lamar USA
C1109. Strube, Gustav GER-USA
Stryja, Karol POL
C1110. Stuntz, Joseph H. GER
C1111. Stupka, František CZE
C1112. Sucher, Joseph HUN
C1113. Suess, Christian GER
C1114. Suitner, Otmar AUS
C1115. Suk, Váša CZE
C1116. Sullivan, Arthur S. ENG
Sulzer, Julius S. AUS
C1117. Surinach, Carlos SPA
C1118. Susskind, Walter CZE-ENG
C1119. Suter, Hermann SWZ
C1120. Svetlanov, Evgeny RUS
C1121. Swarowsky, Hans AUS
Swoboda, Henry CZE
Sygiètynski, Tadeusz POL
C1122. Szell, George HUN-USA
C1123. Szendrei, Aladár HUN-USA
C1124. Szenkar, Eugen HUN-BRA

-T-

C1125. Tabachnik, Michel SWZ
C1126. Taffanel, Claude-P. FRA
Takeda, Yoshima JAP
C1127. Talich, Václav CZE
Talmi, Yoav ISR
C1128. Tango, Egisto ITA
C1129. Taubmann, Otto GER
C1130. Tausch, Julius GER
Tauwitz, Eduard GER
Tchakarov, Emil BUL

C1131. Temianka, Henri USA
Temirkanov, Yuri RUS
C1132. Tennstedt, Klaus GER
Thadewaldt, Hermann GER
Thayer, Arthur Wilder USA
Thomas, Eugen DUT
C1133. Thomas, Michael T. USA
C1134. Thomas, Theodore GER-USA
C1135. Tiessen, Heinz GER
C1136. Tietjen, Heinz GER
Tikka, Kari FIN
C1137. Tilmant, Théophile FRA
C1138. Titl, Anton Emil AUS
C1139. Toldrá, Eduardo SPA
Tomlins, William L. USA
Tooning, Gerard USA
Torkanowsky, Werner GER
C1140. Toscanini, Arturo ITA
C1141. Toye, Edward G. ENG
Toye, Geoffrey ENG
C1142. Trommer, Wolfgang GER
C1143. Trunk, Richard GER
C1144. Tschirch, F. Wilhelm GER
C1145. Turnovský, Martin CZE
C1146. Tuthill, Burnet C. USA
C1147. Tuukkanen, Kalervo FIN
C1148. Tuxen, Erik GER-DAN
C1149. Tzipine, Georges FRA
-U-
C1150. Unger, Heinz GER-CAN
C1151. Usiglio, Emilio ITA
-V-
C1152. Vach, Ferdinand CZE
C1153. Valentino, Henri-J. FRA
Van der Linden, C. DUT
Vandernoot, André BEL
C1154. Van der Stucken, F. GER
Van Slyck, Nicholas USA
C1155. Van Vactor, David USA
C1156. Varviso, Silvio SWZ
C1157. Vàsàry, Tamàs HUN
C1158. Vaughan, Denis E. AUS
C1159. Velasco Maidana, José BOL
C1160. Venth, Carl GER-USA
C1161. Verbrugghen, Henri BEL
C1162. Verhulst, Johannes DUT
C1163. Vianesi, August-C. ITA
C1164. Villa, Ricardo SPA
Villoing, Vasili RUS
Vinogradsky, Alexander BUL
C1165. Viotta, Henri DUT
Vitalis, George GRE
Vladigerov, Alexander BUL
C1166. Vogel, Jaroslav CZE
C1167. Vogt, Augustus S. CAN
C1168. Volbach, Fritz GER
C1169. Vollerthun, Georg GER
C1170. Volpe, Arnold RUS-USA
Von Blon, Franz GER
Vonk, Hans DUT
C1171. Vostřák, Zbynek CZE
C1172. Votto, Antonio ITA
Vrionides, Christos GRE
-W-
Waack, Karl GER
C1173. Waghalter, Ignatz POL-USA
Wagner, Gerrit A. DUT
C1174. Wagner, Joseph F. USA
C1175. Wagner, Richard GER
C1176. Wagner, Robert AUS
C1177. Wagner, Roger USA
Wahlberg, Rune SWE
Wakasugi, Hiroshi JAP
Waldman, Frederic AUS-USA
C1178. Wallat, Hans GER
C1179. Wallberg, Heinz GER
C1180. Wallenstein, Alfred USA
C1181. Wallerstein, Lothar BOH
C1182. Walter, Bruno GER
C1183. Wand, Guenter GER
C1184. Wangenheim, Volker GER
C1185. Wassermann, Heinrich GER
C1186. Watanabe, Akeo JAP
Webb, Charles H. USA
C1187. Weber, Carl Maria von GER
C1188. Weber, Franz GER
Weber, George Viktor GER
Weber, Wilhelm GER
C1189. Weikert, Ralf AUS
C1190. Weingartner, Felix GER
C1191. Weinwurm, Rudolf AUS
C1192. Weinzierl, Max von AUS
C1193. Weis, Karel CZE
C1194. Weisbach, Hans GER
C1195. Weisberg, Arthur GER
C1196. Weissenbaeck, Andreas AUS
C1197. Weissenborn, Guenther GER
C1198. Weissheimer, Wendelin GER
Weld, Arthur Cyril USA
C1199. Weldon, George ENG
C1200. Weller, Walter AUS
Wendel, Ernst GER
C1201. Westerberg, Stig SWE
C1202. Wetzler, Hermann GER-USA
Wenzel, Leopold ITA
Westenburg, Richard USA
Wetzler, Hermann GER-USA
White, John Reeves USA

White, Paul USA
C1203. Whitney, Robert S. ENG
C1204. Whittaker, William ENG
C1205. Wich, Guenther GER
C1206. Wiedebein, Gottlob GER
C1207. Wiklund, Adolf SWE
C1208. Wilkomirski, K. RUS
C1209. Willcocks, David ENG
Williams, David C. ENG
C1210. Williamson, John F. USA
Wilson, Ransom USA
Winderstein, H.W.G. GER
C1211. Windingstad, Ole NOR-USA
C1212. Winograd, Arthur USA
C1213. Wiske, Charles M. USA
C1214. Wislocki, Stanislaw POL
C1215. Wodell, Frederick ENG-USA
C1216. Not in BAKER 7
C1217. Woeldike, Mogens DEN
C1218. Woess, Kurt AUS
C1219. Wohlgemuth, Gustav GER
C1220. Wolfes, Felix GER-USA
C1221. Wolff, Albert Louis FRA
Wolff, Werner GER
Wolle, John F. USA
C1222. Wood, Henry Joseph ENG
C1223. Woodworth, G. Wallace USA
C1224. Wooldridge, David ENG
C1225. Woyrsch, Felix von GER
C1226. Wuellner, Franz GER
C1227. Wuest, Philipp GER
C1228. Wylde, Henry ENG
Wyss, Niklaus SWZ

-Y-

C1229. Yamada, Kosaku JAP
Yansons, Arvid LAT
C1230. Ysaÿe, Eugène BEL

-Z-

C1231. Zach, Max Wilhelm AUS
C1232. Zafred, Mario ITA
C1233. Zallinger, M. von AUS
C1234. Zantonelli, Hans GER
Zaslawsky, Georges RUS-USA
C1235. Zaun, Fritz GER
C1236. Zdravković, Živojin YUG
C1237. Zecchi, Adone ITA
C1238. Zedda, Alberto ITA
C1239. Zemlinsky, A. von AUS
C1240. Zender, Hans GER
C1241. Zenger, Max GER
Zerrahn, Carl GER
C1242. Zillig, Winfried GER
Zimmermann, Gerhardt USA
C1243. Zinman, David Joel USA
C1244. Zoellner, Carl F. GER
C1245. Zoras, Leonidas GRE
C1246. Zulauf, Ernst GER
C1247. Zumpe, Herman GER
C1248. Zuschneid, Karl GER
C1249. Zweig, Fritz BOH-USA

Index of Authors

This index includes authors, joint authors, and editors. Many individual conductors are not included in this listing due to the fact that they did not author published material. Translators and compilers of discographies are also not included here although they are in the citations. References are to individual entries by category in the following order: A0001-A0055 COLLECTIVE WORKS/Books on Conductors; B0001-B0169 COLLECTIVE WORKS/Related Books; C0001-C1249 INDIVIDUAL CONDUCTORS, A-Z.

About the Author

ROBERT H. COWDEN is Professor of Music at San José State University. The author of Concert and Opera Singers: a Bibliography of Biographical Materials and The Chautauqua Opera Association 1929-1958: an Interpretative History, Dr. Cowden has translated several operas as well as authored numerous articles and reviews published in Arts in Society, MLA Notes, The NATS Bulletin, Opera, The Opera Journal, Performing Arts Review, and Theatre Design and Technology. He is presently working on a companion volume to his bibliographies of singers and conductors which will concentrate on instrumental virtuosi including artists in the popular and commercial recording and concert fields.